A Reader's Guide to
Fifty Modern British Plays

Reader's Guide Series
General Editor: Andrew Mylett

A Reader's Guide to
Fifty Modern British Plays

by Benedict Nightingale

Heinemann – London
Barnes & Noble – Totowa, New Jersey

Heinemann Educational Books Ltd

LONDON EDINBURGH MELBOURNE AUCKLAND HONG KONG
SINGAPORE KUALA LUMPUR NEW DELHI IBADAN NAIROBI
JOHANNESBURG KINGSTON PORT OF SPAIN

First published 1982 by Pan Books as
An Introduction to Fifty Modern British Plays
in the Pan Literature Guides Series
First published in this casebound edition 1982

British Library CIP Data

Nightingale, Benedict
    A reader's guide to fifty modern British plays.
    1. English drama—20th century—History and
    criticism
    I. Title
    822′.912′09   PR736

    ISBN 0-453-18725-2

822.9109
N19

Library of Congress CIP Data

Nightingale, Benedict, 1939–
    A reader's guide to fifty modern British plays.
    (Reader's guide series)
    Bibliography: p.
    Includes index.
    1. English drama—20th century—History and
    criticism
    I. Title
    PR736.N5   1982   822′.91′09   82-11448
    ISBN 0-389-20239-8

Published in Great Britain by
Heinemann Educational Books Ltd
22 Bedford Square, London WC1B 3HH
Published in the U.S.A. 1982 by
Barnes & Noble Books

Printed and bound in Great Britain by
Biddles Ltd, Guildford and King's Lynn

Contents

Introduction

I think I agreed to write this book in the same spirit as a schoolboy might pick his fifty favourite footballers, species of food or types of transport. The sheer fun of making a list appealed to me. If so, I was duly punished for my infantilism, because what followed was hard work and, of course, anxiety. How on earth were the choices to be made? If the criterion was merit alone, I might end up with fifty plays by Shaw, Synge, O'Casey, Beckett, Pinter, and perhaps five or six others. If I were to include plays because they represented some trend or fashion, I would inevitably find myself resurrecting justly neglected 'society plays', costume dramas, detective thrillers and melodramas. If the criterion were the extent to which plays were studied in schools and universities, I would end by earnestly expatiating on work in which I had no belief. To make a little grudging space for Bolt's *Man for All Seasons* might be no great sell-out; but was I really to reject *Heartbreak House* for *Androcles and the Lion* or Rattigan's *Deep Blue Sea* for his *Winslow Boy*?

Out of these and other agonies a compromise list eventually emerged, only to be revised as the book progressed. My original selection included Henry Arthur Jones's *Mrs Dane's Defence*, Yeats's *Plays for Dancers*, Rodney Ackland's *Dark River*, Emlyn Williams's *The Corn is Green*, *The Ascent of F6* by Auden and Isherwood, Theatre Workshop's *Oh, What a Lovely War!*, David Mercer's *After Haggerty*, Charles Wood's *H*, Peter Nichols's *Day in the Death of Joe Egg*, and Heathcote Williams's *AC/DC*. Among those to venture briefly on to the list, or come close to doing so, were plays by Pinero, St John Hankin, St John Ervine, Lonsdale, Graham Greene, John Mortimer, Simon Gray and Peter Shaffer. So did Flecker's luxuriant *Hassan* and the revue *Beyond the Fringe*. Perhaps I should have persevered with some of these. Certainly, I feel uneasy at having excluded O'Casey's *Plough and the Stars* and Arden's *Armstrong's Last Goodnight* at the expense of (respectively) the admirable but thinner *Juno* and *Musgrave*, two plays perennially popular with the school examiners. And certainly I feel a little uncomfortable about some of my inclusions. Is Howard Brenton really a better dramatist than his friend and associate David Hare? Is *The Cocktail Party* superior to *The Family Reunion*, or merely more characteristic of Eliot's later, drabber style? Can anything more than deference to Scotland explain the presence of James Bridie? And is it really right so thoroughly to annex Ireland in a book about 'British' drama?

This last question, at least, can be easily answered, and answered without recourse to the obvious excuse, which is that nearly all the 'Irish' playwrights represented here were born before independence. The truth is that without Shaw, Synge, O'Casey, Joyce, Behan and Beckett the book would not be worth writing at all. Actually, only half its plays are by people whose parents were English born and bred. It's as well to remember, when we're tempted to be chauvinistic about our drama, that it has received a substantial blood transfusion from points east and west.

Another anxiety was the starting-point of the survey. A more logical date might have been 1865, when Tom Robertson's *Society* was first performed, or 1867, when he followed it with the better known *Caste*. From such unpretentious beginnings came English 'realism' as Pinero, Jones and many a later playwright knew and developed it. Alternatively, the book could have opened in 1890, or just before. That way, it could have dealt more fully with such augurs as the arrival and slow assimilation of Ibsen and the emergence of Shaw, and offered its obeisances to the best work of Wilde, Gilbert, Pinero and Jones. And yet there is some sense and meaning in starting with the first decade of the new century, since it was, after all, a notable time of revival both for the British theatre and for its written drama.

In 1814 the Jane Austen of *Mansfield Park* could, and did, identify herself with Sir Thomas Bertram's gentlemanly outrage at the prospect of amateur theatricals under his sober roof; in 1828 a sermon could be, and was, preached against the iniquity of the stage in the ruins of the Royal Brunswick Theatre while people killed in its collapse were still being removed. In 1895 the great actor Irving was knighted, followed by Bancroft in 1897. In the intervening seventy years the theatre had gradually become acceptable to Crown and Commons, upper classes and Church of England, indeed almost everyone except the more intransigently puritanical type of evangelical Christian. But it had done so at huge cost to itself. It wasn't only Shaw, William Archer and the 'advanced' people who felt impelled to attack the numbing respectability of late-nineteenth-century drama. As early as 1885 we find H. A. Jones complaining that by 'humble deference to everybody's prejudices we have banished from the stage all treatment of grave subjects but what is commonplace and cursory and conventional', and calling for 'perfect freedom of choice of subject, persons, place and mode of treatment'.

Not that Jones himself was altogether without that 'deference'. Indeed, it's an indication of the moral and intellectual backwardness of the theatre that the crusader for 'freedom' could himself adapt Ibsen's *Doll's House* into *Breaking a Butterfly*, changing the original from a critique into a celebration of hearth and home, complete with happy ending. True, Jones's favourite target was hypocrisy, notably hypocrisy about sex; but his attacks on (say) the 'double standard' came from a point of view hardly more challenging or radical than that of A. W. Pinero. Both men's 'society' plays are full of women who sin and, regrettably but rightly, pay a price that even after 1900 could be high. The protagonist of Jones's *Mrs Dane's Defence* (1900) loses her fiancé; that of Pinero's *Iris* (1901) is reduced to beggary; that of Pinero's *Letty* (1903) is banished to the humdrum suburbs; and that of his *Mid-Channel* (1909) actually commits suicide, like his more famous Second Mrs Tanqueray sixteen years before. That such exercises in prurience could be dignified as 'problem plays', on the grounds that they mildly questioned the over-ferocious enforcement of taboos they fundamentally endorsed, only emphasizes the point: the theatre badly needed to be liberated from its own conformism.

In the Edwardian age that liberation, begun by Shaw in the 1890s, proceeded apace. It was a time of far greater social and intellectual turmoil than we tend now to recognize; and its self-questionings on such subjects as the relationship of the classes, the place of women in marriage and society, and the prescriptive rights of parents, were reflected in the drama. Hankin's *Last of the de Mullins* (1908), for instance, uses a heroine who has had an illegitimate son, and then set up and flourished in business, to attack the prejudices, pretensions and idle habits of her 'genteel' family. The heroine of Ervine's *Jane Clegg* (1913) has all her author's sympathy when she conscientiously rejects her unsatisfactory husband, as does that of Allan Monkhouse's *Mary Broome* (1911), a housemaid married off to the upper-crust wastrel who has impregnated her. The particular contributions made by Barker, Galsworthy, Houghton and others to what was becoming an increasingly far-ranging moral and social debate are noted in the book proper.

At the same time it was becoming widely accepted that drama was an 'art' that needed to be relieved from commercial pressures which, thanks to the cost of increasingly realistic scenery and the disappearance of the old 'stock companies', had become more and more severe. Risky plays could no longer be cheaply tried out by the London managers. Hence the importance of the seasons at the Court launched by Granville Barker and J. E. Vedrenne in 1904

– renouncing expensive sets and stars for interesting drama, presenting the world with some of the best of Shaw, Galsworthy, Hankin and Barker himself – and hence a renewed clamour for a National Theatre. Out of London, too, the repertory movement began to establish itself: at the Abbey in Dublin; at the Gaiety in Manchester; later, in Birmingham, Liverpool, Glasgow and elsewhere.

The general momentum was checked by the First World War, which turned public taste in general towards more escapist styles of drama, stripped the theatre of its young men, and saw the gradual replacement of such actor-managers as Tree, Alexander and Wyndham by show-business entrepreneurs, interested only in the profits they could wrest from their playhouses. Indeed, the period between 1920 and the mid-fifties, and especially that between 1930 and 1950, is a generally unrewarding one for the student of British drama. Of the fifty plays discussed in this book, only three were first performed in the 1930s, three in the 1940s. A continuing fashion for historical drama, especially historical drama with literary links, produced little or nothing worth remembering. There was a resurgence of the interest in poetic drama that earlier in the century had led (or misled) the *cognoscenti* to place faith in Stephen Phillips and John Masefield, the coterie plays of Yeats and Gordon Bottomley, and Hardy's barely stageable *Dynasts*; but, apart from Eliot's earlier work, the achievement hardly matches the hopes expressed. One of the more refreshing realizations of recent years has been that 'poetry' in drama is at least as likely to consist in intense, idiosyncratic prose as in verse.

Critics have seen the influence of European expressionism on C. K. Munro's *The Rumour* (1922), as well as on O'Casey's later work, and of Chekhov on Ronald Mackenzie's *Musical Chairs* (1932), Ackland's *Dark River* (1938) and, later, on the plays of N. C. Hunter; but it is surprising how unsatisfactory these pieces now seem, how insular and closed off the British drama was in general, how little serious work of lasting interest was produced in the century's third, fourth and fifth decades. Indeed, one suspects that posterity will find more that seems revealing both about the period and about people more generally in the comedies of Coward, Maugham and Lonsdale than in Bridie, the slowly declining O'Casey and the senescent Shaw, let alone Bax, Dane, Besier, van Druten and other half-forgotten reputations.

The reasons for this decline may be variously ascribed; but there's little doubt that by the mid-fifties competition from the movies and TV, commercial pressures and lack of subsidy had helped create a stultifyingly middle-class, middlebrow and conventionally minded theatre, shunned as much by the intelligentsia as by the masses. Serious drama in London mainly consisted of classical revivals and foreign imports, usually from France or America. Out-of-town rep was in a state of some dereliction, surviving uncertainly on weekly doses of proven West End successes. The prevalent English genre, engulfing the theatre and (perhaps) expelling better minds, was what the day's leading critic, Kenneth Tynan, dubbed the 'Loamshire' play, comedy, thriller or comedy-thriller: 'a glibly codified fairy-tale world, of no more use to the student of life than a doll's house to the student of town planning'. And there was still a censor, still going by the aptly anachronistic name of Lord Chamberlain, to ensure that orthodox sensibilities were protected from the assaults of such as Arthur Miller's *View from the Bridge* and Tennessee Williams's *Cat on a Hot Tin Roof*, as he had earlier protected them from Shaw's *Mrs Warren's Profession* and Barker's *Waste* and, before his abolition in 1968, was to protect them from Osborne's *A Patriot for Me* and Bond's *Saved* and *Early Morning*. This isn't the place to discuss the effects of censorship in detail; but its presence, combined with public prejudice against homosexuality, explains a continuing twentieth-century phenomenon, the covert, indirect, 'underground' or otherwise camouflaged expression of socially unacceptable proclivities. Coward, Maugham and Rattigan were all

to some extent impelled to translate homosexual experience
and observation into heterosexual terms.

The establishment in 1956 of the English Stage Company, an organization dedicated to promoting new work,
and its presentation the same year of *Look Back in Anger* are
usually cited as the *fons et origo* of what is still sometimes
called the 'renaissance' of British drama in the second half
of the twentieth century. It's a convenient date, and in
many ways an accurate one, since there's no doubt the
excitement generated by Osborne's play had reverberations
far beyond itself. For those potential dramatists who had
seen creative possibilities only in the novel, the film and
TV, for those potential audiences who had felt hopelessly
alienated from it, the theatre was suddenly, in Tom Stoppard's words, 'the place to be'. The drama has had its ups
and downs since, but, bolstered and encouraged by state
financial aid, it has yet to lose the allegiance of those who
believe it should amount to more than escapist entertainment. Thanks to the proliferation of new playhouses, the
revival of repertory in the regions, the emergence of the
Royal Shakespeare Company and then the National
Theatre, and (not least) the growth of a sizeable and energetic 'fringe' in London and elsewhere, there must now
be more well-performed classical revivals and more serious
new plays on offer than at any time in theatrical history.

Smugness should be avoided. In 1981, the commercial
sector was in a sickly state, the health of the theatre as a
whole increasingly and frighteningly dependent on government generosity. Much 'serious' drama had become predictable and dull. The radical had in some cases become
the orthodox, the anti-conventional numbingly conventional. The flow of fresh, original playwrights seemed
largely to have dried up; and few established talents were
at their most prolific and best. It is difficult to think of a
strong candidate for inclusion in the book written after the
last entry, *Comedians*, in 1975: E. A. Whitehead's *Old Flames*,
perhaps, or Peter Nichols's *Passion Play*, or Caryl Chur-

chill's *Cloud Nine*. It would be nice to include a contemporary play which treated sex seriously, as all these do, and especially nice to be able to include at least one work by a woman.

Perspectives shift; judgements of contemporary work are notoriously unreliable; and posterity will, of course, have its own interests, biases and axes to grind. Thirty years ago, Ustinov, MacDougall and Ronald Duncan would probably have been in this book; *Rookery Nook* and *Hay Fever* would have been excluded on grounds of triviality, and Lawrence and Joyce ignored. To speculate about the contents of *Son of Fifty Modern British Plays*, or whatever a parallel volume might be called in thirty years' time, is obviously as much a game as the original list-making itself; but it wouldn't surprise me if it included Churchill, Whitehead, John McGrath, the often-underrated Simon Gray, Michael Frayn, David Rudkin, Stephen Poliakoff, John Spurling, Mustapha Matura and/or Mike Leigh, already the orchestrator of many interesting 'improvised' plays. Perhaps Howard Barker, David Edgar, Barrie Keeffe and Snoo Wilson will have fulfilled the expectations placed in them, and/or Christopher Hampton, C. P. Taylor, Peter Terson, Alan Bennett and Peter Barnes have justified their admirers' longer-term faith. Perhaps a future author will fill what even today may seem to some a glaring gap in this book, my failure to distinguish between 'drama' and 'theatre', or between written work and performance art, and to celebrate the achievements of Steven Berkoff, Pip Simmons and their companies. But then the book would claim to be no more than one critic's view of the twentieth-century British drama as it appeared to him at the beginning of the 1980s; and its contents are to be regarded as provisional only.

James Barrie

(1860–1937)

James Barrie was born in 1860, the ninth son of a sturdily independent Angus weaver and a mother with as strong a belief in the importance of education and self-improvement as anyone in *What Every Woman Knows*. The influence of this gentle but powerful woman on the playwright has been emphasized by his biographers, as has the impact of the death of her favourite son, David, at the age of fourteen. Indeed, it has been suggested that Barrie's first, continuing and doomed ambition was to supersede his elder brother in his mother's affections. Hence many of the idiosyncrasies of his work, as well as much of the unhappiness of his adult life.

Barrie was educated at Edinburgh University, turned to journalism, moved to London in 1885, published a first novel in 1888, began to write for the stage, and by 1910 had some ten successful plays behind him. However, his marriage to the actress Mary Ansell ended in divorce, owing mainly to his impotence and his possessive absorption with the five sons of a close friend, Sylvia Llewelyn Davies. In 1921 his particular favourite, Michael, was drowned, a blow that helps explain the virtual silence between *Mary Rose* in 1920 and the failure of his Biblical drama, *The Boy David*, in 1936, the year before his death.

However, Barrie's work had already become more melancholy with time. In *Dear Brutus* (1917) a gnome-like conjuror gives his human guests a glimpse of the alternative lives they might have led, showing them that their present disappointments come more from inner inadequacy than external chance. *Mary Rose* itself is a rather glum variation on the better-known *Peter Pan* (1904), about a young wife and mother stolen by fairies and then returned to reality, a lost, troubled ghost, to search for a son now older than herself. She fails to recognize him when she meets him – as, in a sense, Barrie's mother failed to recognize Barrie himself. Then she wafts ecstatically off into the 'empyrean' to 'play' for ever – as Barrie would perhaps have liked to have wafted and played. Even in old age he seems to have felt that the ideal answer to a world that unkindly insisted on being adult was simply to escape it. To grow up is sad and bewildering, and brings with it the risk of rejection. If only one could be frozen in everlasting innocence, like the child-sprite Peter Pan or, perhaps, the Boy David whose surname was Barrie.

'Fey', 'coy', 'sentimental': these are the accusations thrown at Barrie from his day onwards. But they are insufficient to describe him. As Max Beerbohm argued, his 'excesses in the sweetly sad' must be measured against 'his humour, his curious inventiveness, his sure sense for dramatic effect'. The annual revival of *Peter Pan* shows that this 'inventiveness' continues to appeal to lively imaginations, at any rate of children. His 'sense for dramatic effect' may be judged by the expertly managed first act of *What Every Woman Knows* (1908), in which a burglar is captured, found to be stealing nothing worse than knowledge from the family library, and coolly bribed into contracting himself to the daughter of the house. And his 'humour' varies from the wry, as in the attack on upper-class self-indulgence gently mounted by *Little Mary* (1903), to the hilarious, as in the second act of *Alice-Sit-By-The-Fire* (1905), a brilliantly taken send-up of the society 'problem play'. Yet even this has its special slant. If we're to laugh at the stage-struck girl-heroine's botched attempts to rescue her mother from an entirely imaginary adultery, we're also asked to care very much whether or not the two of them are reunited in mutual adoration. Indeed, that is the principal source of the play's dramatic tension.

This brings us back to the inevitable question: in what way can Barrie be called sentimental? Is it something to do with his whimsical imagination, his fondness for enchanted forests, magic islands, and never-never lands? To do with the sheer number of sweet and charming people he introduces, sometimes with such gratuitous stage directions as (from the cosy *Quality Street*, staged in 1902) 'the dear woman that she is'? Or to do with his habit of idealizing childhood and, of course, maternal devotion? 'What's a father compared to a mother?' asks the son in *Alice-Sit-By-The-Fire*, summing up an attitude held by Barrie characters of all ages. The pirates in *Peter Pan* seek to capture Wendy, not for the usual reasons, but to make her their mother. Mary Rose looks forward to the day when her son 'takes me on his knee instead of my putting him on mine'. *Little Mary* ends with the girl-heroine telling an elderly but immature peer, 'I can't do without mothering you,' and him replying, 'Stay with me, mother, and try and make a man of me.'

So one might go on, invoking *What Every Woman Knows*, in which an aspiring politician ends by rejecting a romantic attachment for the plain, good woman who knows how to look after him and his career. Barrie was never comfortable with any male-female relationship unless he could persuade himself it was parental rather than sexual. But this is still not quite enough to explain his 'sentimentality'. It is, rather, that one fails to find serious passion of any kind in his plays. Above all, one fails to find a capacity for evil among his characters.

Barrie tends to coo over his nicer characters, and amiably shake his head over his less nice ones, gently mocking their faults as mere foibles. In short, he patronizes his people, as if they were indeed little children and without full moral autonomy. This is so even when he seems at his most 'Scottish' and unsentimental. In *What Every Woman Knows*, for instance, much is made of the hard-headedness of the Lowland girl who manipulates her husband without seeming to do so. But to Barrie this hard-headedness, hiding a soft heart, is itself her most lovable trait. Indeed, one could almost say that he manages to sentimentalize her unsentimentality.

The Admirable Crichton

Barrie's plays may lack virility, but they don't always lack social point or moral edge. 'Think of the future of England if the working classes were to become as stupid as the best people,' declares a character in *Little Mary*, picking on diet, of all things, to explain the upper-class indolence we're shown. If the 'best people' ate more carefully they would function more effectively, being no more than food transformed into flesh. It is a somewhat facetious idea, more so than any to be found in *The Admirable Crichton*. That play offers its upper-class inadequates no alibi. If they are stupid, it is because they were born that way; and they are lucky to be cosseted by a social system which excludes abler men who happen to belong to the lower classes.

Each of the four acts is turned with consummate artistry. Act I introduces the characters to us in a manner witty in itself, and nicely designed to bring out their foibles. Lord Loam, a peer with self-satisfied radical pretensions, is proving his egalitarianism by throwing his once-a-month tea party for his servants. They are uncomfortable, especially the butler, Crichton, who believes that a rigid hierarchy was ordained by Nature. Loam's nephew, Ernest, is a dandy who (as one of Barrie's characteristically prolix stage directions tells us) 'during this last year has probably paid as much in [restaurants] for the privilege of handing his hat to an attendant as the rent of a working man's flat'. He hopes to use the occasion for an epigrammatic speech; and Loam's three daughters, the Ladies Mary, Catherine and Agatha, plan to drift through it as listlessly as possible. By the time the embarrassing little ritual is over, the vital points have been successfully made. The Loams are lazy and selfish, and blithely take their superior status for granted, in spite of the occasional liberal gesture; Crichton is loyal and resourceful. Now they are to go on an ocean cruise accompanied by Treherne, a cricketing cleric ('a clergyman who breaks both ways is sure to get on in England'), and Tweeny, a mousy lady's-maid.

Act II shows us the party just after it has been ship-wrecked on a deserted island. It is soon plain that everyone is reliant on Crichton, who busies himself building a hut. Nature, he announces, will decide the hierarchy that is to emerge under these new conditions, a remark resisted by the Loams as insubordinate. They give him a month's notice, flounce off to another part of the island, but slink back when he begins to cook supper, thus preparing us for Act III, which occurs two years later. A new hierarchy *has* emerged, and is taken absolutely for granted by everyone. Crichton is the respected chief, and has proved his superiority by organizing his followers into a self-sufficient community, complete with electric light. Lord Loam is 'a jolly-looking labouring man', Treherne and Ernest farm-boys. The girls have been transformed into useful citizens, notably Lady Mary, who leaps through the hut window carrying a buck she has hunted across rivers and ravines. Crichton has just proposed to her, and been humbly and gratefully accepted, when a ship's gun is heard. They are rescued. The erect, commanding figure droops back into the ingratiating posture of a servant and addresses Mary, in a notable curtain-line, as 'My Lady'.

Act IV returns us to London, where Ernest has acquired some fame from his history of life on the island, which relegates Crichton to a patronizing footnote. Lady Mary is to marry Lord Brocklehurst, who (according to a stage direction) 'is nothing save for his rank. You could pick him up by the handful any day in Piccadilly or Holborn, buying socks – or selling them.' The *status quo* has been restored, though not without some misgivings on both sides. This is not, of course, quite enough to sustain a whole act: so Barrie adds an entertaining encounter between the Loams and Brocklehurst's grim old mother, who is determined to sleuth out any indecencies that may have occurred on the island. She is thwarted; Crichton gives notice, and seems likely to marry the sensible Tweeny; the play ends.

It is hard to imagine a plot better calculated to fulfil Barrie's intentions. Lord Loam can hold the House of Lords rapt; but he is incapable of recognizing the importance of the hairpin he finds on the island beach. In London Lady Mary is inactive, and permanently exhausted; on the island, she is active, useful and untired. In Act I, thinking she is to be deprived of her maid, she cries, 'How will we ever know it's morning if there is no one to pull up the blinds?'; in Act III she is up with the dawn and finds her life 'gorgeous'. The implication of these contrasts is unmistakable. The English upper class is expiring of too much leisure and too little work. It has become so dependent on the loyalty and labour of others that it is vulnerable and incompetent when the most basic demands are made of it. It needs to be liberated from its own parasitism, and helped to rediscover the qualities it has largely lost – initiative, practical imagination, common sense, physical prowess. But of course, once it begins to compete in these areas, it may well find its supposed superiority largely chimerical, a matter of convention and tradition. The man who runs the house, not the man who owns it, is likely to be the one more capable of creating a new civilization.

It is, of course, a matter of environment. Crichton's philosophy is that it is ultimately impossible to resist what is 'natural' in any particular context. If one is born into a society that is already highly stratified, like the England of 1902, it is, he thinks, 'natural' for such as himself to be butlers and such as Loam to be masters. But in Eden, the opposite is 'natural'. In this, he obviously takes a very conservative view, and indeed admits as much throughout the play. Most people would call the social structure of the England of 1902 not natural at all, but highly artificial. Indeed, some thought so *in* 1902, among them Max Beerbohm, who was moved by the play to muse about the effects of compulsory education: 'Our slaves are still servile enough, superficially, but we know that many of them are in all respects our superiors. And so we feel very guilty and uncomfortable in their presence. We have given to them, and cannot now take away from them, the power to meet us and beat us on our own ground; and who knows how soon they will have the courage to exercise that power?'

Those who take this conclusion from the play will find support from the final exchange between Lady Mary and Crichton.

> *She* You are the best man among us.
> *He* On an island, my lady, perhaps; but in England, no.
> *She* Then there is something wrong with England.

Does Barrie agree with her, or with Crichton's reply, 'My lady, not even for you can I listen to a word against England'? Does he believe the existing class divisions 'natural' or the result of an iniquitous inequality of opportunity? The second, perhaps; yet the play permits a doubt that may help to explain why it was so enthusiastically received in its day by those it now seems to have been attacking. It is possible to see it as Barrie's attempt to strengthen the upper class by awakening it to its weakness and irresponsibility. It is also, of course, possible to laugh all the way through, and refuse to take its implications seriously at all. Barrie was, according to this view, doing no more than mischievously teasing the English; and the English have always liked to think of themselves as able to take a joke.

Yet, for all its humour and charm, *The Admirable Crichton* looks rather sharper than that in the 1980s. It is, after all, one of the few late-Victorian plays that does not start and end with the assumption that the period's social mores and social relationships were broadly the right ones. It offers us different horizons and reminds us of possible alternatives. Here, perhaps, we hear the voice of Barrie of Angus, not the mother's pet this time, but the poor boy of respectable family, born far from the fleshpots of the metropolis, brought up to value good sense, hard work, and thrift. It is a voice still worth hearing today.

George Bernard Shaw
(1856–1950)

Shaw was already thirty-six by 1892, the year his first play, *Widowers' Houses*, was performed. He had moved to London from his native Dublin sixteen years before; he had written five novels and seen them rejected; he had become a noted orator and, in 1884, co-founder of the Fabian Society, that still-influential organization for the promotion of socialism by 'gradualist' means; he had become as successful a critic of music as he was soon to be of the theatre. With William Archer, who at first collaborated with him on *Widowers' Houses*, he was already an acknowledged champion of Ibsen and, like Archer, the enemy of the insipid drama that continued to swamp the London stage. He sat in the stalls and saw, again and again, 'a tailor's advertisement making sentimental remarks to a milliner's advertisement in the middle of an upholsterer's and decorator's advertisement'. His drama criticism he later called 'a siege laid to the theatre of the nineteenth century by an author who had to cut his own way into it at the point of a pen, and throw some of its defenders into the moat'.

Widowers' Houses was his opening thrust, a play that now seems in some ways as dated as those it was designed to supplant. It is conventional in form, naturalistic in style, unsubtle in its characterization, melodramatic in several of its effects, and dependent for much of its tension on a skimpy, implausible romance. But to attack it for these reasons is to miss the point. The 'heroine', Blanche Sartorius, is the daughter of a respectable, hospitable gentleman whose wealth comes from slum rents; and the 'hero', at first glibly appalled by this revelation, is silenced by the discovery that his own unearned income comes from this source, too. The two of them patch up their differences and prepare to marry: landlord, daughter and son-in-law-elect will live off the misery of others. It is a conventional play, and an unconventional one. There are lovers' tiffs, but they are socio-economic in their cause and solution. There is a heavy father, somewhat villainous in aspect, but any evil he commits is public, not private. There is a touching reconciliation, but the couple's happiness-ever-after depends on corruption and injustice. Everywhere Shaw exploited the dramatic orthodoxies of his day, but only in order to manipulate the audience into revising the assumptions about good and evil that prevailed in the London theatre. He gave the well-made play a socialist twist.

Roughly the same point can be made about much of Shaw's work, especially in its earlier stages. Probably the best of the 'Plays Unpleasant' – so called, declared Shaw, because the 'dramatic power is used to force the spectator to face unpleasant facts' – is *Mrs Warren's Profession* (1898). Here is an ironic, 'Shavian' treatment of that favourite Victorian character, the soiled woman, the tragic Magdalen. But Mrs Warren is no wilting repentant. Long ago she became a prostitute. What choice did she have, given her background? Should she have allowed herself to be sweated to death in an East End factory? And now she runs a chain of brothels in Europe, and moves in the best society, mixing with people who know better than to inquire too deeply into the sources of their friends' wealth. All this is revealed to her feminist daughter Vivie, as if in preparation for that well-loved Victorian scene, reconciliation between mother and daughter, preferably with one or other on her death bed. In fact, Vivie ends by rejecting Mrs Warren, though not for the expected reasons. She admires her mother's good sense and courage in having turned to prostitution; she is repelled by her attempt to achieve respectability on money earned from other exploited girls. It is Mrs Warren's conventionality, not her unconventionality, that decides Vivie to pursue a lonely career in accountancy.

Once again, theatrical conventions are used to subvert commonly received attitudes, and the ultimate villain, the true enemy, is revealed as the social, political and economic system. The attack is, as Shaw himself suggested in his preface, fundamentally on his spectators and readers, who are guilty of failing to change a society in which it is not 'possible for all men and women to maintain themselves in reasonable comfort by their industry without selling their affections and their convictions'. The audience is lured into identifying with the romantic aspirations of the 'hero' of *Widowers' Houses* – and then betrayed by the revelation that his seeming decency is a sham. It settles back to enjoy what looks like good, rattling entertainment – and discovers that the plot forces it to ask questions about the bases of its own prosperity. It is invited to blame itself for Mrs Warren's fall from virtue – and then, when the full extent of her shoddy success is revealed, asked whether or not it isn't a sort of Mrs Warren itself.

So one might go on, invoking the 'Plays Pleasant' and the 'Three Plays for Puritans', though the former concern the follies of society, as opposed to its vices, and the latter a series of individuals capable of challenging its orthodoxies. *Arms and the Man* (1894) has many elements of Ruritanian romance, but it has been transformed into a Shavian comedy, an attack on rather than a celebration of the romanticization of sex and war. The fervid, ingenuous heroine fancies herself in love with a swaggering cavalry officer, but ends by rejecting him, with Shaw's evident approval, for a practical Swiss hotelier. *Candida* (1895) is another ironic transmutation, this time of the triangle drama. On the face of it, the heroine does the conventional thing: she gives up the wayward, importunate poet Marchbanks, and stays with her clergyman husband, the sententious Morell. But this decision is made for unconventional reasons. Domestic propriety doesn't interest Candida: she wants to give herself to the man who most needs her and, appearances notwithstanding, that man is already married to her. So far from being covert propaganda for late-Victorian wedlock, the play is an attempt to define the true reasons for living with someone, whether or not society has given the relationship its sanction.

Similarly, the best of the 'Plays for Puritans', *The Devil's Disciple* (1897) is unashamedly melodramatic. Dick Dudgeon is, it seems, the likeable rogue of romantic tradition,

transported to an undeniably romantic setting, America
during the War of Independence. The local minister and,
more especially, the minister's wife disapprove of him; but
when an English soldier comes to arrest the former as a
rebel, Dick allows himself to be taken in his place and,
indeed, is only saved from the gallows at the last moment.
It is melodrama, but Shavian melodrama. A more conventional playwright might have given credence to the explanation of Dick's altruism offered by the minister's wife: he is
in love with her. But that is an idea that leaves him 'revolted'. He sacrificed himself because any other action
would have affronted his deep and personal sense of right
and wrong: 'When it came to the point whether I would
take my neck out of the noose and put another man's into
it, I could not do it . . . I have been brought up standing
by the law of my own nature; and I may not go against it.'
The self-professed diabolist is revealed as a secular saint,
a puritan in a profounder sense than the woebegone church-
goers of Massachusetts. He rejects 'good' as defined either
by society or by the romancers of pulp-plays, and substitutes his own first-hand version of it. He is an example,
more dashing than usual, of the enlightened Shavian man,
a type we'll meet again.

So when we call Shaw a theatrical innovator, we are
talking more of his ideas than of his technique, at any rate
in the plays written before 1900. The point is, in effect,
made by him for us in the preface to the 'Plays for Puritans'.
He remembers how, as a critic, his 'moral sense revolted
. . . to the very fibres at the nauseous compliance of the
theatre with conventional virtue'. He attacks the gentility
of 'nice plays, with nice dresses, nice drawing rooms and
nice people', and the hypocrisy of the imitation-Ibsen play,
'nothing but the ordinary sensuous ritual of the stage become as frankly pornographic as good manners allowed'.
He criticizes the 'pseudo-religious story, in which the hero
or heroine does good on strictly commercial grounds, reluctantly exercising a little virtue on earth in consideration
of receiving in return an exorbitant payment in heaven',

and the romance 'in which the hero, also rigidly commercial, will do nothing except for the sake of the heroine'. He recalls the success of Pinero's *Second Mrs Tanqueray*, suggesting that 'St Teresa would have been hissed off the same stage for her contempt for the ideal represented by a carriage, a fashionable dressmaker and a dozen servants'. He inveighs against theatres conducted 'on the principle of appealing exclusively to the instinct of self-gratification in people without power of attention, without interests, without sympathy: in short, without brains or heart'.

'Heart' we'll come to later; but brains he undoubtedly brought to a philistine theatre. He vastly broadened its range, and greatly increased its seriousness. But he did so by exploiting the theatricality of the very plays his intellect derided: their coincidences, their improbabilities, contrivances, clever twists, effective curtains, and general sensationalism. As he also wrote in the preface to the 'Three Plays': 'My stories are the old stories; my characters are the familiar Harlequin and Columbine, clown and pantaloon; my stage tricks and suspense and thrills and jests are the ones in vogue when I was a boy, by which time my grandfather was tired of them.' His plays were the old plays, reclaimed for the new truths he was determined to propagate.

Naturally Shaw was much criticized. William Archer deplored what he called 'his predilection for love, or at any rate violent love-making, at first sight'. The quickly shifting affections of *Arms and the Man* he regarded as more in keeping with Gilbertian extravaganza – 'in any more serious form of modern drama they would be not only preposterous but nauseous'. But the most common objections to Shaw's dramatic style were two. The first, made by critics throughout his career, was that it was too frivolous. The second, made with increasing frequency after 1900, was that it was too wordy and didactic, better suited to the debating-chamber than to the theatre.

Shaw himself admitted the first charge, and was inclined

to find an explanation in his curious upbringing. His mother was a remarkably cold woman, who ended by rejecting his father for a musician named Lee and moving with him to London; and his father seems to have been able to see the funny side of that and any other adversity. His reaction to the ruin of his wholesale corn business was to 'retreat hastily from the office to an empty corner of the warehouse and laugh until he was exhausted'. The more sacred an idea or situation, wrote his son later, the more irresistibly amusing he found it. He was also an alcoholic prone to delivering pious diatribes against the evils of drink, whose sincerity Shaw at first believed. But one night a suspicion struck the boy and he 'stole to my mother and in an awestruck whisper said to her, "Mama, I think Papa's drunk." She turned away with impatient disgust and said, "When is he anything else?" I have never believed in anything since: then the scoffer began.' Indeed, the situation became so humiliating to the family that 'it would have been unendurable if we had not taken refuge in laughter'. There is a well-known story of the elder Shaw butting the wall of his cottage in the belief that it was the gate, and Shaw the younger being 'disabled with merriment'. Anyone capable of such a reaction, he argued, 'is clearly not a boy who will make tragedies of trifles instead of trifles of tragedies'.

Shaw did not exactly make trifles of tragedies, but, as we'll see, he often tended to underreact to human pain. He also found it difficult to share his contemporaries' gravity about many a social and human problem – 'I always pursued it to its logical conclusion, and then inevitably it resolved itself into comedy.' There was perhaps an element of sheer mischief in this, as he himself admitted: 'Whenever I feel that my great command of the sublime threatens to induce solemnity of mind in my audience, I at once introduce a joke and knock too solemn people from their perch.' But there was something more. Humour is, after all, an effective weapon, especially if you are a dramatist determined to attack the illusions and hypocrisies of society.

Shaw reasonably claimed that he was 'applauded as the most humorously extravagant paradoxer in London', and everlastingly reproached for lack of seriousness, simply because he reported what he saw. The real joke, he claimed, was that he was in earnest.

There are obvious dangers, as well as merits, in Shaw's customary method, which was 'to take the utmost trouble to find the right thing to say and then to say it with the utmost levity'. Conceivably, laughter is the only means by which we can 'destroy evil without malice and affirm good fellowship without mawkishness'. But this claim may also be Shaw's way of rationalizing what was sheer instinct in him, and in some ways a counterproductive one. People may listen more carefully when laughter is on offer, but they do not necessarily listen with respect. Shaw may have hoped to have used humour seriously, but his reward was often to be taken lightly, dismissively: 'I escape lynching solely because people treat everything that I say as a huge joke . . . my fellow citizens stuff their fingers in their ears and drown my words in senseless cackle.' He was Shaw the professional iconoclast, Shaw the clown: a figure easily ignored when he said something genuinely challenging.

Tolstoy, for instance, found him flippant. To Auden, rather later, he was a 'Fabian Figaro'. And yet others took, and take, the contrary view. In his sympathetic study of Shaw, Eric Bentley argues that he consciously chose to be notorious in order to be effective. Hence his pose of 'G.B.S.', an arrogant, irritating figure with a tendency to rhetorical exaggeration and a fondness for playing devil's advocate. He attacked Shakespeare, for instance, but only in order to challenge mindless bardolatry. He created characters like Britannus, the entertaining blimp in *Caesar and Cleopatra* (1901), or Broadbent, the Englishman in the mainly Irish *John Bull's Other Island* (1904), in order to mock his adopted country out of a smug insularity. He spent most of his career teasing the British in one way or another, but always in the hope of awakening them to a sense of their responsibilities both to themselves and to the world outside. His sense of humour was thus a key part of his armoury as *agent provocateur*, gadfly and goad; but whether it was as 'effective' as Bentley suggests remains open to debate. It is a question each reader and spectator must answer for himself on the evidence of the plays themselves.

If indeed they *are* plays. Here is the next important objection, that they would be better described as 'dialogues'. That was Archer's word for them. Shaw, he claimed, could not cut the umbilical cord between himself and his characters. His plays did not occur in the outside, objective world, but within his own brain. He was 'an imperfect ventriloquist, who actuates ingenious and amusing puppets, but can seldom or never disguise his own voice or accent'. And that voice talks and talks and talks.

It is a capsule accusation that raises tricky questions about the nature of drama itself. Is it possible to create an 'objective' world, or liberate characters from their creator's 'brain'? Every play must embody its author's idiosyncratic view of life, and every character is defined and therefore restricted by his imagination. Every dramatist is a 'ventriloquist'. The point is, how 'imperfect' a ventriloquist? And here it is surely difficult to agree with Archer. Shaw's characterization may not have the breadth and depth of Shakespeare's; but it is full of variety. It seems positively ungrateful to patronize the dramatist who presented a barren theatre with Mrs Warren, Lickcheese, Mrs Dudgeon, Crampton, Bluntschli, Marchbanks, Broadbent, Underwood, Tanner, Higgins, St Joan and King Magnus, to make a random selection. It is possible but insufficient to call many of Shaw's characters highly coloured and exaggerated, perhaps even caricatures. The same point may, after all, be urged against Dickens; and Shaw has some of Dickens' ebullience and energy, combined with greater sophistication of mind.

But does that mind express itself too nakedly and directly? That would be a harsh view of the early plays. They are, on the whole, didactic pieces: they exist to pursue certain ideas to a Shavian conclusion. The characters normally represent some point of view in the general debate. But they do not simply stand and spout at one another. They are placed in a particular social context and allowed to interact. The conclusions are reached dramatically, through what are, in most cases, unusually crowded and eventful plots. The purpose of *Captain Brassbound's Conversion* (1900), for instance, may be to illuminate questions of justice, vengeance and self-sacrifice. It is also a desert adventure, full of brigands and sheikhs and tourists in peril. Some of the speeches are rather long and weighty by the standards of the times; but that no more reduces the play to a 'dialogue' than it does *Richard II* or *Henry V*.

In the later plays, however, the balance between event and discussion does shift. A situation is set up, often in extravagant terms, and then debated: if the talk begins to flag, a new character is introduced, often a somewhat sensational one, like the burglars who interrupt both *Heartbreak House* (1920) and *Misalliance* (1910) or the lady aviator who drops in from the sky, again in *Misalliance*. This pattern is by no means invariable. The relatively eventful *Androcles and the Lion* (1913) and *Pygmalion* (1914) come between the relatively uneventful *Fanny's First Play* (1911) and *Heartbreak House*; *St Joan* (1923) between *Back to Methuselah* (1922) and *The Apple Cart* (1929). But it can on occasions be very marked. *Man and Superman* (1905) is sometimes cited as the first of Shaw's 'disquisitory plays': *Getting Married* (1908), which begins with a couple deciding at the last moment they cannot go through with their wedding, and continues with a prolonged debate on the general implications of that refusal, has a better claim to the title. Shaw's own humorous summing-up of this style of drama occurs later still, at the end of the first act of *Too True to be Good* (1932), by which time a hypochondriac girl has been persuaded by a shady nurse and her burglar boyfriend to run away abroad with them and swindle money from her own mother, on the pretence of having been kidnapped. 'The play is now virtually over,' goes the curtain-line, 'but the characters will discuss it at great length for two acts more. The exit doors are all in order. Good-night.' And, indeed, we are then presented with much lively chat about sex, the generation gap, and other topics, ending with a three-and-a-half page speech about the death of traditional values.

Even Shaw's more sympathetic contemporaries sometimes found his verbosity hard to take. Max Beerbohm, for instance, makes an eloquent defence of *John Bull's Other Island* against those who had derided it as 'not a play' – 'This, being interpreted,' he wrote, 'means not a love story, split neatly into four brief acts with no hint that the characters live in a world where other things beside the love story are going on.' But *Misalliance*, whose subjects include creative writing, imperialism, the nature of freedom, government, and much else, seemed to him random and ill-organized – 'about anything and everything that has chanced to come into Mr Shaw's head. It never progresses, it doesn't even revolve, it merely sprawls.' Both judgements still have substance. It is obviously absurd to rechristen a play a 'dialogue' just because the situation raises general ideas, which the characters then discuss: to argue the opposite is to argue that dramatists may only create beings without the capacity to ponder or speculate, that is without minds. There are also times when the situation seems too transparent an excuse for the discussion: the ideas are no more an essential expression of the characters and their conflicts than is the preface to the play in question.

Or is even that too harsh a conclusion? To an *aficionado*, like Bentley, it would seem so. For him, Shaw invented a new kind of drama, one which tends to substitute interaction of ideas for interaction of character. The tension comes less from the traditional source – what will happen to the people on display? – than from its Shavian reformulation – which of the various points of view represented by them will prove the most relevant and cogent? If a more conventional dramatist were writing *The Apple Cart*, for instance, what happens to King Magnus as an individual would be of more interest and importance than what happens to the enlightened ideas he represents. Generalities would emerge by implication only. But here and elsewhere Shaw reverses that emphasis – and not only because a more discursive style allows him much more intellectual range.

It also means he can be more open about his intentions. His objection to the 'naturalistic' play was that it slyly used a special case to propagate its biases and prejudices, its hidden generalities. It was more honest, he came to believe, to move quickly and explicitly to abstraction, and allow the audience to consider the various arguments directly. And whether or not one accepts this as justification for his peculiar style, his achievement can scarcely be disputed. He presented a considerable variety of points of view with wit and energy; he reminded the world that theatrical characters could think, and showed that intellectual conflict could be absorbing. In short, he made ideas themselves dramatic.

But what ideas? Well, much of the early Shaw's thinking should be apparent already. Late-Victorian capitalist society was corrupt and corrupting, and all the more nauseous because of its pretensions. As he wrote in his preface to the 'Plays Pleasant', he could 'no longer be satisfied with fictitious morals and fictitious good conduct, shedding fictitious glory on robbery, starvation, disease, crime, drink, war, cruelty, and all the other commonplaces of civilization which drive men to the theatre to make foolish pretences that such things are progress, science, morals, religion, patriotism, imperial supremacy, national greatness and all the other names the newspapers call them'. His drama would be, and was, very different. Its mission was to expose the moral, political and economic truth from a stance it would be nice to call rationalist and socialist.

Nice, but perhaps misleading, because Shaw was sceptical about all 'isms', including those he himself was generally supposed to espouse. Between *Widowers' Houses* and *Mrs Warren*, two swingeing attacks on the cruelties perpetrated by 'respectable' society, comes *The Philanderer* (written 1893, performed 1905), much of which is set in an 'Ibsen Club', where it is mandatory for women to be 'unwomanly' and men 'unmanly'. It is, in fact, a satire on the 'advanced' people of the day, the more strident feminists and more ostentatious Ibsenites. And the last of the 'pleasant' plays was *You Never Can Tell* (1899), a spirited, charming and often underrated comedy which directs much of its fun at the solemnities of the 'progressives', Mrs Clandon and her daughter Gloria.

The truth, of course, was that Shaw mistrusted those who translated practice into principles and principles into platitudes, however enlightened they might seem. All received wisdom, reactionary or radical, had to be challenged and its illusions exposed. Little-Englanders, like Britannus or Broadbent, had to have the stuffing knocked out of them. So, too, did those who unselfknowingly set themselves up as intellectual, liberated women, like Gloria. And so with the military heroes, the judges, the clergy, the men of science, the vivisectionists, the vaccinationists, the doctors and surgeons. Indeed, one whole play, *The Doctor's Dilemma* (1906), is devoted to demonstrating the ignorance, incompetence, arrogance and bigotry of the medical profession. Wherever Shaw saw evidence of romantic faith or superstitious belief, and he saw it almost everywhere, he dedicated himself to rooting it out.

Is 'Shavianism', then, a mainly negative philosophy? In the early plays it sometimes seems to have little positive to offer except a good-humoured realism, a jaunty commonsense. But Shaw obviously knew then, and felt with increasing force as his career developed, that these virtues, combined with Fabian pragmatism, were hardly enough to change a world that was, as he saw it, squandering its energy on error, illusion and folly. It would take more than a lonely, mocking voice to wean the English from their conceit, their habits of self-deception, their numbing respectability, and (a frequent Shavian emphasis) their obsession with sports, games and other trivialities. It would, most certainly, take more than the election of a Labour government to create a just and responsible society. Genuine change would take time, a long time, perhaps a very long time indeed, and it would demand superhuman efforts of the perceptive, decisive few. It would, in short, demand 'creative evolution'.

'To me God does not yet exist,' Shaw wrote to Tolstoy, 'but there is a creative force constantly struggling to evolve an executive organ of god-like knowledge and power: that is to achieve omnipotence and omniscience; and every man and woman born is a fresh attempt to achieve this object.' Here, in essence, is the philosophy, or (rather) secular religion, Shaw propagated from *Man and Superman* onwards. For Darwinism, it substitutes what he called 'neo-Lamarckianism'; for a mechanical, deterministic theory of human evolution, one which makes man master of his fate. Actuated by necessity, fuelled by will, supported by reason and conscience, and helped by a 'divine instinct' deep inside us, we must, we *will* advance towards our ultimate goal, 'omnipotence and omniscience'. The journey will be arduous, and packed with setbacks, but nature, or the 'life-force', can be relied on to provide enough vital individuals to ensure that triumph will eventually come. It is a faith well suited to Shaw's active, energetic and, for all its short-term scepticism, fundamentally optimistic temperament; and, in so far as it discourages passivity and encourages constructive involvement in the world, it is no doubt a useful one.

But it's obviously hard to credit in some of its essentials and, as we'll see later, disturbing in some of its implications. If God does not exist, what is this 'creative force', with its pantheistic overtones? To what extent are we fulfilling a divine plan, to what extent constructing one for ourselves? More specifically, how literally are we to take a play like *Back to Methuselah*? In this 'metabiological pentateuch', as Shaw called it, we are taken from the Garden of Eden to the year 31,920, by which time the race has evolved to a degree that makes our own time look pig-ignorant, brutish and bad. But it all depends on one key event, which will supposedly occur in the twentieth century. That is, people will start to live for centuries instead of seven decades, thus gaining enough time to acquire knowledge and wisdom. If this is rejected as ridiculous, there is plenty of the play left to appreciate, notably some lively satire of modern moral attitudes and political behaviour. But rather less is left of the philosophy of 'creative evolution'. In fact, it sometimes seems little more than wishful thinking, presented in an exceedingly eccentric way.

Still, there are several respects in which it helps us to understand Shaw – or, to be more precise, fits in with what we know of him from his life or can deduce from his plays. Consider his mistrust of relationships involving sexual or parental emotion. This is evident enough in *Getting Married*, a prolonged critique of love, marriage and that 'cage', the family, and, at the same time, a plea for easier divorce. It is no less apparent in *Misalliance*, though here the subject is the generation gap. 'The fiendish selfishness of the old people and the maudlin sacrifice of the young!' cries a character who clearly has Shaw's sympathy. 'It's more unbearable than any poverty: more horrible than any regular, right-down wickedness. Oh love! home! parents! family! duty! How I loathe them! How I'd like to see them all blown to bits.' One of the discoveries made by the hypochondriac and her mother in *Too True to be Good* is that the closeness of their relationship has been oppressive and destructive. Appearances, habit and convention notwithstanding, they do not really care for each other. Only after they have agreed to 'forget there are such miserable things in the world as mothers and daughters' can a kind of liking develop between them.

Natural mothers are to be resisted or even rejected, as is everyone and everything that cramps individual development; and yet, paradoxically enough, many of Shaw's most impressive characters are surprisingly maternal. The obvious example is Candida, who tends to regard the two men who love her as children in need of care. She ends by giving herself to the one who fulfils her maternal instincts, not the one likely to fulfil her female sexuality and her mind. Shaw's admiration for the character verges on the sentimental, and he is equally uncritical of Lady Cicely, the domineering heroine of *Captain Brassbound's Conversion*, who treats even brigands and Arab sheikhs as small boys to be petted and patronized. Again, it is the motherly Queen, not the sensuous Orinthia, who commands the true allegiance of King Magnus in *The Apple Cart*. It is she who leads away this extraordinarily able man at the end, telling him, 'Now, now, don't be naughty. I mustn't be late for dinner. Come on, like a good little boy.'

Does this reflect Shaw's ambivalent attitude towards his own mother? Certainly, it is tempting to see the Shaw who expresses these conflicting attitudes as the victim of his background: compensating for parental neglect, finding refuge from emotional dissatisfaction in things of the mind, developing what he called 'a frightful self-sufficiency' and becoming 'a treacherous brute in matters of pure affection'. As a young man he had love affairs – that callous yet self-questioning play, *The Philanderer*, supposedly derived from one of these – but his marriage to Charlotte Payne-Townshend, which occurred in 1898, probably remained unconsummated. In other words, he renounced sex altogether, going so far as to declare that 'what people call love is impossible except as a joke (and even then one of the two is sure to turn serious) between two strangers meeting accidentally at an inn or in a forest park'. For Shaw, the most sensible course of conduct was presumably that adopted by the daughter in *Mrs Warren's Profession*, who rejects both mother and lover, since involvement with either would interfere with the burgeoning career which will fulfil her. If the motherly Candida was one ideal, the cerebral and coldly determined Vivie was another. She was, perhaps, an early expression of what Shaw was later to dub 'the life-force'.

Creative evolution, as it is dramatized in *Back to Methuselah*, systematizes much of this. At the play's start, the serpent tells Eve the facts of life, at which point her 'face lights up with intense interest, which increases until an expression of overwhelming repugnance takes its place, and she buries her face in her hands'; but by the end those inconvenient 'facts' have been made redundant by human progress. In the year 31,920 people leap full-grown from eggs, and spend a short time indulging their senses in love, painting, sculpture and the other arts; but by the age of four they have wearied of this 'rag doll' life, and are already developing into 'ancients', sexless, ascetic, bald creatures who spend their very long lives in contemplation and wish only to escape from their bodies. And at the play's end, mankind's mysterious creator, Lilith, comes on stage to prophesy yet another stage in evolution, one in which life will become a 'vortex freed from matter': pure energy and intelligence.

It is the utopia of an arch-Manichee, a man whose faith in the mind and will is matched only by his scorn for the shell in which they are trapped. There is something inhuman about this Shaw, as several of his contemporaries recognized. The dramatist Henry Arthur Jones, for instance, described him as 'a freakish homunculus germinated outside lawful procreation'; and the poet Yeats remembered dreaming of Shaw as a sewing machine, which ticked and ticked and smiled and smiled. Yet if this is the truth, it is scarcely the whole truth. The impression left by the plays is not of a dispassionate man: rather the contrary.

In the first place, he forces us to ask what we really mean by 'passion': he invites us to redefine 'feeling' and 'emotion'. 'The intellect is as much a passion as sex,' he writes, 'with less intensity, but lifelong permanency'; and, at his best, he surely communicates the excitement, even the rapture, of creative thinking. In the second place, more readily recognizable feelings and emotions do mark much of his work. A human robot could not have written *St Joan* or *Heartbreak House*. Behind the poised and witty exchange of ideas, there is sometimes a curious melancholy, nowhere more so than in *John Bull's Other Island*, the play in which, significantly enough, Shaw deals with the follies, foibles and weaknesses of his native Ireland. A 'sewing machine' could have stitched together the speeches neither of the expatriate engineer, Doyle, who returns to regalvanize land and people on behalf of a somewhat sinister 'syndicate', nor of the ex-priest Keegan. The first of these are full of exasperation at the poverty, ignorance and bigotry, the hopelessness, the 'painful' beauty of the countryside, the 'torturing, heart-scalding, never-satisfying dreaming', and the 'horrible, senseless, mischievous laughter': the stage directions become astonishingly outspoken – 'sudden anguish', 'going into a passionate dream', 'savagely', 'bitterly', 'with fierce shivering self-contempt' – as the denunciation becomes more agonized. The second touch a deeper, more sombre note, defining the world itself as 'a place of torment and penance', in short 'hell'. From 'the depths of his being', Keegan proclaims that he does not feel at home on planet Earth.

Shaw officially believed that the world, so far from being hell, could be infinitely improved by evolution. Yet the power and eloquence of these speeches suggest that he also felt the lure of a grimmer view; and no wonder, given the memories a dramatic excursion to Ireland must have awakened in him. He was, after all, the child who was rejected by his mother, and the man who rejected his mother-country. There must have been times when he, too, felt alienated, out of place, 'not at home', frustrated by his failure either to 'belong' or to escape into pure mind and spirit. Yet he reveals so few chinks in his personal armour that it seems tendentious to go even this far, let alone to suggest that creative evolution itself was a way of coping with emotional deprivation. Sufficient to say that *John Bull's Other Island* uniquely demonstrates that revulsion, pain, yearning and even a 'sense of horror' were commodities not absolutely and invariably lacking in G. B. Shaw.

Yet Eric Bentley is right to observe that Shaw 'almost totally' lacks precisely this 'sense of horror'. His metaphysic is one of evolution and error, not of good and evil, and one may read his works from beginning to end without finding one character who could fairly be described as 'bad'. Society may be destructive: individuals are not wilfully so. It is a topsy-turvy world that creates a Sartorius or a Mrs Warren, not any innate malice, vindictiveness, or lust for power or money on their part. It is easy for Lady Cicely to patronize bandits and marauding sheikhs as 'children in the nursery' in *Captain Brassbound's Conversion*: easy for her to ask, 'Why do people get killed by savages? Because, instead of being polite to them, and saying, How d'you do, like me, people aim pistols at them . . . When I met them, I said howdeydo, and they were quite nice.' Easy, because Shaw ensures that they do indeed react like 'children' and are indeed 'quite nice'. In this play, as in others, he twists probability to suit his essentially optimistic beliefs.

Once again, it is enshrined in the theory of creative evolution. What the world calls 'evil' is simply a temporary obstacle on the road to utopia. He makes the point himself in the preface to *Back to Methuselah*. 'The problem of evil yields very easily to creative evolution,' he writes. 'If the driving power behind evolution is omnipotent only in the sense that there seems no limit to its final achievement; and if it must meanwhile struggle with matter and circumstance by the method of trial and error, the world must be full of its unsuccessful experiments . . . If all our calamities are accidents or sincerely regretted mistakes, there is no malice in the Cruelty of Nature and no Problem of Evil in the Victorian sense at all.' In other words, Genghis Khan was an 'unsuccessful experiment' and the First World War an 'error', perhaps even a 'sincerely regretted mistake'. Never mind the suffering as long as the end is in sight.

It is, of course, a dangerous point of view, because it leads easily enough to the idea that it may actually be necessary to be cruel in the short term in order to be kind in the long. If parliamentary democracy, for instance, is an inefficient way of achieving progress, then perhaps it should be replaced with some tougher and more autocratic system. And this brings us to an awkward problem with the later Shaw: his flirtation with the idea of dictatorship, his willingness to countenance violence and even terror, his imperviousness to considerations most people would regard as humane.

Many of the tendencies that became marked in his old age were evident relatively early. In the preface to *Major Barbara* (1905), he proclaims himself a 'revolutionary writer', on the grounds that 'our laws make law impossible; our liberties destroy all freedom; our property is organized robbery; our morality is an impudent hypocrisy; our wisdom is administered by inexperienced or malexperienced dupes, our power wielded by cowards and weaklings, and our honour false in all its points.' Any change at all would probably be for the better, but two, argues Shaw, are particularly necessary. First, there should be a redistribution of wealth and incomes so that 'no crumb shall, save as a criminal's ration, go to any able-bodied adults who are not producing by their personal exertions not only a full equivalent of what they take, but a surplus sufficient to provide for their superannuation and pay back the debt due for their nurture'. Second, our present system of judicial punishment should be abandoned, and persistent troublemakers placed, 'with many apologies and expressions of sympathy . . . in the lethal chamber'. Altogether, it is a hard humanity that Shaw displays, and a tough new world he proposes, one in which sustenance and even life itself would depend on social 'usefulness'.

But how is it to come about? As early as *Caesar and Cleopatra*, Shaw affirmed his belief in the born leader, the exceptional individual inspired, no doubt, by the 'life-force'. Caesar is intolerant of convention, farsighted and wise, witty and ironic, marvellously unpredictable, incapable of vindictiveness or random cruelty, yet firm and commanding when he has to be. Shaw's admiration is obvious, as it is for King Magnus, the hereditary monarch of the much later *Apple Cart*. The two men share many qualities, but there is one crucial difference between them. Caesar exercises complete power, while Magnus is doomed to wrangle for supremacy with an elected government. His ministers are mostly self-interested and incompetent, his Cabinet 'like an overcrowded third-class railway carriage'. It is clear that only he has the capacity and courage to stand up to the great capitalist monster, Breakages Limited, or to an expansionist USA, which plans to annex Britain. Only he stands for 'the eternal against the expedient, the evolutionary appetite against the day's gluttony'. Democracy has not the vision, the ability or the strength.

The Apple Cart was first performed on the very brink of the 'decade of the dictators'; but those who find its implications disturbing will find much more to worry them in *On The Rocks* (1933). Chavender, the complacent, lazy and ineffective PM, suddenly becomes aware of his responsibilities, and presents a radical new programme which includes proposals to nationalize the means of production, build up the police and armed forces, institute compulsory public service, forbid strikes, and attack 'idlers' of all classes. Parliamentary process will be ignored, and power exercised by 'new tribunals and special commissions manned by officials we can depend upon'. There will be 'discipline' and there may have to be 'cruelty', both of which are welcomed by the main representative of the working classes on display, one Hipney. His view is that 'the only man that ever had a proper understanding of Parliament was old Guy Fawkes'. He will, he says, follow 'any Napoleon or Mussolini or Lenin or Chavender who has the stuff in him to take both the people and the spoilers and oppressors by the scruffs of their silly necks and just sling them into the way they should go with as many kicks as may be needful to make a thorough job of it'. And 'to blazes with your elections and your constitution and your democracy and all the rest of it'.

Shaw's regard for Mussolini is well attested, but it isn't easy to accuse him of any sympathy with fascism itself. He believed in the evolution of the human species, not in the supremacy of any breed or colour, least of all that congenitally frivolous one, the Anglo-Saxon. In *Back to Methuselah* the England of the twenty-second century is run by a Chinese-Negro civil service; and in *On The Rocks* itself there is a passionate and persuasive attack on racialism by the Indian who is, significantly enough, the leading business-man in Britain. No, his model is rather Stalin and Stalin-ism, as the preface to the latter play makes apparent. Part of this is an argument for 'extermination', on the grounds of 'incorrigible social incompatibility', a power too grave to be given to any except 'a thoroughly communist govern-ment responsible to the whole community'. And there fol-lows a defence of Stalin's Cheka, which, argues Shaw, could be relied upon not to abuse such power because it 'had no interest in liquidating anybody who could be made publicly useful'.

This is naïve and ugly stuff, embarrassing to Shaw's admirers, who can only comfort themselves with the thought that so personally benign and (as he himself put it) 'old-maidish' an author could never himself put into practice what he recommends in principle. Indeed, he tac-itly confesses as much through Chavender, who admits he isn't the man for the job and, as a 'talker', will have to make way for the ruthless and coercive 'man of action'. But it is, of course, debatable whether this squeamishness makes Shaw more or less admirable. Which is worse, to present the world with blueprints for violence at a particu-larly perilous point in its history, and then to retreat back to your writer's eyrie, or to perpetrate violence yourself?

This is where the philosophy of 'creative evolution' helped to lead Shaw. Theory triumphs over feeling, mind over body, the claims of society over those of the individual, the hoped-for future over the mere present. The mentally subnormal are 'monsters', and it is wrong to allow 'the old doctrines of the sacredness of human life' to terrify us into wasting the lives of capable people caring for them. The Nazis are better than Australians, who kill aborigines out of personal antipathy, because they genuinely believe that Jews 'are unfit to enjoy the privilege of living in a model society founded on definite principles of social welfare'. To be fair, this was written before it was clear precisely how the Nazis were expressing this genuine belief, but later events did not greatly ruffle the ageing Shaw. In *Geneva*, performed in 1938, he gently satirizes characters representing Hitler, Mussolini and Franco when they defend their records before the Court of International Justice. But democracy emerges with no more credit than they, nor does the Jew who comes to complain against Hitler. When a rumour that the world is about to end disrupts the court, his reaction is to bolt to the telephone to sell his gilt-edged securities in order to buy them back as waste paper and die, at least nominally, a millionaire. 'What do you think,' asked Desmond MacCarthy when he reviewed the play, 'of introducing such an incident, *and at this moment in European history*, as symbolic of the Jewish soul when revealed under the stress of disaster? Speaking for myself, it made me ask if it were possible that I had been a fool about Bernard Shaw all my writing life.'

Shaw had a chance to display more humanity in the play's preface, which was published in 1945, five years before his death, at a time when the full monstrosity of the 'final solution' was becoming clear. He did not take it. Hitler, with Mussolini, was patronized as a 'poor devil'. Most of the deaths in the concentration camps were due to overcrowding and lack of food. The guards, who were not fiends, but only incompetents, 'could do nothing with their unwanted prisoners but kill them and burn the corpses they could not bury'. Any atrocities were due to 'the natural percentage of callous toughs among them'. They occur 'in every war when the troops get out of hand'. It is tempting to endorse MacCarthy's suggestion, published seven years earlier, that Shaw was suffering from senility of the heart: 'His recent comments on the state of the world have been marked by a chilling indifference to realities. He has been unable to write a page which did not betray his secret, that he can no longer feel anything much.' Unfortunately, as we've seen, the seeds of the illness had long, very long coexisted with the many qualities that make him enduringly great.

Man and Superman

Shaw described *Man and Superman* as a 'trumpery story of modern London life' and might have been still ruder. It is, on the face of it, a romantic melodrama, full of borrowed devices and shameless implausibilities. There is an eccentric will, putting the heroine in the charge of the man she eventually marries. There is a love-chase through Europe, a kidnapping by Spanish brigands, and a rescue. As a sub-plot, there is a secret marriage, made necessary by a rich and difficult father, who is ready to disinherit his son if he doesn't make the proper match. There are outrageous coincidences: the brigand-chief is in love with the sister of the hero's chauffeur, and has compromising information about the clandestinely wed lovers; he and his men also turn out to have an odd and sinister connection with the heavy father. And there is, of course, a happy ending for everyone involved: an engagement here, a reconciliation there. It is difficult to imagine any Victorian playwright who would have dared pack so many clichés into so small a space.

But the author is Shaw, and nothing is as straightforward as it seems. The father, a *nouveau-riche* Irish–American named Malone, is objecting to a perfectly suitable liaison between his son, Hector, and the upper-middle-class Violet Robinson. He wants his son to marry either well above or well below himself; his social principles insist on what the age would call a 'misalliance'. He is finally reconciled to the match, not by his daughter-in-law's purity and sweetness, but by her hardheadedness, her unflinching realism both about herself and her new husband. And the main plot, too, has been thoroughly 'Shavianized'.

The impediment to romance and marriage is the man's unwillingness, not the woman's qualms. It is not the newly appointed guardian who pursues his timorous ward to the south of Spain, but he who is running away from her, having become belatedly aware that she has designs on his bachelorhood. He, not she, is captured by brigands, and brigands who turn out to be no more predictable than anyone else, since most are political thinkers who spend their evenings in serious debate. She, not he, brings about the rescue, and she, not he, makes sure that everything ends in marriage, which is itself seen as a triumph for her but a defeat for her prospective husband. Add to all this a mysterious something called the 'life-force', and a two-hour philosophical discussion in the form of a dream, and you have something of which the combined forces of Scribe, Sardou, Henry Arthur Jones and Pinero would have been altogether incapable.

The play is a good answer to the accusations sometimes directed at Shaw's capacity for characterization. The less important figures may tend towards caricature but they are still lively and diverse: Roebuck Ramsden, indignantly preserving his self-esteem by proclaiming himself 'an advanced man before you were born', and in fact as ossified in his liberalism as the busts of Spencer and Bright that adorn his stately study; Mrs Whitefield, the heroine's confused and querulous mother, aware that she is being ignored, patronized or manipulated by everyone else, but unable to resist; Violet, steely, haughty and confident, knowing what she wants and more than capable of getting it; her brother Octavius, maudlin and mentally blind, more in love with being in love than with any woman; old Malone, like many of Shaw's more aggressive characters, soft and pliable behind a menacing exterior; Hector Malone, a satiric picture of the sententious American; and, not least, the chauffeur Straker, Shaw's portrait of H. G. Wells's 'new man', unaffectedly proud of his technical skill and somewhat contemptuous of those idlers who suppose themselves his social superiors. It is, however, the two protagonists, John Tanner and Ann Whitefield, who are the play's most complete successes.

To appreciate the latter, compare her with her friend Violet, the colder, more conventional, less likeable character, with none of that sense of fun, that capacity for mischief which apparently made Ann a troublesome child and has kept her a spirited adult. Both women are determined to achieve their ends, but Violet's seems to be largely money and social status, while Ann's is a lasting relationship with a man who attracts her, and attracts her for good reasons. She admires Tanner's obvious abilities, enjoys his eloquence and, perhaps above all, is impressed by his capacity to see through her ruses and deceptions, by that realism which compares so strikingly with the lovelorn absurdities of Octavius. 'Getting over an unfavourable impression is ever so much easier than living up to an ideal,' she says. 'Oh, I shall enrapture Jack sometimes.' Violet would never be capable of such candour.

This may seem an odd word to use about Ann, since she is consistently and deliberately guileful. When it becomes known that Violet is pregnant, her comment is that she 'has done something dreadful – we shall have to get her away somehow': in fact, she knows her friend is secretly married. Her most characteristic trick, as Tanner sees and Octavius cannot, is to present her more calculated selfishness as the wishes of other people. When she decides that Tanner should go for a drive with herself rather than with her younger sister, she suggests that her mother thinks close contact between him and the girl unsuitable. Actually, the old lady's view is precisely the opposite. Indeed, the very choice of Tanner as her guardian, which she piously represents as a paternal decision which she must patiently accept, turns out to have been her own idea, the first move in the plan to secure him as husband. It is the same with the prospective marriage itself: her mother wishes it, and her father's will suggests he wished it too, so she must submit. And yet the result of all this superficial dishonesty is a relationship that promises to be unusually honest and fulfilling.

Ann is less truthful than Tanner, but more in touch with the truth. He voices plenty of provocative and (sometimes) persuasive abstractions, but his grasp of the specific realities immediately around him is less sure. He sees through Ann, and is actually able to call her a liar, a bully, a coquette and (obliquely) a prostitute, but he does not see through her far or easily enough. His chauffeur has to tell him what is 'as plain as the nose on your face', that she is pursuing him, not, as he stupidly supposes, Octavius; and by that time her plans are well advanced. No wonder Ann is able to conclude, with what the stage directions immediately afterwards describe as 'a trace of contempt for the whole male sex', that Tanner may understand what she doesn't understand, but is 'a perfect baby in the things I *do* understand'.

Shaw himself was something of a baby in his dealings with women and sex, and it is tempting to identify him, at least partly, with Jack Tanner. He claimed that the character, with its abruptness and fiery volubility, was based on a prominent socialist of the time, H. M. Hyndman; but his contemporaries weren't convinced. Desmond MacCarthy noted that Granville-Barker, who created the part, was made to look 'as much like Mr Shaw as possible, with a red beard and Mephistophelean eyebrows'; and Walkley, the critic to whom Shaw dedicated the play, observed that Barker intermittently combed the beard with his fingers, a Shavian mannerism. Certainly, Shaw had not long before got married himself, after a bachelorhood no less dedicated than that of Tanner. And certainly many of Tanner's opinions are his. A ringing denunciation of the 'vile abjection of youth to age', for instance, is quintessential Shaw. What is interesting about this speech, however, is that it is based on a complete misapprehension: that it is Ann's mother, not Ann, who is trying to prevent the girl Rhoda from going out with him. Whatever its wider wisdom, in this particular context it is deluded drivel, and, ironically enough, it puts the unknowing Tanner still further into Ann's power, since it ends with his inciting her to 'break your chains' and drive with him across Europe to Africa, an invitation she is happy to accept.

Intelligent and eloquent though he may be, Tanner is perpetually making a fool of himself. He praises Violet for her courage in becoming pregnant outside wedlock, only to find that she is married already and exceedingly angry at being confused with 'one of the wretches of whom he approves'. Much later, he commends Hector for flouting morality by paying court to the married Violet, not knowing that the boy is in fact her husband, and, once again, is embarrassingly disabused. It is as if Shaw were deliberately sending up his own rebelliousness, his perverse, busybodying and garrulous temperament. Again and again Tanner is exposed as what Shaw himself was often accused of being, a brilliant windbag, a gifted waffler. 'You talk so well' is Ann's not inappropriate put-down after his speech about the 'abjection' of youth to age. And his denunciation of wedding rituals at the play's end only succeeds in provoking her to look at him 'with fond pride' and say 'Go on talking', as if the content of his words were infinitely less important than the figure he cuts while delivering them. 'Talking!' cries Tanner to 'general laughter', and the curtain comes down.

Part of the play's purpose, then, is to chronicle a resourceful and cunning woman's conquest of a man hardly less clever and emotionally unaware than Shaw himself. Briefly, Ann uses Jack's status as guardian to reestablish some of their childhood intimacy, even getting him to admit that their old friendship was an 'unconscious love compact'; and then she pursues him to Grenada, corners him, charms him, implores him to marry her, teases out of him an admission he loves her, and finally, when the others come in, declares that the two of them are engaged and dramatically swoons, momentarily recovering to check whether or not Jack has dared deny it. There are obvious reasons why he succumbs to her ruse: he likes her, he is sexually attracted to her, and, not least, he has been socially compromised. The enemy of convention is, ironically enough, defeated by the conventional expectations of his friends and acquaintances. But another and, for Shaw, far more important explanation rises to Tanner's trembling lips: 'The Life Force enchants me.'

To explain. Both protagonists are intended to represent

impulses beyond themselves, Ann the female need for security and a family, Tanner the male desire for personal achievement. Her attempts to trap him aren't just a matter of individual preference, but of biological compulsion – as Shaw remarks in his Epistle Dedicatory, 'every woman is not Ann, but Ann is Everywoman'. And Tanner's resistance isn't just his own masculine old-maidishness, but the urge to preserve the freedom that alone can allow him time and opportunity to develop his intellect and express it fully, imaginatively and to the benefit of society. When Ann patronizes him as a 'talker', and forecasts a future for him harmlessly letting off steam in Parliament, she isn't only making gentle fun of his loquacity: she is displaying a female voracity dangerous to his male integrity. As Shaw sees it, with a clarity we would nowadays call over-simple and perhaps even sexist, the two impulses are incompatible and doomed to remain in conflict until the man is overwhelmed by the woman or the woman rejected by the man.

Yet both impulses are also, of course, beneficent. *Man and Superman* isn't simply a deromanticized love-story, nor just a paradigm of the continuing battle between the sexes. The 'moral passion' for which Jack makes such high claims and the procreative, vitalist instinct which Ann represents are two cosmic forces, interdependent if embattled expressions of the 'life-force', each as necessary as the other to the future of the race. The play as a whole is heavily imbued with Shavian metaphysics; and the third act consists of little else. This is, Shaw later declared, 'a new book of Genesis for the Bible of the Evolutionists', a 'dramatic parable of Creative Evolution', the expression of a 'new religion'.

Don Juan in Hell, as the act is called, gives a characteristically Shavian twist to received opinions of the hereafter. Hell is, on the face of it, a happy place: a place of love and beauty where there is 'nothing to do but amuse yourself'. In Heaven happiness is irrelevant. It is the home of the 'masters of reality', to whom the business of life (or afterlife) is to work, struggle and strive towards that state of being in which the individual is 'omnipotent, omniscient, infallible, and withal completely, unilludedly self-conscious, in short a god'. Hell, on the other hand, is a place of illusion and convention, where men still worship the 'seven deadly virtues', honour, duty, justice and the like. Heaven is the home of the intellect, Hell of those 'greasy commonplaces', flesh and blood. In other words, Hell is life as most people live and see it. Heaven is life as Shaw believes it should be. And the act puts these warring stances into a dialogue, with Don Juan, the lover who never found satisfaction in love, speaking up for the evolutionary aspirations of the intellect, and the Devil cynically defending the view that man is incapable of moral improvement, that the world is incapable of progress, and that therefore the one would do best simply to enjoy the other. Dona Ana and the statue of her father are also on hand, though their contribution to the discussion is less important.

It is a lively debate, if not one that stands up to the closest analysis by those seeking foolproof consistency: through Don Juan Shaw talks to win, and win by any means he can. The question to be faced here, however, is its precise relevance to the rest of *Man and Superman*. Should it, like Tanner's 'revolutionist's handbook', be regarded as an unorthodox version of the Shavian preface, that is, an elaboration of the ideas raised within the action, a series of intellectual afterthoughts? Or is it more integral? Shaw declared in his Epistle Dedicatory that he published the 'revolutionist's handbook' at full length in order to avoid being accused of failing to prove that Tanner was, in fact, the genius he claimed to be. Can a parallel case be made for *Don Juan in Hell*? What *is* its impact on the plot proper, and the plot's impact on it?

Well, it is Tanner's dream, and it is peopled with characters identifiable with Ramsden, the leader of the brigands, and Ann, though in the last case the resemblance seems faint. Only when Dona Ana cries 'A mother for the superman!' and joins Juan on his exit to heaven do the two women begin to merge into one. There are, however, other obvious attempts to link the act to the play outside. Octavius's sentimental promise to Ann that 'one white hair of the woman I love will make me tremble more than the thickest gold tress from the most beautiful young head' precisely echoes the fraudulent promise the Statue remembers making to those who attracted him. Again, Ann rather bewilderingly refers to Tanner's 'famous ancestor, Don Juan'. Tanner's denunciation of a 'lifetime of happiness' as 'hell on earth' is at once a definition of the hell we are to see and a pre-echo of some of the conversation heard there. Above all, Tanner and Juan share the view that female sexuality is one of nature's least resistible forces, but one from which men must escape if the world is to progress on the most important level, the mental one.

In the dream, Juan wins the debate and is followed on to his higher plane by the woman he has, so to speak, intellectually seduced. In the play, Ann wins the battle, and is joined in her more ordinary world by the man she has rather more literally seduced. If we're to equate Tanner with Juan, and from both play and preface it's clear that Shaw expects us to do so, we can conclude that the dream partly exists to give Tanner a larger, more mythic significance, partly exposes his overweening, conceited image of himself, partly expands his philosophical ideas, partly demonstrates that those ideas cannot survive totally intact unless they are removed from the pressures of reality itself. Only in an imaginary world, an afterlife, can his theory remain unsullied. The dream is the thesis, the play the evidence that tends to challenge that thesis.

Man and Superman is usually played without *Don Juan*; but, without it, something is lost. Some have argued that the play trivializes the dream: which is true, if by 'trivialize' they really mean satirize by putting to the test of experience. It can as convincingly be claimed that the dream gives the play the more serious dimension its author wanted. Shaw may overstate things when he says that Tanner is a 'true Don Juan, with a sense of reality that disables convention, defying to the last the fate which finally overtakes him'. Most certainly, he fails to make the collision between male and female egos the 'tragic' affair he believes it can be. But Tolstoy surely exaggerated almost as greatly when he accused Shaw of speaking 'jauntily' of the purpose of human life in *Man and Superman*. After all that has preceded it, do we simply feel the ending to be the punch line of a prolonged jest? Isn't there something just a little despairing in Tanner's last cry, 'Talking!', and just a little cruel in the 'universal laughter' that follows it?

It may be extravagant to claim that one of nature's 'life-forces' has been crushed by another: it is an absurd understatement to talk as if no more has happened than that a windbag and emotional fool has received his just deserts. The impression with which the play leaves us is ambiguous, teasing. A man's ideals have been dented, yet so have his myopia, complacency and folly; he has lost himself, he has the opportunity to find himself in a new and perhaps profounder way; marriage may mar him, marriage may make him. There is reason to feel pessimistic about his future, reason to feel optimistic, and reason to respect a play that ends by making us feel both at the same time.

Major Barbara

Shaw was already becoming accustomed to the accusation that his plays were 'not plays' when he wrote *Major Barbara*, so he half-satirically subtitled it 'a discussion in three acts'. It is a caveat that the piece itself renders largely unnecessary. The most professional of dramatic craftsmen would be proud of the neat exegesis, in which Shaw quickly and amusingly fills in the background and characters of Lady Britomart and her son, Stephen, and prepares us for the appearance of their long-absent husband and father, the armament tycoon Andrew Undershaft; and the second act, occurring as it does in a Salvation Army shelter in the East End, is packed with character, colour and incident. Even in the third act, when the rights and wrongs of Undershaft's profession are most thoroughly debated, the 'discussion' never loses touch with the somewhat sensational situation that has provoked it. Will Cusins, the foundling, become heir-elect to the armourer's empire? And, if he does, will Barbara, the apostate Salvation Army major, marry him?

It is a tremendously lively play, but, Shaw being Shaw, it is the 'discussion' that finally matters. All the main characters, and several of the minor, have parts to fulfil in what becomes first a conflict, then a synthesis, between realism and idealism. Lady Britomart and Stephen, for instance, represent aspects of orthodox morality, with its myopia, its lack of realism and its misplaced idealism. She is a majestic and rather likeable hypocrite, to whom the profession of virtue is much more important than its practice. He is a smug prig, who believes that merely being an English gentleman is virtue, wisdom and religion enough. Both owe their prosperity to the Undershaft millions, that is to the profits of war and slaughter: a truth that discomforts Stephen rather more than the serenely self-assured Lady Brit. But his instinctive chauvinism ends by reconciling him to the Undershaft factory of death. Its efficiency makes it 'a credit to our country'.

But obviously it is the exceptional and extraordinary, not the conventional, that really interests Shaw; and the key moment in the first act is the challenge his two most vital characters offer one another. Barbara invites her father to her Salvationist shelter, declaring that the experience may move him to renounce the manufacture of weaponry. Undershaft invites his daughter to his cannon works, giving her a parallel warning. Which will prevail, and how?

The answer is Undershaft, who successfully adds his considerable weight to what becomes a pretty damaging critique of the Army and its methods. Shaw himself had watched William Booth's organization at work in the East End, where he had been impressed by its energy and determination: 'It marches to fight the devil with trumpet and drum, with music and dancing, with banner and palm, as becomes a sally from heaven by its happy garrison.' But its social impact he found suspect. It blackmailed starving men with bread and promises of heaven. The effect of its soup-kitchens, of its sermons about a better hereafter, and of the sometimes fraudulent and always melodramatic public confessions of its converts, was to pacify the rebellious poor and draw teeth that, perhaps, ought to be snapping at an unjust social system.

In Act II we are introduced to a cross-section of the East End proletariat the Army was in business to help: Peter Shirley, one of what the Victorians liked to call the 'deserving poor', a respectable, industrious and temperate worker thrown out of employment for no reason except middle age; Bill Walker, representing the 'undeserving poor', brutish enough to lash an inoffensive girl across the face; and Snobby Price, fly, sly and an opportunist, who exploits the Army's gullibility and kindness. It is the last of these who most clearly sees what is happening to all of them. The Army 'combs our 'air and makes us good little blokes to be robbed and put upon'. And this point of view is confirmed by the arch-robber, Undershaft, when he pays his promised visit. 'You see how we take the anger and bitterness against you out of their hearts,' says the Army commissioner, Mrs Baines, after Price has walked offstage, telling a pious lie and, incidentally, stealing a sovereign. 'It is certainly most convenient and gratifying to all large employers of labour' is Undershaft's reply.

But Undershaft's attack on the Salvation Army isn't limited to double-edged applause. His chance comes when it is revealed that Bodger, the whisky king, will give it £5,000 provided others make the figure up to £10,000. He, the armaments king, will be those 'others'. Now, the Army's attitude to such gifts was (and is) that it gets the money out of the Devil's hands into God's. As Mrs Baines cries, 'Who would have thought that any good could come out of war and drink? And yet their profits are brought today to the feet of salvation to do its blessed work.' The preface indicates that Shaw, too, saw the practical sense of this; and yet the play is at pains to point out its irony. Bodger is actually offering a pittance of his profits in order to rescue some of those who have become ruined in the process of producing those profits. He is securing his conscience, and perhaps his salvation, by handing over money the Army knows to be contaminated.

At any rate, this is the way Barbara sees it. Her father has demonstrated that the Army is dependent on corruption; and, still more significantly, he has exposed its spiritual claims. This is the importance of Bill Walker, one of those rogues in whose blackheartedness Shaw could never entirely believe. Little Jenny Hill, the Salvationist he has hit, is quick to forgive him, precisely the reaction he cannot accept. He wants to atone, and the Army won't allow him to do so, except by giving it himself. Specifically, Barbara turns down his offer of a compensatory sovereign, informing him that 'the Army is not to be bought: we want your soul, and will take nothing less'. Her father's offer to increase his gift to £100 she also resists. But her superiors eagerly accept his proffered £5,000, leaving Bill to conclude, reasonably enough, that the Army *can* be bought, provided the bribe is large enough. He promptly reverts to his old cynicism, crying 'Wot prawce selvytion nah?', and, as Barbara sees it, his soul is lost. 'My God, why hast Thou forsaken me?' she wails, and hands in her Salvation Army insignia. Undershaft has won.

But in what guise has he won? Is it simply a victory of Mammon over God? At the end of Act II it might appear so. Undershaft is the unscrupulous capitalist, different from his ilk only in the size of his success and the degree of his honesty. 'Unashamed' is his motto, and he bears it out by emphasizing his dedication to slaughter. Offered the standard excuse for his trade by the amiable fool Charles Lomax, that 'the more destructive war becomes, the sooner it will be abolished', he replies that it will rather become more fascinating. To Mrs Baines he boasts of 'the men and the lads torn to pieces with shrapnel and poisoned with lyddite, the oceans of blood'. Money and power are what matter to him. His 'religion' is to be a millionaire. And

those millions, and that power, are spent on refining weaponry, so that a hundred will be killed today where ten
were yesterday, and a thousand tomorrow.

In the first two acts he is not greatly interested in justifying himself. Altogether, he seems a very wicked man,
Sartorius of *Widowers' House* expanded to a positively satanic
size; and, indeed, he is actually described, only half-comi-
cally, as 'Mephistopheles', 'devil', 'demon' and 'the prince
of darkness'. Destruction is his profession, in every sense of
the word. He destroys his daughter's faith and he destroys
what she sees as Bill Walker's soul. All that can be said in
his favour is that Barbara's faith was, at least in Shaw's
eyes, a false faith, depending on ignorance of the economic
system and an illusory heaven; and, for Shaw, ignorance
and illusion are always to be rejected, whatever the personal cost. As Undershaft later tells her, 'You have made
for yourself something that you call a morality or a religion
or whatnot. It doesn't fit the facts. Well, scrap it, and get
one that does fit.' But, at the end of Act II, all he has to
offer in place of her punctured idealism is a 'realism' that
consists of the ruthless acquisition of money and gunpowder: unrestrained laissez-fairism.

It is in Act III that Undershaft is allowed to justify
himself, and he does so in a way markedly reminiscent of
Shaw's Mrs Warren. She, you recall, became first a prostitute, then a madame, in order to escape abject penury.
He was an East Ender who 'moralized and starved until
one day I swore that I would be a full-fed free man at all
costs; that nothing should stop me except a bullet, neither
reason nor morals nor the lives of other men'. In other
words, he reacted sensibly to an England which offered him
no other path to security, let alone prosperity. It isn't
surprising that Shaw thought of calling the play *Andrew
Undershaft's Profession*, as if to emphasize its similarity to the
earlier one. Both would thus be an attack on the crimes,
not of the individual, but of the society which drove the
individual to crime.

If Shaw had clung to such an intention, he would clearly

have had to tell us far more about Undershaft's bastard origins and deprived upbringing. But he seems to have changed his mind about the character and its meaning as the play progressed. The result is still, to be sure, very centrally an attack on the 'crime' of poverty, which, as Undershaft says, 'blights whole cities, spreads horrible pestilences, strikes dead the very souls of all who come within sight, sound or smell of it'. Shaw himself told Beatrice Webb that the play's subject was 'the need for a preliminary good physical environment before anything could be done to rescue the intelligence and morality of the average sensual man', and his preface reiterates the idea, insisting that 'our first duty, to which every other consideration should be sacrificed, is not to be poor'. Economic security must precede everything, because without it man's spirit is in chains or (worse) brutalized.

Walker, Shirley and Price are examples of the destruction and demoralization spread by poverty, and so, it at first seems, is Undershaft himself. But in the third act he changes from being the ugly effect of an evil system to being a constructive response to that system: Sartorius as hero, or Mrs Warren as life-force. It is a curious transformation, and one that needs brief elaboration.

Something of the old Undershaft does remain. He proclaims the 'good news' that three hundred men have been killed by his new aerial battleship, 'brutally' kicking a dummy soldier out of the way as he makes the boast. But his attitude to such slaughter is now that of the Shavian evolutionist. He declares that the 'best' of the mottos emblazoned in the Undershaft armoury by his predecessors is 'Nothing's ever done in this world unless men are prepared to kill one another if it is not done.' A little later he develops the idea: 'Poverty and slavery have stood up for centuries to your sermons and leading articles: they will not stand up to my machine-guns. Don't preach at them: don't reason with them. Kill them.' It is only a short way from this to the kind of attack on constitutional change with which Shaw's audiences were to become increasingly familiar in the years ahead. The ballot paper that really governs has a bullet in it. When you vote, you only change the names of the members of the Cabinet. When you shoot, 'you pull down governments, inaugurate new epochs, abolish old orders, and set up new'.

Suddenly the villain who emphasized to Mrs Baines that no drop of blood split by his weapons was 'shed in a really just cause' is discovering conscientious reasons for his trade. The 'factory of death' stops being simply the malign creation of 'unashamed' capitalism, and starts being the means by which capitalism may one day be overthrown, the 'crime' of poverty eradicated, and peace and equity established. Undershaft actually puts forward the very self-justification he had repudiated when it was offered him by Lomax. 'Dare we make war on war?' he asks his heir-apparent, Cusins, meaning that only violence today can prevent violence tomorrow. And all this is given the sanction of Shaw's developing religion. Undershaft is the super-man, and his armoury the expression of 'a will of which I am a part'.

It is pretty inconsistent, but it does provide a philosophy to fill the gap left by Barbara's loss of faith; and this is developed by Cusins, the Greek philosopher who will one day take over the munitions factory and reconcile her idealism with Undershaft's realism. Under his control the business will become still more beneficent, because he will give the 'common man' weapons to use against those elitists who have long oppressed them. This power will be 'strong enough to force the intellectual oligarchy to use its genius for the general good'. And Barbara, the ex-Salvationist, concurs. She not only supports Cusins's decision to become Undershaft's heir; she would never have married him if he had refused the offer. A sort of Blakean mysticism informs the pact: 'Then the way of life lies through the factory of death?' 'Yes, through the raising of hell to heaven and of man to God, through the unveiling of an eternal light in the Valley of the Shadow.'

There is room for several objections here. First, Cusins

does not strike us as a superman in embryo. When he introduces the characters, Shaw describes him as a 'most implacable, determined, tenacious, intolerant person who [is] considerate, gentle, explanatory, even mild and apologetic, capable possibly of murder, but not of cruelty or coarseness'. The responsibility placed on him at the end means he must possess these qualities, but they remain a matter of assertion by Shaw rather than of concrete proof by the play. Mostly he comes across as jaunty, frivolous and lightweight, not an impressive candidate either for Undershaft's heir or for Barbara's husband.

Second, Barbara herself makes a pretty feeble impact in Act III, perhaps because the play is virtually finished for her. In the Salvation Army she was powerful, commanding and, if we can judge by her manipulation of Bill Walker, supremely competent. Now her days are to be spent with the well-fed people of Perivale St Andrews, winning converts for a God in whom she scarcely seems any longer to believe and whose revealed word Shaw indisputably rejects. Compared with that of her husband, her work is clearly of minimal importance. It seems an altogether inadequate replacement for the vocation whose ruin in Act II led her actually to repeat Christ's words on the cross.

But the real objection is to the philosophy Shaw offers in the play and expands in the preface. As often, he takes it for granted that everything is to be judged, not by any intrinsic value, but by its practical effects, and in this case by its likely success in eradicating poverty. The Christian virtue of humility is thus simple cowardice. Pity, 'the scavenger of misery', is dismissed with contempt, and love with disgraceful brusqueness. 'Honour, justice, truth, love, mercy and so forth' are, in Undershaft's view, simply the luxuries of security and prosperity. 'Money and gunpowder' are the real virtues now, because they can create that security and prosperity later.

Here are two assumptions whose glibness recent history has tended to expose. The first is that the eradication of poverty will in fact make men less brutish and violent. A society that has become familiar with the 'problem of leisure' knows that a prosperous Bill Walker won't necessarily become a model citizen with a 'tall hat and a chapel sitting', as Undershaft prophesies: he may well prove as vicious in his suburban semi as in his Stepney slum. The second is, of course, that the weapons Undershaft offers with such evenhandedness are infinitely more likely to end with established tyrannies than with idealistic revolutionaries. Oppression rather than liberation would surely be the final effect of his policy; and Cusins's determination to arm the 'common' people, even supposing such an aspiration possible, is a recipe for Stalinism or some other variety of 'popular' autocracy. Indeed, the evidence Shaw himself offers tends to cast doubts on his political expectations. In the utopian Perivale St Andrews everything is strictly hierarchical, not by Undershaft's design, but because of his employees' wishes. The carmen snub the sweepers, the artisans the unskilled labourers, and so on up to the clerks, who snub everyone. Is a 'revolution of incalculable beneficence' likely to come from people whose inclination, when they have any prosperity or power at all, is to use it to dominate those about them?

So here we have Shaw the armchair revolutionary, with his intellectual bloodthirstiness; but also Shaw the intellectual provocateur, inciting debate and disagreement on a considerable range of subjects. Not many English plays have managed to be simultaneously serious about politics and religion. In 1905, *Major Barbara* was as unique as, let us at least admit, it remains entertaining.

Pygmalion

Pygmalion gives the Shavian treatment to two romantic stories. In its reworking of Ovid's *Metamorphoses*, Galatea is not brought to life and happily married to her maker. Rather, she is reduced by her Pygmalion to something not unlike a statue, and then, when she has acquired some confidence and independence, she rejects him. Again, the play may be seen as a modern *Cinderella*, with several of the familiar ingredients. There is a nasty stepmother in the background, but one who, we're told, becomes strangely benign once her economic fortunes have changed for the better. There are slippers, which are thrown at the head of the fairy godmother, or (rather) godfather, the symbol of whose complacent egocentricity they have become. There is a ball, but one which leaves its star and belle disillusioned. There is no certainty of marriage at the end, no promise of happiness. Indeed, the heroine actually threatens to go into partnership with the bad fairy, who has tried to outwit the godfather and expose the girl herself as a fraud.

But we are jumping ahead of the play, which has three approximate phases of development. In the first Professor Higgins, expert on phonetics, transforms Eliza Doolittle from a flower-girl into a superficial imitation of a lady. Her life before then has been unenviable. Half-a-crown is a day's wages, a sovereign a fortune. The short scene Shaw added for the film version of the play reveals that she lives in a single room of depressing poverty. More importantly, she lacks the experience to see the limitations of her lot and the language to express any but the shallowest thoughts and most generalized feelings. Wonder, fear and pain in her mouth become an indiscriminate 'Ah-ah-oh-ow-ow-oo!'

Yet at least she has a capacity for emotion. She is not as demoralized and numbed as her predicament might lead one to expect. She earns her own living with resourcefulness and pluck. She has the spirit and pride promptly to hire herself a cab with some of the loot Higgins has offhandedly dropped into her basket. More to the point, she has the enterprise and ambition to go to his house demanding, in a surprisingly highhanded way, that he teach her to speak properly. By the time he has agreed to accept the challenge, we have seen enough of her to know that she cannot simply be summed up as a 'baggage', a 'draggletailed guttersnipe', or any of the other insults he proceeds to direct at her. Such remarks mainly reflect on his insensitivity, and, indeed, suggest in advance that what he and his friend Pickering are pleased to call their 'experiment' may not be more than a limited success. To Higgins Eliza is at best a child, to be compulsorily bathed and coaxed with chocolates, at worst a thing, an object, fit to be thrown 'in the dustbin' or, when the lessons are ended, 'back into the gutter'. To believe, as he does, that she has 'no feelings we need bother about' is to risk creating no more than an automaton or, as his mother says, a 'doll': exquisite to see and hear, nothing else.

And that is precisely what Eliza is, or tries to be, at Mrs Higgins's tea party, where she causes consternation by saying all the wrong things in absolutely the right accent. This amusingly demonstrates that a nice voice and fine clothes are not enough to make a lady, let alone a plausible person. But the scene also indicates that Eliza will not, in fact, easily be transformed into the well-spoken robot of Higgins's hopes. Her conversation, which becomes a saga of poverty, disease, theft, alcoholism and murder culminating in the swearword that shocked the play's original audiences, is too robust and resilient. What is clearly desirable is some fusion between the old Eliza and the new; but, equally clearly, this isn't the correct one. At the moment the ingredients fail to congeal, creating a mix of crudeness and clockwork.

By the time Eliza returns from her triumph at the ambassador's ball she is neither crude nor clockwork. Her accomplishments are not a matter of mere elocution. She can express herself articulately and, as her conduct at Mrs Higgins's the next day confirms, she is at ease in a difficult social situation. Indeed, she can manipulate, even control it. This is partly due to her quick-witted absorption of the cultural crash-course that has been added to her lessons in phonetics. But Shaw emphasizes a rather subtler explanation. As Eliza says, 'Apart from the things anyone can pick up (dressing and the proper way of speaking and so on), the difference between a lady and a flower-girl is not how she behaves, but how she is treated.' It is Pickering's un-

failing courtesy, consideration and kindness that has given
her self-respect and confidence, and taught her those
aspects of gentility that are worth learning. If she had been
left to the rude, inconsiderate and unkind Higgins, she
could never have become what at last she is, a true lady.

So ends the second phase of Eliza's and the play's development, at which point a lesser dramatist would have
stopped. After all, Shaw has made an important point,
which is that gentility is a matter, not of heredity, but of
education and environment. By proving that a flower-girl
can learn to pass herself off as a duchess – or, to judge from
the excitement Eliza generates at the ball, a princess – he
has suggested that duchesses are in no important respect
better than flower-girls. In fact, duchesses are only
flower-girls with good clothes, good accents, and social
savoir-faire. It is an attack on the class system rather similar
to that Barrie mounts in his *Admirable Crichton*. Give the
downtrodden equality of opportunity, and many of them
will surely outpace their 'superiors'.

But Shaw is interested, not in readjusting the class system, rather in creating a world in which the concept of
'lady' or 'gentleman' is meaningless. What, after all, is
Eliza to do with her social acquisitions? Do they fulfil her
adequately? Do they even enable her to earn a living?
Higgins's sensible housekeeper, Mrs Pearce, insists from
the start that her employer think of Eliza's future, and Mrs
Higgins, who is as near to a moral touchstone as the play
offers, neatly sums up the danger. 'The manners and habits
that disqualify a fine lady from earning her own living
without giving her a fine lady's income!' she expostulates
to her son. One of the functions of the Eynsford-Hills, a
family which clings to gentility without the economic wher-
ewithal to sustain it, is to draw attention to precisely this
trap; and by Act IV Eliza has affirmed her new maturity
by seeing it for herself. She has been educated to be dissatisfied with her old life, and she is disgusted by the main
recourse her new one offers impecunious ladies, that of
catching a wealthy husband. 'I sold flowers, I didn't sell

myself,' she tells Higgins. 'Now you've made a lady of me I'm not fit to sell anything else.'

However helpless she feels, her behaviour now indicates that the third stage of her development is in progress. She is becoming a person, independent enough to criticize her master, stand up to his domineering contempt, and even throw slippers at him. By Act V, she is ready to leave him, though whether she actually does and (if so) for whom is left unclear. Her threat to work with Higgins's professional rival is presumably meant only to annoy. The asexual *ménage à trois* that attracts Higgins himself, in which he, she and Pickering will live together like 'old bachelors', seems improbable, though Eliza's parting shot ('What you are to do without me I cannot imagine!') suggests that it is conceivable. What's surely certain is that she does not marry her Pygmalion, in spite of the electricity that undoubtedly passes between them on the occasions she succeeds in riling him, upsetting him, and showing him that he is not as indifferent to her as he pretends. When Beerbohm Tree, who created the part, suggested a sentimental *rapprochement* by tossing Mrs Patrick Campbell's Eliza a rose, Shaw was outraged; and rightly so.

His view was that she eventually married the penniless, vacuous but adoring Freddie Eynsford-Hill. At any rate, his curiously cosy sequel to the play visualizes their setting up a thriving flower and vegetable shop. Now, this possibility is certainly prepared for by Eliza herself, who declares that she might 'make something' of Freddie and that his love for her 'makes him king enough for me'. But we must distinguish a play from its author's gloss on it, just as we must distinguish Galatea from her creator; and the ending of *Pygmalion* itself is, as it surely should be, less clear cut. To dispatch Eliza to a happy marriage and a successful job is to provide a solution to a predicament that has much more truth, significance and impact if it is left as a problem. After all, what *was* the place for a 'lady' who combined Eliza's energies, adornments and educational limitations in the society of 1912? What is it now?

But the play isn't only Eliza's story. Higgins changes, too; or, to be more exact, we see him in a new light at the end. From the start he is one of Shaw's liveliest creations: an egoist and bully with a genial manner, no malice, and a blithe unconsciousness of his worst faults. A point persistently made is that his manners are no better, and probably worse, than those of the slum Eliza. He is indiscriminately rude and boorish, pretty foul-mouthed by the standards of his day, and capable of such improprieties as using his sleeve as his napkin; and yet, of course, he is a prescriptive 'gentleman' and accepted by everyone as such. The character thus allows Shaw to emphasize the illogic of a society that can embrace an ill-mannered person with money and the right accent, and reject perfectly amiable people without those credentials. That such a one should set up as a teacher of polite behaviour is, of course, one of the play's ironic jokes.

But at the end Higgins has more importance than that. From the first he has claimed and demonstrated an uninterest in women, sex and romance. He takes what we may nowadays find an offensive and even vulgar attitude to such matters, but not necessarily one that would be altogether repudiated by Shaw, who regarded any emotional involvement that distracted a man from intellectual fulfilment as a temptation to be resisted. Higgins's single-minded devotion to his career has made him less unsympathetic than might otherwise have been the case, and now it helps make him Shavian. He cares for 'life, for humanity' rather than for importunate individuals. He dismisses Eliza's complaint that he has brought her 'trouble' with the assertion that 'making life means making trouble'. He proclaims the virtues of work, asceticism, 'coldness', and finally he congratulates Eliza on her new-won independence from him. She is no longer an emotional 'millstone': she is at last 'a woman', meaning a self-sufficient individual. At last she has deserved what he has always withheld, his respect.

A final word must be said about one of Shaw's most arresting and amusing characters, Eliza's father, Alfred

Doolittle, because he has a place in the play's meaning, if not in its plot. When he first arrives in Higgins's house, the attitude he strikes is that of the aggrieved father of melodrama, coming to defend a daughter nefariously abducted. But he is promptly revealed as yet another Shavian inversion. Actually, he wants money and, as he cheerfully admits, he wants money in order to enjoy himself. He proclaims himself a member of that class to which the Edwardians took so punitive an attitude, the 'undeserving poor', meaning those who refused to practise thrift but squandered their money on drink or other forms of 'irresponsibility'. Through him, Shaw attacks middle-class prudence, which may indeed be, as Doolittle claims, 'just an excuse for never giving me anything'. Through him and his hedonistic philosophy, Shaw also puts Eliza's social aspirations in wry perspective. Perhaps she will lose as well as gain something by renouncing the one English class that may still, if only sometimes and selectively, be capable of unselfconscious fun.

Certainly, Doolittle exposes the emptiness of some of those aspirations on his second appearance, at Mrs Higgins's. He has been left £3,000 a year, and dare not reject it, because the workhouse is the long-term alternative. The consequence is that his 'happy', 'free' days have gone: he is 'ruined', 'destroyed', 'delivered into the hands of middle-class morality'. A life of responsibility and obligation lies ahead of him. He must even 'learn to speak middle-class language' instead of 'proper English'. The immediate relevance of this to Eliza, who is also discovering the perils and pains of her new status, is obvious. Perhaps she has done no more than sell out to social convention. But Doolittle's words may also look forward to Higgins's last speeches. What is important is individual freedom and fulfilment, whether it is to be found in Higgins's work, Doolittle's play, or elsewhere: to trap someone in a social straitjacket is to wrong and diminish him.

This, perhaps, is the play's basic stance. It is a much more elaborate and less clear-cut critique of society than

Shaw himself implied by his claim that the bulk was written 'merely to call public attention to the importance of the study of phonetics' as a means of breaking down class barriers; and it is not only a critique of society. It is also a defence of a person's right to own and develop his or her soul.

Heartbreak House

Shaw called *Heartbreak House* his *Lear*, provoking critics to find ironic parallels between Ellie and Cordelia, the Shotover girls and Goneril and Regan, Shotover himself and Shakespeare's mad king, Hector Hushabye's second-act cry of 'fall and crush' and Albany's 'fall and cease', and, less fancifully, the title of the play and Lear's 'Break, heart, I prithee, break'. Actually, all he probably meant was that it was his most sombre work and perhaps his greatest. A comparison with the Chekhov of *The Cherry Orchard* is more apt, because Shaw himself made it in the preface to *Heartbreak House* and subtitled the play itself 'a fantasia in the Russian manner on English themes'. The subject, a cultured, leisured world near its end, is obviously Chekhovian. So is one of its main themes, the prevalence of illusion and illusions, and some of its detail: for instance, explosions no less ominous and symbolic than the famous breaking of the cello string. The difference is that Chekhov's characters are more realistic, richer and more resonant, Shaw's the representatives of ideas, points of view, that shift and alter during the play, but do not become more credible as sentient, suffering people. Perhaps he should have subtitled it, 'a fantasia in the Shavian manner on Chekhovian themes'.

The plot is thin. In so far as there is one at all, it involves Ellie, the penniless girl invited by Captain Shotover's younger daughter, Hesione Hushabye, to his Sussex home for the weekend. Soon after her arrival, she admits to being in love with one Marcus Darnley, who turns out to be Hesione's husband, Hector, in one of his many romantic disguises. Disillusioned, she becomes harder and more go-getting, and affirms her intention of marrying the successful financier, Mangan, even though she does not care for him. Later still, she rejects the prospect of money, discovers a spiritual dimension in herself, and declares herself married to the aged Shotover. The meaning of this curious match will be considered in a moment. The pattern of Ellie's development in the play is, however, a continual discovery of new, truer identities.

This stripping-away of fraud, pose and illusion occurs in other characters, too. Shotover is said to have sold his soul to the Devil long ago in Zanzibar: it was just a ruse, a rumour spread by himself to intimidate unruly sailors. Now he strives to attain the 'seventh degree of concentration', which turns out to mean that he is tippling rum in the kitchen. Hector's vaunted exploits are, of course, false. So is Hesione's exquisite, admired hair. Even Mangan's reputation for toughness and wealth is a façade. He never goes near his factories, because the workers alarm him, and anyway they belong to the 'syndicates and shareholders and all sorts of lazy good-for-nothing capitalists'. And a flirtation with Hesione reduces the great entrepreneur to abject misery: rejected, he blubs helplessly, as unimposing a figure as it is easy to imagine.

This particular transformation is characteristic of Shaw, who found it hard to believe in human evil and always preferred to belittle it. To him, as to the women, Mangan is fundamentally 'Little Alf', an overgrown child. It seems a self-indulgent view. Nevertheless, Shaw does go on to distinguish between the inadequate individual and his social role, making it clear that Mangan is also, as Shotover claims, one of those 'hogs to whom the universe is nothing but a machine for greasing their bristles and filling their snouts'. He has ruined men while pretending to help them. Indeed, Mangan himself admits that his main achievement, since being invited to bring his business skills to the government, has been to 'stick a ramrod' into the departments of people he feared would 'do me out of the credit and out of my chance of a title'. If he represents pretence and illusion in the play, he also represents misused power.

This brings us to Shaw's main purpose, which he elaborates in a preface that divides the English élite into the representatives of Heartbreak House and of what he calls Horseback Hall. Hesione's elder sister, Ariadne Utterword, makes roughly the same distinction in the play itself when she declares that good society consists of 'the equestrian classes and the neurotic classes', adding that 'everybody can see that the people who hunt are the right people and the people who don't are the wrong ones'. Shaw, of course, sees the situation the other way round. Horseback Hall consists of boorish, ignorant philistines, and Heartbreak House of people in whom, as he remarks apropos Chekhov, 'The pleasures of music, art, literature and the theatre have supplanted hunting, shooting, fishing.' Unluckily, the cultured people in England, as in the Russia of *The Cherry Orchard*, are politically and socially futile. They shrink from contact with the public world, thus ceding power to the barbarians.

Heartbreak House is an exposure of, and a lament for, precisely this folly. Those characters whose spiritual home is Horseback Hall are Mangan, the ultra-conventional and hypocritical Ariadne, and her husband Hastings Utterword, a colonial bureaucrat so faceless that he never actually appears in the play but so powerful that he dominates much of the conversation in his absence. This faction's ideal solution to England's problems would be, according to Ariadne, to 'get rid of your ridiculous sham democracy; and give Hastings the necessary powers, and a good supply of bamboo to bring the British native to his senses'. This would, of course, be anathema to the representatives of Heartbreak House; yet they have no alternative solution and don't even seem interested in discovering one.

For instance, Ellie's father, Mazzini Dunn, began adult life with the revolutionary hopes his name suggests, but is now happy to believe that the nation will 'blunder and

muddle on'. Hector enjoys playing the romantic hero, prac-
tising thrusts with his swordstick, dressing up as an Arab
sheikh, mythologizing his imaginary exploits, and even
dashing off upstairs, eyes blazing, when he hears a burglar
has been discovered; and behind the tales and lies he
actually has imagination, energy and courage. Yet he is as
publicly ineffective as his own name indicates. Hector
Hushabye: a Trojan warrior, snoozing in a cradle; a force
for political good rendered null by Hesione, the seductive
Trojan woman whose sacrifice to a sea-monster was demanded by Poseidon, and unwisely refused. If Shaw singles
out anything to blame for this character's dereliction, and
hence for the dereliction of Heartbreak House in general,
it is an over-absorption with love, sex, personal emotion.
'Fool, goat!' cries Hector in self-hatred after making a play
for his sister-in-law; yet he cannot help himself, and Hesione, who boasts that 'we live and love and have not a
care in the world', actually encourages his amours. He has
been reduced to a 'lap-dog', 'a household pet': Heartbreak
House is ultimately governed by 'the lovely women'.

The result, suggests Shaw, is drift, and the danger ship-
wreck. This metaphor is insistent from the opening of the
play, which confronts us with a room like part of an old-
fashioned schooner; and in the mouth of Shotover, the
retired naval captain, it becomes an explicit warning. What
hope is there for a ship of state yielded to 'Mangan, chance
and the devil?' Is it wise to trust in providence either in
seamanship or in politics?

> The captain is in his bunk, drinking bottled ditchwater; and
> the crew is gambling in the forecastle. She will strike and sink
> and split. Do you think the laws of God will be suspended in
> favour of England because you were born in it?

The only solution, says Shotover, is 'navigation – learn it
and live, or leave it and be damned'.

But where are we to find the navigator? And is it too
late? These are the questions that become paramount at
the end of the play. Ellie, in particular, provides an example

for the inhabitants of what she herself christens Heartbreak House. Loss of illusion, she finds, is painful. It breaks the heart, yet burns the boats, and so constitutes 'the beginning of peace'. Her first reaction to this discovery is, in fact, the one recommended by Shaw in *Major Barbara*, a principled avoidance of the evil of poverty: 'It is just because I want to save my soul that I am marrying for money.' But the prospective husband, Mangan, is not an Undershaft or Cusins. Indeed, Shaw is no longer naïvely excited by the idea of a union between the Barbaras and those with economic power. Shotover, so often his spokesman in the play, declares that Ellie and her generation have rejected the 'romance and sentiment and snobbery' of their elders for nothing better than 'money and comfort and hard common sense'. He warns her that if she sells herself, she will 'deal your soul a blow that all the books and pictures and concerts and scenery in the world can't heal'.

She listens. In fact, she renounces all personal expectation and finds a strange new happiness: 'I feel now as if there was nothing I could not do, because I want nothing.' The mystic marriage with her 'natural captain, spiritual husband and second father' follows. Now, obviously Ellie's development is very improbable in psychological terms; but it has its place in what's best seen as a dream-like debate, a sometimes nightmarish morality play. So, of course, does the eccentric, perceptive, misunderstood Shotover, conceivably Shaw's half-satirical self-portrait as well as his mouthpiece. His plans for destroying the Mangans by psychic ray sound like a wry burlesque of his author's own reliance on the power of a mind whose political impotence had become only too apparent; his terror of mental softening, of yielding to 'the sweetness of the fruit that is going rotten', may reflect Shaw's fear of weariness, weakening, senility. Whether or not this is so, however, a union between him and Ellie combines youth and age, vitality and wisdom, and the spiritual and social realism that both now represent.

But it is all very symbolic. How is such an ideal to come

to power? Shaw does not answer the question, but he does prophesy a social crisis, perhaps a cataclysm, out of which a new world will come. He wrote the play in 1916 and 1917, at a time when the Zeppelin raids were bringing a little of the reality of war to the English civilian. Hence, perhaps, the curious and sudden violence of the ending. A bomber reduces the neighbouring rectory to rubble, and then scores a direct hit on the gravel pit, where Mangan has gone to hide, along with the Shavian burglar who has interrupted the proceedings, not altogether relevantly, in Act II. It leaves Heartbreak House itself untouched, in spite of the efforts of Hector, who has been busily turning on the lights; but it will, it appears, be back again. Hesione, like her husband, would clearly welcome another such visit, and Ellie is 'radiant at the prospect'.

The play has given Shaw the opportunity to explore his mixed feelings about many subjects, from women to revolution to money; but nowhere is ambivalence more evident than here. The behaviour of some characters, notably Hector, suggests that Heartbreak House has a death-wish. Even the prospect of destruction is better than a 'damnably dull' existence. It was, perhaps, in this mood that many of England's sons hurried off to be killed in the trenches of France, a loss to civilization eloquently mourned by Shaw in his unusually grim and angry preface. On the other hand, it does offer the possibility of change, renewal. The Church has been symbolically bombed for, in Shotover's words, failing to head 'for God's open sea'. As Mazzini points out, 'the poor clergyman will have to get a new house'. At the same time, 'the two burglars – the two practical men of business' have been no less symbolically destroyed. What Shaw seems to be forecasting is breakdown, chaos, and a vacuum which, conceivably, the Ellies may have the opportunity to fill. That is presumably why she ends the play 'radiant' and talking of hope.

It is not, then, a hopeless play; but it is as dark a one as Shaw ever penned. Such solutions as Fabian socialism, creative evolution, or Undershaft's guns and money, were clearly looking inadequate to him, given the depth of the national disease that the war was continuing to demonstrate. What could be done for a land that remained complacent even in the middle of disaster? Must 'the heavens fall in thunder and destroy us', as Hector suggests? Will 'some new creation come to supplant us as we have supplanted the animals'? Or have we still an outside chance of correcting things for ourselves by ourselves?

St Joan

Although one would hardly go to *St Joan* for an objective history lesson, Shaw takes only one major liberty with the facts of the Maid's brief career. He transforms her first important miracle, which was knowing the outcome of the Battle of Herrings several days before the official messenger arrived at Vaucouleurs, into the mere bewitching of a henhouse. It becomes a comical coincidence, regarded as magical by the credulity of the time, and indicates very early in the play what its preface makes clear, that Shaw didn't believe Joan had any paranormal powers at all. Elsewhere, De Stogumber is given an importance his few recorded remarks scarcely justify, and Dunois and d'Alençon have been welded into a single character and given the former's name. The trial is greatly compressed, and the gap between Joan's capitulation to her accusers and her reassertion of belief in her voices, which was actually several days, is reduced to a few lines. But Shakespeare often took dramatic licence further than that, as Shaw himself pointed out.

Yet of course the play is calculatedly anachronistic when it comes to expressing and interpreting the facts. Its people talk in a modern idiom, heightened at times, but flexible enough to allow the intrusion of 'howlers', 'dug-outs', 'deliver the goods' and other 'regrettable lapses into the slang of today', as the critic of *The Times* originally called them. More to the point, they think and argue with an awareness of the issues and their historical significance impossible in the later Middle Ages. Shaw admitted this in his preface, suggesting that they say 'the things they actually would have said if they had known what they were really doing' and claiming that this was a necessary convention in order to 'make a twentieth-century audience conscious of an epoch fundamentally different from its own'. Different; yet, perhaps, similar as well. As Desmond MacCarthy argued in 1924, Joan's struggle is essentially that of Jesus, Galileo, or one of many lesser and later men and women. The play's 'spiritual and intellectual anachronisms are therefore in a sense artistic merits, for they help to generalize the case'. It could all be happening now.

What *is* Joan's struggle, both in its particular and more general aspects? It is with the French military practice of her day, which, we're told, reduced war into a mercenary tournament, with knights knocking other knights off their horses in order to claim the ransom. It is with received ideas of the station and behaviour proper to women. It is (as the English leader, Warwick, emphasizes) with a political system in which power tended to be exercised locally by barons rather than nationally by kings. It is against imperialism, in particular that English expansionism justified by De Stogumber because of his country's 'peculiar fitness to rule over less civilized races for their own good'. More importantly, it is against the Catholic Church's absolute hegemony on matters of faith and conscience. It is the struggle of Napoleonic realism against military romance, nationalism against feudalism, Protestantism against religious orthodoxy, the individual against the collective, the woman against sexual compartmentalization, youth against age, imagination against myopia, the spiritual against the numbly doctrinaire, the vital against the stagnant, the future against the present: in short, the questioning, rebellious, crusading temperament against every aspect of the *status quo*. It is this mind, spirit, talent and energy, not her martyrdom, that gives Joan her place in Shaw's pantheon. She is a saint because she represents what he calls 'the evolutionary appetite'.

Some critics have felt that Joan is too representative a

figure, too much a spokeswoman for her author's vitalist philosophy. T. S. Eliot went so far as to accuse Shaw of committing sacrilege, 'for instead of the saint or the strumpet of the legends, he has turned her into a great middle-class reformer, and her place is a little higher than Mrs Pankhurst'. Now, no one would claim that his Joan comes across as an unusually complex character, or deny that the play she dominates is as strongly didactic as Shaw declared all great art must be. Yet the effect she creates in the theatre is hardly of a series of ethical attitudes. Indeed, one of the traits that humanizes her is a blithe unawareness that she represents anything abstract and daunting, anything (indeed) except native common sense guided by God. Thus she can innocently believe herself a faithful daughter of the very Church her insistence on the primacy of her 'voices' is outraging. A jaunty, irrepressible enthusiasm, verging at times on gaucheness, marks her early scenes: a growing vanity and arrogance her later ones. True, she is disconcertingly single-minded throughout the play, as she must be; single-minded to the point of pig-headedness. But one only has to compare the naïve excitement of her first reaction to the Archbishop ('You are filled with the blessedness and glory of God himself') with her later impudence to him ('Speak, you, and tell him it is not God's will') to see the opportunity Shaw offers an actress to show change, development, within an emotionally consistent and consistently emotional personality.

This development also shifts the play from what Shaw himself admitted to be 'romance' towards what he and others have claimed as 'tragedy'. The mood of the first three scenes is gay, upbeat, optimistic. Joan charms and befuddles Baudricourt into sending her from Vaucouleurs to Chinon; she cannily picks out the Dauphin from among his courtiers, and somehow persuades him to give her power; her arrival at the Loire changes the unfavourable wind, allowing her and her companions to storm offstage to take Orléans. It is the sort of stuff that the anti-romantic Shaw would never countenance in fiction; but it actually happened, and so he records it, injecting into his fabric all the sceptical correctives he can – the Archbishop's cynical explanation of miracles in terms of public relations, for instance, or Dunois's patient demolition of Joan's wilder military ideas. But in Scene *iv*, the tide begins to turn. Warwick plots with Cauchon to capture and perhaps burn one now described as a 'heretic'; next, the Dauphin she has just crowned rejects her, and her other 'friends', military and ecclesiastic, indicate that she cannot rely on them; and then comes the trial and her execution by fire.

'An irresistible force met an immovable obstacle,' wrote Shaw, 'and developed the heat that consumed poor Joan.' Her faith was that force; the Church and law the obstacle; and Aristotle himself might have regarded the conflagration as tragic. True, the *Poetics* regard the passing of a 'virtuous man', let alone a saint, from prosperity to adversity as shocking and immoral; and much of Joan's sanctity survives Shavianization. Even though her author tends to think her 'voices' evidence only of an uncommonly receptive imagination, he recognizes that her beliefs were intense and profound: she is 'in love with religion'. Indeed, a believer could leave the play, for all Shaw's scepticism, concluding that what her imagination was receiving was, in fact, God. Yet Joan still fulfils the Aristotelian prescription for a tragic hero, because she has a 'hamartia', or flaw, principally a presumption 'beyond that [in the preface's words] of the proudest pope or haughtiest emperor'. Her habit of translating her own lights and graces into peremptory orders from above verges on hubris, a word explicitly used by the not-altogether-contemptible Archbishop. Her riposte to this accusation, 'I am not proud: I never speak unless I know I am right', amusingly exposes both this and a naïvety that itself accelerates her doom. Her extraordinary virtues bring about her destruction. But so do her ignorance of the realities of power, her failure to take account of the often sensible views of others, her wilfulness and obstinacy, not to mention the small but significant vanity that takes her into battle in a cloth-of-gold surcoat, thus causing her capture.

Whether her death provokes those traditionally tragic emotions, pity and fear, is another matter. Several critics have attacked Shaw's handling of the end of the trial scene, notably the famous speech in which she chooses death rather than an imprisonment that would deny her 'the wind in the trees, the larks in the sunshine, the young lambs crying through the healthy frost'. Raymond Williams, an extreme voice, feels that these 'mechanical evocations of nature' help turn Joan into a 'simple romantic heroine' and take the play itself into calculated pathos and melodrama. Yet Pirandello, perhaps not so responsive to the nuances of English, found a 'noble poetry' in this passage, and wondered why the New York audience did not burst into 'frenzied applause' at its emotional power. My own view falls somewhere between the two. I find it difficult to react strongly to the warrior-saint's sudden pastoral enthusiasm; but Shaw's handling of Joan's death seems to me enterprising and successful. First, he makes us aware of its horror and pain, through the unexpected ruse of bringing back the arch-chauvinist De Stogumber, who has hitherto displayed a caricatured lust for Joan's blood, in frantic regret and self-accusation. Then he allows the sympathetic Ladvenu to emphasize its nobility and spirituality. Whether or not a Christian martyrdom, bringing with it hope of a hereafter, can inspire pity and terror in Aristotle's sense, this one is surely very moving.

But it is for its intellectual sophistication rather than its emotional power that the sixth scene is best remembered. Indeed, Shaw's talent for thinking his way into opposing points of view, for presenting the same subject from different stances, is well illustrated by *St Joan* as a whole. We've already observed the complexity of his attitudes towards his protagonist and her spiritual claims. We should also have noticed the play's nice balance between high serious-ness and wry comedy, apparent even in the trial scene and itself the expression of a flexible, questioning mind, capable of discriminating between men, their acts and the abstractions they express or represent. As Shaw himself said, 'the angels may weep at the murder, but the gods laugh at the murderer'.

More specifically, he adamantly resists the glib thinking that brands the Inquisitor as iniquitous and Joan's conviction as a travesty of justice perpetrated by moral monsters. The distinction between Cauchon, who hopes to reclaim Joan from heresy, and Warwick, who sees her death as a political necessity, is as evident in Scene *vi* as in Scene *iv*. The girl is, as the Inquisitor claims, judged by 'her most faithful friends, all ardently desirous to save her soul from perdition'. She is given a fair trial, perhaps even a necessary one. Her principal judge's great speech, in which he justifies the Inquisition's apparent cruelty on the grounds that it prevents larger evils and replaces mob-justice with the rule of law, is not simply an instance of Shaw's perversity, his supposed fondness for finding white where others found black and vice versa. The Inquisitors had a strong case in their own day, perhaps even one worth hearing in the twentieth century. After all, the audiences of 1924 had recently seen appalling evidence of the world 'of blood, of fury, of desolation' prophesied by Cauchon if Joan's 'heresies' prevailed. Shaw, though of course ultimately on the side of the primacy of the individual soul and the saint who died for it, is openminded enough to recognize the attractions of the universal order that the Cauchons were desperately trying to impose and protect.

The 'comedy' of the epilogue shows the same sophistication and open-mindedness. Indeed, the very character of the former Dauphin, whose dream it is, simultaneously constitutes a justification of Joan, who did so much to transform him from a down-at-heel weakling into Charles the Victorious, and a critique of her intemperate zeal, since he has ruled long and well by keeping 'my nose pretty close to the ground'. The scene was much criticized in its theatrical period, which was less used than ours to switches of mood and tone; but it justifies itself in two ways. Obviously, it points out that this isn't, in Shaw's words, 'only a sensational tale of a girl who was burnt, leaving the spectators plunged in horror, despairing of humanity'. The words of the executioner at the end of Scene *vi*, 'You have heard the last of her,' are proved ironic by her rehabilitation and canonization. Her exemplary, inspirational qualities are now recognized by all and celebrated in a pastiche Te Deum, recited by the principal characters.

Second, it means that Shaw can close the play on a note, not of despair, nor even of celebration and hope, but of challenge. 'Tell me,' Joan asks her kneeling admirers, 'shall I rise from the dead, and come back to you a living woman?' They all 'spring to their feet in consternation'. Even the Vatican bureaucrat who has come by time-warp from the 1920s makes his excuses and leaves. As Shaw suggested in a radio-talk, many of his modern listeners would probably have voted for Joan's conviction if they had lived in the Middle Ages. Similarly, many would find the kind of threat she posed to established order intolerable nowadays. The shrewd Charles's words, that 'if you could bring her back to life, they would burn her again in six months, for all their present admiration of her', is aimed at more than the fifteenth century. Some have found the speech that ends the play mawkish, but it is surely inevitable: 'O God, that madest this beautiful earth, when will it be ready to receive Thy saints? How long, O God, how long?' The struggle between the Joans and the world will, *must*, continue: Shavian philosophy in a nutshell.

Harley Granville-Barker
(1877–1946)

Harley Granville-Barker was as near to a complete man of the theatre as Britain has produced: actor, director, scholar, theoretician, polemicist, and a much underrated dramatist. He was born in 1877, the son of a property speculator, first appeared on the London stage in 1892, and went on to take leading parts in many of the plays of his friend and mentor, Shaw: among them Marchbanks in *Candida*, Dubedat in *The Doctor's Dilemma*, Tanner in *Man and Superman*. The two latter performances were at the Court, during the famous period, from 1905 to 1907, when Granville-Barker managed that theatre with J. E. Vedrenne. There, too, he produced Galsworthy, Masefield, Yeats, Maeterlinck, several of Gilbert Murray's translations of Euripides, and his own best known play, *The Voysey Inheritance*.

But his next play, *Waste*, was banned by the Lord Chamberlain for its frankness about abortion (and, one suspects, politics), and, with Shaw, he became a leading crusader against censorship. He also helped lead an equally important and unsuccessful campaign for a National Theatre. But by the time the Great War broke out his practical involvement with the stage was virtually over. His marriage to the actress Lillah McCarthy collapsed, and he remarried an American poetess, Helen Huntington, who appears to have encouraged him to break with his previous associates, notably Shaw, and to cultivate his diplomatic and political ones, such as Asquith. His later years were spent lecturing and writing, most famously the *Prefaces to Shakespeare*, which uniquely combine literary intelligence and theatrical experience. He was Director of the British Institute of the University of Paris, and a Reader at Liverpool University. His death occurred in 1946.

Today he is mainly remembered for his four early plays – *The Marrying of Ann Leete* (1901), *The Voysey Inheritance* (1905), *Waste* (1907) and *The Madras House* (1910) – though the two he wrote in the 1920s, *The Secret Life* (1922) and *His Majesty* (1923) have their admirers. They have rarely been performed, because of the generally accepted wisdom that most were too intellectual, subtle and untheatrical. A. B. Walkley, for instance, dismissed *Ann Leete* as 'a practical joke', which showed 'no skill in building up the framework of a drama, no coherence, no clearness'. But it was always Granville-Barker's view (expressed in his preface to

Lear) that 'we need no more expect to receive . . . the full value of a great drama at a first hearing than we expect it of a complex piece of music'. The answer to those who find *Ann Leete* bewildering on first reading is, simply, to read it again.

It is a very interesting play, not least in its dénouement, when Ann Leete, daughter of a prominent eighteenth-century politician, rejects a highly convenient aristocratic marriage for her father's gardener. As he and she awkwardly face each other over the cottage fireplace, the reader may feel he has been peremptorily whisked from the world of Sheridan to that of Lawrence. But a closer look at the text should show him how many opportunities there are for the performers to prepare us for Ann's decision, by emphasizing the cynicism and emptiness of her father's circle and her own growing dissatisfaction with it. It is, in fact, a play for the theatre, not the study. When William Archer accused Granville-Barker, apropos *The Secret Life*, of 'drifting away from the theatre that is understanded by the people, even the fairly intelligent people', he replied that 'I protest I never have – I cannot – write an unactable play, it would be against nature, against second nature, anyhow; I act it as I write it.' His plays *are* incomprehensible – by those who take no pains comprehending them. They *are* unactable – by incompetent or unimaginative actors.

Several seem well worth attention. *Waste* is a perceptive, if overlong, study of another politician, the tough, able Henry Trebell. His mistress dies after an abortion, an event that persuades the government to disown him; and the play ends with the 'waste' of his suicide. *The Madras House* is more comic in tone, but hardly less serious in its concerns. 'The theme throughout is the present and future of women,' wrote an enthusiastic Max Beerbohm, 'women regarded from various standpoints, moral, aesthetic, economic, and so on.' Specifically, the sale of a drapery shop to an American chain-store gives Granville-Barker the opportunity to introduce a remarkably rich array of relevant characters,

principal among them Constantine Madras, a sensual Mo-
hammedan who believes that women can only find fulfilment in satisfying a particular (and possibly polygamous)
man, and his cool, aloof, highly Anglicized son, Philip,
whose 'way with a woman is to coax her on to the intellectual plane, where he thinks he can better her'. The final
two plays, though intricate and subtle, have not the abundance and energy of these. *His Majesty*, about a deposed
monarch half-heartedly trying to regain his kingdom, declines towards its end; and *The Secret Life*, about Evan
Strowde, a politican rendered ineffective by unattainable
longings and a sharp awareness of his errors and deficiencies, tends to become wordy, meditative and dull. Both
plays give some support to Maugham's view that
Granville-Barker needed 'more force, more go, more bluntness, more guts, more beef'.

But his work as a whole must have seemed marvellously
refreshing in a period when most British playwrights,
Maugham among them, were capable of little more than
bluntness and beef. Shaw did not exaggerate when, looking
back from 1946, he called Granville-Barker 'altogether the
most distinguished and incomparably the most cultivated
person whom circumstances had driven into the theatre at
that time'. He was, perhaps, ahead of his age. There is no
glibness about his characterization, no unnatural neatness
about his dialogue, no simplification of the moral issues, no
clean-cut conclusions for an indolent reader to carry home.
Today, too, one leaves his plays with a sense of having
encountered an unwontedly large, open and supple mind.
For instance, Granville-Barker achieves startling perspective by allowing Constantine to give a sort of mocking
Martian's-eye-view of European civilization; he then gently
accuses the same man of sexual greed and other not-very-
civilized vices; and that's by no means all there is to the
character and its meaning. His audiences are constantly
being asked to reassess the witnesses and the evidence they
so lavishly present.

But Granville-Barker's enthusiasm for and receptiveness

to ideas don't mean he has no convictions of his own. On the contrary, all his plays concern self-discovery and self-fulfilment: moral imperatives to him as to his most important influence, Ibsen. Ann Leete feels she can find herself only if she moves out of her milieu and, indeed, her class. In her case, this involves an escape from a public to a private life, from politics to domesticity and an embryonic love; but in most others the two worlds are inextricably related, dual objects of desire and need. It is vital to Trebell to steer his Disestablishment Bill through Parliament. He also discovers in himself emotion, part-sexual, part-paternal, that he has long been repressing, 'something in me which no knowledge touches, some power which should be the beginning of new strength': 'new strength' in his political life as well as his personal one. According to Evan Strowde, only inner satisfaction can give outer achievement meaning and value. But both men make this discovery too late: in Trebell's case, the woman he casually seduced and the child she was carrying are dead. Emotion, he declares, 'has been killed in me unborn before I had learned to understand it – and that's killing me'.

Not all Granville-Barker's protagonists are as ruthlessly logical as Trebell, who, seeing no future for himself in either inner or outer world, simply opts out of both. But they usually tend that way. They are detached, witty, ironical, observant, intellectual, honest, honourable, responsible, and (not least) dissatisfied. They rarely make as much of themselves as they think they should – precisely, it is said, Granville-Barker's own predicament. There was about him, too, the sort of unease, even melancholy, that afflicts his characters as they struggle to find fulfilment in a world that seems inherently unfulfilling. And as time passed he grew, if anything, more sceptical, both about relationships and public achievement.

Ann Leete may perhaps find contentment with her gardener; Philip Madras decides to seek election to the London County Council and fight for social change at the humblest level; Trebell has a burning sense of mission. But Evan

Strowde and 'His Majesty' always seem doubtful of the value of what they have to offer, and half-resigned to political failure; and, in Strowde's case, there turns out to be no emotional sanctuary to which he can escape. It could be that the dramatic slackness of the two last plays is a symptom of loss of confidence, faith and optimism on Granville-Barker's own part. Yet even there a distant and elusive vision may be glimpsed: of human wholeness – the inner and outer man reconciled, the individual in harmony with a society that uses him gladly. It is this attractive, improbable prospect that informs Granville-Barker's work and gives it its unity.

The Voysey Inheritance

Granville-Barker himself described *The Madras House* as 'far more universal than *Voysey*, and incidentally far better written'. Possibly he was right; but it is the earlier play that has excited the more admiration, perhaps because it is more easily accessible. Certainly, it is one of the very few British plays of the time, or indeed any time, that genuinely earns those familar hurrah-words, 'provocative' and 'controversial'. Not only does Granville-Barker mount an attack on middle-class 'respectability' and Edwardian self-satisfaction, taking that most morally pretentious of institutions, the law, as his particular target. Insidiously but irresistibly he manoeuvres us into agreeing that a good end may justify a criminal means, and, indeed, that a 'swindler' may be a higher moral being than the man whose money he misuses. Nor, Granville-Barker being the author, is that all.

Act I plunges us into the situation without fuss or preparation. Old Voysey, a flourishing and respected solicitor, has let his son and partner, Edward, into a secret: he has been speculating with his clients' trust funds while paying them interest. A large number of depleted accounts are the 'inheritance' he received from his own father and proposes handing over to the next generation of Voyseys. Edward is appalled and censorious, and listens incredulously as his father presents himself first as a martyr, then as a sort of hero, whose 'labour and devotion and self-sacrifice' have supported a large family, kept a celebrated business afloat, and ensured that no client has lost a penny of income or a night of sleep.

Unconventional questions are already being asked. Act II, which takes us into the family's comfortable Kent house, intensifies them. Could old Voysey possibly be right when he claims that his experience has made him a 'bigger, better, stronger man'? Isn't Edward rather too inclined to rest his objections on abstract 'principle'? Isn't he something of a prig? Who, really, is being harmed by Voysey's defalcations? Who is being endangered? At this point Granville-Barker introduces one of his most important characters, George Booth, an old gentleman who has led a life of contented inertia on unearned income. The highest virtue he can claim is, as Margery Morgan suggests, harmlessness, and that only 'with dubious right'. But Granville-Barker is a fair dramatist, and does not try to convince us that all investors are George Booths. There are also references to a 'nursie' whose £500 Voysey stole *in toto*, paying her a regular £75 a year.

Edward, who loves his father, agrees to share the 'inheritance' for the old man's lifetime, though he tries to make conditions that clearly will not be honoured. Voysey will not even lower the marriage portion he plans to give one of his daughters. He is a naturally generous character, and also something of a 'buccaneer': the inference is that he has come to relish his life of Inns-of-Court piracy. Later, it becomes apparent that he once managed to make good all his father's defalcations, only to find the urge to go on gambling irresistible. But by the beginning of Act III he is dead, and the family has just returned from his funeral. Suddenly, hysterically, Edward confronts them with the truth, declaring that he will accept public disgrace and (possibly) prison, while they must renounce their fortunes. This is not an idea that greatly appeals to them, and, as Max Beerbohm wrote,

Their attempts to reconcile their distaste for it with the
rectitude on which they pride themselves, and their
bewildered doubts as to how to reconcile their virtuous
indignation against their father with a decorous attitude
towards the deceased whom they have been so sincerely
mourning, and all the other elements of doubt that are
battling in their souls and making them dimly ridiculous even
to themselves, suffice to furnish what I am tempted to regard
as the finest scene of grim, ironic comedy in modern English
drama.

Major Booth Voysey, who now boorishly regards himself
as head of the family, tries to bully his brother into perpetuating the 'inheritance'. The girl to whom Edward has
unsuccessfully proposed marriage, Alice Maitland, criticizes him for his reliance on 'principle'; and he himself,
perhaps too quickly for credibility, agrees to try to make
good the 'smaller' accounts, restoring the capital as and
when he can. Act IV takes us back into the same office we
saw in Act I. Edward, it seems, is keeping his word – and
some of his principles. He refuses to pay the chief clerk his
regular Christmas bribe; he interviews his brother Hugh,
the artist of the family, who has decided that wealth has
spoiled him, and wishes to renounce his allowance; then
George Booth appears, insisting on withdrawing his entire,
huge fortune. Edward responds with a mixture of hysteria
and relief. The pretence is all over – or is it? Act V, which
returns us to the Voysey mansion, brings old Booth back
on stage with an offer. He has talked to the local vicar,
Colpus, whose trust money is also held by Voysey & Son,
and they have a joint proposition. If Edward will restore
their money first, they will say nothing. He contemptuously
refuses; and at the end of the play the inference is that the
'inheritance' will become public knowledge, mainly because
the vicarage has a reputation for not keeping secrets.

But now Edward has Alice. She has decided to marry
him, feeling that he has lost his priggishness and grappled
courageously with his burden. It is a conclusion that the

audience, too, should find difficult to resist. Edward, like Philip Madras, has learned that detached idealism is not enough. A man, to be justified, must involve himself in the practical problems around him. Trebell and Strowde come to realize that private fulfilment would make them better and more effective as public men; Edward's discovery is similar but opposite, that his work in Lincoln's Inn Fields has matured him as a private man. Once again, the ultimate vision and promise is human wholeness, a fusion of the public and private, something (we feel) Edward has come closer than most to achieving. The irony, of course, is that he does so by means usually considered dishonest.

But Granville-Barker is not only suggesting that dishonesty may sometimes be honourable. The questions he wants us to ask go far beyond that. What is wealth in the first place? Where did it originally come from, and why should individuals be able to accumulate it without regard to their actual needs? What is Edward sacrificing himself to protect? Isn't the ultimate effect of his heroism to bolster and reinforce an evil economic system? These points are raised in Act III by Alice, and Act IV by Hugh, who describes walking through London, disgusted by the filth of the streets and the children – 'It's no use preaching and patching up any longer, Edward. We must begin afresh. Don't you feel, even in your calmer moments, that the whole country is simply hideous?' It is not only that wealth is unjustly acquired: it is also badly used. The possession of it tends to corrupt the owner; the lack to dehumanize the deprived. At all events, it defines people: which is why Hugh wishes to renounce his fortune. He wants to discover 'whether I even exist or not. Am I only a pretence of a man animated by an income?' 'But you can't return to nature on the London pavements,' Edward reasonably replies. No – 'but is there no place on this earth where a man can prove his right to live by some other means than robbing his neighbour? Put me there naked and penniless. Put me to that test. If I can't answer it then turn down your thumb.'

Once again Granville-Barker's scope and perspective are remarkable. *The Voysey Inheritance* is as complete an essay on the subject of money as *The Madras House* on the subject of women. There, he contemplated Western civilization from the stance of the East; here, at least passingly, from that of the Garden of Eden. The objection, perhaps, is that the debate is too explicit and abstract. This was the point originally made by Walkley, who accused Granville-Barker of being over-influenced by Shaw. 'Mr Granville-Barker has a story to tell, an interesting story in itself, and as long as he lets the parts speak for themselves, all is plain sailing,' he wrote. 'But at periodic intervals, overcome by the atmosphere of the Court theatre, he feels impelled to offer you a gloss, a "Shavian" gloss, on the facts. Then all is confusion, "new" morality, Nietzschean "transvaluation", and goodness knows what.'

The indictment is exaggerated (where is the 'confusion'?), but not entirely unfair. Yet how, one wonders, could Granville-Barker possibly explore his subject so broadly without a certain spelling-out of the issues? The plot itself takes him a long way, and the very existence of some characters illustrates his chosen subject. George Booth is the obvious example. Another is Colpus, there to demonstrate how far some Christians are prepared to compromise with capitalism. Still another is Hugh's wife, Beatrice, there to balance his somewhat ingenuous idealism. She is a budding authoress, who has known poverty and sees nothing but self-indulgent folly in the voluntary rejection of money and security: a hard or (rather) hardened character, and one with an important contribution to make to the argument. But these people are not quite sufficient for Granville-Barker's purpose. He cannot say all he wants without venturing out of his naturalistic framework – and so, regrettably but inevitably, we get the excessive explicitness of which Walkley complained. But the blame isn't to be put on Shaw, Nietzsche, or any 'new morality': rather, on a style of drama ultimately incapable of containing elaborate thought.

Yet the play as a whole has sufficient sense of life to make this objection seem niggling. Granville-Barker excelled at creating the atmosphere, the 'feel' of a large family; and, though the first act of *The Madras House* is his principal triumph, *The Voysey Inheritance* is not far behind. Note, for instance, the care he has taken with the small part of the eldest daughter, the overburdened, unimaginative Honor, who has long accepted that her task in life is to attend to everyone else's smallest needs. Each character is at once credibly individual and suggestively representative of something larger than itself. 'There congregate at Chislehurst persons who speak for the Army, the Law, the Church, the gentlemen of England, masters and servants, Commerce and Art,' writes Miss Morgan; and her analysis of the play's careful structure, with its parallels and contrasts, is well worth reading. Major Booth Voysey she sees as a 'hollow imitation of his father, force without brains'; Trenchard Voysey QC, the old man's eldest, estranged son, is brains without heart, or 'legality divorced from moral values'; and both men are clearly to be compared with one another, with the ineffectual Hugh, and with Edward, who ends by synthesizing heart, brain and strength.

Characters who, like George Booth, might be mere caricatures are humanized. So is Hugh, who could easily be no more than a series of moral attitudes. The only exception to this rule is Alice Maitland, who, as Miss Morgan writes, 'is too consistently right to be dramatically tolerable'. She is, we feel, a mere mouthpiece of her author's moral sentiments – 'She shows no signs that she is in love with Edward,' wrote Beerbohm, 'or could possibly be in love with anyone except herself.' It may be significant that Granville-Barker, who was apt to tamper with his plays long after their first appearance, changed the scenes between her and Edward more than any others in *The Voysey Inheritance*. He seems to have been aware of what is, perhaps, his main failing as a dramatist: a certain coldness in his more intimate scenes between men and women. Like Shaw, he was more confident with ideas than with feeling, especially sexual feeling. But it is a failing that flaws *The Voysey Inheritance* only slightly. The achievement remains.

John Millington Synge
(1871–1909)

J. M. Synge was born in a Dublin suburb in 1871, his father a barrister, his mother an evangelical Christian whose oppressive Calvinism no doubt helps explain the dramatist's later agnosticism. He was a delicate child, was educated largely at home, and developed a strong and lasting interest in nature, country-walking and bird-watching. He took a degree in languages, including Celtic, at Trinity College, Dublin, travelled widely in Europe, and ended in Paris, where he wrote poetry and met W. B. Yeats, who advised him to go to the Aran Islands, off the west of Ireland, in search of 'a life that has never found expression'.

Accordingly, he took his violin and notebooks off to Aran, punctiliously recorded life as he discovered it or heard it in stories, and wrote two short plays that were then produced by the company Yeats had helped to found in Dublin, the Irish National Theatre Society at the Abbey Theatre. *The Shadow of the Glen* (1903) is a sombre comedy about a neglected girl who, believing her husband dead, starts talking of marriage to a local farmer, whereupon the old man leaps from beneath his winding-sheet and banishes her from his house. *Riders to the Sea* (1904), one of the few modern plays with any claim to be called a tragedy, involves the death of the sixth son of an old peasant woman, who has already lost his five brothers and her own husband to the sea. She ends beyond despair, in a spirit of simple stoicism: 'No man at all can be living for ever, and we must be satisfied.'

The Well of the Saints followed in 1905, a longer play which, though a failure at the Abbey, remains arguably his finest and certainly his most sardonic. A beggar and his wife, both blind, are given their sight by a peripatetic holy man. Unluckily, this destroys the illusion which has sustained them, that they are both exceptionally handsome. When the saint returns, and offers them a permanent cure for the blindness that has again overtaken them, the old husband deliberately dashes the holy water to the ground. As the couple is chased from the parish by an outraged populace, to what will probably soon be their deaths, they are already finding a new happiness in somewhat emended myths, she in the beauty of her white hair, he in the grandeur of his silvery beard.

The Playboy (1907) was the last of Synge's plays that he himself was to see on the stage. He died of cancer at the age of only thirty-seven, leaving unperformed the early *Tinker's Wedding*, in which a woman's plan to marry her travelling companion is thwarted by the demands of a mercenary priest and the irresponsibility of her drunken mother-in-law-elect, and the unrevised *Deirdre of the Sorrows*, the one play in which he deserted the peasantry for romantic lore. It tells of the desire of Conchubor, High King of Ulster, for the beautiful Deirdre; of her surreptitious marriage to Naisi and escape to seven years of bliss overseas; and of their fateful return. Naisi is killed by Conchubor's treachery, Deirdre commits suicide.

It is a frustratingly slim *oeuvre*, but a remarkably distinctive one, not only because of Synge's idiosyncratic use of language, but because of the grim yet ecstatic view of life his plays convey. Their people are unsophisticated and unsentimental, expressing simple feelings without self-consciousness, acting on them without fuss, and somehow scratching a living from land or sea. Isolation, loneliness, is a constant dread. Change, decay, old age and death are omnipresent, and there is no evident hope of a hereafter. These people invoke the Christian totems incessantly, but more from custom than deep-seated belief. The comforting promises the priest is reported as offering in *Riders to the Sea* are proved illusory. His God seems simply irrelevant, given the power of a nature which is always harsh, sometimes destructive.

Yet if nature is cruel, it is also a source of exhilaration and joy. At the end of *Shadow of the Glen* a passing tramp offers to take the rejected wife with him: 'You will be hearing the herons crying out over the black lakes, and you will be hearing the grouse and the owls with them, and the larks and the big thrushes when the days are warm.' The girl knows there will be hard times too, but she decides the risk is better than the safety of the local workhouse, and Synge clearly approves her choice. Wildness attracts him, in people as well as in the natural world to which, perhaps, they properly belong. Far better the rough, wayward travellers of *The Tinker's Wedding* than the dull, disapproving priest who wants their money. Neither social form nor Christian ritual has meaning for such as these. Synge believed there was an essential and inspiriting paganism in the Irish peasantry, heavily camouflaged though it might be.

But not everyone can or should become a tramp or tinker; and in the world in which his people commonly find themselves trapped, there is only one way in which this wildness, this paganism can find expression, and that is through imagination, dream, fantasy. The tension between an Irish imagination Synge found to be 'fiery and magnificent and tender' and an often numbing Irish reality is perhaps his principal concern. In *The Well of the Saints* the two beggars retreat permanently and by choice into fantasy rather than face a world they find ugly and punishing. When they see, they are blind: when they are blind, they see. Again, the seven happy years Deirdre spends with Naisi at Alban are, as she herself says, a sort of dream; and dreams, they both know, cannot last for ever. Naisi begins to fear he will tire of Deirdre. Deirdre, too, foresees decay, age, ugliness. So they return to Ulster knowing that Conchubor will almost certainly dishonour his promise and murder Naisi. It is a kind of suicide pact. Better a beautiful dream that ends in death than a slow awakening and the disillusion Synge regards as inevitable.

These are, of course, the extreme cases. Synge's other

characters do not simply opt out of reality. But, as we shall see in *The Playboy*, they can still feel the lure of the dream and experience the difficulty of reconciling it with everyday existence; and this may, perhaps, help to explain their very individual speech. Anyone who wants detailed information about the way the playwright anglicized Gaelic will find some in Alan Price's *Synge and Anglo-Irish Drama* and rather more in Nicholas Grene's *Synge*. Sufficient to say that he fashioned a prose poetry which manages to be concrete, vivid, rhythmically captivating, and yet plausible enough to use in plays that the Irish themselves sometimes found unpleasantly realistic.

He has been accused of exploiting it somewhat indiscriminately, and it is true that the grammar and perhaps even the cadences do not alter markedly from character to character. On the other hand, a comparison of Old Mahon's blunt, brutish language in *The Playboy* with that used by Pegeen Mike should be enough to show that he had other ways of distinguishing verbally between different people. A subtler accusation is that Synge is over-dependent on simile, and often very elaborate simile. Unlike the Elizabethans, with whom his language has so often been compared, he avoids metaphor and uses imagery as decoration, extrinsic to the idea that is being communicated. Now, there is truth in this, but not perhaps quite the truth the criticism suggests. It is, after all, not Synge who is speaking, but his characters: not he who is elaborating ordinary experience, but them.

The verbal excess, the extravagance if you like, is the logical expression of minds who find it difficult or painful to synchronize with objective truth. To escape into rhetoric is the imagination's protest against reality and its means of negotiating it. It is a way of investing the world with wonder and somehow surviving in it. As such, it adds depth and resonance to Synge's prime theme and a continuing Irish concern, the gulf between the wish, the hope, the dream, and the bald facts of daily life.

The Playboy of the Western World

Life in the remote village in whose pub, or 'shebeen', the
play occurs is clearly drab and unfulfilling. The men find
what solace they can in gossip and drinking, and the women
look for it in the men. Unfortunately, the only bachelor
who appears to be available to the publican's daughter, the
'wild-looking but fine' Pegeen, appears to be the gormless
and cowardly Shawn Keogh. Soon they will marry, in spite
of her obvious contempt for him and boredom with her lot.

All this is established within a few minutes of the opening. So is a certain callousness on the part of the local
peasantry. A man is groaning in the ditch outside, maybe
'getting his death' there, and no one seems interested in
helping him. As quickly, we learn two of the main characters' attitudes towards authority. Pegeen speaks approv-
ingly of a tearaway who 'knocked the eye from a peeler'.
However, Shawn is in total thrall to the local priest and
fearful of breaking his smallest taboo. This Father Reilly is
mentioned often. The Holy Father is invoked, too. One
might say that the very word 'father' sums up everything
Pegeen finds oppressive. This is a patriarchal society whose
official morality is determined by the Catholic hierarchy.

So when the stranger climbs out of the ditch, stumbles
into the pub, and then lets slip that he is on the run after
killing his father, Pegeen's reaction is not altogether surprising. To her this is exciting and liberating. It demonstrates initiative and courage, not malignity. And the men
are impressed, not the least horrified, even though Christy
Mahon, as the young man is called, has no better excuse
to offer than that his father was 'a dirty man, God forgive
me, and he getting old and crusty, the way I couldn't put
up with him at all'. They recognize that he may be caught
and hanged, because that is the law. But they see no connection between law and justice or law and morality. Indeed, Pegeen's father, at her suggestion, promptly hires
Christy as potboy, and his friends agree that he is just the
man to look after her while they are carousing at a local

wake: 'By the grace of God, herself will be safe this night, with a man killed his father holding danger from the door.'

This is one of several lines that rubs in the irony of the situation. A more celebrated one occurs when Christy is asked if he really killed his father: 'With the help of God I did, surely,' goes his reply, 'and that the Holy Immaculate Mother intercede for his soul.' This accentuates the gap between Christian profession and what Synge would see as the instinctive paganism of his people. It also dramatizes the naïvety, one might say innocence, of Christy himself. But it is perhaps too exaggerated to be totally plausible, and it is interesting to note that the play's original audience took offence at the first act only retrospectively. Not until the word 'bloody' was used did it begin to show its indignation, and not until 'shifts' were invoked did it turn into what W. G. Fay, actor and co-manager of the Abbey, called 'a veritable mob of howling devils'. Up to then it had given the appearance of enjoying a play that Synge himself had told a friend was to be 'an extravagant comedy' and which was not, it seemed, to be taken altogether seriously.

More of the *Playboy* riots in a moment. What needs to be said here is that the audience, even if triggered by trivialities, must have felt a growing mistrust. 'Extravagant comedy' is not, after all, adequate to sum up the play as it progresses. Pegeen fêtes the bewildered Christy; so does the Widow Quin, whom the death of a wild, boisterous husband has left sadly in need of male comfort; and the village girls bring him gifts. Then on comes his father, bruised but alive, and hunting down his runaway son. Attempts by the Widow, first to direct the old man elsewhere, then to pass him off as a madman, both fail. Christy, now victor of the local sports and affianced to Pegeen, is exposed as a liar at the very moment of his triumph. He tries to batter his father to death with a spade, just as he had done before, only to be seized by the villagers, who fear they may be accused of the murder if they do not hand him over to the police. Pegeen turns violently against him, the indestructible Old Mahon crawls on to the stage once more, and the play ends with father and son leaving for home.

So much for the outline of the plot. Let us consider the part played in it by the two main characters. The contrast between the impression Christy makes at first and the heroic qualities the villagers attribute to him is wide indeed. He is 'very tired and frightened and dirty' when he enters, and the way he proceeds to present and describe himself suggests that in his own parish he was a Shawn Keogh: mild, timid, despised by the girls, and in absolute thrall, not perhaps to the priest, but to his natural father. He presumably struck the old tyrant with his 'loy' in a moment of desperation, and ran in panic, not even checking that his victim was dead. And now he finds himself acclaimed for precisely those qualities he never had or, more accurately, never knew he had. Soon he is telling everyone what they want to hear, and talking of the ugly little assault as if it was an epic tussle between giants. He begins to believe in his own myth and, more interestingly, actually to *become* his own myth. Because Pegeen thinks of him as a desirable lover, he finds in himself a passion and eloquence quite missing before. Because he is expected to triumph in the sports, he promptly triumphs. Other people's confidence in him gives him self-confidence, their esteem makes him estimable. The mouse gradually transforms itself into the man for which it was mistaken.

He is, however, subjected to two big tests. One is the arrival of his father and the other the defection of Pegeen. The first test he begins by botching, not because his second attempt at murder fails, but because murder is not the solution. The second he passes, painful though it is. He turns out not simply to have substituted dependence on Pegeen for dependence on his father. On the contrary, he shows his new self-sufficiency by threatening, 'almost gaily', to kill any villager who dares apprehend him. And he proves his courage and independence, not by trying to kill his father a third time, but by making the old man understand that from now on their positions are reversed and he himself will be the master. As Christy leaves with an impressed and not displeased Mahon, he thanks the villagers, as well he might. They have indeed 'turned me into a likely gaffer in the end of all'.

In this case romance has become actuality, myth truth, the dream reality, and Pegeen is left wildly lamenting the man she has lost. Her fault all along has been that she has let herself be seduced by that romance, myth and dream, and to a degree the cannier and more experienced Widow Quin never allows herself to be. Hardly has she met Christy before she is calling him 'a fine, handsome young fellow with a noble brow', which he clearly isn't, and thinking of him as one of the poets: 'fine, fiery fellows with great rages when their tempers' roused'. She is a little disappointed to hear that he hasn't been 'living the like of a King of Norway or the eastern world', but she is firmly convinced he has the 'mighty spirit' she has been craving. Before long she has agreed to marry his 'poet's talking' and 'bravery of heart'. It isn't surprising she should be disappointed and angered by his 'treachery' in *not* having killed his father. Nor is it really surprising that Christy should fail to win her back by his desperate attempt to kill the old man now.

When the murder was invisible behind a cloud of heroic rhetoric, when it could be dignified by the imagination, it was possible to admire it. Now its sordid brutality is clear to see, that reaction is impossible. There is, as Pegeen says in perhaps the play's most important line, 'a great gap between a gallous story and a dirty deed'. She is right about that and, given her wild, proud character and extreme disillusion, it is logical that she behaves more vindictively than anyone else to Christy. Yet, in a sense, she is still the victim of her romantic imagination. If she had not submitted so entirely to it, she might now see him in a clearer, more balanced way. But it is not until too late that she realizes that Christy has, indeed, become the man she wanted. Her imagination has made him – and unmade herself.

Those who want a detailed résumé of the first reactions
to the play should consult James Kilroy's *The Playboy Riots*.
Enough to say that it provoked many of its spectators,
especially those with strong nationalistic feelings, to displays of fury never since matched in the theatre, even in
Dublin. History has tended to dismiss the protestors as
philistine fools; but there may be more to be said in their
defence than history has recognized. The play clearly reflects some ambivalence of aim on the part of Synge himself.
On the one hand, he defended it as 'an extravagance, made
to amuse'. On the other, he had reacted to the hostile
reception of *The Well of the Saints* by promising that 'the
next play I write I will make sure will annoy them'. And
if, as we have seen, the original production began by fulfilling his first intention, it ended by deliberately and consciously fulfilling the second.

William Fay saw *The Playboy* as 'wrath disguised in a
grin' and 'anger in excelsis'. To him and his brother Frank
it was a realistic satire that went too far. In fact, they tried
to persuade Synge to cut the scene in which Pegeen burns
Christie with lighted peat in order to accelerate his capture;
but to no avail. It was said that in the original production
this moment was itself akin to a murder attempt. Moreover,
Pegeen was very sensual, Christy unpleasant-looking, and
the bloody head of his father rather horrible. In other
words, it was an extremely realistic interpretation of the
play, and remained so until after Synge's death, when the
Abbey company began to emphasize its comic aspects, cast
a more romantic actor as Christy, and underplayed the
violence of the last act. Revivals since have usually erred
on the sentimental side, with the consequence that theatrical tradition has come to accept that *The Playboy* is a less
cutting play than Synge actually wrote and the first audience saw.

Yet even with its edge thus blunted, it is a provocative
piece. It still shows Christian savages unselfquestioningly
romanticizing, not just violence, not just murder, but the
great sin of patricide. In effect, it accuses at least some of

the Irish of extremes of self-deception and brutality. And if it is performed with unusual verisimilitude, the accusation obviously becomes more insistent, more serious. Nowadays audiences seem willing to be challenged and even insulted without demur, as if what they were seeing had no substance or relevance whatever. A more combative reaction at least suggests that the dramatist has struck home and his play actually matters. Thus it might be said that the outrage of the patriots was testimony to the power of the theatre in general and Synge in particular. As Malcolm Kelsall concludes in the October 1975 number of *Theatre Research International*, essential reading for anyone wishing to pursue this suggestion, 'the riots were natural, even, dare one suggest, healthy'.

John Galsworthy
(1867–1933)

Galsworthy was born in 1867, into the kind of upper-middle-class prosperity that was to be the wryly perceived subject of many of his novels and plays. He was educated at Harrow, where he excelled as an athlete, read law at Oxford, and was called to the bar: hence (it has been suggested) his balance and sense of fair play, his readiness to do justice to each side of any dramatic conflict. But he never actually spoke in a courtroom, preferring to travel – once, on a ship whose first mate was Joseph Conrad; later, in the company of his cousin's wife, Ada. This liaison, soon to lead to her divorce and a lasting marriage with him, doubtless increased the young man's embryonic rebelliousness, and encouraged him to renounce both the law and the family business for writing. A volume of short stories appeared in 1897; and in 1906 he published *The Man of Property*, the first volume of what was to become *The Forsyte Saga*, that 'satire' of middle-class values so seriously compromised, as it progresses, by Galsworthy's success, his reabsorption into the class he had once scandalized, his reacquired conservatism. In the theatre, too, his later work often lacks the bite of the earlier: compare *Escape* (1926), with its glib idealization of a dashing young patriot, with *The Silver Box* (1906), *Strife* (1909) or *Justice* (1910).

The first of these was presented by Granville-Barker at the Court; and it was widely admired for the restraint with which it demonstrated that there was one law for the rich, another for the poor, one for the unemployed man who is drunkenly given a valuable cigarette box, another for the MP's son who steals a girl's handbag. Here, as in the more accomplished *Eldest Son* (1912) and *Loyalties* (1922), Galsworthy condemned 'double standards', reminded audiences of a common humanity transcending class and caste, and did so without deviating from judicious naturalism into polemic. There are no heroes, no villains in his best work. As Max Beerbohm wrote of *Justice*, he 'carefully eschews any show of sympathy with one character or of antipathy towards another . . . he strives unremittingly to be quite impartial. He knows that a suspicion of special pleading would jeopardize his case.' The method worked, too. *Justice*, with its famous scene of a crazed young man trapped in a cell, is credited with having ended the practice of putting freshly convicted felons into solitary confinement. Had this young man not been weak, unprepossessing and unquestionably guilty of fraud, had his trial not been fairly conducted and the prison not run by a relatively humane man, the play would doubtless have been far less effective. Galsworthy's great forensic strength is his apparent impersonality.

Those who look for revolutionary zeal in his early work are doomed to disappointment, from every point of view. He was essentially a reformist. In his life, he crusaded for many liberal causes, from women's suffrage to the abolition of censorship to the humane slaughter of cattle, and gave vast sums to charities. His plays, too, were designed to help improve the *status quo*; and goodwill and common sense generally seemed to him sufficient weapons. There's no suggestion in them that society must be radically, painfully reconstructed if social enemies are to be reconciled and social ills remedied.

There is a good deal of enmity in his plays, some of it surprisingly intense. Moderate Galsworthy may be, dispassionate he may appear – mild his work certainly isn't, at any rate when negative emotions are on display. Class and caste divisions cause bitterness, envy and anger, a hatred at its most implacable in *Strife*, *Loyalties* and (especially) *The Skin Game* (1920). 'If ever I can do you or yours a hurt I will,' the *nouveau-riche* Hornblower tells the snobbish Mrs Hillcrist after she has blackmailed him into submission; and one believes him. Who would imagine that a dispute over land could generate such heat, and in an English play of the 1920s? And here it is the innocent who mainly suffer, as in many of Galsworthy's plays. A woman loses her unborn baby, another is left a widow, another made destitute, yet another starves to death, and all because of other people's quarrels, other people's intransigence.

Galsworthy died in 1933, loaded with honours, among them the Nobel Prize. He left twenty-one full-length plays, of which all those mentioned are still worth reading, even if many of the social malaises they describe are solved, or at least improved. They are not technically adventurous, but they show that documentary precision can be reconciled with serious argument and pointed analysis. They are not enormously provocative, but they perpetuate an honourable liberal tradition, perhaps carry it a little further forward. They are decent, humane, and often theatrically gripping as well. And the best and most characteristic of them is *Strife*.

Strife

We spend the first act in the house of Francis Underwood, manager of the Trenartha Tin Plate Works and husband of Enid, who also happens to be the daughter of the company chairman, John Anthony. Anthony and his fellow-directors, including his son Edgar, are down from London in hopes of settling a factory strike that has dragged on throughout the winter. Everyone on the management side wants compromise except old Anthony, and so does almost everyone on the workers' side, the main exception here being the strike leader, David Roberts. Both refuse to move an inch, and a meeting between directors and men ends in deadlock.

Act II takes us first into the Roberts's cottage, where we meet women of the village and hear stories of suffering and near-starvation. The sickly Annie Roberts was once maid to Enid Anthony, who now visits her, offering food that is refused. Enid is abused as a 'spy' by one Madge Thomas, who then persuades her admirer, George Rouse, to desert his ally Roberts at the next strike meeting. Although every character in the play is at least to some extent individualized, most also have a more general, representative function. Enid is the middle-class 'do-gooder' who cannot understand why her help should be spurned as patronizing and she herself hated as a class enemy. Madge is an updated version of Aristophanes's Lysistrata. She shows how women's pressure can, and in strikes often does, undermine men's solidarity.

The act's second scene is the strike meeting itself. The Union leader, suggestively named Harness, has withdrawn support for the men because some of their demands are too great, but he promises to restore it if they are moderated. Rouse and Madge's pious and chapel-fearing father also edge the majority towards compromise; but their impact is far less than that of Roberts, who launches into a fiery denunciation of capitalism and urges absolute intransigence on the crowd. Then comes news his wife has died. He goes, and in his absence the moderates triumph. The men instruct the union to negotiate a settlement.

Act III returns us to an increasingly fractious and divided board. Old Anthony is unmoved by appeals on behalf of the shareholders and by an emotional attack by Edgar, who feels the directors must take responsibility for the suffering of women and children. When the vote goes against him, he resigns in disgust. The men file in, followed by Roberts, who berates them for cowardice. Harness and the company secretary sit down to work out an agreement which, it appears, is identical to the one they put to both sides four months ago. It has all been a destructive waste, killing a woman, breaking 'the two best men' and leaving a residual bitterness summed up by Madge's final threat to Enid, 'When a person hurts us we get it back on them.'

First of all, the play shows Galsworthy's mastery of naturalism. True, we must accept such plot-tightening improbabilities as a close relationship between the chairman's daughter and the strike leader's wife; but, that done, it is impossible not to admire the quick, unobtrusive way he feeds us the essentials of the situation and distinguishes between the characters, piecing together a structure plausible in its detail and yet so shaped as to keep the action and argument moving forward smoothly and arrestingly.

Indeed, the naturalism is part of the argument. The tenor of the plot and the nature of the ending strongly suggest that Galsworthy is on the side of the moderates. But he never visibly intrudes or manipulates; the conclusion is reached without obvious bias or special pleading; and the case for compromise is the stronger as a result. The suffering women are not romanticized, and Anthony's fellow-directors are no worse than vacillating, unimaginative and perhaps a little selfish. One grumbles about the food in the local hotel, forgetting that his workpeople are eating almost nothing. Another worries about whether or not he will get away in time to take his wife to Spain, though (a touch indicative of the author's fairness) he needs to do so, because she is ill and might not survive the English winter. Enid and Edgar are both humane people thrust by circumstances on to a side of the barricades that makes them thoroughly uncomfortable. And Galsworthy does equal justice to the two main combatants, Anthony and Roberts.

The characterization of these is perhaps the play's principal strength. It is not done in great depth, first, because they are both seen mainly in their public roles, second, because Galsworthy was not a psychologically penetrating writer at the best of times. But it is done with great intensity. Anthony is one of those rock-like old men for whom Galsworthy always had a grudging admiration; and the speech in which he warns his fellow-directors that concessions will lead to new demands, until they are 'floundering in the bog [with] the very men you have given way to', retains some power today. Much the same can be said for Roberts's charismatic oratory, his eloquence when it comes to denouncing the 'thing that buys the sweat o' men's brows, the tortures of their brains, at its own price – capital!' Each man represents a stance that the play suggests is too extreme and uncompromising, yet each has a force of personality that makes the moderates seem insipid. Galsworthy's head may be against them; his heart, paradoxically enough, is with them both.

As the reviews of the National Theatre revival in 1978 recognized, *Strife* has obvious aptness at a time of industrial turmoil, such as the last decade. It is often surprisingly prescient in its analysis of 'the trouble of the century', and it has considerable theatrical virtues, too. Beerbohm, who pronounced it a 'great play', particularly noted the moment at the end when the two beaten fanatics look each other in the eyes and slightly bow, in recognition and respect. Then there is the strike meeting of the second act. Galsworthy is always gripping in quasi-documentary set pieces: the courtroom scene in *Justice*, for instance, or an auction in *The Skin Game*. But here passion combines with authenticity to a rare degree. One feels oneself – as with the board meetings, too – thrust into the rough-and-tumble of practical politics.

But the play does, of course, date somewhat. Changing attitudes have been kinder to Roberts than Anthony. From the stance of the 1980s his radicalism seems far less extraordinary than audiences of 1909 would have considered it, and the other's conservatism far more reactionary. To accept them as equal if opposite extremists is more difficult now than then. Moreover, a contemporary socialist is likely to be irritated by the emphasis Galsworthy places on personal motivation. Anthony is perhaps actuated by the mere desire to win a fight; Roberts feels a real, deep bitterness. He was paid only £700 for an invention that made the company £100,000, and the suggestion is that it was this grievance which politicized him. Some may think this a sly way of casting doubt on social and economic views that seem perfectly tenable nowadays.

Beside such great plays about social upheaval as *The Cherry Orchard* or Gorki's *Enemies*, *Strife* seems somewhat insular and lacking in resonance. It is not so much that we have only a limited sense of the characters in their private capacities, away from the industrial dispute that brings them together (one might almost say, as D. H. Lawrence did of the Forsytes, that they are all economic beings, defined by money or the lack of it). It is rather that a Chekhov or a Gorki would have put the characters into a deeper perspective, and asked larger questions about the fate of the society to which they belonged. Galsworthy has no cosmic vision. Early twentieth-century English society is his interest, the practical ordering and humanizing of it his concern. But within those self-imposed limits he is trenchant and assured.

Stanley Houghton
(1881–1913)

Stanley Houghton was born in Cheshire in 1881, and, after leaving Manchester Grammar School, went into his father's cotton business, regarding this as a stop-gap before he became a full-time writer. This last step he was not, however, to make until the London triumph of *Hindle Wakes* in 1912, after which he had barely another year to live. He died of meningitis in December 1913, if not the most famous of the playwrights based on Miss Horniman's Gaiety Theatre, in Manchester, certainly the one of whom most had come to be expected.

His short life was unusually productive. Besides prose

fiction, essays, and theatre reviews for the *Manchester Guardian*, he wrote eight full-length plays and as many one-acters, the most celebrated of which is *The Dear Departed* (1908). Anyone approaching Houghton would do well to start with this succinct and amusing anecdote about the grasping daughter who seeks to outwit her no less avaricious sister by stealing their deceased father's chest of drawers, and then to out-mourn her, only to discover that the prone figure on the bed upstairs is not only not dead, but about to re-marry. 'These things,' wrote C. E. Montague, his mind perhaps on Synge's rather similar *Shadow of the Glen*, 'are a kind of dramatic common or open space. Every playwright has equal rights over them. What matters is the way the rights are used.' Appropriately enough, he drew attention to Houghton's 'pretty turn of observation', 'fresh, quick relish for the harsh humour of the situation', and 'capital sense of theatrical values', meaning neat construction, dramatic economy, and deft timing of comic effects. He might have added a strong sense of place, in this case lower-middle-class Manchester.

These remain Houghton's prime qualities, though he tried to develop others. The short *Master of the House* (1910), for instance, is understated melodrama, generating a rather morbid menace from (once again) death and greed. *Phipps* (1912), *Fancy Free* (1911), and the full-length *Partners* (1911) are comedies of manners, the last of them a sort of dramatic dance in which two husbands and two wives weave intricate patterns with one another before returning to the safety of marriage. The knowing, cynical, selfconsciously aphoristic dialogue owes something to Gilbert, something more to Wilde: one never feels that Houghton, witty though he sometimes is, has managed to concoct a style of his own. His plot is more sophisticated than he is himself.

Houghton is more at home when he is dealing with unheightened reality and with the subject that links many of his plays, namely the oppression of the young, and especially of young women. In *Marriages in the Making* (1909) a spirited girl breaks her engagement to the priggish and embryonically tyrannical young man her mother has thrust upon her, and realigns herself with a relaxed and tolerant suitor. In *The Younger Generation* (1909), like several of the plays set in 'Salchester', an obvious amalgam of Manchester and Salford, a repressive, chapel-going father is pointedly reminded of his own youthful imperfections and persuaded, much against his will, to give his grown-up children more freedom. In *The Perfect Cure* (1911), a girl is released from total subjection to a valetudinarian father by the intervention of a north-country cousin, and married to the young man she had felt it her filial duty to reject.

The moral of these plays is, as the Lancashire cousin tells her protégée, that 'it's your duty, and everybody's duty, to be free, first of all'. Parents cannot fully understand the aspirations of the young. Youth must be allowed to make its own mistakes, trusting in its own instincts, because 'they're a truer guide in the long run than the cut-and-dried wisdom of the older generation'. Sometimes this message has a distinctly feminist slant to it. The most forceful character in the early *Independent Means* (1908) is a young wife who eloquently attacks her nearly bankrupt father-in-law both for his domineering behaviour and for his reliance on the lottery of the stock market, and proceeds to leave her weak, spoiled husband, declaring that 'I must be loyal to myself, first of all.' She will return only when he respects her freedom to take the job and participate in the political activities she wants. The later plays are, however, less specific and doctrinaire, more concerned with what Houghton clearly feels to be a general issue of human rights.

These plays leave us with the impression of a craftsmanlike author with an amiable temperament, a nice sense of humour, and some capacity for indignation; but they are uneven. *Independent Means* is derivative, obviously indebted to Ibsen and Shaw. The better *Younger Generation* and *Perfect Cure* have plots that are not only neat, but pat. His friend and fellow-dramatist Harold Brighouse reported that he 'knew the full course of his play before he wrote a line of dialogue'. Perhaps as a consequence, one feels that his characters are carefully manipulated to a predetermined conclusion. They do not often blaze into first-hand life – or, more accurately, they do not do so until *Hindle Wakes*. Nothing in Houghton's previous or subsequent *oeuvre* quite prepares us for the excellence of that.

Hindle Wakes

The play starts, prophetically enough, with thunder and lightning offstage, and there is an unexplained tension in 137, Burnley Road, Hindle, Lancs. Mr and Mrs Hawthorn are waiting for their daughter Fanny, who has been spending the 'wakes' holiday in Blackpool. For some reason they are worried. The conversation turns, casually but (again) prophetically, to the rich mill owner Nat Jeffcote and his son Alan, who has been off motoring in Wales; and then Fanny arrives, explaining that she has just returned with her friend, Mary. This, they say, is a lie. She keeps up the pretence, and then her parents hit her (and the audience) with their news. Mary is dead, drowned: where has Fanny been? In her distress, she mentions Llandudno, and the truth is out. She has been weekending with Alan Jeffcote: a shocking revelation, given the standards of respectability by which this tight-knit community lives. Her mother's instant reaction is that Fanny is a fool not to have exploited the situation to her economic advantage: 'What did you do it for if you didn't make him promise to wed you?' Her more considered view, however, is that Fanny may have been slyly preparing Alan for marriage. Her father, kinder and less crass, nevertheless agrees that wedlock is the only answer, and prepares to tackle Nat Jeffcote, who is, in fact, his old friend and one-time workmate, though since risen far beyond him in wealth and status.

It is a neatly constructed opening, one which, like the play as a whole, confirms Brighouse's view of Houghton as a 'first-rate technical artist'. The characterization is deftly and economically done, not least that of Fanny, who shows some toughness and spirit in resisting her parents' assault; and there is more to come. Nat Jeffcote's love of the power and influence he has achieved combines with his pride in his flinty integrity to produce the first of the play's dramatic ironies. Not knowing the seducer is his son, he announces he'll personally make sure he'll marry Fanny; and the truth makes him, first furious, then resolved. Promises must be kept. Right must be done. Alan must break his engagement to Beatrice Farrar, daughter of the second richest mill owner in Hindle and an acquisition on whom Nat has set his heart. When the boy's mother demurs, she's told she doesn't wear the breeches. When the boy himself tells his father to mind his own business, he is warned he'll be cut off without a penny. While old Jeffcote's intentions are to some extent honourable and even admirable – 'honestly' is the word with which he three times reminds his palpitating son of his duty – it becomes increasingly clear that he is determined to get his own way simply because it *is* his own way, a proof of his strength and an end in itself.

He comes close to getting it, too. Alan may stand up to his father; he may even stand up to Farrar, who quickly reneges on his promise to 'back you up' when the boy's prospective fortune disappears; but he cannot hold on to Beatrice herself. The scene between these two is, however, generally conceded to be the play's weakest; and one sees why. Houghton's plot demands that Alan does indeed propose to Fanny. It must also seem likely at the end that he will marry Beatrice. He has to be weak, for reasons soon to become apparent, but not too weak, or he will seem simply contemptible. He must love Beatrice, and be sincere in his attempt to remain engaged to her, or the play's conclusion will seem hollow. Therefore Beatrice must temporarily reject him, rather than vice versa, but not for any cause that would diminish her in our eyes. Her reason must not be lack of love, still less fear of acquiring a penurious husband. So Houghton falls back on the somewhat implausible expedient of a principled renunciation. Fanny, she says, has more 'right' to Alan than herself: 'Can't you see what a splendid sacrifice you have it in your power to make? Not only to do the right thing, but to give up so much in order to do it.' Both Alan and Fanny think this disingenuous, and it sounds it; but Beatrice's author has no better explanation to offer.

If a more orthodox mind than Houghton's were responsible for the play, there would now be several possibilities. Jeffcote could somehow be induced to take a less intransigent stand. Fanny might turn out to have an earlier lover, one with better claims to her. She might be conveniently mangled to death in a loom at her workplace. Or she and Alan might discover they did indeed love one another, and marry with some show of joy. Indeed, the earlier Houghton would probably have opted for this last choice, thinking their 'natural' liaison better than the parentally encouraged one between Alan and Beatrice. Conceivably, Fanny herself might have played the post-Victorian angel, and self-sacrificially renounced Alan herself. That she should, in fact, reject him for her own sake, and that only, is not at all what we have been expecting; yet when this revelation comes, it is logical enough to leave us murmuring 'of course'. Everyone on stage has taken Fanny's consent so much for granted that we have tended to do so, too. But, as she points out, appalling her mother and impressing the Jeffcotes, 'It doesn't suit me to let you settle my affairs without so much as consulting me.'

The scene that follows is justly famous. Alan has been deputed to talk her into marriage, and, so far from doing so, he is morally bested and emotionally crushed. Earlier, Alan had reassured Beatrice that his affair with Fanny was 'an amusement, a lark'. Now Fanny uses precisely the same words when he asks her if she ever loved him. Of course she didn't, she says. He was fun, amusement, a lark. This shocks him, since he thinks it a male prerogative to have sex without love. 'You're a man, and I was your little fancy,' is Fanny's prompt response. 'Well I am a woman, and you were *my* little fancy.' This he thinks 'jolly immoral', but worse is to come. She won't marry him because 'you're not good enough for me'. Alan is too much in thrall to his father. There's 'summat lacking – you're not man enough for me'.

As an attack on the double standards of morality held by everyone else in the play, it is ringingly eloquent, and still has power to surprise us today. The obvious question is whether it is also artistically truthful: is she speaking in her own voice or have these views been foisted on her by an author with, as we've seen, a crusading belief in the liberation both of women and of the young? Each spectator (or reader) must decide for himself; but it seems to me that Fanny's wilfulness and stubbornness have been amply established already, both by her own demeanour and by others' comments. Her father, at one of those amusingly observant moments that give the play much of its character, ruefully remarks that he 'had a dog just like her once'. She herself actually enters the Jeffcote household wearing her weaver's shawl instead of a hat, as if to emphasize her lower social status and to show that she proposes to make no concession to theirs. Defiance is her nature, and it is perfectly plausible that she should express it at her greatest crisis.

Houghton knows, however, that her decision would lose impact if it were altogether easy and painless for her. Some Edwardian critics thought it evasive of him not to land her with a pregnancy; but it is hard to see how that could be managed within the play's time-span. There is, in any case, a hint that this is a possibility in Jeffcote's warning that her refusal of Alan might leave her 'in the cart'. As it is, her mother swears to throw her out of the family home, and promises to make life 'hot' for her father if he resists. Fanny's riposte is in character. She doesn't want to remain with her parents after this: 'I'm a Lancashire lass, and so long as there's weaving sheds in Lancashire I shall earn enough brass to keep me going . . . I'm going to be on my own in future.' There will clearly be difficulties, but by now we've no doubt she'll surmount them. Hindle, in the ambiguous words of the title, has woken.

D. H. Lawrence
(1885–1930)

In 1968 an important new playwright was discovered, to uniform acclaim from the English theatre critics. The oddity was that he had been dead for nearly forty years, and that the best of his plays had lain more or less untouched for twenty years longer than that. This phenomenon was, of course, D. H. Lawrence, the facts of whose short but productive life are too well known to need detailed recitation here and whose work has, if anything, suffered from a surfeit of critical attention. It is hard to believe that until recently there was a glaring gap in the general picture, but within a few weeks an imaginative young director had proved this to be the case. Without the efforts of Peter Gill, who staged what became known as 'the Lawrence trilogy' at the Royal Court, we might still be talking of a major novelist and essayist who happened to write a few 'literary' and 'unactable' plays.

So vivid and gripping in performance were *A Collier's Friday Night* (1909), *The Daughter-in-Law* (1912) and *The Widowing of Mrs Holroyd* (1914) that it is difficult to understand why only the last was staged in Lawrence's lifetime, and then without any public impact. The reason, presumably, was the theatrical climate of the time. Lawrence may have been right to declare, as he did in 1913, that audiences were 'sick of the rather bony, bloodless drama we get nowadays', and that it was 'time for a reaction against Shaw and Galsworthy and Barker and Irishy (except Synge) people – the rule and measure mathematical folk'. But the managements did not share his view, and one can see their point. Metropolitan audiences were not used to plays that were set in mining communities or were quite so serious about the emotions of working-class people. Only in Manchester was an earthier drama in vogue; and perhaps Lawrence might have achieved recognition as a playwright had some relationship been established between him and Miss Horniman's Gaiety Theatre. But that did not happen.

The three plays don't only have in common their Nottinghamshire setting. All have as their main characters strong and educated women who have married 'beneath' them, precisely the situation in Lawrence's own home. The most complete and satisfying picture of that unhappy place is, of course, to be found in *Sons and Lovers*; but *A Collier's Friday Night* is no less autobiographical than the novel and in some ways more balanced as a work of art. We have the ignorant, drunken and brutish father, the weary, long-suffering mother finding emotional fulfilment in her children, and particularly in her sickly, gifted son. But our sympathies are not so strongly directed away from one parent and towards the other. From the evidence offered it is apparent that the father has reason to feel neglected and rejected. The dramatic form has forced on Lawrence a degree of objectivity and detachment often missing when he is present as narrator.

Too much detachment, perhaps. The play looks like a mere 'slice of life', the casual events of a Friday night. There is little plot. The father comes in from the mine and argues with his wife; his son arrives home from college, and his girlfriend comes to spend the evening with him; the two of them, left alone, allow the family bread to burn, provoking the mother to a possessive, jealous outburst; and the father totters in from the pub, spoiling for a fight. But appearances are deceptive, and the play is by no means as thin as it seems. It shows us, in some detail, relationships in action, and invites us to consider how and why they became what they are. Like any work of art, it is selective and somewhat manipulative; but it gives us plenty of opportunity to speculate for ourselves.

In other words, Lawrence asks for something rarely demanded by the drama of his time: emotional intelligence, or at least intelligence about the emotions. He has it himself, and wants us to find it in ourselves. This is equally apparent when he comes to the second play in the 'trilogy', *The Daughter-in-Law*, about the disruption caused a newly wed couple, partly by the revelation that the young husband has impregnated another woman, but mainly by the wife's justified resentment of her oppressive mother-in-law. The feelings implicitly expressed are to be found in much of Lawrence's work, including *A Collier's Friday Night* and *The Merry-go-round* (1912): fear of castration or at least a sense of emotional impotence, a suspicion that one's heart will always be maternal property. As the young wife, Minnie, puts it in *The Daughter-in-Law*, 'How is a woman ever to have a husband, when the men all belong to their mothers? It's wrong.'

It is wrong, no doubt. But Lawrence is not a dramatist who deals in heroines or villainesses; and Minnie herself is in some respects as open to reproach as her mother-in-law and her neglectful husband, Luther. Indeed, she embryonically displays those qualities she dislikes in the old lady. She has become possessive and somewhat cruel, and was always proud. If Luther must renounce his ignominious dependence on his mother, she must reject those things that set her apart from him, specifically a legacy that gives her pretensions above those of a miner's wife. They must come together as equals, and so perhaps they do at the end, though Lawrence is too sensitive and honest a writer to suggest that the relationship will ever be easy. Once again, he is ruled, not by the dramatic habits of his day, but by an instinct for emotional complexity, an awareness that life itself is rarely clear or conclusive.

None of Lawrence's other plays is as satisfying as the 'trilogy', and some have never been performed. It is difficult to visualize an audience for *The Married Man* (1912), a plea for honesty even in adultery, or for *David* (1926), with its luxurious Old Testament rhetoric and unsubstantiated suggestion that its hero bequeathed civilization 'cunning' and 'shrewdness', a cerebral bias from which we have yet to recover. *The Fight for Barbara* (1912) made little impact when it was first performed at Leicester in 1967: unsurprisingly so. It is a dramatized version of Lawrence's early days with Frieda Weekley, the professor's wife with whom he eloped and whom he eventually married; but though he claimed that 'much of it is word for word true', it is curiously unfelt and shallow, a personal anecdote from which all personal pain has been extracted.

Nor did Peter Gill repeat his earlier triumph when he staged *The Merry-go-round* in 1973. It, too, is set in a Nottinghamshire mining community, and the most successfully handled character is a young man trying to build an emotional life for himself after the death of his mother. The trouble is that the play seems unsure whether it is a serious study of relationships or a comedy of manners, a genre for which Lawrence was temperamentally ill-suited. The tone becomes self-consciously humorous, even facetious, especially when the stage is occupied by the censorious, voyeuristic German baron and baroness who, for no clear reason, are also the local vicar and his wife. Gill, very wisely, trimmed and tidied up these characters; but even he could not disguise the play's many awkwardnesses, notably an ending which conventionally and flippantly pairs off all the main characters, as if there had been nothing significant in their dealings with each other.

It has been plausibly suggested that Lawrence failed to become the dramatist he might have been, not only because of an alien theatrical climate, but because he spent so much of his life abroad, away from those parts of England which would have nourished the kind of play for which he had special aptitude. That, combined with the change in social status that success had brought him, would have made it difficult for him to have written another *Daughter-in-Law* or *Mrs Holroyd*. And, indeed, when he returns to Nottinghamshire mining country in *Touch and Go* (1920) something has been lost. A strike occurs, as it does offstage in *The Daughter-in-Law*, but this time it is seen from the stance of the masters and their friends: we do not venture into a miner's cottage or get to know a member, as opposed to a representative, of the working class. There are some strong scenes, notably one in which the mine owner quietly menaces his disaffected office staff and then physically attacks a trades union leader; but one is left with the impression of two plays, one a politically unsophisticated version of Galsworthy's *Strife*, the second an earnest and rather untheatrical examination of personal relationships, neither complete in itself nor satisfactorily integrated with the other.

By the formidable standards of *Women in Love*, to which it has obvious similarities, *Touch and Go* is clearly no great success; and yet it has passages which make Lawrence's contemporaries seem woefully stunted by comparison. It ventures into areas of feeling, and of speculation about feeling, quite closed to them: for instance in the curious, even bizarre scene in which the young mine owner's mother surprises him with his former mistress, and, so far from reacting in the socially predictable way, enjoins her to be rough and hard – 'a woman who was good to him would ruin him in six months, take the manhood out of him. He has a tendency, a secret hankering, to make a gift of himself to somebody . . . keep a solitude in your heart even when you love him best. Keep it. If you lose it, you lose everything.' What dramatist but Lawrence could have written that? Who else could have written the reconciliation between Minnie and Luther in *The Daughter-in-Law*, or the charged scenes between son and mother in *A Collier's Friday Night*, the last ending with 'a dangerous gentleness – so much gentleness that the safe reserve of their souls is broken'? Indeed, who but Lawrence could have written that stage direction?

The Widowing of Mrs Holroyd

The Widowing of Mrs Holroyd was rejected by Granville-Barker in 1911, rewritten by Lawrence, and professionally staged in its familiar form in 1926. To *The Times*, it seemed 'stagnant and tormented'; but Desmond MacCarthy, expressing what's now become the general view, praised Lawrence for 'austerely keeping his gift for lyric expression within the bounds of naturalism'. Though the subject was the eternal triangle, 'there runs through it a new conviction and an exceptional intensity'.

The components of the triangle are Jack Holroyd, a 'tipsy and lawless' miner; his wife Lizzie, better educated than her husband and dissatisfied with their marriage; and Blackhouse, a young electrician, also Holroyd's social and intellectual superior. A drunken attack by Holroyd on his rival precipitates the crisis that has long been building. Lizzie agrees to desert her husband for Blackhouse. But before they can go, Holroyd is dead, suffocated in a pit fall. The play ends with characteristic inconclusiveness. Lizzie thinks the accident 'a judgement on us', Blackhouse promises to return the next day, and it's unclear if their embryonic liaison is irretrievably blighted.

The precision and love with which Lawrence evokes the working-class setting is equally characteristic. This is a kitchen where clothes are dried and ironed, loaves baked, and meals prepared and, all too often, left uneaten by the master of the house. This (we feel) is how people lived in Nottinghamshire mining country, and how some of them died. The scene in which Holroyd's body is brought home – 'by Guy, but 'e 'ings heavy', 'Yi, Joe, I'll back my life o' that' – has a blunt, unaffected authenticity; and its ritual washing, as we'll see, a truth that goes far beyond the documentary.

Considering his lack of dramatic experience, Lawrence proves remarkably adept at feeding us necessary information, shaping his material and maintaining relevance without spoiling the naturalistic veneer. Notice the rat that appears in the second scene. It has obvious symbolic resonance; it emphasizes that the environment is relatively poor, in spite of Lizzie's pretensions; and it provides the first indication that there is more between herself and Holroyd than mutual discontent. She momentarily suspends hostilities, instinctively anxious to protect him from something 'poisonous'. Notice, too, how credibly and pointedly Lawrence differentiates between the two children, the boy siding uncritically with his mother against his father, the little girl pathetically wiser: 'If you said something nice to him, he'd happen go to bed and not shout.' Indeed, there's little in the play that doesn't contribute to what's presumably its overall end, to provoke us to assess the main characters with all the understanding we can muster. We are to see the 'triangle' in the round, if that isn't a geometric contradiction, accumulating evidence from every available source, however seemingly inconsequential.

From Holroyd's mother, for instance: hardly a convincing witness, with her numbing fatalism and obvious bias, yet not one we can ignore. Didn't her son perhaps 'only want a bit of coaxing and managing, and you clever women won't do it'? Certainly, we believe the old woman when she calls Holroyd 'a taking lad, as iver was', and claims that 'some women could have lived with him happy enough'. And then there's Clara, one of the 'paper bonnets' Holroyd foolishly brings home from the pub in the second scene. Her intrusion provokes Lizzie's justified resentment, but also exposes something excessive in her pride and hostility. Should she withhold all fellow-feeling from a woman who has also suffered, and far worse, from a bad husband? Clara is carefully, judiciously observed in herself, and serves a dramatic function, creating a crisis between the Holroyds and casting light on both of them.

And when Lawrence deals more directly with his three principals, the fairness, balance and emotional intricacy of his play is, not unnaturally, more evident still. Blackhouse's virtues are responsibility, reliability, a determination to look after Lizzie's children as well as Lizzie herself; his most obvious vice, a certain slyness. His main method of advancing his own cause is, it seems, to undermine Holroyd's already shaky status without appearing to do so. When a child suggests he should move in, he replies 'You've got your own dad to live here,' but is 'looking swiftly at Mrs Holroyd' as he speaks. Soon he is asking whether they 'like [Holroyd] to shout when you are in bed?', hardly a question one expects of a disinterested family friend, and answering Lizzie's 'You're different from most men' with an 'all men aren't alike, you know'. Why, she asks rather later, has he bothered to bring the drunken Holroyd home? 'Well, I thought you'd be upset about him,' he explains. 'I had to drink three whiskies – had to, in all conscience.'

This disingenuous advertisement of his own altruism and sobriety leaves an ugly taste. Here is Blackhouse the eponymous predator, the canny rat on the loose. His excuse, of course, is that he thinks he loves Lizzie, or (more accurately) has come as close as such a man can to loving her. All along, it's suggested that he is a slightly cold, cerebral character, over-controlled where Holroyd is uncontrolled. He 'hates mess of any sort'. He can credibly claim to have resisted his growing involvement. His idea of lovemaking is to suggest that his and Lizzie's hands 'sort of go well together'. It isn't surprising that his general approach to wooing a married woman should be cautious, politic, devious.

But if Lawrence's handling of Blackhouse demands alertness, 'emotional intelligence', of the audience, that of the crumbling marriage demands more. Lizzie wed 'the first man that turned up' in order to escape loneliness, but she did also 'care' for Holroyd and 'want to be a wife' to him. He was a big, strong man and a good dancer, like Lawrence's own father; and he had a 'rare smile', which she found lovable. But then the familiar troubles developed. The intelligent, genteel woman became increasingly disappointed by aspects of what first attracted her, her man's intellectual limitations and social crudeness. He reacted to her dissatisfaction by escaping to the pub and becoming still more aggressively boorish. She became more contemptuous, he more contemptible; and by the beginning of the play it's hard to say who is more at fault. Both partners are allowed to put their sides, though she more fully. He has made himself ugly and loathsome to her. More subtly, 'there's nothing at the bottom of him . . . you can't get anywhere with him. There's just his body and nothing else.

Nothing that keeps him, no anchor, no roots, nothing sat-isfying. It's a horrible feeling there is about him, that nothing is safe or permanent.'

This is an over-explicit little speech, the one point in the play when the author, rather than a living character, seems to be speaking; but at least Lawrence knows that it's alto-gether insufficient to sum up the situation as a whole. Holroyd might have proved more 'safe and permanent' if Lizzie had ever accepted the implications of the marriage she herself made. But she seems entirely unable to identify with him, his class or his background. To her the local people are 'as common as they're made'. She 'stands speechless' at the suggestion that the 'paper bonnets' are 'women as good as you'. And by the standards of her husband's place and time she has clearly been 'too big for your shoes, in my house'.

Nowadays we would be far less sympathetic to those standards. We'd say that it isn't exactly 'his' house, and that she's right to declare, as she tearfully does over the washing, that she is 'not going to let him have it all *his* way'. Besides, if she should have accepted his character, he should equally have recognized he was marrying a woman with higher expectations than most of those available. On the other hand, criticism must clearly give *some* weight to the social assumptions which Lizzie is, in effect, challenging when it seeks to assess the two combatants. It would be unjust to call Holroyd a 'bad' man, and anachronistic to dismiss him as a worthless husband. He is fond of his children. After the 'paper bonnets' have left he is 'ashamed yet defiant, withal anxious to apologize', and a less intran-sigent wife would have let him do so. He has good reason to feel jealous and angry, and there is no doubt he is suffering, perhaps more than she. Indeed, it's misery that causes his death, since that is why he stays unsocially apart from his fellow-miners, and remains behind when they leave for the surface. Is it because this misery becomes suicidal or because he was so quickly asphyxiated that he 'didna seem to ha' strived much to get out' of his rock trap?

Probably the latter; but it is significant that one momentarily wonders.

Each Holroyd, then, has a point of view powerful to him or her. Each is right, and also lamentably selfish. The scope of Lawrence's sympathies is considerable; but there is depth here too. Whether or not 'the play suggests there is some tie . . . . more primitive and deep than love', as Desmond MacCarthy claimed, it certainly leaves us feeling that there's a mysterious bond between the Holroyds that will always be denied to the more mental Blackhouse. He himself seems to sense it when he looks at the drunkenly sleeping Jack and says he 'supposes you really care about him, even now', and questions her claim to have lost her feeling for him: 'I don't believe he can destroy it'. And his scepticism is justified by the extraordinary scene in which Lizzie washes her husband's corpse.

The superficial resemblance is to Synge's *Riders to the Sea*, a play Lawrence greatly admired. A more useful comparison is with his own short story, *Odour of Chrysanthemums*, which describes a similar marriage and comes to a similar climax. According to the critic Raymond Williams, the prose version is much the stronger, especially in the scene over the dead body, because it allows Lawrence to use several voices: report what the young widow looks like and does, describe what she consciously thinks, assay her deeper feelings. 'In dread she turned her face away . . . her mind, cold and detached, said clearly, "Who am I? What have I been doing?" . . . Her heart was bursting with grief and pity for him'; and so on. In this last crisis, claims Williams, the story 'moves into a different world'.

This is surely questionable. After all, the theatre has a crucial advantage over the short story, which is that it lets us *see* its widow. Here is a living anguish, happening now, not one verbally painted for us. And don't the words Lawrence provides allow Lizzie to express a great deal? 'I can't bear it . . . the children's father . . . I wasn't good to you, but you shouldn't have done this to me . . . Did it hurt you? . . . I never loved you enough . . . You didn't try . . .

You couldn't help it . . . My dear, my dear, what can I do for you?' There is pain and grief, self-pity and recrimination, horror and helplessness, all (and more) brought together in an astonishingly concentrated and intense span. There is bitter irony, too, since Mrs Holroyd cannot face the death she openly wished for, and, as Sylvia Sklar argues in her study of Lawrence's plays, at last cedes him some of the victory he sought in life. The dead Holroyd forces her to ask, as never before, where and why she went wrong.

Much of the last act makes tremendous demands on an actress. Not every emotion is spelled out. The language is mostly banal. Such stage directions as 'stares witless around' must be enacted. With a second-rater in the part, the story will doubtless seem superior. But a good actress could suggest considerable subtlety and complexity of emotion, and a great one leave us feeling we have intruded upon something appallingly intimate and profound: beyond words, in spite of the words. Indeed, the play at this point touches a chord which no modern playwright but Lawrence could possibly have sounded. It is this passage which, more than any other in his *oeuvre*, justifies Sean O'Casey's claim, made apropos *A Collier's Friday Night* in 1934, that 'had Lawrence got the encouragement [he] called for and deserved, England might have had a great dramatist'.

Harold Brighouse
(1882–1958)

Harold Brighouse, born in 1882, the son of a Manchester businessman, began adult life in a shipping merchant's warehouse, became an enthusiastic theatre-goer, and started to write after seeing an 'outrageously bad' play and deciding he could do better. The first of his pieces to be staged was the short *Doorway*, put on in 1909 at Miss Horniman's Gaiety, the Manchester repertory theatre whose most celebrated product he was to become; the first of his full-length works, *Dealing in Futures*, was presented the same year in Glasgow. By his death in 1958, he was the author of some twenty plays, many produced with success but only one revived with any frequency nowadays. As he himself wryly remarked in his autobiography, he was a 'one-play man'.

Actually, intimations or echoes of *Hobson's Choice* are to be found in much of his work. Gormless but capable young men appear in *Zack* (1920), *Dealing in Futures* and *The Game* (1913), in the last as a brilliant footballer under the thumb of his mother. Strong and determined young women may be found in *Zack*, *Coincidence* (1929), *Dealing in Futures*, *The Northerners* (1914) and *Behind the Throne* (1929). A dominating and oppressive parent or (sometimes) step-parent appears in several of these plays, as well as in *Garside's Career* (1914), *Odd Man Out* (1912) and *The Sort of Prince* (1929). The title of the last of these invokes *Cinderella*, and some others seem as indebted to fairy stories as to life. The archetypal Brighouse play involves a victimized young adult released from his or chains and celebrating the liberation with marriage. Indeed this actually happens, not only in *The Sort of Prince*, but in *Zack* and *Odd Man Out*.

Brighouse's strength was his entertaining characterization of northern people: his weakness, that he cheapened serious and potentially fruitful themes with gratuitous love-interest and glib dénouements. To various degrees this tendency mars *Dealing in Futures*, about a chemical-dye firm that is poisoning its workforce; *Garside's Career*, about a young MP spoiled by success; *Graft* (1912), about civic corruption; and *Coincidence* (1930), about an election campaign. Even *The Northerners*, which involves Luddites in the Lancashire cotton industry of the 1820s and is probably the best of his serious plays, ends as a domestic melodrama, with the young wife of a ruthless factory owner reasserting her working-class origins by shooting him dead. Brighouse had sufficient originality to tackle subjects neglected or ignored by British dramatists of his generation, but not enough to resist the romantic conventions of the well-made play. Consequently he is best remembered for a comedy, one in which the love-interest, as well as being more earthily handled than in his 'serious' plays, is essential to the plot and meaning: *Hobson's Choice*.

Hobson's Choice

Hobson's Choice is the best-known creation of the 'Manchester school', though it was first performed in the USA and given its British première in London in 1916, when Miss Horniman's Gaiety, though still in existence as a repertory theatre, was in decline and her company soon to be disbanded. It is also generally regarded as the most characteristic work of its genre, if only because it deals naturalistically and humorously with ordinary people living in an unpretentious northern milieu and using a distinctively northern argot. In fact, it is more representative than that, as we shall see.

The situation is set up with admirable deftness and economy. Within two pages we know that Hobson is a drinker and that his daughters, who run his shoe business for him, regard him as a nuisance. We know that Alice hopes to marry young Albert Prosser, probably against her father's wishes; that she and Vickey, who reads a book during opening hours, are uninterested in their work; but that Maggie, regarded by her sisters as an 'old maid', is tough, determined and capable. She can, and does, sell poor Albert a pair of shoes he doesn't want. And when Hobson himself enters, *en route* to his drinking cronies, we begin to suspect that Maggie *is* Hobson's shoe shop and Hobson's household.

And so, of course, she is. Hobson, though he likes to regard himself as the unfortunate victim of 'uppish' women, is no better than a drone, living off their unpaid labour. Certainly, he plays no significant part in the business that bears his name. The best of his shoes, those that sell themselves, are made by Willie Mossop in the basement, and the worst, those that no one else could sell, are somehow foisted on the customers by Maggie upstairs. To the unsentimental thirty-year-old the situation seems 'to point one way'. After a wealthy customer has praised Mossop's work (and, not incidentally, treated Hobson as the irrelevance he is), she summons him into the shop and puts a proposition to him. They are 'a pair'. He is 'a business idea in the shape of a man', and she will 'invest' in him; and to Mossop's consternation, this means more than a 'working partnership'. She is determined on marriage and will brook no refusal.

The humour of the scene comes from its inversion of convention. The woman, not the man, is the wooer; and business, not romance, impels her. Its weakness is the relative improbability, not of Maggie's approach, but of Mossop's consent. The absence of love, mentioned by him, is too quickly shrugged off – 'We'll get along without.' His fiancée is too speedily disposed of. Within four or five minutes he is declaring that there 'seems like there's no escape', when there obviously is. Still, Brighouse does seem aware of the problem, and ends the act with some skill. Hobson, whose characteristically coarse-witted response to the suggestion of such a marriage is to take off his belt and threaten Mossop, only succeeds in arousing the young man to rebellious indignation. Indeed, he embraces Maggie and promises to 'stick to her like glue'. This adds some plausibility to their liaison, and also has a second function: it shows us that there is, as Maggie says, 'the makings of a man' in her future husband.

There is one other significant event in the play that the sceptical may find hard to swallow. Hobson, drunk, falls through a cellar trap into the warehouse of the corn-merchant whose son, Freddy Beenstock, is in love with Alice; and the ever-resourceful Maggie persuades the boy and his friend Prosser, who is a lawyer, to exploit the mishap. They must sue the trespassing Hobson for damages, and then, by offering a settlement out of court, wangle from him the dowries for both Alice and Vickey he would not otherwise give. But of course such a suit could never succeed, and it is hard to believe that the mere threat of it could prise £500 out of the tight-fisted Hobson, however deep his horror of lawyers (established, incidentally, early in the first act) and however great his fear of losing his reputation, his position as a vicar's warden and, as a consequence of both, much of his trade.

Still, accusations of improbability are perhaps rather nit-picking, since the play's principal strength is its characterization, and the twists of its plot do, on the whole, emerge naturally from that. Consider the dénouement. Deserted by his daughters, Hobson succumbs more and more to drink, and falls seriously ill. His business declines no less dramatically. Someone must come and look after him – but who? Not the vapid and snobbish Alice. Not the equally ineffective Vickey. Both are, predictably enough, nervous in case their father should will his money elsewhere; but neither has the stomach for the work involved. No, clearly it can only be Maggie. And, equally clearly, Hobson must in some way defer to her and Willie, who have prospered by natural talent and hard work. The Hobson shop must become the Mossop shop, or at least the Mossop–Hobson partnership.

Of the three relevant characters, Hobson himself is probably the richest, or at least the most entertaining. Actors of the calibre of Laughton and Redgrave have been attracted to play the part of the Salford Lear, rejected by two daughters, reconciled with the third and, because this is a comic cosmos, able with her help to avoid the madness and death that threaten him. He is a memorable picture of unjustifiable complacency and illusory power. Hobson thinks of himself as a solid bastion of the imperishable British middle class, though in fact he neglects everything that merits him that status. He also is, or tries to be, a domestic tyrant. In fact, he is all bluster and no action. Maggie runs the house, allowing her father, for the sake of peace, to believe that her decisions are his household rules. His only victories are minuscule: he refuses, for instance, to wash his hands when asked. And not only does he fail lamentably to impose his will on those technically depen-

dent on him: he proves ignominiously dependent on Maggie
whenever trouble or sickness threatens. He is stingy and
sly, weak, self-pitying and essentially passive; and all his
misfortunes, from Maggie's original desertion to his commercial downfall and physical ruin, are at once caused and
merited by this combination of flaws. With nice logic and
justice his own character punishes him.

It is no less logical that Maggie should end by taking
over him and his business. No less satisfying, either. All
along, Brighouse is careful not to succumb to the obvious
danger, that of making his heroine too hard, bossy and
go-getting. She is, to be sure, candid to the point of bluntness, determined to get her way in all essentials, and emi-
nently practical, not caring whether her wedding-ring is
made of brass or if she furnishes her cellar-flat with ser-
viceable odds and ends from Hobson's lumber-room. But,
as with her father, her bark is worse than her bite. She
commits no unkind or unjust act, and, indeed, is responsible for the only wholly unselfish one in a play that is, on
the whole, rather cynical about people's capacity for altruism: she secures for her sisters the marriage settlements she
herself has done far more to earn. Nor is she without personal affections, though she tends to express them in furtive,
embarrassed ways, like sneaking a wedding-day flower to
press in her Bible. If we don't altogether believe her when
she tells Willie, near the beginning, that she has 'got the
love all right', we are ready to accept by the end that she
is fond, as well as proud, of him. We should also have
noticed how important the family and family rituals are to
her: hands must be shaken and kisses exchanged to seal
her sisters' and father's acceptance of Will. Altogether, we
feel that more than business expansion dictates her return
to Hobson's shop. The old man can look forward to a firm
but benign rule.

Maggie has the ability to discriminate between good
sense and convention, never more so (of course) than in
her choice of a bootmaker as husband and partner. She has
what the stage directions say is necessary, the 'very keen

eye' which can see that he is the 'raw material of a charming man'. But how successfully does Brighouse validate this judgment? To what extent does he bring off the transformation of Mossop from wage-slave to master, and from gormless nonentity to adequate husband? The answer to these questions depends largely on the ability of the actor playing the part to pick up and emphasize the few opportunities offered him. He has little chance to be anything but timid and meek until the end of the first act; but then, when Hobson threatens him, he can show that he has some spirit, even if he has been 'stunted mentally by a brutalized childhood'. Act II provides him with the chance to show warmth, capacity for affection and increasing regard for Maggie – 'You're growing on me, lass.' By the end of Act III, we have seen him talk, or try to talk, to his father-in-law as an equal; we have seen him buckle down to his lessons in literacy; and, less positively, we have seen him nervously led off 'by the ear' by Maggie to their marriage bed. But enough should have been suggested to leave us unsurprised by the newly confident Mossop who appears in Act IV, after twelve months of conjugal life, education and business success. It is logical enough, given their temperaments, that he and Maggie should so evidently be enjoying a real marriage, not just a commercial partnership. It is also logical that by now he should be sufficiently convinced of his own abilities, and sufficiently sure of his status, to drive a hard bargain with his father-in-law. It even logical that, to her evident satisfaction, he should stand up to Maggie. If Brighouse had not given him some qualifying lines after Hobson's abject exit – 'I'm afraid I bore on him too hard', 'I weren't by half as certain as I sounded' – we might not find the transformation so plausible. But it is clear that the character's toughness is still somewhat superficial and incomplete. It is also apparent that, continue to change though no doubt he will, a kindly, sensitive and essentially humble individual will survive somewhere inside the future shoe-king of Manchester.

It is a rather sentimental ending; but it is one that Brighouse has made efforts to justify, and it clinches several themes characteristic, not just of his òwn work, but of the more enlightened British drama of the early twentieth century. The play chronicles a shift in the balance of power between the generations and between the sexes. Its view is that parents have no prescriptive rights over their offspring, and that heavy fathers must be resisted. It suggests that women, as much as men, must assume responsibility for their destinies, and it insists that intelligence, determination, strength of will and even business acumen can no longer be regarded as male prerogatives. It has little time for the man who lives off other people's labour or at their expense, as Hobson does, and not much more for women who do the same, like Alice and Vickey. It regards work as a merit and perhaps a duty. It is indifferent or even hostile to many of the day's conventions, from the one that declares that men must always take the sexual initiative to the one that says they must never do the washing-up.

Not least, it reiterates in rather more extreme terms the idea put forward in *The Admirable Crichton*. Inside a butler may be a man with infinitely greater powers of leadership than his master. Inside the lowliest worker, the one whose father was 'a workhouse brat', may be a craftsman of imagination and a businessman of resource: one who (as Maggie prophesies) will eventually be 'thought more of at the bank' than his middle-class brothers-in-law, in spite of all their advantages. The social system may be repressing talent and stifling ability. It may, in short, be completely awry. Brighouse's achievement in *Hobson's Choice* is to raise all these ideas in an unpretentious and amusing play about the ownership of a Salford shoe shop.

James Joyce
(1882–1941)

James Joyce, born in Dublin in 1882, died in Zurich in 1941, is, of course, mainly important as the author of the

novels *Portrait of the Artist*, *Ulysses* and *Finnegans Wake*. However, he was always interested in drama, as a youth almost
fanatically so. In his teens he visited the theatre whenever
he could afford it, writing reviews of what he saw; and as
a student at University College, Dublin, he delivered a
combative public lecture on his idol, Ibsen, and published
an account of that playwright's *When We Dead Awaken* in
the London *Fortnightly Review*.

The view of these is that drama is the highest of the arts,
because it deals with the underlying laws of mankind, 'in
all their nakedness and divine serenity'. It presents the
'everlasting hopes, desires and hates of us', and 'will be for
the future at war with convention'. The modern playwright
'stands a mediator in awful truth before the veiled face of
God', projecting 'deathless passions, human verities'. But
he can also achieve this through the portrayal of ordinary
life, as Ibsen does with particular success in his later plays,
to criticize which 'verges on impertinence'. His style, added
Joyce in a later essay, should be 'noble and bare'.

It is heady stuff; and he first tried to put it into practice
in a play called *A Brilliant Career*, dedicated to 'my own
soul' and evidently indebted to Ibsen's *Enemy of the People*.
He sent it to the critic William Archer, who had relayed to
the delighted eighteen-year-old Ibsen's gratification at the
Fortnightly article, and got a polite if puzzled assessment
back. He tore the play up, and thereafter wrote only one
other, *Exiles*, in 1915. W. B. Yeats, whom Joyce thought
'a tiresome idiot', rejected it for the Abbey Theatre in
Dublin, calling it 'sincere and interesting' but not as good
as the *Portrait*; the Stage Society in London also turned it
down, one member calling it 'reminiscent of Strindberg at
his most putrid'; and Joyce failed to secure a production
even from the English Players, which he himself helped
found in Zurich during the First World War. Instead, the
company performed Synge's *Riders from the Sea*, Houghton's
Hindle Wakes and Wilde's *Importance of Being Earnest*, a production that led to the bizarre lawsuit between Joyce and

the consular official Henry Carr which Tom Stoppard has chronicled in *Travesties*.

Notwithstanding the enthusiastic advocacy of Ezra Pound, and the more erratic support of Shaw, *Exiles* didn't find a stage until 1919, when it was performed without success in Munich. Productions in New York in 1925 and London the following year failed to make much impression and the play had to wait until Harold Pinter's production in 1970 before its theatrical, as well as its literary, merits were recognized. What sort of playwright, then, did the English-speaking theatre manage to lose?

Exiles

Midway through *Exiles* a character proposes to another 'a battle of both our souls . . . against all that is false in them and in the world. A battle of your soul against the spectre of fidelity, of mine against the spectre of friendship.' The speech, holding out a fierce and demanding honesty as an ideal, might have been lifted from Ibsen. But consider the somewhat Strindbergian context. The speaker, Robert Hands, has been making advances to the common-law wife of his oldest friend, Richard Rowan, and has actually invited her to the Dublin cottage in which the two men long ago entertained women and discussed progressive ideas. Now Richard comes to tell Robert he knows. Bertha has all along been telling him everything. Robert is horrified, embarrassed, apologetic, and all the conventional things; and then discovers that Rowan, if not exactly a mouthpiece for Joyce, holds opinions about personal freedom Joyce would substantially share, at least in principle. If this is where love is to be found, so let it be.

There are many parallels, large and small, between Joyce's and Rowan's predicaments. In 1904 the writer had left Ireland for Italy with Nora Barnacle, and in 1905 they had an illegitimate son. In 1909 a visit to Dublin was seriously spoiled by the false claim of a 'friend', Vincent Cosgrave, to have made love to Nora while Joyce was courting her; another visit, in 1912, the year in which *Exiles* is set, proved so unsuccessful he never again returned. Rowan, too, is a writer, ran off with a social and intellectual inferior, had a child in Italy; but his return may be more permanent, because a senior university post is on offer.

The Ireland of *Exiles* seems uninviting. It was the home of Richard's hard Catholic mother, who died without forgiving his sexual transgressions; and it has reduced Robert's Protestant cousin and Richard's intellectual confidante, Beatrice Justice, to what Joyce called 'an abandoned cold temple'. But the play's emphases aren't social. Its subjects are rather the power of mind and will over body and passion, the difficulty of emotional honesty, and the limits of human tolerance in vital relationships.

Why does Richard hold his doctrine of freedom and how far can he push it? His principled view is that Bertha belongs to herself, can give herself, and may decide she is more Robert's than his: 'Who am I that I could call myself master of your heart or of any woman's?' The question, however, is whether these fine sentiments are disingenuous. Bertha suspects that her infidelity will enable Richard more happily to pursue an affair with Beatrice, whose letters apparently helped inspire his last book; but this isn't so. Beatrice is patently too closed and repressed for anything physical. Bertha also accuses Richard of telling Robert that she has been feeding him news of his sexual advances in order to alienate Robert from herself; and in this she may be partly correct. Richard is not Joyce, who was reportedly 'shattered' by Cosgrave's insinuations. He cuts a colder, more austere figure, and talks of sex with intellectual disdain, as a 'death of the spirit'. Yet it's evident he does feel anger and jealousy, and comes to feel so painfully betrayed he is tempted to 'despair'.

The conflict is not, however, simply between Richard's mind, which wants to want Bertha's freedom, and his instincts, which don't. In his character, mind, will, instinct and much else merge into something far more complex. For instance, Richard claims to feel he stole Bertha's girlhood innocence, youthful beauty, hopes and loyalty. Moreover, he appears to have neglected her in Italy, and to have been unfaithful 'grossly and many times'. Perhaps his professed desire to make reparation could be more accurately called a ruse to rid himself of guilt by loading her with some guilt, too. But this possibility isn't explored in the play, because Richard proceeds to accuse himself of darker motives still. 'In the very core of my ignoble heart I longed to be betrayed by you and by her,' he tells Robert, 'in the dark, in the night – secretly, meanly, craftily . . . to be dishonoured for ever in love and lust.' And he has, he says, 'a deeper motive still'.

The nature of this 'deeper motive' is unclear. Perhaps there's a clue in Joyce's notes for the play, which define jealousy as 'the very immolation of the pleasure of possession on the altar of love'; perhaps a more solid one when he writes of Bertha's infidelity giving the two men an 'almost carnal contact' they could not otherwise achieve 'without dissatisfaction and degradation', and of Richard wanting 'to feel the thrill of adultery vicariously and to possess a bound woman Bertha [sic] through the organ of his friend'. This last idea is not, of course, explicit in the play, but even there it's frequently suggested that Richard is sexually unorthodox. He is obsessed with the physical detail of Robert's advances. He seems ready to cause others pain, and perhaps even courts it himself. Indeed, Joyce called the play 'a rough and tumble' between Sade and Masoch. Back in 1919 the *Little Review* organized a symposium on *Exiles*, at which a psychiatrist analyzed Richard's 'homopsychism', emphasizing his sadistic, 'intensely' masochistic and voyeuristic impulses. However, he did Joyce some disservice by suggesting that the play was a 'dream' in which he acted out unconscious longings. It's apparent that the dramatist was largely aware of his protagonist's pathology.

It's also apparent that the impurity of Richard's motives makes his ideal of freedom and truth look naïve, dishonest,

or worse. This ideal is, however, more thoroughly undermined by the characters of those he expects to put it into
practice. Robert, for all his grandiloquence, makes a sly,
shoddy impression. Given his record, apparently a long line
of casual affairs, both his Nietzschean belief in the primacy
of passion and his ardour to Bertha come across at least
partly as a seducer's ploys and rhetoric. He proclaims
friendship to Richard, and promises to help him secure his
university post; yet he says some remarkably subversive
things about him to Bertha ('It makes you happy . . . this
gift of freedom he gave you nine years ago?') and he introduces a blatant smear into the newspaper article he writes
supposedly promoting Richard's cause. This isn't simple
treachery. It's evident that in many respects Robert means
well, or wants to mean well, or cannot help himself, and is,
as Bertha says, 'honest in his way'. But it's the way of the
mean sensual man ('Secrets can be very sweet, can they
not?') rather than that of the emotional Ibsenist.

The impracticability of this Ibsenism is, however, most
evident when we come to Bertha herself, who regards it
with scepticism and outrage. To her, it's mainly evidence
of Richard's lack of love. Why doesn't he defend her against
Robert? Why leave her with him? She speaks of her potential lover with pride, but it's an unconvincing pride, nearer
an attempt to salvage some dignity and self-respect. Her
main motive in accepting Robert's attentions and informing
Richard about them has, it would seem, been to excite
Richard's jealousy. She wants the 'strange wild lover' he
was in the early days back again. In short, the 'battle of
souls' grandly mooted by Richard and Robert is largely an
attempt to exploit her for the private gratification of each,
and something she herself tries rather pathetically to exploit
in hopes of re-establishing her relationship with her
'husband'.

This may be to take a harsher, simpler view of the claims
of the ideal than Joyce would wish; yet it's one the play
itself tends to substantiate. Its people cannot cope in prac-

tice with the freedom their principles, or purported principles, enjoin on them. In other words, *Exiles* comes to a somewhat conventional conclusion, nearer to the Ibsen of *The Wild Duck* than of *Rosmersholm*. But it is hardly a conventional play. What other English-speaking dramatist of the earlier twentieth century dared investigate the pathology of sex at all, let alone as trenchantly and daringly as this? The play, it has been observed, is a series of confessions. Who else could have written the one Richard ignominiously makes to Robert? How many others the scene in which Bertha coolly describes, down to minutiae of lips, tongue and sexual excitement, Robert's advances to her?

This scene, surprising, shocking, yet true, also helps answer those early critics who accused Joyce of lacking theatricality, of offering theories and attitudes rather than people, and of over-elaborating those theories. It is a very dense play; but its three 'cat and mouse acts' (Joyce's own description, referring presumably to the way Richard manipulates the others) were proved by Pinter's production to work well on the stage. Even the melodramatic language – 'I am living with a stranger!', 'I have murdered my soul for you' – is given substance by the emotional authenticity, by Joyce's evident involvement in the situation, by the understanding he brings to it.

The piece was ahead of its time in other respects, too. Exile is, after all, not only a recurring theme in Joyce's work, but a quintessential one of the twentieth century itself. Admittedly, Joyce's notes refer only to the obvious variety, explaining that Robert is the elder brother in the parable of the Prodigal Son, that 'a nation exacts a penance from those who dared to leave her', and suggesting that the 'new' Ireland cannot contain both a Robert and a Richard. Either intellectual or sensualist must go into exile, as, in fact, Richard does at the end. But the play itself would seem to define the condition more sweepingly. All the characters are in exile from something or someone, Richard from his society, his family, his friend, his wife, from the cerebral Beatrice, from his feelings, his body, even love: a disintegration as total as any endured by, say, David Storey's characters.

At the same time, the nature, degree and depth of his alienation remain tantalizingly unclear, even to himself. He spends the play trying to puzzle it out, and, by the end, is in some ways more lost than when he started. No wonder Pinter was attracted to the play. The relationships prove as elusive and unfathomable as those in *The Collection*, *Old Times* or *Betrayal*. We do not even know if sex occurs between Bertha and Robert when she visits his cottage. Most critics assume there wasn't time; but Joyce's notes show he wanted to 'cloud' the issue, and both the suggestive end to Act II – light playing from Robert's bedroom into the darkened living room, Robert kissing Bertha's hair, she silently submitting, the rain falling outside – and the ambiguous conversation they hold in Act III leave one suspecting that something more than a heated flirtation may have been crammed into an admittedly busy evening. That is, of course, partly why Richard ends the play with 'a deep, deep wound of doubt which can never be healed'. But the 'doubt' obviously goes beyond this. Indeed, it would be vulgar to suggest that Richard wonders only if copulation literally occurred.

What surely torments him is that he can never know, and isn't even sure he wants to know, how near Bertha and Robert came to achieving, not merely physical contact, but the spiritual nakedness he himself regards as the essence of a true relationship. And what gives this conclusion an even more markedly contemporary ring is that this doubt itself appears to give Bertha new power over him. There is hope for him in her love. There is also, the play suggests, hope in the vitality and affection of his young son, Archie. There is also a 'restless, living, wounding doubt' that half-hurts, half-exhilarates him, and both opens and closes him to her. Characters, and play, rarely come as elaborate and resonant as this.

W. Somerset Maugham

(1874–1965)

William Somerset Maugham, born 1874 and died 1965, was scarcely less successful as a dramatist than as a writer of prose fiction. In 1908 he had four plays running simultaneously in London; and he continued to captivate the theatrical public with some regularity thereafter, or at any rate until 1933, when he retired from the stage. By then he had twenty-two dramatic pieces behind him, ranging in style from melodramas (such as *The Letter* and *The Sacred Flame*) to comedies of manners (such as *Lady Frederick* or *Home and Beauty*) to satiric moralities (such as *The Breadwinner* and *Sheppey*).

'Cynicism' has always been the accusation directed at him; and it was one he himself accepted, since to him cynicism was only a discomforting candour. To a reader of the prefaces to his collected plays, however, it may look closer to contempt. A theatre audience, he suggests, has a sort of corporate stupidity. It 'can only receive ideas when they are placed before it in their simplest form, and even then only when they agree with its own instinctive convictions'. It is not interested in thinking, only in being touched or amused. And so the function of the dramatist is to secure 'the entertainment of the audience, not its improvement'. Prose drama 'is one of the lesser arts, like wood-carving or dancing, but so far as it is an art at all, its purpose is to afford delight. I do not think it can usefully concern itself with the welfare of humanity or the saving of civilization.' Some of Maugham's own plays may, he concedes, draw a moral, 'but with a shrug of the shoulders as if to invite you to lay no stress upon it'.

This is unsubtle stuff, to put it no lower, which tells us more about Maugham than about drama. And, to be fair to him, he is as 'cynical' about his own aspirations and achievements as about anything else. 'I wanted money and I wanted fame,' he tells us. 'I reflected upon the qualities which the managers demanded in a play: evidently a comedy, for the public wish to laugh; with as much drama as it would carry, for the public liked a thrill; with a little sentiment, for the public liked to feel good; and a happy ending.' Add a 'star part for an actress', and the formula was more or less complete. It was one from which Maugham never ventured very far.

Was he simply rationalizing his own limitations? Was he just a hack, giving the public what a condescending view of its capabilities told him it wanted? To a reader of the slimmer comedies, such as *Lady Frederick* (1907) or *Mrs Dot* (1908), it may seem so. And yet even the severer critics were forced to concede that there was some quality in *Home and Beauty* (1919) when the National Theatre revived it in 1971. It is, no doubt, pretty cynical about marriage, a condition described as never 'happy' but sometimes 'tolerable'. An officially 'dead' husband returns from the Great War to discover that his best friend has married the 'dear little thing', his wife. Both men naturally compete with one another, but, in spite of appearances, not to keep her. The joke is that both are maddened by her knack for passing off extreme selfishness as total selflessness, and each would like to fob her off on the other.

It is lively stuff, and includes a nice, ironic attack on the hypocrisy of the English divorce laws, voiced by the Jewish lawyer, A. B. Raham, a name and a character reminiscent of comedies long preceding those of Maugham. Indeed, critics have often compared his work to that of the seventeenth and eighteenth centuries. Grein, for instance, suggested that the people of *Lady Frederick* would have been more naturally attired in powder and wigs; and Maugham himself confessed that he wrote 'in the tradition which flourished so brightly in the Restoration period and was carried on by Goldsmith and Sheridan'. His term for much of his work was 'artificial comedy', which 'treats with indulgent cynicism the humours, follies and vices of the world of fashion'. *Home and Beauty* is probably the wittiest example of the type: cynical, perhaps, but no more objectionally so than Wycherley or Congreve.

It is also one of his least pretentious plays. What is surprising about Maugham's work is the frequency with which it does, in fact, moralize about society, and not always with a 'shrug'. Take *Smith* (1909), for instance, a comedy about a Rhodesian farmer who returns to the old country, and is so disgusted with his sister's shallow, brittle and greedy set that he decides to marry the parlourmaid, a straightforward, wholesome girl who will willingly fulfil what he assumes to be a wife's proper functions, bearing children and looking after him. Take *Our Betters* (1923), a more successful treatment of the same theme, about Americans in Britain. The young protagonist, more attractive and less priggish than the hero of *Smith*, whisks his one-time fiancée back to moral safety across the Atlantic, after the corruptions of London 'society' have been satisfactorily exposed. Or take *The Breadwinner* (1930), about a stockbroker who allows himself to be 'hammered' and ruined, thus winning the freedom to leave home, take odd jobs and discover the world, and obliging his predatory wife and children to become more self-reliant. Students of Maugham's life may suspect there's something disingenuous in what he insistently protests in these plays, that money is a moral danger and fashion a snare, that simplicity and kindness are to be valued above all; but, if so, his mask does not slip. Indeed, his last play, *Sheppey* (1933), is in some ways the most obviously 'moral' of all: the tale of a benign old barber who wins a small fortune and uses it to perform the charitable works enjoined by holy writ, only to have his practical Christianity undone by his family and friends. 'A sane man isn't going to give his money to the poor,' announces the doctor invited by them to commit him to the asylum, 'a sane man takes money from the poor.'

These plays are uneven. Indeed, only *Our Betters* is especially successful at reconciling comedy with social comment. Maugham is, on the whole, more effective when he is writing about personal relationships, though here his celebrated 'cynicism' is often evident. He is, in particular, cynical about love. It may be a delight and it may be a disease, but either way it is entirely out of people's control. 'It wasn't me that deceived you,' explains the murderess in *The Letter* (1927), 'it wasn't me that loved that other. It was a madness that seized me, and I was as little my own mistress as though I were delirious with fever.' And it may disappear as quickly as it came. The young wife in *The Sacred Flame* (1929) cannot, as her all-seeing mother-in-law gladly agrees, in the least help falling out of love with her crippled husband and in love with his brother. Love, for good or ill, comes when it chooses, and wisdom is to embrace it while you can and try not to regret its almost inevitable passing. It is an odd way of looking at relationships, which may (surely) be more firmly grounded and weather with time into something far more complex than Maugham likes to believe. Perhaps a better word for his attitude to love is not so much 'cynical' as 'shallow'.

Still, there is pleasure to be had from *The Constant Wife* (1926). Constance and John, married for fifteen years, have had an 'extraordinary stroke of luck: we ceased to be in love with one another simultaneously'. He starts an affair with her best friend. She affects not to notice, feeling that loyalty is a commodity natural only when you're 'in love'. How, anyway, can she complain when she is economically dependent on John, and therefore (as she announces) a 'kept woman', a 'prostitute', a 'chattel' he has the right to dispose of as he wishes? And so the play turns into a debate about economic and sexual inequality, culminating with Constance, now fully self-supporting thanks to a job with an interior-decorator friend, going off on holiday abroad with an old admirer. She is not in love. She pays her own way. Why shouldn't she, too, have an affair? Her husband, albeit reluctantly, is obliged to agree. It is pretty cold-blooded stuff, but not without a saving wit and energy. You can feel Maugham enjoying himself as he presses towards a consciously provocative, 'cynical' conclusion; and, for better or worse, he communicates some of that glee.

The last point to be made about him is perhaps precisely this: he evidently relished his role as a controversialist, or,

more accurately, as a commercial playwright with a reputation for confronting his audience with slightly shocking
truths. He made 'cynicism' part of his formula. Thus we
have *The Constant Wife*, putting the case for adultery, and
by a woman. Or *The Breadwinner*, openly declaring that
paternal and filial affection count for nothing once the
children have reached puberty. Or *The Sacred Flame*, defending euthanasia and insisting on the relativity of all
morality. Or *For Services Rendered* (1932), which foreshadows
Priestley in its attack on the chauvinistic complacency of
a small-town lawyer who cannot see that his family is
disintegrating. This includes a denunciation, put into the
mouth of a blinded veteran and of an intensity unique in
Maugham's plays, of the 'incompetent fools' who conducted the First World War.

The trouble is, however, obvious enough: yesterday's
controversy is today's orthodoxy, and what shocks one generation is liable to be shrugged off by another. But to say
that Maugham has dated is not to say anything that would
have surprised him: he did, after all, describe drama as
'the most ephemeral of the arts', adding that 'the day before
yesterday's newspaper is not more dead than the play of
twenty years ago'. The defensive pose of a playwright who
suspected that he was, indeed, something of a hack? Or
that cynicism of his yet again? A hard truth, or a self-
indulgent fib? His best play, *The Circle*, may show.

The Circle

One of the perils of 'naturalistic' plays is the awkward
exegesis. 'The facts are lamentably simple,' says Arnold
Champion-Cheney MP to his wife Elizabeth. 'She had a
husband who adored her, a wonderful position, all the
money she could want. And she ran away with a married
man.' 'She' is Arnold's mother, Lady Kitty, and the 'married man' is Lord Porteous, once a rising star in the government. Both are about to arrive at Aston-Adey, Arnold's
house. It will be the first time he has seen his mother since

he was five, and the first time his wife has met either. However, Elizabeth has expectations. As she explains to Arnold's father, Clive, who has returned unexpectedly to the cottage he occupies on the grounds, 'When you've loved as she has loved you may grow old, but you grow old beautifully.' She will have a grave, pale face, exquisitely thin hands and white hair: her dress will be black silk, 'with old lace round her neck and old-fashioned diamonds'.

Not a bit of it. Romantic predictions are usually dashed in Maugham's work, and they are so here. Lady Kitty has 'dyed red hair and painted cheeks', is 'somewhat outrageously dressed', and has a scatter-brained, shallow style of speech. Porteous, once the most handsome man in London, is now 'a very bald, elderly gentleman in loose, rather eccentric clothes'. He is 'snappy and gruff', not least with Lady Kitty, who clearly gets badly on his nerves. Before long, she is flinging out of the room, crying 'You brute, you brute,' and the two of them are quarrelling about the 'sacrifices' each has made for the other: his career, her reputation. By the end of Act II you might suppose there is nothing but sourness between them.

By this time, too, their relevance to the play's central situation is evident. Arnold is clearly not a very fulfilling husband, especially for someone of Elizabeth's temperament. The stage directions describe his home as 'not a house, but a place', and him as 'intellectual but somewhat bloodless'. He fusses over the furniture, giving the impression it matters more to him than any personal relationship. 'Effusiveness' he dislikes, and marriage exists 'because [a man] doesn't want to be bothered with sex and all that sort of thing'. It's no wonder Elizabeth feels out-of-place and purposeless. And given Maugham's belief in sudden and irresistible passion, it's no wonder she falls for the house-guest, one Teddy Luton, in England on a visit from the Malay States.

The play's construction is neat. Early in Act I there is a hint of attraction between the two of them ('I thought I'd been asked for my blue eyes', 'Vain beast! and they

happen to be brown') and later in the same act they admit
it. At the same time the parallels between the women begin
to make themselves apparent. Elizabeth looks very like
Lady Kitty when she was young. Lady Kitty, too, was 'so
gay and so natural' – and (suggests Clive) might not have
turned into a 'silly worthless woman' if she had not been
seduced into leading 'a silly worthless life'. Soon we are
ready for the logical next step, and it is duly taken in a
scene described by the anonymous *Times* critic as 'one of
Mr Maugham's happiest inventions . . . They never doubt
their love – nor do you. It is a very subtle scene, all nuances
and reticences, indicating the deepest passion in the timid,
awkward avoidance of its expression.' It is, in short, a very
English love-scene. Teddy tries to be businesslike: will she
'chuck all this and come to me'? Elizabeth chummily teases
him as he flounders, describing him as a 'dear old thing',
an 'owl', a 'perfect duck', an 'idiot'. The English mistrust
of the romantic is displayed in all its gawkiness, and yet
somehow turned to an advantage: the gawkiness *is* the
feeling. And the play is successfully brought to its crisis.
Will history repeat itself? Will the 'circle' continue un-
checked? Or can Elizabeth be prevented from succumbing
to Lady Kitty's fate?

Act III concerns the others' efforts to stop her. A photo
album is produced by Clive, who wants to show Elizabeth
the difference between the former and the present Lady
Kitty; and Lady Kitty herself describes life with Porteous.
Love faded, and life abroad, in a fairly corrupt and corrupting society, began to weary. Porteous was unfaithful to
Kitty, she to him. 'A certain horror' seizes Elizabeth 'of
this dissolute, painted old woman'; and then in comes Arnold to press the advantage. His first reaction to Elizabeth's
proposal to leave him has been hurt, petulant and negative.
Now he tries a subtler method, enjoined upon him by his
father, who fancies himself 'a downy old bird'. He presents
himself as loving, selfless and magnanimous, and promises
her the divorce that will ruin his career. The idea, as Clive
explains, is to impress Elizabeth with his self-sacrifice:

'What makes a prison? Why, bars and bolts. Remove them, and a prisoner won't want to escape.'

Here, perhaps, is a weakness in the play. Certainly, Maugham himself believed so: 'I have always thought the device suggested by Clive Champion-Cheney to his son to prevent Elizabeth running away not very happy. I should have liked at that point a more substantial and dramatic invention.' It is indeed improbable that Arnold would chance all on such a gamble, and perhaps improbable that Elizabeth would credit his sincerity. But she does so, and decides to reject Teddy, only to be won back by his force-fulness. 'I'm giving up all my hope of happiness,' she tells him, to which his reply is simple: 'I don't offer you peace and quietness. I offer you unrest and anxiety. I don't offer you happiness. I'm offering you love.' After Arnold's cold-ness, the barren perfection of his house and the boredom of both, this appeal is irresistible. Elizabeth cannot face the prospect of continuing to be an animate art-object stuck among inanimate ones. She opts for trouble and unease – in short, for life.

It is felt to be the right decision, not least by Porteous and Kitty, who have, rather improbably, witnessed this last encounter. They have, they agree, 'made rather a hash of things'. But perhaps that is 'because we were rather trivial people'. Teddy and Elizabeth may fare better. 'You can do anything in this world if you are prepared to take the consequences,' says Porteous, 'and consequences depend on character.' And off the two of them go into the night – to a life of social snubs, isolation abroad, but also, for a time at least, love.

The Circle has obviously dated greatly since sections of the first-night audience booed it in 1921. It can hardly be expected similarly to shock an age in which social ostracism is unlikely to be the result of adultery, let alone divorce. Yet a revival at Chichester in 1976 did well when it was transferred to London: testimony, perhaps, to Maugham's success in avoiding both the sentimentality that could have resulted from his lightning-bolt view of love and his customary 'cynicism'. Indeed, the play's most obvious cynic, Champion-Cheney Senior, is exposed as smug, cold, conceited, and finally wrong-headed. He does not 'know what women are', as he condescendingly claims. Considering the author, the play is surprisingly warm-hearted and compassionate.

And nowhere more so than when Porteous and Lady Kitty are on stage. True, Maugham has much fun at their expense, and their quarrel in Act II is the play's most entertaining scene. Their reconciliation in Act III is, however, its most touching. According to Lady Kitty, the tragedy of love isn't death or separation: it is 'indifference'. But this awkward, rather pathetic encounter – she reassuring Porteous he would have become Prime Minister, he insisting she would have been wife of the Governor General of India – suggests that 'indifference' isn't adequate to sum up their latter-day relationship. They are a weak, sad, sottish couple, full of regrets about the past; but they have suffered together, and something survives, something has grown between them, something replaced the passion they remember so nostalgically. Quarrels and recriminations notwithstanding, they are as much an argument for the action Elizabeth proposes to take as against it.

That ambivalence, that depth, such as it is, makes *The Circle* a play uncharacteristic of Maugham. It suggests that he wasn't simply a 'cynic', still less a 'hack'. If he had continued to combine his talent for comedy with the same penetration of feeling, we might now regard him as a dramatist of some importance instead of what he finally is, a gifted entertainer occasionally capable of seeing beneath the surface of things.

Sean O'Casey
(1880–1964)

Sean O'Casey was born into the Dublin slums in 1880, the son of Protestant parents, a father who died when the dramatist-to-be was six and a mother whose toughness and resilience are reflected in such plays as *Juno and the Paycock* and *Red Roses for Me*. No less than eight of his twelve brothers and sisters failed to survive infancy, and he himself contracted serious eye trouble which left him permanently poor-sighted and made it difficult for him to attend school regularly. However, the education he received at home developed a talent for painting, music and acting, and an interest in drama, especially Shakespeare, the Irish language and, eventually, radical politics.

He joined the Gaelic League and the clandestine Irish Republican Brotherhood as a young man, but came increasingly to believe that the important struggle was more with international capitalism than with the imperialist English. As an unskilled worker himself, whose jobs had varied from caretaking to hod-carrying, he joined the Irish Transport and General Workers Union and rose in its ranks, writing for its newspaper and acting as secretary of its paramilitary Irish Citizen Army during the great 1913 lock-out. He was rounded up too early to take part in the Easter rebellion of 1916, but its failure, combined with what he regarded as bourgeois bias in the nationalist movement, left him disillusioned with revolutionary republicanism. He joined the Socialist Party of Ireland, remained aloof from the civil war that followed Irish independence, and began to write plays, one of which was eventually accepted by the Abbey Theatre and performed with success in 1923.

This was *The Shadow of a Gunman*, set in a Dublin slum in 1920, when the Black and Tans were terrorizing the populace in a last-ditch effort to keep Ireland British, and somewhat similar to Synge's *Playboy of the Western World*. The tenement dwellers convince themselves that a young poet, Davoren, is a gunman on the run, and, pleased with the hero-worship of the pretty, impressionable Minnie, he fosters the illusion. When the Tans raid the house, it is she who hides a bag of bombs that a republican friend of Davoren's companion has, unknown to them, left in their room. She is discovered, arrested, and killed trying to escape. But Davoren, so far from being transformed into the decisive man-of-action Synge's Christy eventually became, ends feebly and self-indulgently lamenting his guilt: 'Oh Davoren, Donal Davoren, poet and poltroon, poltroon and poet!'

It is in essence the same contrast that marks so much Irish drama, the one between romance and reality, the imagination and the facts. What distinguishes O'Casey's treatment, at least in the earlier plays, is his starker view of reality and the trivial, even shoddy nature of his characters' romancing. For instance, the alcoholic clerk Adolphus Grigson is humiliated by the Tans, who terrify him into singing hymns while they drink his liquor; but when he comes to recall the episode, the Tans are congratulating him on his coolness in the face of their guns, and he himself is beginning to believe the myth. O'Casey's slum characters are for ever boasting, posturing and spinning tall stories in what is, perhaps, their attempt to avoid suffering and retain self-respect in an urban environment poorer and more abject than Synge's rural counterparts.

All three of the so-called 'Abbey plays', the second of which is *Juno* and the third *The Plough and the Stars* (1926), look at major events in recent Irish history from the point of view of the slum tenements, a stance which inevitably demythologizes, deromanticizes. In *The Shadow* the tenants bring Davoren a grandiloquent letter addressed to 'the gentlemen of the Irish Republican Army': it turns out that all they want is the loan of a hit-man to evict an unruly neighbour. The second act of *The Plough* is set in a pub, where a prostitute competes for attention with a nationalist 'figure in the window', heard hailing bloodshed as a 'cleansing and sanctifying thing' and calling on Ireland to welcome war 'as she would welcome the Angel of God'. Some of the slum men drop in for a drink, flushed with a momentary patriotism; that does not, however, prevent them using the Easter Rising itself, which follows in Act III, as an opportunity for looting. The tenor is anti-heroic, but the effect not simply cynical and negative. Such ironic contrasts do, after all, make the perfectly serious point that the real needs and desires of the oppressed poor were much more basic than those of the bourgeois patriots seeking to 'liberate' them.

The Plough caused the most serious disorders the Abbey had seen since *The Playboy*, bringing an ageing Yeats on-stage to ask the rioters if such behaviour was to be 'an ever-recurring celebration of the arrival of Irish genius'. Once again, it may be argued that the audience's anger was unsurprising, conceivably even healthy. As Raymond Williams writes, we are bound to note 'how little respect, except in the grand gesture, the Irish drama had for the Irish people'. The two most sympathetic characters in *The Plough*, both women, take a hostile view of the nationalist rebels. One, Nora Clitheroe, is allowed to comment eloquently on the fear, and the fear of seeming afraid, she perceives behind their bravado. There is a suggestion that the husband she seeks to drag home from the barricades is fighting for no better reason than this fear of shame. All along, O'Casey draws attention to the unsentimental truths behind the sentimental rhetoric. All along, it is clear that his heart is not with a 'figure in the window' provocatively designed to resemble and echo the rebel leader and martyr Pearse, but with the low-life braggarts, drunks and wastrels, forever wrangling about issues they hardly understand, and somehow surviving in the cracks of the civilization whose superstructure others are trying, and dying, to change. No wonder the original audiences were outraged.

They must also have found the play's tone disconcerting. The 'reality' with which it contradicts romantic pretension is sometimes comical, sometimes extremely painful, and sometimes both at once. In Act III a rebel fighter is carried in, dying in agony of a stomach wound, just before and after we see the looters at their most preposterous. And in Act IV the men tattle, bicker and play cards beside a coffin containing Nora's stillborn baby and a child dead of consumption, a scene interrupted by news of Jack Clitheroe's death and the appearance of Nora herself, three-quarters insane. It is hard to think of another twentieth-century dramatist capable of the breadth of sympathy, range of tone, and truth to life in all its contradictory aspects, that O'Casey displays here. If the term 'tragi-comedy' means anything, this is its modern summit, because he touches extreme points both of pain and of hilarity and somehow fuses the two into a single experience.

'To the gay laugh of my mother at the gate of the grave' was his apt dedication to *The Plough*. Apart from anything else, that sterling woman may have contributed to one of his most striking characters, Bessie Burgess. This is, to be sure, a most unsentimental creation, but the more effective for being so. Bessie is drunken, quarrelsome and violent. As a Protestant and loyalist, she spends part of the third act bawling promises of grisly retribution at her Catholic neighbours. She is the first of the tenement people to begin looting. And yet when Nora is angrily rejected by her guerilla husband, and collapses on the steps of the tenement, it is Bessie who brings her inside, Bessie who goes out among the bullets to find a doctor, Bessie who spends night after night looking after her in her madness, Bessie who is shot trying to pull her away from a dangerously exposed window — but also Bessie who screams 'You bitch, you' at her as she collapses dying. This is a marvellously rounded creation. Like his Juno, it's also O'Casey's tribute to the strength, endurance and selflessness of which he believed women more capable of men.

O'Casey never wrote so well again, a decline that many have attributed to his decision in 1926 to exile himself to England, where he lived until his death in 1964, and to the Abbey's rejection in 1928 of *The Silver Tassie*, an event which completed his alienation from Ireland. It is idle to speculate about what might have been. In any case, some of the later plays are far from negligible. But it has to be admitted that the changes he introduced into his work, both in style and content, were often for the worse.

Simplification sets in. That is to say, his people are more easily identified with the attitudes they profess, and sometimes simply *are* those attitudes. *Within the Gates* (1933) is a morality play, set in a microcosmic park, in which various religious and intellectual interests battle for the soul of a young prostitute. *The Star Turns Red* (1940) is a didactic piece set at Christmas during a strike and, as the title suggests, becomes O'Casey's attempt to reconcile his unorthodox Christianity with his unorthodox Communism. It might, however, prove more effective if its conflicts – fascists versus communists, communists versus trade union oligarchs, Church power versus charity and humility – were not presented so starkly in terms of moral blacks and whites. This is a play in which a worker's 'last dying sigh is swelling with the great chant of the Internationale', and even his corpse 'has on it a stylized look of steady determination'. After this, the comic *Purple Dust* (1938) is a relief; yet the principal objects of its satire, two Englishmen seeking pastoral perfection in Ireland, are outrageous caricatures. So pat and predictable is the running conflict between this patronizing, arrogant, ignorant, hypocritical and emotionally defunct pair and the idiosyncratic Irish around them that O'Casey is obliged to ginger up the plot with make-weight farce: panic when a cow is mistaken for a bull, accidents with antique furniture, and so on.

Red Roses For Me (1942), in spite of a dream-sequence in which Dublin is transformed into an enchanted utopia, marks a return to naturalism, if not to the anti-heroic vision of the 'Abbey plays'. 'There's no woman gives a son or husband to be killed,' cried Nora Clitheroe in *The Plough*. 'If they say it, they're lyin', lyin', against God, nature, and against themselves.' And O'Casey himself explicitly defended her: 'Nora voices not only the feeling of Ireland's women, but the women of the human race. The safety of her brood is the true morality of every woman.' In the play he came close to suggesting that no political idea was worth the suffering caused her and her ilk. Yet in *Red Roses*, set during a strike similar to the one O'Casey himself experienced in 1913, we find the mother of Ayamonn Breydon sending him to face the militia with 'go on your way, my son, an' win: we'll welcome another inch of the world's welfare'. By the definition offered in *The Plough*, she is 'lying', and doing so with her author's evident approval; and, by that play's concept of suffering, her grief at his eventual death is muted, dignified. O'Casey, we may feel, is telling us what he wanted to be the truth rather than what he knew *was* the truth.

On the whole, O'Casey's concerns in his later plays tilt from the particular towards the general. He felt the need to preach a philosophy of joy, in love, in beauty, in the good things of life, and of freedom from fear, guilt, clerical pressure, and the oppression of tradition and the past. Unfortunately, this is often put over by protagonists ranging from the insipid to the self-righteous, opinionated and even priggish: Ayamonn Breydon, the Dreamer in *Within The Gates*, O'Killigain in *Purple Dust*, and, worst of all, Drishogue, the communist hero of O'Casey's celebration of the Battle of Britain, *Oak Leaves and Lavender* (1946). Fortunately, it also gives energy and thrust to his late attacks on Irish parochialism, philistinism, hypocrisy and religiosity, *Cock-a-Doodle Dandy* (1949) and *The Bishop's Bonfire* (1955). In the second and lesser of these the villagers prepare, in agreeably chaotic style, to welcome their prelate by burning undesirable books; and in the earlier and better a magic cock, aided by the local women, teases and harasses the puritanical Father Domineer and his loveless followers. O'Casey pronounced this his favourite play, and it certainly expresses a fine Dionysiac glee, while retaining the honesty to give the victory to those forces of gloom and repression he felt to the end were murdering his native country.

At the time of *Within The Gates* O'Casey announced his intention of releasing the drama from naturalism 'and sending her dancing through the streets', filled with 'beauty, fire and poetry'. However uneven his success with the drama *in toto*, his dialogue often has great sparkle. Blacklegging, according to Ayamonn, is 'to blast with the black frost of desertion the gay hopes of my comrades'. A character in *The Star* warns against 'walking on a country road with a sex-hilarious lassie eager to pillage him bare of all his holy hesitation'. A workman in *Purple Dust* accuses the ancient English of 'gathering dried grass, an' dyin' it blue, to hide the consternation of your middle parts'. 'You're not trying to convince me that your bank account isn't increasing by the week' becomes, in *Cock-a-Doodle Dandy*, 'You're not goin' to magicfy me into th' dream of believin' you're not addin', every hurryin' week, a fine bundle of notes to the jubilant store you've there already, forcin' overtime on th' poor men o' th' bank, flicking th' notes into imperial order.' The effects aren't usually achieved with elaborate metaphors or Syngesque similes. It is more a matter of the unexpected, ambitious, yet strangely judicious verb, noun or adjective: blast, gay, pillage, hesitation, consternation, magicfy, jubilant, imperial.

Even here, however, objections may be made. Where the low-life people of the Abbey plays used rhetoric as part of their armoury against reality, a means of evading material poverty by the richness of the imagination, the rhetoric of the later plays seems more simply decorative, and is somewhat promiscuously shared among the characters. But why end on so negative a note? 'There are plays in which O'Casey will bore you stiff,' writes Saros Cowasjee, 'and just when you are about to give him up as hopeless he will strike a note or a sentiment which will require you to re-examine your opinion.' Into the understated heroics of *Red Roses* steps the marvellous character of Brennan, Protestant, loyalist and landlord, obsessed with the fear that the Bank of Ireland isn't a sound enough haven for his money, yet sufficiently generous to spirit away the statue of an Irish saint, transform it with a new coat of paint, and allow the women of the house to acclaim the result a miracle. A conversation about the possibility of Russian paratroops landing in Ireland, in search of asylum either political or lunatic, suddenly lights up *The Bishop's Bonfire*. Even *The Star Turns Red* is happily and unexpectedly interrupted by a prolonged argument between two workmen about the 'aljaybra' of hanging decorations in the mayor's parlour. Lofty though his aims and aspirations became in later life, O'Casey never lost what is surely his great talent, for evoking ordinary people and ordinary life in all their colour and confusion.

Juno and the Paycock

The emergence of the Irish Free State in 1922 did not end the fighting in southern Ireland. On the contrary, the civil war intensified between those who were satisfied with the dominion status offered by Britain and those 'die-hards' who wanted all Ireland an independent republic. The atrocities committed by both sides were appalling. By the end of the war in 1923 the Free State government had executed far more nationalists than the British occupying forces had done in their last bout of repression between 1919 and 1921. O'Casey, as we've seen, held aloof from the conflict himself, but nevertheless used it as the background to *Juno and the Paycock*, set in 1922 and first performed in 1924. Indeed the play was conceived as the tale of Johnny Boyle, the campaign-crippled IRA quartermaster who betrays Bobbie Tancred, commandant of his battalion, to the Free-Staters and is himself murdered in reprisal by his former comrades.

The emphasis of the finished play, however, is the disintegration of the Dublin-tenement family of which Johnny is part. Juno is his mother and Jack Boyle, or the 'paycock', the wastrel father who is told he has inherited £2,000. The family gets heavily into debt on this expectation, only to discover that a fault in the will's wording means it will receive nothing. The new furniture is repossessed. Bentham, the young clerk responsible for the bad will, abandons the Boyles' daughter, Mary, whom he has impregnated. Johnny is taken away and shot. Juno and Mary then desert Jack, who ends the play obliviously drunk with his crony, Joxer Daly.

It is a grim story of destruction inflicted both from outside and from inside, by political nemesis, sexual exploitation and paternal fecklessness; and yet laughter is almost everywhere. The fear and foreboding of Johnny is constantly reiterated, possibly to excess, preparing us from the very beginning for his last-act death. At one point he screams, and runs pale-faced into the room, claiming to have seen the ghost of Tancred kneeling before the picture of the Virgin. This interrupts a conversation in which the Catholic Boyles try to comprehend Bentham's professed theosophy; it is followed by the arrival of a garrulous neighbour. This juxtaposition, or coexistence, of the painfully serious and the perceptively comic characterizes the play as a whole.

How could it be otherwise with Jack Boyle as a protagonist? This is the Irish version of Shaw's Doolittle, a shiftless layabout living in a world of almost permanent make-believe. His deceptions and self-deceptions range from the claim that the pain in his legs prevents him working, to the pretence that he understands philosophy, to the fantasy that he has been an ocean sailor, often 'fixed to the wheel with a marlin-spike an' the win's blowin' fierce an' the waves lashin' and lashin', till you'd think every minute is goin' to be your last'. In fact, as his long-suffering wife reveals, this strutting 'captain' took one voyage only, 'in an oul' collier from here to Liverpool'. And the more absolute he is that such-and-such is so, the less he is to be credited. In the first act he swears he has not been in a bar, and is promptly exposed as a liar. He takes his Bible oath that Joxer has not visited the flat, when Joxer is hiding from Juno on the roof outside. Exposed again, this time at the end of the second act, he extravagantly promises never to see Joxer again. No sooner has the curtain risen on the third act than he is inviting him out for a drink.

Joxer himself has no more respect for the truth, though perhaps from different motives. He doesn't give the impression of deceiving himself in order to bolster his ego, like Boyle: rather he falls in with other people's pretences to ingratiate himself with them. Much of the time, he is simply Boyle's echo, one that assents with equal vehemence whether the 'captain' is denouncing the Irish clergy for 'having too much power over the people in this unfortunate country' or, having just been flattered by the local priest, is praising the same clergy as 'always in the van of the fight for Ireland's freedom'. His pet word is 'daaarling'. Everything is 'daaarling': tea, books, even a funeral. His indiscriminate use of what is, after all, a strongly emotional word is O'Casey's way of telling us how little Joxer actually feels.

As this suggests, O'Casey's portrait of this twosome, though funny, isn't simply funny. Superficially engaging they may be: they are also moral cretins, in their relations with each other, with the rest of the world, and internally with themselves. Truth, to them, is what most suits their vanity or greed. Underneath the posturing and the rhetoric, there is a dreadful coldness and callousness. Boyle's response to the news of his daughter's pregnancy is a mixture of self-pity and threatening bluster. His reaction to the Tancred funeral procession, which passes in Act II, is 'them thugs . . . don't affect us, an' we needn't give a damn', words that turn out to be painfully ironic. As for Joxer, the degree of his affection for his boon companion is indicated by his remark to the local tailor, who has discovered that Boyle will not receive the legacy he has been using to cadge credit: 'Who, in the name of God, would leave anything to that oul' bummer?' And on the two occasions the pair bicker, Joxer has no qualms about puncturing the very illusions he has just been enthusiastically reinforcing: 'I have to laugh every time I look at the deep-sea sailor, an' a row on a river would make him seasick.' Yet such quarrels turn out to be as insubstantial as the dreams and fantasies. There is no evident correlation either between perception and fact or between feeling and experience: just a haze of words that camouflage the near-nothingness of both characters.

Altogether, the men do not emerge from the play with

much moral plausibility. All can be accused of some blend of fraudulence, hypocrisy and treachery. Bentham, though able to say that Tancred should have been destroyed like 'a mad dog', treats Mary with quiet brutality, wooing her largely for the legacy he himself botched and escaping to England when she turns out to be both penniless and pregnant. After this defection, Jerry Devine, the trades-union activist she earlier rejected, comes with promises of love and high-sounding talk of humanity, yet deserts her when he hears of the coming baby. And Johnny, who has brought about a comrade's murder, is self-righteously indignant at his hopeless father and positively vindictive towards his sinning sister: 'She should be driven out o' th' house she's brought disgrace on.'

The excuse for many of these men is, no doubt, their environment. Poverty helps explain Boyle's habitual escapism and Joxer's sycophantic collaboration in it. Sexual puritanism explains the limitations of Devine and the apparent callousness of Johnny. Indeed, O'Casey twice draws attention to the family's oppressive 'circumstances' in the stage directions at the play's beginning. What is interesting, however, is that he uses the word in relation to the women: Mary, whose lively mind is being held back by circumstances, and Juno, whom they are preventing from becoming the 'handsome, active and clever woman' she could be. And yet Mary and Juno are the most sympathetic characters in the play, and Juno is by far the most admirable.

She is not the idealized creation Ayamonn Breydon's mother comes close to being in *Red Roses for Me*. She has little sympathy for trades-union militancy, and thinks Mary foolish to have sacrificed her job out of solidarity with a victimized fellow-employee. She makes an embarrassing fuss of Mary's supposed fiancé, solicitously calling him 'Mr Bentham' three times in one sentence. She considers Mary's pregnancy 'worse' than a wasting-away by consumption. In other words, she has what O'Casey would probably have thought a bourgeois cast of mind; and yet, of course, her courage, common sense, industry, reliability, compassion and capacity for self-sacrifice are never in doubt. If Jack is the drone, she is at once queen and worker bee, keeping the family together, fed, and as self-respecting as circumstances permit. She defends her disgraced daughter against others, and will clearly stand by her to the end. Even the death of Johnny, which she has said would make her 'lose me mind', does not crack her rock-like strength and solidity. When Mary reacts by declaring there can be no God, Juno promptly corrects her, putting what is evidently O'Casey's view: 'Ah, what can God do agen the stupidity o' men!' And she actually accuses herself of selfishness in taking for granted that Mary will come with her to identify Johnny's body: 'No, no, you mustn't come – it wouldn't be good for you.'

Her very name suggests that she belongs in some pantheon: the matriarch unsentimentally deified. It is also she who gives the play the unity some critics have accused it of lacking, since she is the common factor linking (and suffering) the plot's principal events: the disappearance of the legacy, Mary's pregnancy and abandonment, Johnny's death. Moreover it is she who, without ever ossifying into a mere mouthpiece, voices what are surely the play's fundamental attitudes. Others talk piously of the importance of principle. Her pragmatic riposte, made to Johnny, is that 'you lost your best principle, me boy, when you lost your arm'. And after his murder she repeats the lament Mrs Tancred had made over the boy Johnny betrayed:

> Blessed Virgin, where were you when me darlin' son was riddled with bullets, when me darlin' son was riddled with bullets? Sacred heart o' Jesus, take away our hearts o' stone, and give us hearts o' flesh. Take away this murdhering hate, an' give us Thine own eternal love!

It is the women who ultimately pay for men's convictions, as for most other things. Nothing justifies the suffering inflicted by conscientious hatreds. It is our common humanity, not our ideological differences, that really matters. The word 'darling' can, and should, mean something.

Perhaps this is to simplify O'Casey's point of view. It is, however, one which his *Plough* tends to validate; and, if he had wished to qualify it, he would surely have given us a deeper, more sympathetic insight into Johnny and his comrades. As it was, he actually cut the roadside death-scene he had intended to include, and limited the Republicans to two characterless goons and the young 'mobilizer' who tells the severely disabled Johnny, in a line whose cold fanaticism is surely meant to freeze our ears, that 'no man can do enough for Ireland'. An impotent boast from Johnny, that 'Ireland only half-free'll never be at peace while she has a son left to pull a trigger', and some empty rhetoric vaguely in favour of freedom and the Fenians from the equally discredited Boyle, is as near as the play gets to explaining, justifying or applauding either the ideologues or the fighters. Unsurprisingly, the nationalists did not like it, and actually burned the film version in the streets of Limerick in 1930.

All the same, it is possible to argue that the character of Johnny is somewhat thinly realized. So, perhaps, is that of Mary. Her final scene with the play's most wooden creation, Devine, seems particularly lifeless. Lines such as 'My God, Mary, have you fallen as low as that?' might have been lifted from a nineteenth-century sexual melodrama. Yet there are notes that no other twentiety-century dramatist could have struck, especially at the play's conclusion, much criticized in its day by those unable to see the truth-to-life, depth and resonance that O'Casey's peculiar blend of laughter and pain was capable of producing.

Another playwright would probably have rung down the curtain after the climactic exit of Juno and Mary. O'Casey allows a pause, then brings on the anti-climactic figures of Boyle and Joxer, both drunkenly mouthing the usual fraudulent nonsense. It is the more honest conclusion. To leave the play's muddled, foolish world on a note of high anguish, uttered by a clearsighted and noble character,

would be a distortion. We need to end with the egoists and
bunglers, the idle drifters and greedy braggarts, those who,
in O'Casey's sceptical but compassionate view, make life
the disillusioning comedy of lies and evasions it mostly is.
The conclusion is also, of course, hauntingly ironic. Here
is Boyle spouting meaninglessly about Ireland and patriotic
death when, unknown to him, his son lies murdered; here's
Boyle, whose own small world has finally fragmented,
proudly proclaiming his favourite platitude, that 'th' whole
world's in a terrible state o'chassis'.

These words are posturing, and yet we feel them to be
literally true as well. They are the last we hear, and somehow they encapsulate the fundamental tensions of the play:
the confusion, the fear, the agony; the reduction of that
confusion, that fear and agony, to extravagant rhetoric;
and, consequently, the improbability of anything happening to order that confusion, remove that fear, cure that
agony.

The Silver Tassie

W. B. Yeats's reasons for refusing *The Silver Tassie* a production at the Abbey are puzzling. The play, he wrote, has
no subject. O'Casey isn't interested in the Great War,
which 'obtrudes itself upon the stage as so much dead wood
that will not burn with the dramatic fire'. Instead, he writes
from his 'opinions', which are illustrated 'by a series of
almost unrelated scenes'. There is 'no dominating character, no dominating action, neither psychological unity nor
unity of action'. Altogether, the poet's letter of rejection is
a tissue of untruths, half-truths, and accusations which, if
true, do not matter. Its importance is, not so much that it
distressed and infuriated O'Casey, rather that it deprived
him of the close collaboration with an Irish company he
had enjoyed before. Afterwards his plays were usually published before they were performed, probably to their
detriment.

Actually, the play has two 'dominating characters'. One

is the war itself and the other is Harry Heegan, the Dublin footballer whose skill wins his club the 'silver tassie' three years running. The war cripples him, paralyzes the lower half of his body, and loses him his fiancée, thus giving the play its 'unity of action'. His progress from triumph to raging desperation to a grim serenity is chronicled with perfect psychological truth and in what is, most of the time, O'Casey's best naturalistic manner. There is, however, one of the four acts in which Harry does not appear at all, one mainly written in a heightened, liturgical style. It is important in O'Casey's development, because his drama afterwards became more expressionistic, less realistic. *Pace* Yeats, who presumably regarded it as undramatic 'opinion', it is also deeply impressive in itself.

R. C. Sherriff's *Journey's End* evoked the pain and poignancy of the First World War by showing an unheroic heroism: ordinary people repressing their feelings of protest behind jokes, reminiscences, routine, food, drink. But such miniaturism could not begin to reflect O'Casey's apocalyptic outrage, his feeling that the war was an affront to everything holy. Moreover, he wanted to show that it overwhelmed the personal, depriving people of all individuality. Hence his second act. Having just seen Harry run boisterously offstage to the boat for France, we find ourselves confronted with a starkly emblematic landscape: the jagged ruin of a monastery, a stained-glass Virgin at whom an askew Christ is pointing, the words *princeps pacis* beneath this crucifix, a vast gun, a soldier with a face like a death's head and skeletal hands crouching above, and, tied to a gunwheel as if to a cross, Harry's friend Barney, who is being punished for stealing a chicken. The quality of the verse that follows is admittedly uneven, sometimes poor. But the visual and aural impact in the theatre can be devastating.

The anonymous soldiers chant our their weariness, bewilderment and cynicism, their longing for home, and their distaste for those who do not share their lot, here represented by a boastful, sanctimonious but cowardly 'visitor' and a 'staff-wallah' who issues absurd orders in parody militarese. These chants are, by O'Casey's instructions, 'simple plainsong'; and the total effect, up to and including the great attack that ends the act, is of a religious service gone horribly awry. The 'Croucher' intones an inversion of Ezekiel 37, substituting destruction for God's creation of an army in the 'valley of dry bones'. The sound of the Kyrie and the Gloria drifts in from the shattered monastery. The soldiers make an act of obeisance to the great gun: 'We believe in God and we believe in thee.'

Reminders of the divine are omnipresent in this scene, and never far away elsewhere. In Act I, Harry raises the silver cup he has won 'as a priest would elevate a chalice', indicating, perhaps, that he is worshipping false gods. In Act IV he drinks red wine from it, sardonically invoking 'the blood that was shed for you and for many for the commission of sin', and a little later crushes it in what is, at least in part, a symbolic rejection of those very gods. O'Casey's Christianity may have been unorthodox, violently anti-clerical and strongly humanist in emphasis; but *The Silver Tassie*, questioning and sometimes sceptical though it is, is surely a deeply religious play. Its view, roughly, is that man has betrayed God's generosity and Christ's sacrifice. As one soldier incants, 'Christ, who bore the cross, still weary, now tracks a rope tied to a field gun.' Another sings of God masking 'His paling countenance from the blood-dance of His self-slaying children'. And we end on a note markedly similar to Juno's 'Ah, what can God do agen the stupidity of men!' The resolution reached by Harry and his blinded comrade, Teddy, is this: 'The Lord hath given and man hath taken away', 'Blessed be the name of the Lord'.

Yeats thought the play gradually deteriorated. For Shaw, however, it was 'a new drama rising from unplumbed depths to sweep the nice little bourgeois efforts of myself and my contemporaries into the dustbin', a play in which there was 'no falling-off, no loss of grip – the hitting gets harder and harder right through to the end'. The truth is

probably somewhere between these extremes. It is arguable
that the third act could have been cut, or fused with the
fourth; yet Harry's despair is as forcefully presented as
Shaw suggests, and the contrast between his agony and the
amiable triviality of the lives around him is as pointedly
observed as in the earlier plays.

We have met Harry's father, Sylvester, and his crony,
Simon, in Act I. They are a more harmless and sympathetic
version of Boyle and Joxer, chattering, mildly bickering,
forever squandering time in one another's company. Now,
by happy coincidence, they are together in a hospital which,
like the army, reduces its inmates to so many impersonal
numbers. Two operations are scheduled, a minor one on
the frightened Sylvester, a crucial one on Harry. The latter
reintroduces himself to us in a moment of some theatrical
power, suddenly and silently crossing the ward in a wheelchair. He is nervous, touchy, irritable, and obsessed with
his girlfriend, Jessie, whom we have reason to believe is
betraying him with the very man who earned the VC rescuing him under fire, his old friend Barney. When she
refuses to see him, he howls her name. As the nuns who
run the hospital sing 'Salve Regina' offstage, he cries 'God
of the miracles, give a poor devil a chance.'

The chance does not materialize, at any rate physically.
We find Harry, legs useless, among the hale couples at the
football club dance. His sexual jealousy becomes sexual
vindictiveness as he propels himself after Barney and Jessie,
catches them love-making and impotently brags of his own
past encounters with the girl. Some of the 'hitting' is certainly 'hard' enough here. 'Stretch me on the floor fair on
my belly,' says Harry, 'and I will turn over on my back,
then wriggle back again on to my belly; and that's more
than a dead, dead man can do.' 'You half-baked Lazarus,'
snaps Barney, provoked to violence, 'don't force me now to
rough-handle the bit of life the Jerries left you as a souven-
ir.' The depth of Harry's suffering, and that of the sightless
Teddy Foran, pushes the dialogue once more into an expressionistic, liturgical style: 'I never felt the hand that

made me helpless', 'I never saw the hand that made me blind', 'Life came and took away the half of life', 'Life took away from me the half he left with you'.

What makes this suffering acute, ironic and instructive is, of course, that it hits Harry where he is most vulnerable. He was the glorious athlete, the warrior-hero, admired (as we learn from the conversation that opens the play) for his prowess in breaking chains, beating up policemen and scoring goals. His virility was an idolatrous totem which he, like his society, uncritically venerated, ignoring the things of the mind. As O'Casey pointedly remarks, 'He has gone to the trenches as unthinkingly as he would go to the polling booth.' So his paralysis may be seen as a hideously apt punishment for hubris. At first, he can only react with self-pity, bitterness and blasphemy, having no inner resources with which to cope. Only at the very end does he discover a new heroism, a deeper virility: 'What's in front we'll face like men.'

Shaw saw the play as anti-war propaganda, bringing 'the voodoo war-poetry with an ironic crash to the earth in ruins'. It is certainly that, but also more. War (it suggests) is monstrous and calamitous, yet not all the changes it causes are altogether for the worse. Harry's gain does not justify his loss: nevertheless there *is* a gain. Teddy Foran, who violently terrorizes his wife in Act I, ends up wholly dependent on her censorious goodwill. Barney, Harry's disregarded hanger-on at first, ends confident and commanding, if also as hard and callous as 'friends' in O'Casey's plays often turn out to be. The one character who indisputably grows as a result of the war is Susie Monican, in the first act a hell-fire evangelist moping covertly for Harry, in the third a capable nurse, and in the fourth the queen of the ball, dancing with her doctor-admirer. It is to her that O'Casey gives the play's conclusion:

We can't give sight to the blind or make the lame walk. We would if we could. It is the misfortune of war. As long as wars are waged, we shall be vexed by woe; strong legs shall

> be made useless and bright eyes made dark. But we, who
> have come through the fire unharmed, must go on living.

And off she and the others waltz.

It is a remarkably honest and mature summing-up for 'anti-war propaganda'. It is also one that looks forward to such plays as *Purple Dust*, which insists we cannot let ourselves be trapped by the past. Guilt, regret, nostalgia, must not prevent the present and future being lived as fully as possible. Even Barney and Jessie, treacherous, cruel and shallow though we may think them, are surely right to seize their chance of love. There is joy as well as pain, laughter as well as horror, comedy as well as tragedy.

It is in many respects the same vision as that of *The Plough*. Great events, such as the War or the Easter Rising, destroy some and damage others. But somewhere in the background there are always the survivors, small and sometimes ignoble people with paltry concerns, who manage to avoid or deflect the blows, to remain apart from and even oblivious to the agony and anguish: why, and yet why not? Life is about Surgeon Maxwell flirting offhandedly over his patients, and about Sylvester and Simon hilariously arguing about baths or failing to come to terms with that daunting invention, the telephone, as well as about Teddy eyeless and Harry mutilated. O'Casey saw, lamented and celebrated life as a whole. What twentieth-century dramatist cam compare with him in size and scope?

Noël Coward
(1899–1973)

When the National Theatre revived *Hay Fever* in 1964, the critical reception surprised and delighted Noël Coward. No longer was he dismissed as 'a jester, a foolish, superficial, capering lightweight with neither depths nor real human understanding': his own words and his own wry self-accusation, reflecting both what he called his 'deep Christian

subconscious' and the common view of the British intelligentsia in the forties and fifties. At last, he was forgiven
for having been fashionable before the Second World War
and for having become unfashionable after it. According to
Ronald Bryden, writing in no less austere a journal than
the *New Statesman*, *Hay Fever* proved him 'a national treasure
. . . demonstrably the greatest living English playwright'.

Perhaps that was to overvalue him; but there is no doubt
his stock had fallen undeservedly low, as successful revivals
of *Private Lives*, *Design for Living* and *Blithe Spirit* have since
proceeded to prove. His characters are not very profoundly
realized – yet isn't Madame Arcati, the brisk and hearty
medium in *Blithe Spirit*, a splendidly original caricature?
His wit is scarcely ever epigrammatic, and rarely as daz-
zling as enthusiasts have claimed – yet don't those downbeat, understated exchanges commonly generate more than
the predictable quota of laughter? His commitment to entertainment as the supreme dramatic virtue means that we
rarely leave the theatre with much to ponder afterwards –
yet isn't *Design for Living*, with its bright, defiant and yet
logical defence of a *ménage à trois*, still a morally challenging play? Coward himself suspected that 'immediately after
my death, if not a long while before, my name would be
obliterated from public memory': he died in 1973, and his
prophecy remains unfulfilled.

He was born in 1899, the son of a piano salesman, and
was brought up in genteel poverty in the London suburbs.
Very early he showed what he was to call his 'talent to
amuse': he sang, took dancing lessons, and, at the age of
eleven, appeared on the professional stage, as Prince Mus-
sell in *The Goldfish*. Other engagements followed, and he
also began to write, first short stories, then an unpublished
novel, then plays . . . *The Rat-trap*, *I'll Leave it to You*, *The
Young Idea*, *Sirocco*, and, in 1926, *The Vortex*, the scandalous
success that established him as a playwright of prominence
and also as (his own pen-portrait) 'a weedy sensualist in
the last stages of physical and moral degeneration'.

This was largely because he himself played Nicky Lancaster, the young drug-addict tormented by his mother's adulteries and her neglect of him. The climax is an updated version of the closet scene in *Hamlet*, a confrontation that seemed remarkably frank to audiences raised on Pinero and Barrie. People, as often, confused subject with message, and concluded that Coward himself was at worst a decadent, at best an apologist for the wild, anarchic generation that was supposed to have grown up since the Great War. In fact, the play is hardly less conventional morally than technically. Florence Lancaster, told by her anguished son that 'you're going to be my mother for once – it's about time I had one before I go over the edge altogether', ends up by agreeing to reform her ways and do her best to 'save' him. It is a strangely immature conclusion – isn't it odd to find a twenty-four-year-old man so ignominiously dependent on his mother, and odder still that his Oedipal fixation should receive his author's blessing? It is an improbable and sentimental conclusion, since we never believe that Florence has the strength of character to 'save' anyone. It is also, of course, a thoroughly respectable conclusion and, as such, uncharacteristic of the earlier Coward.

As several critics have observed, powerful and sometimes wayward mothers are often to be found in his plays. Judith Bliss in *Hay Fever* (1925) is another example, akin to Florence in her vanity and fondness for flirting with young men, but less destructive, more attractive, and a great deal funnier. Coward seems to have shifted attitudes in the year between the composition of the two plays. Perhaps he realized there was something melodramatic about Nicky's anguish. Perhaps he decided that his own view of Florence's behaviour should be more tolerant and accepting. Perhaps he also recognized that the proper place for two-dimensional character is comedy, not domestic tragedy. *Hay Fever*, we might say, is Coward's maturer version of *The Vortex*, the one in which he is glad to countenance unorthodoxy and refuses to strike moral attitudes.

Not that his subsequent comedies are amoral. They have a morality of their own, but one at odds with that implicit in *The Vortex*. It is, roughly, that people have a right to their own predilections, especially their sexual predilections, whether or not others disapprove. Most of all, they should accept love where and when they find it, rejoicing while it lasts and avoiding recriminations when it passes. The point is most clearly made in *Design for Living* (1933), with its symbiotically close main characters, Otto, Leo and Gilda. Leo sleeps with Gilda when she is supposed to be living with Otto, and Otto walks out in a conventional rage. Then Otto invades the household she has set up with Leo, provoking a similar outburst from him. Then she makes a conventional marriage with an old friend, Ernest; but it is no good. Otto and Leo arrive, reconciled, and carry her off. Emotions, it seems, transcend conventions, and the emotional logic of the situation is that all three should live together – and why not? People, admits Otto, would accuse them of being loose-living degenerates.

> But the whole point is, it's none of their business. We're not doing any harm to anyone else. We're not peppering the world with illegitimate children. The only people we could possibly mess up are ourselves, and that's our lookout . . . a gay, ironic chance threw the three of us together and tied our lives with a tight knot at the outset. To deny it would be ridiculous, and to unravel it impossible. Therefore, the only thing left is to enjoy it thoroughly, every rich moment of it, every thrilling second . . .

So honesty and affection are the supreme virtues, hypocrisy and cant the great vices. It is a pretty simple-minded philosophy, but Coward is a lively and sometimes passionate advocate, capable of a defiance, a moral bravado that adds undeniable energy to his work and contradicts the commonly held view of him as imperturbably cool and urbane.

This is so, for instance, in *Easy Virtue* (1925), on the face of it no more than an updated version of Pinero's *His House in Order*. A divorcée marries into a rigidly orthodox 'county' family, to be patronized, snubbed, and, when her past indiscretions are brought to light, cruelly abused. But Coward is more contemptuous of the smugness, insularity and hypocrisy of the 'respectable' people than Pinero dared be. He records the inanities of their conversation and the tastelessness of their dress with some venom, and gives their victim all those qualities of wit, sophistication and feeling that they so signally lack. Since it is an early play, the conflict is more clearcut, perhaps more crude, than in *Design for Living*; but Coward's sympathies and antipathies are not essentially different. The later play ends with the humiliated Ernest barking 'unscrupulous, worthless degenerates' at Otto, Leo and Gilda, while they 'break down utterly and roar with laughter'. Conventional morality, if not destructive, is likely to be ridiculous: it is the unconventional, the gay, stylish, witty and carefree who should capture our hearts, minds and imaginations.

There are many such characters in Coward's work. The first examples are Sholto and Gerda in *The Young Idea* (1921), two clever adolescents who reconcile their divorced parents by separating the father from his disagreeable second wife and from 'county' society: the last is probably Gary Essendine, the temperamental actor who is the protagonist of *Present Laughter* (1942). Such characters are invariably attractive, rarely 'good'. They are selfish, difficult, even maddening, but (suggests Coward) valuable because of their intelligence and capacity for life. They are unreliable, untrustworthy, painful to live with; but it is more painful to live without them, whatever the damage they cause. As Ronald Bryden has observed, Elvira in *Blithe Spirit* (1941) sums them up. She is 'a kind of poltergeist of human energies', sexually fickle during her life and, even after death, captivating, quarrelsome and dangerous. Indeed, she actually attempts to kill her widower in order to perpetuate their edgy but fulfilling relationship on the astral plane.

At the same time there is something immature about many of these characters. 'Coward's drawing rooms are nurseries,' writes John Russell Taylor, 'where overgrown children can take refuge, safe from the world, to play at being grown-ups for as long as they care to and on exactly what terms they choose.' Few of them have to earn their own livings, look after real children, or, indeed, do anything but indulge their talent for irresponsibility. They quickly fly into tantrums, and, when they do, they tend to use schoolboy or schoolgirl language. 'I should like to shake you, Julia, shake you and shake you and shake you until your eyes dropped out,' cries Jane in *Fallen Angels* (1924), fearful that her friend will make off with the glamorous Frenchman for whom they are both waiting. We feel we are in the presence, not of jealous adults, but of two sticky-fingered infants, bickering over the possession of some household pet. The world of Coward's comedies, for all its absorption with sexuality, is a curiously innocent one. Bitterness, hatred, or any other emotion that could be subsumed under the heading of 'evil', does not intrude into it.

Of course, not all Coward's plays are comedies. Among his considerable *oeuvre* are musicals, notably *Bitter Sweet* (1929), revue sketches, the patriotic pageant *Calvalcade* (1931), and numerous 'straight' dramas, of which the most noteworthy are the late *Song at Twilight* (1966), a study of a homosexual writer in old age, *This Happy Breed* (1942), about a lower-middle-class family between the wars, and *Peace in Our Time* (1947), an imaginative picture of Britain under Nazi occupation. The last two may surprise people accustomed to Coward's 'sophisticated' comedies, since both are marked by admiration for 'ordinary' citizens, 'little' people. In *Peace in Our Time* the smart intellectuals and London literati become collaborators: the lower middle class gives its children to the Resistance and is there, its integrity intact, to welcome the liberators when they land at Dover.

So perhaps there are two Cowards: Coward the Teddington piano salesman's son, and the clever, successful Coward, who couldn't escape the suburbs fast enough. To put it another way, there's Coward the sentimentalist, and there's Coward the wit. Criticism has tended to prefer the second of these, but it would be unwise to ignore the first. There always was a conventional side to the apostle of unconventionality, and, as he grew older, it began to affect even his 'sophisticated' comedies. In *Present Laughter* there is an Elvira-figure, an unscrupulous charmer who tries to lure the actor Essendine from his friends and his devoted but unexciting ex-wife, Liz: she is firmly rejected by him, and by the end of the play it is clear that he and Liz will remarry. In *Relative Values* (1951), Coward sides with the Countess of Marshwood in her determination to prevent her son marrying a Hollywood star. The 'county' people have his sympathy, the attractive intruder is dismissed as shallow and deceitful: a precise inversion of *Easy Virtue*.

His reputation, then, mainly rests on some five or six comedies written between 1923 and 1941: *Fallen Angels, Hay Fever, Private Lives, Design for Living, Blithe Spirit*, perhaps *Present Laughter*. As he himself claimed, they 'mirrored, without over-exaggeration, a certain section of the social life of the time'. Some of them shocked and provoked. All were extraordinarily theatrical. In them, Coward proved himself the master, not only of timing twists of dialogue and plot so as to keep an audience amused and eager for more, but of making much from little, or even something from nothing. Who else could have sustained *Fallen Angels*, which almost entirely consists of two women waiting for the arrival of their ex-lover? In his philosophy the great sin was to bore people, the great virtue to give delight, however transitorily: he invariably avoided the first, and often achieved the second, never more successfully than in his two best-known plays, *Hay Fever* and *Private Lives*.

Hay Fever

Coward wrote *Hay Fever* in 1925, some three years after getting to know the actress Laurette Taylor and her husband Hartley Manners in their New York setting. 'To be a guest of the Manners was evidently an altogether un-nerving experience,' writes Sheridan Morley in his *Talent*

to Amuse. 'They were a highly strung family, deeply theatrical and prone to elaborate word-games which always
ended in hysteria and the entire family abandoning their
guests to cope as best they could.' And that, roughly, is the
situation of *Hay Fever*. Each of the four Blisses separately
asks a friend for the weekend. These arrive on Saturday
afternoon and, after an evening of games, insults and his-
trionics, are only too glad to sneak away on Sunday morning, hours before they might have expected to leave.

It's a simple, even thin idea, and Coward transformed
it into a play in three days, rewriting not at all. But the
effect is neither awkward nor skimpy. For one thing, *Hay
Fever* is, as Coward himself claimed, 'quite extraordinarily
well constructed'. The events are shaped, patterned. Indeed, there's a sort of formality about them; and yet they
seem perfectly logical, given the situation, and natural,
given the people. The rivets that hold the structure together
are visible only if we consciously look for them.

So let us look. We begin by being introduced to the
family: first the son and daughter, Simon and Sorel, then
their mother, Judith, a retired actress vaguely planning a
comeback, and their father, David, a writer. The bohemi-
anism of the family is quickly established. Sorel, the most
self-critical of the four, wishes they were all 'more normal
and boring', and Simon thanks God they are not. Judith
emerges from the garden, where she has been learning the
names of flowers in order to cultivate her image as 'the
squire's lady', and promptly reveals her remoteness from
mundane reality by forgetting the name of the scullery-
maid. One by one they casually drop the information that
a weekend guest may arrive at any moment, to occupy 'the
Japanese room'. Sorel has invited down Richard Greatham,
a diplomat, and Simon Myra Arundel, an ageing beauty
who is said 'to go about using sex as a sort of shrimping
net'. Judith's guest is Sandy Tyrell, whom her son sums
up, without great inaccuracy, as 'some dreary, infatuated
young man', one of the sort she is apparently prone to
encouraging. Then down the stairs comes David, to

announce that he has asked 'a perfectly sweet little flapper', Jackie Coryton: 'She can sleep in the Japanese room,' he declares, and disappears.

By the time the guests arrive, we know that the Blisses are quarrelsome, self-absorbed and casual to the point of rudeness. We have also some sense of their individual characters, particularly that of Judith, who has already begun to indulge her favourite habit, striking theatrical attitudes ('I don't know what I have done to be cursed with such ungrateful children!'). The reception of the visitors is all we expected. Sorel and Simon snub Sandy, Judith is vaguely insulting to Myra, Jackie and Richard are ignored. Each of the Blisses has eyes only for the guest he or she has personally invited, and even these relationships are clearly not too promising. Sorel finds talking to Richard difficult, the precious and urbane Myra finds Simon's attentions 'too demonstrative', and David quickly loses interest in Jackie. The curtain to Act I falls on the embarrassment of the guests, who try to make conversation simultaneously, and the imperviousness of the hosts, who gorge the afternoon tea.

What's meant by 'formality' should by now be clearer. Each of the Blisses is about to reject the guest he or she invited, and to get off with another. This happens in Act II, during and after a version of charades called 'adverbs', which gives Coward the opportunity to show how easy the Blisses find role-playing and how difficult and discomforting it is to their visitors. It is subtly, at times imperceptibly, done. When Sandy says he does not understand the game, it is Sorel who says 'I'll show you'; and when Jackie proves stupid, Simon who 'pats her hand in a fatherly fashion'. Soon each Bliss has a new partner, a situation they exploit for all the fun and drama they can. Before long Judith is asking a flustered Richard to 'wait for her', Sorel is announcing that she 'loves' a bewildered Sandy, Simon has decided he is 'engaged' to Jackie, and David promises to run away with an appalled and finally furious Myra. The declarations become more theatrical and evolve quite naturally into a joint performance of the climax of *Love's Whirlwind*, the melodrama in which Judith became famous. The curtain falls on cries of 'You cur!!!', and 'Don't strike! He is your father!!!!', as the guests look on 'dazed and aghast'.

The pattern is now nearly complete. Each of the guests has endured the attentions of the two Blisses of the opposite sex, and it has been made apparent to them that those attentions are entirely meaningless. So nothing remains but for the guests to go, in much the same casual and unannounced way as they came. Down they come to breakfast, plot to leave in Sandy's car, and do so while the Blisses, who are late risers, quarrel with histrionic fury over the marmalade about (of all things) the precise geography of Paris. 'People really do behave in the most extraordinary manner these days,' says David, as the sound of the engine dies away.

They are now alone together, as they always were, and happy together, as they also always were. It is surely no accident Coward called them Bliss. Nothing, it seems, can crack their blissful self-regard. Everything, even relationships with people outside the family, are games they play for and with each other. Ronald Bryden is surely wrong when he describes them as examples of the 'aristocracy of talent' that replaced the 'old, hopeless gentry' in the 1920s, cultural meritocrats newly ensconced in country houses, like the one at Cookham where the play occurs. They have no such social allegiances. If they belong to any class, any group, it is to that motley clan of essentially private individuals that people Coward's imagination: self-indulgent, hedonistic, mannered, irresponsible.

Perhaps one could say they reflect and incarnate the irresponsibility and hedonism of the 1920s, or at any rate of those members of the younger generation in reaction against the 'old men' supposedly responsible for the First World War. In other words, they may represent, not a new élite, but a state of mind, a generalized desire to be rid of all social ties and of all obligations except personal ones. That seems a more defensible interpretation, and is more easily reconciled with Russell Taylor's description of Coward's drawing rooms as 'nurseries'. The Blisses refuse to engage with the real world: they refuse, if you like, to be adult. They prefer to remain in the world that they have invented, absorbing grown-up mannerisms into essentially immature rituals. The language of love is used, but never meant. An adult flirtation or affair becomes a game of let's-pretend that can be started or stopped at a whim, without any impact on the emotions. Sooner or later a quarrel breaks out, usually for no reason, and then equally abruptly stops, allowing the fun to continue. In so far as the play has any social edge, it accuses Coward's own generation of childishness.

'You haven't got one sincere or genuine feeling among the lot of you,' cries Myra as Judith and David discuss the imaginary divorce in which she, presumably, will be the 'other woman'. And Sorel tends to agree: 'We none of us ever mean anything.' This is possibly, as Bryden claims, the central line of the play, and it has technical as well as moral import. Coward generates a considerable amount of laughter from the Blisses' habit of putting the English language, especially its cliché and platitude, into invisible inverted commas. 'Life has dealt me another blow,' says Judith. 'What?' asks David, and she repeats the sentence, exposing its vacuity. Words are for parodying, for playing with. The Blisses pick them up and make us look at them closely, like children showing off strangely shaped stones: 'I don't flaunt', 'You are tawny', 'I always longed to leave the brittle glamour of cities and find rest in some old-world nook.'

Of course, it may be said that all Coward's people do this to some extent. There is, for instance, a characteristic exchange between Richard and Jackie, full of the embarrassment of being thrust together and having nothing to say.

Richard	Spain is very beautiful.
Jackie	Yes, I have always heard Spain is awfully nice.
	[*Pause*]
Richard	Except for the bullfights. No one who ever really loved horses could enjoy a bullfight.
Jackie	Nor anyone who loved bulls either.

The difference, and part of the joke, is that these people are unaware of the banality of their conversation. Coward is still making fun of platitude, but is also making fun of those who use platitudes without knowing what they are. Here, perhaps, is another way of distinguishing between his characters. The attractive, interesting ones use the English language as if permanently marvelling at its absurdity: the ordinary ones take it for granted. Both approaches, needless to say, can be hilarious.

Here, too, we have an example of Coward's ability to make much out of little. The flattest of lines can be suddenly illumined by the wry perspective in which he puts it. This is one reason why Coward is always best seen in theatre and, if read, must be read with imagination, and preferably aloud. As an actor and director as well as writer, he knew that the most innocent remarks could come to comic life with the right intonation and, above all, with the right timing. 'You can see as far as Marlow on a clear day, so they tell me,' says Judith to Sandy: the reader might skim over those last four, seemingly unimportant words, but in performance they can become a devastating comment on the character's uninterest in the country, on a metropolitanism that survives in spite of her pretence to be the squire's lady. She has, it seems, never seen the view from her own drawing-room window.

Similarly, there is Jackie's line as she sits nervous and embarrassed, trying to ignore the rudeness of passing Blisses. 'I expect tea will be here soon,' says Richard. 'Do you think they *have* tea?' she asks. According to Bryden's review of the National Theatre production, Lynn Redgrave's pause at this point was 'just long enough for a

whole abyss of stricken adolescent panic to yawn'. All Coward's high comedies contain tiny hints from which a good
actor or actress can, not just achieve laughter, but build
character. He was a master of the theatre.

Private Lives

'Of Coward's skill there is no doubt,' concedes Allardyce
Nicoll, the doyen of theatrical historiographers, just after
he has delivered himself of the opinion that the dialogue of
Private Lives hardly moves 'farther below the surface than
a paper boat in a bathtub, and, like the paper boat, [is]
ever in imminent danger of becoming a shapeless sodden
mass'. It is an inadequate account, though characteristic
of academic criticism of Coward at the time it was first
published, 1949. But at least there is a grudging qualifi-
cation. The bathtub idler is allowed to have skill. But how
much, of what kind, are questions that Nicoll does not
think worth investigating.

He could have made a useful start with the first act of
Private Lives, as elegantly executed a piece of comedy of
manners as the twentieth century has produced. We are
confronted with the balconies of two suites in a French
hotel. One is occupied by honeymooners, Sibyl and Elyot,
the second of whom has been married before. Within five
pages of economical and entertaining dialogue, Coward not
only provides us with all the necessary background about
them, but uses it gently to suggest that the match is not all
it might be. Why does Sibyl harp so much on Amanda,
Elyot's first wife? Why does she need to be reassured about
the miseries of that marriage and the charms of this? Isn't
she perhaps a little insecure? Hasn't she reason to be so,
given Elyot's over-vehement denunciation of Amanda and
faint mistrust of Sibyl herself, who (he suggests) will try to
'run me without my knowing it'? When Elyot declares that
he loves Sibyl 'more wisely' than he did Amanda, and that
their life together will be 'tremendously cosy, and unflurried
by scenes and jealousy', anyone familiar with Coward will

grasp the ominous message. Wise, unflurried, unjealous love simply is not love.

And who should promptly come on to the second balcony but Amanda and her new husband, Victor, to hold a markedly similar conversation? This time, it is he who is seeking reassurance, and she who is giving it, though, like Elyot, in a way that makes us suspect her of disingenuousness. She constantly rowed with Elyot. Once she broke four gramophone records over his head, which was 'very satisfying'. She loves Victor 'more calmly'. In other words, she does not really love him, which is scarcely surprising, given the differences of temperament Coward points out. Victor has, as she tells him, a tendency to be pompous. He declares 'I'm glad I'm normal,' which strikes her as an odd thing to be glad about and certainly not true of herself. He is, we begin to suspect, a male variation of Sibyl: solid, reliable, humourless, a bit dull, and out of his emotional depth in this unlikely marriage.

It is equally clear that Elyot and Amanda have more in common with one another than with their spouses. They seem humorous, ironic, knowing, perhaps a little flippant, more intelligent, aware and experienced than Victor and Sibyl, and also less placid and even-tempered. Tiny parallels reinforce the larger ones. Both Amanda and Elyot propose to go gambling in the local casino, a plan that fills the others with apprehension. Elyot suggests that he and Sibyl should bathe tomorrow, and her immediate response is that she must not get sunburnt: 'I hate it on women,' she explains, when he seems surprised. Amanda, on the other hand, plans to get sunburnt, to Victor's distress: 'I hate sunburnt women,' he explains. Coward's love of pattern may also be seen in the very names the characters call one another. Sibyl calls Elyot 'Elly', Victor calls Amanda 'Mandy', cosy abbreviations in which their more rigorous spouses do not indulge when they remake one another's acquaintance.

By now we are ready for this to happen. Both Amanda and Elyot are appalled to find each other in neighbouring rooms, and both instantly turn to their new spouses, in each case demanding that the two of them should promptly leave for Paris. This the commonsensical Victor and the commonsensical Sibyl predictably refuse, provoking parallel rows with Elyot and Amanda, which end with Victor and Sibyl flouncing downstairs, and Elyot and Amanda left alone on their neighbouring balconies. The inevitable happens, in one of Coward's more celebrated and inimitable scenes. A terse, seemingly banal conversation ensues:

> 'I went round the world, you know, after. . . .'
> 'Yes, yes, I know. How was it?'
> 'The world?'
> 'Yes.'
> 'Oh, hugely enjoyable.'

Once again, Coward's deadly ear for platitude is apparent, but the effect this time isn't only humorous. This faintly ludicrous small talk is the way the two characters seek to conceal their feelings. The dialogue is actually charged with emotion, and evolves quite credibly into an open profession: 'Darling, darling, I love you so.' Off they go to Paris together, leaving empty balconies which are immediately filled by Victor and Sibyl, who are starting a stiff, awkward conversation when the curtain falls.

The rest of the play is scarcely less technically accomplished. Act II takes us to an apartment in Paris, and shows us Amanda and Elyot relaxing after dinner. They are, it appears, very happy, though they feel some remorse and some apprehension. But Coward has no great regard for or belief in a serene, tranquil happiness. It is, after all, based on love, and love means conflict, trouble. So the affectionate conversation is punctuated by four quarrels, roughly similar in character. All involve sexual jealousy or sexual anger, frustrated possessiveness: subjects rarely aired so openly in the British theatre of the 1920s. It isn't surprising that the censor objected to this act as 'immoral', though his qualms were eventually allayed by Coward.

Each quarrel is of ascending intensity, each more difficult

to check, and the last is not checked at all. It is allowed to
reach its ignominious peak, at which point the door opens,
Victor and Sibyl appear, the natural climax and end of an
act with, once again: its own clear pattern. And so to the
inevitable sorting-out of relationships. It is the morning
afterwards, and Victor and Sibyl are nervously waiting for
the others to appear, which they soon do. Confrontations
and recriminations, each with each, are followed by an
understanding of sorts. Victor will let Amanda divorce him;
Sibyl, who clearly hopes for a reconciliation, will postpone
divorcing Elyot for a year. So far the only two people who
have not properly conversed are Amanda and Elyot, who
don't regard themselves as being on speaking terms. But it
gradually becomes clear that a thaw is setting in between
them, and when Victor and Sibyl, who have been getting
on one another's nerves for some time, begin openly to
quarrel, and quarrel with increasing abandon, they seize
their chance. They slip out of the apartment with their
suitcases, unnoticed, and the curtain falls.

'Skill' is manifestly the right word when one contem-
plates the unobtrusive elegance with which the plot is
shaped – and yet, of course, an obvious question remains.
Is the play simply an exercise in technical bravura? Are the
characters interesting, or even credible? Does Coward penetrate any further below the surface than the paper boat
dismissively postulated by Professor Nicoll?

Not, perhaps, when he is involved with Victor and Sibyl,
characters for whom he has no temperamental sympathy.
He himself thought them 'little better than ninepins, lightly
wooden and only there at all in order to be repeatedly
knocked down and stood up again'. That is too harsh, but
there is some truth in it. It is, for instance, difficult to
believe that these two dull, pained people would tear into
one another quite so rumbustiously at the end. Coward
wants a parallel with the close of Act II and a good, neat
final curtain. He wants an excuse for getting Amanda and
Elyot offstage together. Possibly he wants to suggest that
Sibyl and Victor, who have so much in common, have

hopes themselves of achieving a living relationship together, like the ever-quarrelsome Amanda and Elyot. But, for the only time in the play, one is more aware of his intentions than the logic of the characters he has created.

That cannot be said of his handling of Amanda and Elyot, both of whom are as complete as he could make them and neither of whom could possibly have been created by anyone else. They are, perhaps, Coward's archetypal characters: witty, hedonistic, thoroughly irresponsible; attractive egoists with strong sexual drives and very little respect for conventional morality; people whom the world, with some justification, would regard as 'impossible'. They are destructive to outsiders, and probably to each other as well; but it is difficult to dismiss them as worthless. In their urbane and sophisticated way they represent anarchic, Dionysiac impulses, a spirit that cannot easily be absorbed into society and its sanctioned relationships, such as marriage.

At one point only the stage direction 'seriously' is placed after Elyot's name, and, aptly enough, he is talking about one's duty not to be serious. One must defy 'all the futile moralists who try to make life unbearable. Laugh at them. Be flippant. Laugh at everything, all their sacred shibboleths. Flippancy brings out the acid in their damned sweetness and light.' But what if one or the other of them dies, asks Amanda. Does the survivor go on laughing? Yes, declares Elyot. Nothing is sacrosanct.

> Let's be superficial and pity the poor philosophers. Let's blow trumpets and squeakers, and enjoy the party as much as we can, like very small, quite idiotic schoolchildren. Let's savour the delight of the moment. Come and kiss me, darling, before your body rots, and worms pop in and out of your eye-sockets.

Carpe diem. There, in that speech, is the newly liberated and rebellious spirit of the 1920s, and there, too, is the philosophy of Coward's most accomplished comedies: a counter-puritanism, rejoicing in laughter and fun and in-

sisting on the freedom of the individual, however unorthodox the form that freedom might choose to take. It is,
surely, simple-minded to accuse Coward of being 'shallow'.
It would be more accurate to say that shallowness, as
defined by his comedies, is a conscious and perhaps even
serious response to a dull, convention-ridden world. And,
as such, shallowness is not altogether shallow.

Ben Travers
(1886–1980)

At the end of 1975, Britain suddenly realized that a dramatist always associated with the twenties and thirties was
still alive, still writing, and still worth hearing. What made
this shock of recognition greater was that the play that Ben
Travers, at the age of eighty-nine, was offering the nation
was a 'sex comedy' – indeed, an unequivocal celebration of
the power of Eros. *The Bed Before Yesterday*, as he called it,
was received with something approaching rapture, and a
revival by the National Theatre of his early *Plunder* (1928)
was almost as successful at the beginning of 1976. We had
checked ourselves on the very brink of forgetting a major
contribution to the English comic tradition.

The Bed Before Yesterday was set in the high period of
Travers farce, the 1930s, and it had the feel of a play that
had been fermenting for a long time. In fact, the author
himself confirmed that it made explicit much he had been
obliged to keep implicit in the old days. It was the departure of the Lord Chamberlain that had liberated him, the
end of censorship that now allowed him to tell his tale of
the starched and irritable spinster who enters marriage
mainly for companionship, belatedly loses her virginity,
recovers her good humour, and becomes something of a
nymphomaniac, making up for lost time with a zest that
leaves her husband bewildered and helpless. The subject
could easily have been smuttily handled: instead, it brought
an affectionate, kindly humour out of Travers. He had

sympathy both for the husband's inability to become a sex-athlete overnight and for his wife's artless and eager promiscuity, partly because it left her dangerously vulnerable to unscrupulous predators. In no way did Travers sentimentalize sex; and yet he insisted that it was a need and a joy, a means of enhancing life for both men and women.

That is precisely the attitude that underlines his 'classic' farces, and may well be one reason for their continuing attraction. They, too, are plays of a period busy throwing off taboos and inhibitions, this time of the age in which Travers himself was brought up. He was born into well-to-do but conventional circumstances in 1886, went to public school, and, not long before his death in 1980, could still ruefully remember 'being flogged for things that seemed absolutely natural'. He found more freedom when he went into the family sugar business, and was sent to Malaya, a setting he was to use in one of his liveliest works, *Banana Ridge* (1938). After a distinguished war career in the air force, he turned to publishing, thence to writing novels, one of which he eventually adapted into the first of a long series of 'Aldwych farces', *A Cuckoo in the Nest* (1925).

As in most of the genre, beds are never far away. Indeed, the hilarious second act is set in the bedroom of an inn to which a young husband has brought a girl with, be it emphasized, the most innocent of intentions. This being 1925, adultery does not actually occur. But a great deal of fun is generated by the two characters' subterfuges, since they must convince their pursuers that nothing 'immoral' has occurred and at the same time persuade the lady innkeeper that they are, in fact, a respectable husband and wife. This last character is the first of the many aggressive puritans, usually female, who haunt Travers's plays. His people may be divided between those who accept and enjoy their sexuality and those who dislike it, reject it, and enjoy depriving others of it.

Those who want confirmation of which side had Travers's allegiance should read *Rookery Nook* (1926) or *Turkey*

Time (1931), with its rather similar plot. A penniless actress, Rose, seeks sanctuary with two young men, Max, an amiable ne'er-do-well from the colonies, and David, who is engaged to be married to Louise. There are (of course) puritans about, in the forms of Ernestine Stoatt, a tyrannical gossip, and Rose's landlady, Mrs Gather, who declares that 'what you sowed in sin I mean to reap in rent'. Nevertheless, sex has its way. David falls for Rose, and Max conveniently relieves him of Louise, who turns out to be a very enlightened and accepting girl. 'Any man who *is* a man,' Max tells her, 'ought to want to take every pretty girl he sees to Brighton.' Similarly, every man, married or single, enjoys watching attractive women: 'Nature intended that sort of thing: that's why the neck is made to turn.' Louise's reaction, that Max is 'wonderful', isn't altered when, a few moments later, she catches him fondling the parlourmaid. 'What do you think of him now?' asks Ernestine, who has also witnessed the encounter. Louise (smiling at Max): 'I think he's a world beater.'

The peculiar tension of Travers's farces comes from the conflict of strong sexuality and those forces which want to repress it, from the collision of anarchic impulses and a morally inflexible society. Now that we have thrown off most of our taboos against premarital affairs, and even some against adultery, this tension cannot easily be created. Today the arrival of a village gossip is not going to send would-be lovers into cupboards, or under beds, as so often happens in Travers. But in the twenties and thirties, the possibility of this variety of farce still existed, and Travers, with his unconventional sympathies, was clearly the man to take advantage of it.

He also had the necessary skill. It often takes time for the laughter to arrive, but this is because he has prepared so thoroughly for it. His view was that the situation must first be carefully established, the characters filled out, and all events emerge naturally from a credible plot. He always opposed Feydeau's brand of farce, regarding it as too mechanical. Everything must be 'absolutely real'. Indeed,

Travers blamed his few flops, for instance the late *Corker's End* (1968), on a temporary failure to observe this principle.

Of course, 'reality' is a relative commodity. Travers's people may be more 'real' than Feydeau's, but they are usually less so than, let's say, Alan Ayckbourn's. There's an element of caricature in many of the supporting parts, as we might expect from their bizarre names: Meate, the oafish factotum in *Turkey Time*, or Death, the sinister butler in *Thark* (1927), who brings the 'last post' and darkly promises to 'call' the house guests. There is also a degree of predictability about some of the leading characters: the result, no doubt, of the consistent and regular casting at the Aldwych. Tom Walls would play the young hero, Ralph Lynn his raffish friend, Winifred Shotter the pretty heroine, Mary Brough an aggressive Amazon, Robertson Hare an oppressed husband, and so on.

Clearly, the familiarity of these faces was one reason for Travers's success. Robertson Hare's cry of 'Oh misery me' amused people simply because it was what they expected of him, and naturally we miss such more or less automatic laughter when Travers is revived nowadays. This is one respect in which he dates. Another is his social attitudes. He has little sympathy for those with ideas above their station, such as the housekeeper who marries and survives a rich man in *Plunder*, disinheriting his granddaughter. This woman and her ill-bred kin are made to atone for their envy and presumption; but the 'pukka' people are allowed to commit robbery and even manslaughter as they seek to recover their invested wealth. Raffles may triumph, being a gentleman: Mosca and Tartuffe must be punished.

Much of Travers's verbal humour may seem too punning for modern tastes, too. 'My name's Inspector Monkhouse,' says a policeman in *Outrageous Fortune* (1947), and back comes the answer, 'Oh, from the zoo.' 'Rats,' says one of the upper-crust robbers in *Plunder*, talking to another policeman. 'You'd be well advised to be a little less discourteous,' the officer replies severely, provoking the inevitable, 'Very well, then – mice!' But if Travers's wit can be frankly schoolboy, it can also be more sophisticated. He is amused by clichés, verbal mannerisms, slang, and often contrives to parody them. Much is made of Max's Americanisms in *Turkey Time*: 'You'll crack a boo. You'll go and snout it to your frau' . . . 'Tell the stiff to lay off the Jane' . . . 'I should like to noss that big sap'. In *Banana Ridge*, a visitor to Malaya discusses hunting with a local resident:

'What is there? Buck or pig? What about pig?'
'Yes, you might easily strike hog . . . At dawn you'd not only strike hog. You'd be pretty certain to spot croc.'

It is easy to see how skilled acting might extract a good deal of hilarity from these knowing monosyllables.

Whether or not aspects of Travers date, the laughter that greeted *Plunder* in 1976 suggests that enough remains to make him worth reviving. Even in the study – and he was, overwhelmingly, a man of the theatre – his confusions still seem amusingly inventive. *Thark*, for instance, rises to a hilarious climax in a purportedly haunted house. *Banana Ridge* exploits the embarrassment of a group of men suddenly presented with a young adult who may be the son of any of them – and, at the same time, extracts laughter from the boy's irresistible attraction to older women, including the wives of his supposed fathers. But the most characteristic and celebrated of all Travers's farces is *Rookery Nook*.

Rookery Nook

This is the situation, and these the characters. Clive, 'a sport in his thirties', is staying with Gertrude and Harold Twine, and not enjoying the experience at all. Gertrude, 'a critical, suspicious type of seaside resident', is a natural bully, and easily dominates Harold, 'a short, feeble man' forever saying 'Yes, dear' and 'No, dear'. We are not, however, in the Twines' home, but in Rookery Nook, a house they have taken for Gerald Popkiss (Clive's cousin) and his new wife Clara (Gertrude's sister but, it seems, altogether more pleasant and prepossessing). With Mrs

Leverett, a large and lugubrious charlady, they wait for their guests' arrival – or at least for that of Gerald, since Clara is looking after her sick mother, and will be delayed.

In comes Gerald, 'a young, smiling and cheerful man', and before long he has been left alone. Then something surprising happens. A 'young and very pretty girl in pink silken pyjamas' appears. She is Rhoda Marley, who has been thrown out of her home by her stepfather, a 'very Prussian and masterful' gentleman called Putz. He puts in a menacing appearance a moment later ('You t'ink you can command me. Herr Gott! I show you . . .') before returning to the darkness outside. Thus Travers prepares us for farce. Rhoda will have to stay the night, and there is no way of retrieving her clothes. And so we come to the play's first climax, which has Gertrude wandering around the house, just missing Rhoda, then Clive and Harold discovering her to their mutual astonishment, and then the two of them keeping this news from the ever-curious, ever-officious Gertrude.

If Rhoda is discovered, Gerald will be compromised. If Gertrude finds that Harold knows about Rhoda's presence, and has been concealing it from her, his life will not be worth living. This is the tension implicit in the situation, and it is with the latter possibility, in particular, that Travers holds our interest. In fact, Mrs Leverett sees Rhoda next morning, and, being one of Travers's prurient busybodies, she tells Gertrude. Gertrude appears, falsely pleasant, and we have the climax of Act II, which has Twine hiding in terror with Rhoda, barely escaping discovery by his wife. The farce comes from the closeness of the call.

Nor has Travers done with Harold. Indeed, it could be argued that he gradually becomes the play's central character – or, at any rate, its chief butt and victim. If Gertrude oppresses him, the two young men exploit him. First, they bully him into going and fetching Rhoda's clothes from Putz, who terrifies him and drives him away. Then they bamboozle him into stealing some of Gertrude's clothes which, when he returns, are stolen by Putz. The third act finds him deeply confused and exceedingly flustered, a marvellous opportunity for Robertson Hare, the actor who originally portrayed him. If one is to get the full flavour of the play, one needs to imagine this 'sepulchral bittern', as J. C. Trewin called him, creeping around Rookery Nook like a criminal and feverishly failing to explain himself to Mary Brough's brawny Leverett.

> Tell me, do you know something?
> Do I know what?
> Oh! I don't know – I'm sure I don't know.
> Do I know what you don't know?
> Yes.
> Well, if you don't know what you know, how do I know if I know it?

And so on. Hare, it seems, was a master at keeping an audience on tenterhooks, wondering whether or not he'd be rumbled.

In fact, he never is, because Gertrude secretly fetches Clara to see her husband's disgrace for herself. This brings us to the funniest moment of Act III. Clive and Gerald begin to explain the truth. They will only have to show Rhoda to Clara to be believed, because she 'radiates purity and innocence'. Alas, unknown to them Rhoda has found her own solution with the help of a chance visitor, a girl selling flags 'for the lifeboat'. She lends Rhoda her dress, while Rhoda fetches her own. As always, Travers increases the impact of the inevitable by keeping us waiting for it. 'Come out of that room,' calls Gerald, and, in front of the whole company, 'Poppy Dickey enters in cami-knickers, singing and dancing, "Oh, sir, she's my baby".'

It takes the arrival of the appalling Putz to prove Gerald innocent; and though Travers was never one to wrap up the plot neatly, preferring to end it in mid-career, it is clear that Gerald and Clara will resume their life together, and Clive and Rhoda may be expected to marry. Gertrude has been satisfactorily humiliated, and, indeed, explicitly denounced by Clive for her 'vile scandals and venomous libels and dirty little tattling tea parties'. Once again, sexuality triumphs over puritanism and convention, even though that sexuality has in the end to take a conventional form, namely wedlock. This is, after all, 1926, and there is still a censor and a shockable audience to appease. Nevertheless, Travers manages to emphasize how desirable the pyjama-clad Rhoda is found, not only by Clive, but by the married Gerald. Before long, the two men are quarrelling over her like greedy schoolboys; and it is only the chastening appearance of Clara that gives Clive the victory.

The discomfort of Harold provides most of the comic tension; this, its romantic counterpart. Who will get Rhoda, how, and when? Travers keeps these interdependent plots going simultaneously, and with all his usual attention to timing. Every climax is amply prepared for and arrives in precisely the right place. There is a good deal of spirited dialogue during the preparation, too, some of it amiably and harmlessly vulgar.

Mrs Leverett	Those are my quarters. You don't want to see them, do you?
Gerald [*to Clive*]	I don't think we want to see her quarters, do we?

In general Travers is less than usually dependent on puns and doubles entendres, and those he introduces are more than usually amusing.

With Hare and Brough, Tom Walls as Clive, Ralph Lynn as Gerald, and Winifred Shotter as Rhoda, the characters must have seemed relatively predictable to the original audiences at the Aldwych, and they hardly seem very surprising or complex now. Travers's attachment to 'absolute reality' could only go so far. Nevertheless, Gertrude is an original creation, not altogether unattractive in spite of her obsessive meddling; Putz is a splendid grotesque, with his roars of '*Himmel*' and '*Donnerwetter!*' and his constant, exasperating injunction, 'Speak!'; and so is another bellicose intruder, Admiral Juddy. He comes first to find Harold, who is supposed to be playing golf with him, next to lay his lascivious hands on Rhoda. Both times he is disappointed. Indeed, he leaves 'disgusted, swearing in Chinese', but not before he has delivered himself of the sort of slang in which Travers, the connoisseur of linguistic oddity, always delighted.

> 'Bridge – now, bridge. Yesterday at the club he was my
> partner. I dealt and called a brace of shovels. No – no – no.
> Right. Two shovels it was. This fellow here had something –
> I don't know – a small sparkler. Twine, if you please, lays
> down a hand stiff with blood-thumpers!'
> 'Not really? Stiff?'
> 'Yes, stiff. And never a murmur! Don't you understand – he
> ought to have called!'
> 'Called! He ought to have screamed.'

There, in that little exchange, you can hear the voice of Ben Travers: spirited, mischievous, funny.

R. C. Sherriff
(1896–1975)

R. C. Sherriff was born in Kingston-on-Thames in 1896, followed his father into a local insurance office, rose to the rank of captain during a year's service in the trenches of the Western Front, and began writing plays to raise money for his rowing club. The seventh of these was *Journey's End*, a triumph in Kingston, the West End of London, and New York, and the work by which he continues to be remembered.

Actually, he produced some eight more original plays before his death in 1975, ranging in content from *St Helena* (1936), a not-insensitive and scrupulously unromantic study of Napoleon in exile, to *The White Carnation* (1953), a moral ghost story about a stockbroker who comes to recognize only after death the misery his callousness caused his wife in life. Some were modest commercial successes in their day, but none has the lasting quality of the first. It is often hard to believe they and *Journey's End* come from the same mind; yet perhaps there are interests and attitudes that link them.

Most obviously, war memories sometimes obtrude. The ghost in *The White Carnation* was killed by a flying bomb. The solution to the domestic thriller *Home at Seven* (1949), about a banker who believes he may have committed a murder during the twenty-four hours he lost his memory, is that he spent the time being looked after by friends after a sudden bang in the street reactivated a kind of shell shock. Less superficially, the nostalgic delight in the minutiae of English life that Osborne and Trotter show in their conversation about gardening, and some of the camaraderie the characters of *Journey's End* find in the trenches, reappear in several of the plays.

Badger's Green (1930), for instance, is an amiable if weakly plotted piece about wrangling local bigwigs who draw together when their beloved village is threatened by speculators. It is a celebration of parish-pump life and parish-pump people with a cricket match for a climax. *Miss Mabel* (1948) is more technically accomplished and rather more unorthodox in the way it expresses its affection for England, in this case represented by a small country town. The main character murders her twin sister with toadstool soup, having forged a will in which this cantankerous crone leaves everything to the local people and good causes she despised. To Sherriff, as to the doctor, vicar and other characters, this is a virtuous act. Loyalty to a quintessentially English community is all. Those at odds with it – and the bad sister actually presumes to hanker for Australia and even plans to marry an Australian adventurer – cannot expect to go unpunished.

Would it be going too far to suggest that Sherriff's experience in the trenches left him a little insensitive to the death of the un-English? Probably. In any case, his plays display a kindly, undemanding and, on the whole, unjudging temperament. The worst one can say of most of them is that they are a little cosy, a little complacent, a little too satisfied with a life spent coming 'home at seven' to a quiet, orderly wife and spending the evening pottering in the garden and the weekend chatting in the golf club. But one has to add that *Journey's End* makes the mundane rituals of peace seem very attractive indeed.

Journey's End

When *Journey's End* was revived in London in 1972, at a time when we were hardly likely to be as impressed by a deglamorized picture of war as our forefathers evidently were in 1928, it still proved a remarkably moving experience. The question to be answered is, simply, why?

The plot is not particularly sensational or even unusually eventful. The place is the officers' dug-out in the trenches before St Quentin, some hundred yards from the similarly entrenched Germans, and the time March 1918. Captain Stanhope and his men return from furlough. A new young lieutenant, Raleigh, who knows Stanhope's family and hero-worshipped him at school, has wangled himself into the company, much to the annoyance of Stanhope himself, who is afraid his heavy drinking will disillusion the boy. In fact, he suspiciously opens Raleigh's letter to his sister, to whom he is unofficially engaged. Another lieutenant, Hibbert, tries to report sick, only to be thwarted by Stanhope. Raleigh successfully captures a prisoner in a raid on the German lines, but Osborne, Stanhope's second-in-command, is killed. The night before the big enemy offensive is expected, the surviving officers have a party. The next morning the attack duly occurs, and Raleigh dies of wounds. The play ends as the battle continues.

Bernard Shaw, to whom Sherriff sent the play, saw it primarily as a piece of reportage: 'as interesting as any other vivid description of a horrible experience' and 'useful as a corrective to the romantic conception of war'. This judgement does insufficient justice to Sherriff's skill in setting up his situation, building up tension, varying the intensity, timing his climaxes, and so on. The play is far from an amateurish 'slice of life'. On the other hand, Shaw was right to suggest that it possesses autobiographical authenticity and, hence, authority. Sherriff knows about the rats, the smell, the bad cooking, the Verey lights, the weaponry, the dreadful dullness, the sudden, frightening happenings. He even knows that the reaction of men about to go on a perilous mission is, of all things, to yawn. It is the play of a man who has seen it all; and that, of course, is one reason for its potency.

The authenticity extends to the characterization. The nearest to an idealized creation in the play is Osborne, older than the others, steady, dependable, benign, and extremely tactful and sensitive in his handling of others; and the nearest to a villain is Hibbert, who has almost certainly invented the neuralgia he hopes will get him invalided out of the army. There is perhaps, as J. C. Trewin says, 'a trifle too much sweetness-and-light' in the first. But we feel that the second is simply a rather weak, naturally frivolous young man who has tried hard to become the soldier he was expected to be, and cannot manage it except under compulsion. It is a not-unsympathetic picture.

There is also sympathy, and some subtlety, in the portrayal of Trotter, the officer who has risen from the ranks. He talks interminably about his great obsession, food, and generally presents a comfortable, unruffled front to the world. Stanhope patronizes him for a lack of imagination – all his life he 'feels like you and I do when we're drowsily drunk', he remarks to Osborne – and up to a point he is right. Yet when Stanhope tells him he envies his equanimity, Trotter's reply is a sigh and 'little you know'. He is not perhaps as insensitive as he has had to make himself in order to keep going. And his description of Hibbert as a 'poor little bloke' and 'poor little feller' is rather more apt than Stanhope's dismissal of him as a 'little worm'.

Not that Stanhope lacks insight. In one of the play's most arresting scenes he browbeats and threatens Hibbert, breaks his defences and exposes his deception, reduces him to tears – and then proceeds to restore and bolster his ego with understanding, kindness and the generous admission that he, too, is a 'blasted funk', often half-paralyzed with fear. It is this combination of sensitivity and strength, plus military excellence, that makes him an effective leader of men. We see his quality, not only in the obvious good sense and conscientiousness he shows by reinforcing the protective wire others have left holed, but in such minutiae as his self-denial in giving the best bed, the one the previous company commander had made his own, to the older Osborne, whom he believes needs it more. Osborne's own testimony is that he would 'go to hell with him'. The men, too, are said to 'love him', because he's 'always up in the front line . . . cheering them on with jokes and making them keen about things'. By the end we believe what we are told at the beginning, that he is 'a long way the best company commander we have got'.

And one reason we believe it is, paradoxically, that he is living on nerves that are already three-quarters shattered. Stanhope is no military automaton, but a very young man who has lived through three years of constant terror, cannot sleep, shows symptoms of mental breakdown both in the perceptual oddities he describes to Osborne and in his paranoid behaviour to Raleigh, has been obliged to turn to whisky in order to sustain courage and sanity, and is keenly and painfully aware of his general deterioration; and yet he still somehow forces himself to do what he believes he must, whether or not it takes him up to or even beyond the limit of endurance.

What drives him on is a sense of duty, a strong loyalty to those around him, and perhaps the remnants of that pride which, as the young hero of his public school, he presumably brought out to the trenches: notice, for instance, that when the colonel suggests that an officer from another company might take the inexperienced Raleigh's place in the near-suicidal raid on the German lines, Stanhope quickly refuses an offer he presumably finds somewhat humiliating. What does *not* actuate him is any burning patriotism or principled belief in the British war aims. In fact, he presents only two arguments in favour of fighting to the wretched Hibbert. One is that the next world may well be better than this: 'Think of all the chaps who've gone already: it can't be very lonely there.' The other is that Hibbert will lose his self-respect if he deserts his comrades: 'They all feel like you do in their hearts, and just go on sticking it because they know it's – it's the only thing a decent man can do.'

'The only thing a decent man can do': theirs not to reason why, theirs but to do and die. That would seem to be Sherriff's view, too. His is not a play that openly criticizes war, or even questions this war. To be sure, it communicates a certain cynicism about the way the top brass directs it. Stanhope hints that the fatal raid may have been scheduled for the afternoon rather than the safer evening so that dinner at headquarters will not be disturbed. He speaks with obvious bitterness when the colonel's first reaction to its success is, not to ask about the men lost, but to exclaim excitedly that 'It's a feather in our cap, Stanhope.' 'How awfully nice if the brigadier's pleased,' he says and sarcastically repeats. There is also a suggestion that these men, who are actually fighting the war, are increasingly kept ignorant of its progress. 'Still, my wife reads the papers every morning,' remarks Trotter, 'and she writes and tells me.'

Again, Raleigh is allowed to suggest that 'it all seems rather *silly*, doesn't it', and Osborne to agree, when he hears how hostilities resumed with their usual fury the morning after an enemy officer had helped the British recover a wounded soldier. There is no personal animosity towards the German soldiers, who are 'really quite decent'. The 'boy' (he is no more) captured by the raiding party is treated in a kindly, considerate manner, as befits one who has been in precisely the same predicament as his captors. And yet everyone takes for granted the inevitability of the fight. As Sherriff himself said, there is 'not a word spoken against the war . . . no word of condemnation uttered by any of its characters'. If we ourselves wish to conclude that it is morally unacceptable to ask men to face such an ordeal, we may no doubt do so, citing in evidence the terrible change the war has wrought in the golden boy, Stanhope, the awful disillusion of the eager, ingenuous Raleigh after the raid, and the young man's own random death. But Sherriff is counsel neither for the prosecution nor the defence. His job is to evoke war as honestly and unsentimentally as he can; and, on the whole, he succeeds.

But is this, combined with the killing of two characters we have been lured into liking and admiring, enough to explain the play's potency? Not quite. There is something strangely moving in the sight of men of less than heroic stature displaying a perseverance that, though they would certainly disclaim the word, must seem to a luckier generation indisputably heroic. The case of Stanhope, stifling the voice of protest with the help of hard liquor, we have already considered. Other strategies for moral and emotional survival include the wry, plodding jokes in which Trotter specialises; conversations about food, gardening, England, anything normal and reassuring; and (of course) the somewhat drunken party that follows the death of Osborne and is justified by Stanhope as an opportunity to 'forget'. The flat language and dated slang only add to the effect. These are unpretentious, unglamorous people, tolerating the intolerable and enduring the unendurable.

What's more, they tolerate and endure without, it seems, really understanding why. They have been swallowed by a vast machine of whose workings they see only a little and whose destruction they can do nothing to halt. Many have been killed already, and many more will clearly die before it grinds inexorably to its close. As the time of the German offensive gets nearer and nearer, and the tension builds, we realize that most, if not all, of the men we have got to know are doomed, from the punctilious sergeant-major to the amiable cook to Stanhope himself. In Sherriff's own words, 'they are caught in a trap with no hope of escape'. Whether the play's dramatic conflict – ordinary people bravely and helplessly defying an implacable fate – can be defined as 'tragic' is debatable and perhaps does not greatly matter. It still has the power to make one feel the pity and the waste.

James Bridie
(1888–1951)

James Bridie was the pen-name of Dr Osborne Mavor, a prominent physician in the city where he was born in 1888, Glasgow. He did not begin writing seriously until he was forty, but became enormously prolific, and by his death in 1951 had completed forty-two plays and was regarded as the grand panjandrum of Scottish theatre. Indeed, he was often described as a second Shaw, a comparison that is helpful only in so far as it draws attention to his intellectual curiosity, his somewhat similar belief in a 'life-force', and the range of his subject-matter. Much of his better work, though naturalistic in style and content, eschewed the contemporary world for the historical, mythological or biblical. It varied in mood from the sunny *Tobias and the Angel* (1930) to *Daphne Laureola* (1949), an unromantic study of a lonely woman whose character and context some have identified with the exhaustion and dereliction of post-war Britain. In general, it darkened with time, though never so greatly that it could easily be called pessimistic, let alone tragic. The impression left is of a good doctor beside the bedside of an ailing but fascinating world: detached yet genial, inquiring, benign, and not without hope.

Bridie's plays were criticized by George J. Nathan for their 'unmeditated air and slapdash preparation', and by almost everyone for last acts that sometimes seemed off-handedly tossed away. But both faults, if such they were, reflected his view of the playwright's purpose, which was primarily to entertain, secondarily and importantly to leave the heads of the audience 'whirling with speculations':

You should be lovingly selecting infinite possibilities for the

characters you have seen on the stage. What further interest
have they if they are neatly wrapped up and bedded and
coffined? It makes me angry to hear these doctrinaire duds.

Conclusiveness he regarded as dishonest and dull: 'Only
God can write third acts, and He seldom does.'

God is often invoked by Bridie, but invariably in ways
that raise rather than answer questions. In *A Sleeping Clergyman* (1933) He is symbolized by the cleric of the title,
who spends the play snoozing in a club while a raw tale is
told about a gifted but wayward family whose capacity for
destruction outweighs their genius for two generations, but
who end by saving the world from plague and war. God,
explains Bridie, set the process in motion, then withdrew:
His ways, here and elsewhere, are mysterious, unpredictable, even whimsical. In *The Black Eye* (1935) a young man
worries how best to use the creative energies he feels he
possesses: he then proceeds to gamble his last £3 into a
fortune of over £8,000, thus saving the family business from
bankruptcy. The moral, said Bridie, was that of the Prodigal Son and many fairy stories, that 'we are not justified
by a catalogued series of sensible, social acts, but by something very much more extraordinary'. In *Jonah and the Whale*
(1932) Jahveh transports the prophet to Nineveh, but only
to demonstrate to him that his forecasts of doom are inaccurate. 'Forgive me, little man,' the whale tells him, 'you
are an instrument of God in your fantastic way, but you
are not in all His secrets.'

Bridie's God, assuming he exists at all, is an ironist and
joker, who enjoys exposing pride and presumption. The
protagonist of *John Knox* (1947) also ends by admitting that
he was wrong to think himself divinely inspired. Men must
not be ashamed to confess themselves ordinary and helpless: they are 'poor creatures, when all's said'. Yet, paradoxically, a select few can achieve much through an effort
of will aided by what Raphael, in *Tobias and the Angel*, calls
their 'daemon', that mysterious and perhaps God-given
force 'by whose agency you write immortal verse, go great

journeys, leap into bottomless chasms, fight dragons, starve in a garret'. It is this that presumably comes to fruition in *The Sleeping Clergyman*; inspires Daniel in *Susannah and the Elders* (1937), and enables him to save the heroine from the vindictiveness of the Babylonian lechers; actuates the formidable, far-sighted and obnoxious Robert Knox, protagonist of *The Anatomist* (1930), and puts him into conflict with the stupidity of a period that regards him as scarcely better than the body snatchers, Burke and Hare; and is perverted by the sinister but charismatic murderer, *Dr Angelus* (1947).

This life-force can be used for good or ill, and sometimes challenges the distinction between the two by partaking of both. The devil who calls himself *Mr Bolfry* (1943) is allowed to argue, first, that evil is necessary for good to exist, develop and grow, second, that he himself stands for the liberation of the whole man: 'How long, O Lucifer, Son of the Morning, how long? How long will these fools listen to the quaverings of impotent old priests, haters of the Life they never knew?' The only answer offered by the antagonist he has intellectually bested, a hard-line Calvinist minister, is to pursue him with a knife into the night. As this suggests, Bridie always mistrusted institutionalization, whether in politics or religion. His ideal, perhaps, was some Blakean marriage between heaven and hell, reason and instinct, order and disorder.

This may, however, be an over-simple summing-up, because it is hard to find philosophic consistency in Bridie's elusive but suggestive little entertainments. Indeed, those who attribute set opinions, formulated conclusions to him should bear in mind the punishment he hands out to the cast of his last play, the Punch-and-Judy morality, *The Baikie Charivari* (1951). The protagonist uses his stick to kill 'all those fools who pretended to know'. As Gerald Weales remarks in his *Religion in Modern English Drama*, Bridie 'preferred to approach an idea skippingly, to run around it rather than build it slowly and carefully'. He gave the impression of wanting to find out for himself what consistutes good and evil, choice and fate, truth and illusion, realism and romanticism, pride and humility. Above all, he wanted to discover whether the progress of the universe was, as he put it, simply 'towards destruction and nothingness' or whether, as Jupiter suggests in the Homeric *Queen's Comedy* (1950), we 'little objects' may one day 'attain to the properties and activities of the Immortal Gods themselves'.

'Who knows?' goes on the Creator. 'I have not nearly completed my universe. There is plenty of time. Plenty of time.' Condition intriguing, diagnosis unclear, prognosis uncertain: that, perhaps, is the essence of Dr Bridie's quirky, diverting case-notes on humanity.

Tobias and the Angel

This quaint and seemingly slight piece, long the most popular of Bridie's plays, was described by its author as 'a plain-sailing dramatic transcription of the charming old tale in the Book of Tobit in the Apocrypha'. It is a fairy story in biblical guise, complete with adventures, magic, and a happy ending. It is a description, with what it would probably be pretentious to call existential overtones, of the process of growing up. Finally, it is an attempt to discover a little of the nature of God and his ways to man.

As fairy-tale, it is a variation on the familiar myth of the boy dispatched by his poverty-afflicted mother, or in this case mother and father, in search of good fortune. The wizard watching over Tobias, who goes to recover a debt from the wealthy spikenard-manufacturer Gabael, is actually the archangel Raphael, disguised as the Nephthalite, Azarias. Helped by this supposed servant, the boy survives various perils and eventually brings home both wealth and a wife. His father, who is blind, is given back his sight, and the play ends in a mood of gratitude and rejoicing.

Without Raphael none of this could have happened; yet he directly involves himself in only one of Tobias's adventures. He chases the demon Asmoday, who has strangled all seven of the husbands that have preceded Tobias into Sara's marriage-bed, across Asia Minor and binds him fast in Egypt. At all other times he inveigles, cajoles or brow-beats the boy into action. 'Don't be a coward,' he tells him, and Tobias somehow manages to overpower the monstrous mud-fish which is attacking him. 'Answer him, be a man,' he says, and Tobias frightens off a bandit with a 'face like a devil'. 'Here comes her father, you had better ask him,' is his blunt response to the would-be husband's nervous scruples. Tobias is even persuaded to go to bed with his bride, though he has little faith in the charm which Raphael promises will protect him.

The point is that it is Tobias who acts, and acts in spite of being a remarkably unheroic hero. He is small, fat and bald to look at, and painfully unassuming to meet. His words are full of anxiety and self-doubt, and he seems seriously lacking even in self-respect. He tells Sara that he is 'only a poor little worm, really', and, later, that he is 'a miserable cowardly little whelp'. But, as she points out, events have tended to contradict him. 'Oh my beautiful, what do I care whether I die or not,' he has cried to his bride, and, with no Raphael to egg him on, has gone com-pliantly upstairs with her. She is right to tell him that he's a 'brave little man', and that if he insists on calling himself a coward he 'will begin to be a bore'. Tobias never learns to believe in himself; but by the end the experiences he has voluntarily undertaken have transformed him from a boy into a man.

But of course self-abasement is not very romantic, and, though she comes to appreciate him, Sara is not exactly in love with Tobias. This is the main difference between Bridie and the Book of Tobit. Sara, so long the obsession of a jealous devil, not surprisingly regards herself as special, 'different'. She feels dissatisfied with a husband who is 'commonplace' and 'mean about little things', and 'snores in his sleep'. Instead, she falls for Raphael, or rather for his 'daemon', and is severely rebuked by him for doing so. She must learn not to be impatient with the ordinary. She must learn to love Tobias for his mundane qualities and 'for his little round body'.

The angel's dissertation (which begins with the definition of 'daemon' we've already heard) raises at least as many questions as it answers; and modern audiences may find it irritating, since it suggests that a woman should seek fulfilment in her husband, children and 'household tasks'. But it does also embody one of Bridie's familiar ideas, that both men and women must face their own insignificance with humility. Such self-denial will produce its own rewards: he (or she) who loses his (or her) life will find it. If Sara loves what she understands, says Raphael, she will 'understand more and more until your life is so full there will be no room for anything else – torturings and itchings and ambitions and shames'.

It is the sort of paradox that pleases a God who, as Tobias's father Tobit says, 'is full of unexpected moments'. Jahveh rewards this faithful and deserving servant: Tobit, said to have been based on Bridie's mother, but, by the end, almost a caricature of goodness; Tobit, whose unremitting generosity has been responsible for his poverty, who has never failed to give thanks or do his duty however great his suffering, who always finds excuses for his people's persecution, who is so lacking in pride that he actually accuses himself of 'selfishness' in wanting to court danger by burying a fellow-Jew; Tobit, who characteristically talks of his now-cured blindness as 'a slight temporary affliction of my eyes – nothing much, but it prevented me travelling and undertaking any engagements for eight years or so'. But Jahveh also rewards Tobias: Tobias, whose early exchanges with his father proclaim him a very different moral creature; Tobias, who has complained, and trembled, and mistrusted, and deceived his bride about his family's standing in Nineveh; Tobias, who has spent more than two months with an archangel without even beginning to suspect it, a spiritual insensitivity that may be compared with Sara, who senses that 'there is a God in the garden' before she has met Raphael; Tobias, whose lack of imagination is further demonstrated by a last speech that woefully under-reacts to the angel's sudden revelation of himself – no wonder, he says, his dog was frightened!

Human justice might decide otherwise. But Raphael tells *both* Tobit and Tobias not to fear, for it will 'go well' with each of them. Jahveh has heard the father's prayers and seen his deeds that were also prayers: he has not forgotten the selfish little son. Whether or not this is enough to send away an audience with its collective head 'whirling with speculations', it ends the play on a note of mystery as well as joy. All is well, but for reasons we cannot thoroughly explain.

A last word about the characterization, much admired in its day, and the language, much criticized. The praise still seems just, because even the more unlikely parts give opportunities to their players. Raphael, who might be mon-otonously perfect, is humanized (if that's the word) by his exasperation with Tobias, his slight if justified arrogance, and the boyishness of his enthusiasm for the encounter with 'stinker' Asmoday. Sara's father Raguel is a particularly nice comic creation, with his not-unnatural awkwardness when it comes to welcoming a son-in-law whose grave he spends the wedding night fatalistically digging. As this suggests, the play is consistently lively and diverting – and partly because of its idiomatic dialogue, not despite it.

According to *The Times*, Bridie constantly betrayed his mood 'by some piece of clashing cleverness, by some forcing of the contrast between biblical and modern language'. Some may think the complaint validated by such occasional facetiousness as Sara's reference to a song about 'the Bonny, Bonny banks of the Tigris' and to herself as 'a poor Highland girl', ignorant of that 'standoffish' pristine Edin-burgh, Nineveh. It may also be that Tobit's exchange with Tobias about the new generation – 'much more tempera-mental and highly strung' – is, like others in the play, an over-deliberate attempt to suggest that the people and con-cerns of 700 BC were not vastly different from those of AD 1930. But in general the convention does not seem difficult to accept nowadays. How much easier it is to deliver and to absorb Bridie's downbeat idiom, with its 'sonny', 'yattering and yammering', 'by gum' and so on, than the artificiality and archaism of, say, Lawrence's *David*. Most of the time the language simply lets us forget it and attend to more important matters, and, even when it doesn't, it may often be justified in other ways:

Raphael	Once upon a time there was a king's daughter who had eyes like two full moons, teeth like a flock of Angora goats, and cheeks like a parcel of pomegranates swimming in blood.
Tobias	By gum, she must have been a pretty girl.

That tells us something about both characters, and with a wry, kindly humour all Bridie's own.

T. S. Eliot
(1888–1965)

Thomas Stearns Eliot was born in St Louis in 1888, came to live in England at the outbreak of the First World War, worked in a bank and then in a publishing house, founded and edited the influential *Criterion*, took British citizenship and joined the Church of England in 1927, and died in 1965. The misery and guilt of Harry Monchensey in *The Family Reunion* may perhaps reflect the prolonged disaster of his first marriage, which ended when his wife died in a mental hospital, long after their separation; the serenity and emphasis on love of *The Elder Statesman*, the happiness of his second, which occurred in 1957. Behind these bald facts and presumptuous speculations lies a writer who is, of course, more important as a poet and critic than as a playwright. Nevertheless, he was always fascinated by the drama, and came to feel called to restore to it some of the depth, energy and verbal life he had found in the Elizabethans and Jacobeans.

Before 1920 we find him suggesting, in an essay actually

called *The Possibility of a Poetic Drama*, that it might be feasible to 'take a form of entertainment, and subject it to the process which would leave it a form of art'; and in *A Dialogue on Dramatic Poetry*, published in 1928, he takes his thinking further, arguing that realistic prose drama tends to deal with appearances rather than fundamentals, the ephemeral rather than the 'permanent and universal'. Besides, 'the human soul, in intense emotion, strives to express itself in verse'. One of the essay's imaginary speakers, suggestively identified as 'E', even recommends a poetic drama which respects the unities of time, place and action. 'We want more concentration,' he explains. 'An hour and a half of *intense action*.' If *Murder in the Cathedral* takes minor liberties with time, *The Family Reunion* does indeed obey all three unities.

Several critics have drawn attention to the instinct for drama, the embryonic theatricality, suggested by 'Prufrock', 'Sweeney among the Nightingales' and parts of 'The Waste Land'. But Eliot's first formal foray into 'dramatic poetry' was the fragmentary *Sweeney Agonistes* (1932), interesting for its use of a chorus, its jazz rhythms, its protagonist's disgust with a seemingly meaningless world, the sense of dread ('the hangman's waiting for you') it conveys, and, not least, its epigraph. This is a quotation from St John of the Cross – 'the soul cannot be possessed of divine union until it has divested itself of the love of created beings' – and has obvious relevance to *Murder in the Cathedral*, *The Family Reunion* and *The Cocktail Party*.

The Rock (1934) was Eliot's first complete play, though others collaborated on it and he himself chose to perpetuate only its choruses in his collected works. It is a pageant, largely written in prose, and involves the building of a particular church and, by analogy, the Church itself. Blackshirts, Redshirts, plutocrats and other 'shady and rapacious individuals' of the 1930s try to impede or divert this enterprise; there are historical flashbacks, involving Nehemaiah, the first Bishop of London, Christopher Wren and others; and the play ends with a triumphant affirmation of faith and hope. It is generally conceded that much of the dialogue is poor, especially that between some condescendingly conceived Cockney workmen, but the verse is often recognizably Eliot's, whether it is sardonically attacking modern apathy ('and the wind shall say: "Here were decent godless people: / Their only monument the asphalt road / And a thousand lost golf balls" ') or acclaiming spiritual struggle ('Nothing is impossible, nothing, / To men of faith and conviction. / Let us therefore make perfect our will. / O God, help us'). Again, the relevance to *Murder in the Cathedral* is evident.

This was Eliot's next play, performed in 1935; but, as he later wrote, it was something of a 'dead end'. It proved that verse might be suitable for a historical play on a religious subject, written specifically for 'those serious people who go to "festivals" and expect to have to put up with poetry'. But Eliot wanted to 'bring poetry into the world in which the audience lives . . . not to transport [it] into some imaginary world totally unlike its own'. He wanted a poetic drama 'in overt competition with prose drama', one by which 'our own sordid, dreary daily world would be suddenly illuminated and transfigured'.

The first fruit of Eliot's aspirations was *The Family Reunion* (1939), which presented the audience with the same upper-class drawing room it had seen on a hundred stages and proceeded to subvert conventional expectations both of content and style. Harry, who claims to have murdered the manic-depressive wife who was destroying him, is to be seen as a modern Orestes, pursued by Furies who materialize on two occasions. His aunts and uncles intermittently abandon dialogue to become a chorus, commenting fearfully and helplessly upon the action in the Aeschylan mode. And throughout the play they and everyone else speak in rhythms that are analyzed and justified by Eliot himself in the important *Poetry and Drama*, published in 1950.

Blank verse he rejected, as too redolent of Shakespeare, too inflexible, too remote from colloquial rhythms. Instead, he chose 'a line of varying length and a varying number of syllables with a caesura and three stresses', the only rule being that there must be one stress on one side of the caesura and two on the other. This is so free a scheme that, especially in his later work, it can be hard to believe what we're hearing is verse at all. But the idea was that, while remaining 'close to contemporary speech', it would have a subliminal impact on its audiences' ears and minds. They would rightly object to poetic effects suddenly interpolated into prose, but they would, thought Eliot, be prepared to accept a verse that intermittently intensified into poetry. This would happen when the emotional or spiritual temperature rose sufficiently to justify it. The result would, or could, be a new 'perception of order in reality'. A crowd of unclassifiable and unnameable feelings, beyond the grasp of prose drama, might be revealed, and the audience brought 'to a condition of serenity, stillness and reconciliation', ready for new spiritual insights.

Whether *The Family Reunion* achieves this is dubious, though it certainly handles complex and elusive feelings with discrimination and subtlety. Moreover, much of its 'poetry' is bleak, chilly and by no means intense. Eliot is at his most characteristic when he is evoking childhood fears, subterranean dreads: 'the wind's talk in the dry holly tree', 'the unspoken voice of sorrow in the ancient bedroom', 'the sobbing in the chimney, the evil in the dark closet', 'a concrete corridor in a dead air'. The moments of spiritual self-discovery, when the verse should be most 'poetic', are not the most metaphorically alive and verbally arresting.

Spiritual self-discovery is the subject, as it is of all Eliot's plays. A man (or woman) painfully comes to realize the truth about himself, his background and environment, and, divested of all deception and distraction, sets out on a lonely journey towards union with the divine that may and may not end in triumphant death. He (or she) loses life in order to find it. Specifically, Harry Monchensey rejects the comfortable but stultifying roles offered him by his family. He learns that it was his father, and probably not himself, who plotted to escape from an oppressive marriage by murder. He renounces the remorse that is crushing him, embraces his inherited guilt, and goes off to purge himself of what we might call original sin, encouraged by Furies whom he now realizes to be benign, not vindictive. He will, we're somewhat bathetically told, become a missionary.

This was hardly what audiences expected in the theatrical drawing rooms of 1939. As Carol Smith argues in her *T. S. Eliot's Dramatic Theory and Practice*, every device is used to 'shake [their] confidence in the validity of that world of surface reality as a total representation of existence'. The triviality of uncles and aunts who might have strayed in from Pinero or Lonsdale is exposed, and new, higher, more intense levels of awareness revealed. Eliot was never so revolutionary again. His subsequent dramatic work also uses naturalistic settings for spiritual debate and, doing so, tries to show that debate's relevance to ordinary life. Unluckily, its impact is weakened by a reliance on convention that goes beyond drawing-room settings.

It is a loss of nerve well illustrated by the attack on *The Family Reunion* Eliot himself makes in *Poetry and Drama*. His description of Harry as an 'insufferable prig' may not be wholly inaccurate. The coldness of his earlier spiritual heroes, their tendency to patronize or even hector lesser souls, is certainly disconcerting. But Eliot's main complaint, that the chorus, the Furies and much of the poetry are too intrusive, can be rejected by an age, like ours, more tolerant of imaginative exuberance and incongruity of style. Indeed, a revival of *The Family Reunion* in 1979 proved that the elements which Eliot regretted were precisely its strength. Beside it *The Confidential Clerk* (1953), about a young man who resists others' plans for him and seeks fulfilment in church music and (perhaps) Holy Orders, seems flatly written and dull. It tries to build a comedy about disputed paternity into a chronicle of spiritual discovery, but ends by reducing the latter into the former. In Raymond Williams's damning phrase, it becomes 'a repertory of West End gestures'.

The Elder Statesman (1958) is better, and has even been described as Eliot's *Oedipus at Colonus*, his serene farewell to the theatre. In it, a politician faces out the inadequacies and evils of his mainly misspent life, and, purged and reconciled, goes out in vague imitation of Sophocles's hero, to die under a beech tree. The importance of love is much and sometimes movingly stressed, in interesting contrast with those plays whose epigraph is, or ought to be, St John of the Cross. The road to salvation exemplified by the Chamberlaynes in *The Cocktail Party* evidently came to seem increasingly admirable to Eliot in his old age. Yet the language still lacks invention, the action momentum, and the sum effect, if not quite that of (Kenneth Tynan's phrase) 'Pinero on stilts', is hardly Sophoclean in its beauty and grandeur. The crusading poet had, alas, allowed himself to be intimidated by the theatrical practice of his day; and we can only speculate, ruefully and impotently, about the major dramatist he might have become if he had continued to apply the full armoury of his talents to the stage.

Murder in the Cathedral

Murder in the Cathedral was first presented only fifty yards from the actual spot where Thomas à Becket was assassinated in 1170, and designed to raise money for Canterbury Cathedral itself. Both the setting and the Christian commitment of the audience clearly made Eliot's somewhat revolutionary aims easier to fulfil. A chorus was, after all, analogous to a church choir, and this one actually incanted variations on the Dies Irae and Te Deum. Verse could be presented without incongruity to a public accustomed to the liturgy. A soliloquy could be transformed into a sermon. In short, archaic forms could be turned to modern religious purposes without enormous strain on anyone's aesthetic credulity. And the Greek cult of gods, heroes and sacred places, which Aeschylan tragedy substantially is, could become a ritualistic celebration of a Christian martyr.

Analysis, however, as well as celebration. Eliot later ex-

plained that he excluded much of Becket's story and background because he 'wanted to concentrate on death and
martyrdom', and his 'concentration' can be spiritually subtle and intellectually demanding. The audience, or congregation, is asked, not just to participate in an act of worship,
but to think about knotty and paradoxical theological issues, notably the relationship of the individual will to the
divine plan. Consider Thomas's very first speech, addressed
to the chorus:

> They know and do not know, that acting is suffering
> And suffering is action. Neither does the agent suffer
> Nor the patient act. But both are fixed
> In an eternal action, an eternal patience
> To which all must consent that it may be willed
> And which all must suffer that they may will it,
> That the pattern may subsist, for the pattern is the action
> And the suffering, that the wheel may turn and still
> Be forever still.

This isn't easy to paraphrase and, as a 'mystery', may not
even be susceptible to reason. It seems to mean that 'suffering', whether it is defined as pain or passive consent,
may be a cause or 'action', and action itself may lead to or
actually be 'suffering'. But the circle of human cause and
effect, of effects that are causes and causes that are effects,
is subsumed into a larger 'pattern', one in which the will
achieves perfection in self-surrender and true freedom consists of subjection to a God who is the unmoving mover,
the still point at the hub of the turning world. Just to add
to the difficulty, the speech is later thrown back at Thomas
by the last and subtlest of his tempters, perhaps mockingly
or perhaps ironically, perhaps to expose to him his failure
to fulfil his own prescription for perfecting the will, or
perhaps to suggest that his words arrogantly imply that he
believes he has perfected his will already. The purpose of
the repetition is disputed by critics.

By the time Becket is presented with this tempter, it is,
however, clear what his principal fault is. He has returned

to his archbishopric from exile abroad expecting an attack and, in a way, welcoming it. He has said that the 'consummation', meaning his impending death, will be less burdensome than a wait spent battling with 'shadows'. Already, the inference is that he expects to triumph with ease over insubstantial enemies, and this is perfectly true of his confrontation with the first three tempters, respectively representing courtly hedonism, temporal power, including power to do good, and an alliance with the barons against Henry II. Yet each of these recognizes or exposes what is, in fact, Becket's flaw. 'I leave you to the pleasures of your higher vices,' says the first, 'which will have to be paid for at higher prices.' 'Your sin soars sunward,' adds the second, 'covering king's falcons.' And Becket himself rejects the third with a similar image: 'Shall I who ruled like an eagle over doves / Now take the shape of a wolf among wolves?.' His sin, his potentially costly vice, is pride.

There is historical basis for the accusation, as there is for very much of the play. In pursuit of his quarrel with the king, originally about the excessive power of clerical courts, but eventually about the political power of the Church itself, Becket often behaved immoderately, highhandedly. In the very Christmas Day sermon which Eliot rewrites in *Murder in the Cathedral* he dwelt angrily on the evil of king's men who had cut off the tail of one of his servants' horses, and excommunicated them there and then. But the pride for which the fourth tempter attacks him is much more insidious than that. 'Seek the way of martyrdom,' he suggests. 'Make yourself the lowest / On earth to be highest in heaven'; and Thomas admits that this does indeed reflect 'my own desires'. Is there no way, he asks, that 'does not lead to damnation in pride'? Must worldly pride be replaced by a deeper and more dangerous variety of the same sin? Is untainted action and suffering impossible?

The battle with the desire to be a martyr and saint is the only inner conflict ascribed to Becket, and it is soon over. After a short passage in which the tempters propagate what Eliot would regard as the illusion of disillusion, the priests recommend caution, and the chorus expresses foreboding and horror, Thomas speaks again. The greatest treason, he tells us, is 'to do the right deed for the wrong reason'; but it is a temptation that 'shall not come in this kind again'. He will no longer presume deliberately to act or suffer, but submit to 'my good Angel, whom God appoints / To be my guardian'. He now knows why and how he must, as he expresses it later, 'make perfect my will'.

Some critics have questioned whether he completely succeeds in doing so, and wondered if there is, in fact, some weight in the conclusion of the fourth knight, whose approach is similar to that of the fourth tempter and who was actually played by the same actor in the original production. After all, the line between martyrdom and suicide is as narrow as that between sanctity and pride, and the slightest intrusion of personal will or self-consciousness could indeed reduce the one into the other. According to the historian Paul Johnson, for instance, getting himself killed became the only way the original Becket could damage the king. So he deliberately baited the knights; he 'chose to be assassinated'.

Eliot's Becket is, of course, very different. He may resist being carried by his priests into the supposed safety of the cathedral, and, once there, insist (as the historical Becket insisted) that the doors be flung open; yet he responds to the knights' insults with polite argument and solemnly warns them of the spiritual dangers they are courting both here and in the hereafter. It might be claimed that, so far as is consonant with his integrity, he actually attempts to deflect them from their purpose. And yet Eliot, asked by his producer Martin Browne whether Becket triumphed over the fourth tempter, answered that none of us 'can attain final victory while we live'. While his Becket will only be dismissed as a suicide by those who cannot believe in any martyrdom, the degree of his sanctity at the time of his murder is open to debate.

It is, however, a sanctity more than sufficient to prevent the play being regarded as a tragedy in any Aristotelian sense. Becket is not destroyed by the hamartia, or flaw, of pride; his death, as his own sermon presciently suggests, is at least as much a cause for joy as mourning; and he can no doubt look forward to his reward in the hereafter. Nor can the play easily be classified as the Christian thriller that was at the back of Eliot's mind when he considered calling it *The Archbishop Murder Case* and actually introduced into it echoes of Conan Doyle's 'Musgrave Ritual'. Bluntly, it lacks tension. We are told very early by Becket that the 'hungry hawk' will soon strike; everything proceeds to an end we always feel (indeed, know) to be inevitable. If Eliot had taken us further inside his protagonist, and drawn out the conflict with those internal voices that are represented by the Fourth Tempter, there would have been a gain in dramatic excitement; and some critics have attacked him for failing to do so. But that would, of course, have given us another kind of play. Eliot is not interested in exploring the psychology of Becket as an individual. Rather, he makes him an archetypal figure, representing faith and integrity, in almost ritualistic confrontation with the world, the flesh and the devil.

This may not, however, wholly explain the cold and forbidding impression he makes. At times we feel that his devotion to renunciation is inhuman rather than superhuman. There is an obvious parallel, invoked in his own sermon, between his sacrifice and that of Christ; and yet there is only one moment when he partakes of Christ's love for humanity, and that is when he forbids the rampaging knights to touch his priests. We do not find him forgiving his enemies at the point of death. He rids himself of egoism, but replaces it, not with altruism, but with a sort of negative capability, an openness to the divine will that is based on detachment and withdrawal. In other words, he lacks charity – and without charity, St Paul tells us, it profits a man nothing to give his body to be burned. But this is a criticism of Eliot's theological emphasis – at this stage, a matter of purgation, rejection of things human, atonement through self-denial and self-sacrifice – and beyond the scope of this book to pursue.

Certainly we do not feel that St Thomas is 'one of us' in the way that some of the minor characters are. The garrulous, self-important messenger and the nervous, cowardly first priest have rather more individuality than him. No, he is the emblematic hero of a spiritual morality play, and one with an obviously exemplary function. Eliot wanted, he said, to 'bring home to the audience the contemporary relevance of the situation.' And this brings us to the three elements of the play that remain to be discussed: the language, the knights, and the chorus.

The need for relevance manifestly excluded an archaic style of speech: historical considerations excluded modern conversation. The language, decided Eliot, had to be 'neutral, committed neither to the present nor to the past', and cast in very flexible verse. Accordingly, he tells us, he kept in mind the medieval morality *Everyman*. He avoided too much iambic, and introduced some alliteration and the occasional rhyme into lines whose rhythms vary considerably from place to place, depending on speaker and mood. Compare, for instance, the tripping dactyls with which the First Tempter introduces himself, the concentrated violence of the rhymed repetitions of the tipsy knights, the psalmic last chorus, and the abrupt, finger-pointing emphasis of Thomas as he rounds on the spectators, warning them that for every wrong 'you and you / And you, must be punished. So must you'.

This last is an obvious attempt to involve the audience in the play, to insist on the permanence of its truths. Another is Thomas's sermon, the point at which the spectators are most clearly identified with the congregation at a service. But the most important is the self-justification of the knights, who buttonhole the audience in contemporary prose and subject it to a temptation parallel to that faced by Becket himself. The scene was as much criticized in its day as the epilogue to *St Joan* to which it is indebted; but nowadays it seems, not just theatrically acceptable, but a wonderfully inventive and entertaining way of debating the meaning of a play that is now all but finished. To what extent, we're asked, did Becket's political conduct and personal temperament make him responsible for his fate? The knights argue reasonably, plausibly. Eliot is remarkably fair to them, and that, of course, makes their appeal the more dangerously insidious. They are, in fact, rationalizing an atrocity, an increasingly frequent occurrence in the 1930s. The polite menace of their exit-line – 'Please be careful not to loiter in groups at street corners, and do nothing that might provoke any outbreak' – was often to be heard in the years to come.

The play is of its period, propaganda for Christianity at a time when shrill and combative voices were crusading for fascism, communism and other materialist causes. When the third knight asks the audience to applaud him and his comrades for helping to achieve 'a just subordination of the pretensions of the Church to the welfare of the State', Eliot may well have had in mind Hitler's growing interference in ecclesiastic affairs in Germany. But clearly a more sweeping relevance is intended. The knights, said Eliot, were there to 'shock the audience out of its complacency', and they do so by implicating it in their crime. If nowadays we approve of the continuing secularization of society, we owe it to people like them, and must therefore share their guilt. Might not we, too, prefer a modern Becket dead?

But the audience is not only asked to examine its Christian conscience: it is also to share the experience of a chorus which begins the play as apathetic, as mechanical in its religious observance –

> We have kept the feasts, heard the masses,
> We have brewed beer and cyder

– as spiritually derelict as many Anglicans now and in 1935. It consists of 'the scrubbers and sweepers of Canterbury', 'types of the common man', or, as Eliot expressed it elsewhere, 'excited and sometimes hysterical women'. It increases the play's power, he claimed, while concealing its dramatic defects. It 'mediates between the action and the audience; it intensifies the action by projecting its emotional consequences, so that we as the audience see it doubly by seeing its effect on other people'. More specifically, it moves from distress at the disturbance it foresees, to the demand that it be left alone to pursue its tiny concerns in peace, to terror at the prospect of being abandoned to fend for itself in a hostile world, to an awareness of its own guilt and responsibility for evil, to a sense of emptiness and horror at being separated from God, to a feeling that the whole world is polluted and must be purified, and finally to the great affirmation of the Te Deum that closes the play.

The words and rhythms of this bear out the third priest's summing-up, 'the Church is stronger for this action, / Triumphant in adversity'. The women express joy, gratitude, awe and contrition, and end by asking St Thomas to pray for them, much of the time using the imagery of nature, animal creation and the seasons that characterizes Eliot's poetry throughout the play. The world has been renewed by blood sacrifice. They themselves have been renewed by Christian martyrdom. And off goes the audience into the twentieth-century darkness, itself perhaps invigorated by the same spirit of renewal.

The Cocktail Party

Eliot could not resist a classical allusion, even if it added little. *The Confidential Clerk* owes something to Euripides's *Ion*; *The Elder Statesman*, something more to *Oedipus at Colonus*; and *The Family Reunion* much to the *Oresteia*. The reference made by *The Cocktail Party* is elusive, perhaps too elusive, and unconnected with the play's one foray into non-realistic ritual, the 'libation' scene that ends the second act. It is to Euripides's *Alcestis*, in which Heracles, having unwittingly caroused in a house of mourning, atones for his blunder by rescuing Alcestis from the dead and reconciling her with her husband Admetus. This helps explain why the

Uninvited Guest, having spent the first scene drinking gin, suddenly bursts into the drinking song whose title was originally supposed to be that of the play itself, 'One-eyed Riley'. This is because, as Eliot explained, the character wants to 'mystify' his host, Edward Chamberlayne; but also because he is to be identified with Heracles. And later, true to myth, he attempts to 'bring someone back from the dead'. He resurrects Lavinia Chamberlayne, so to speak, and reconciles her with Edward, himself suffering from 'death of the spirit'.

This occurs towards the end of the second act, by which time Eliot has shown the dereliction of their marriage in considerable detail. Indeed, Lavinia, who has been having a somewhat unfulfilling affair with the aspiring film director Peter Quilpe, has actually left Edward, whose own affair with the fashionable Celia Coplestone is, it seems, more successful. Moreover, she has deserted him just before one of their cocktail parties, obliging him to invent unconvincing explanations for her absence and face awkward questions from his guests, who include the nosy and garrulous Julia and the professional traveller, Alex. Yet left alone with the Uninvited Guest, alias the psychiatrist Sir Henry Harcourt-Reilly, he suddenly unburdens himself and discovers that he does, after all, want Lavinia back, if only to unravel the truth about their five-year marriage and cure his feelings of bewilderment, insecurity and self-doubt. He also reveals himself as an emotionally dishonest man and a thoroughly apathetic husband, who brings no more than mechanical reflexes to a meaningless relationship: 'a set of obsolete responses', as Reilly puts it.

This impression is reinforced when he is confronted with Celia, who is looking forward to his divorce and their marriage. He is self-absorbed, self-pitying and feeble. His professed 'love' for her is revealed as self-deception and sham. All he can foresee, if he and Lavinia are indeed reunited, is boredom and misery, made worse by what he now recognizes as his own 'indomitable spirit of mediocrity'. Celia watches the man she had adored wither into a 'mummy', his voice shrivel into that of an 'insect'; but then she sees that she has been in love with someone who never existed, but was invented by herself. Edward is, after all, only Edward.

There follow two meetings of husband and wife, the first in their London flat, the second in Reilly's consulting room. The tone is recriminatory, unpleasant. To Lavinia, Edward is a weak and passive poseur, actuated by the desire to think well of himself; to Edward, Lavinia is cold, hard and socially ambitious, a bitch who has simply made a convenience of him. To Reilly, they are both liars, who have sought to deceive themselves, each other and everyone else about both past and present. What really frightens Edward, he says, is that he may not have the capacity to love: what frightens Lavinia is that no one can love her. Why not 'reverse the propositions and put them together'? And off they go to try to do so.

But this doesn't end Reilly's morning. Three lives have been threatened with 'ruin', and need revival; and the third is that of Celia, quietly aghast at having made an icon of Edward and worshipped that, not him. Her reaction to this discovery has been characteristically humble and magnanimous. She has, in fact, apologized for 'using' him, thus bolstering the good impression she has already made. We have the testimony of Peter Quilpe, who has fallen for her, that she can make others extraordinarily peaceful, happy. And we've the testimony of our own ears that she has a capacity for love, for pity, and for facing hard truths honestly and self-critically. But how is she to use that capacity, how express the love she has manifestly misdirected, the need she has been seeking to fulfil in the wrong place?

These are the problems she apologetically brings to Reilly. She feels, she says, a great sense of solitude, an awareness of the insufficiency of human relationships. She also feels a sense of sin, not because of the obvious 'immorality' of adultery, but because of 'emptiness, of failure / Towards someone, or something, outside of myself'; and she wishes to atone for it. Finally, she reports having felt an 'intensity of loving', for an unknown entity. What all this adds up to is obvious to Reilly, as to anyone who knows his Eliot; and he offers her a choice. Either she can be helped back to humanity, normality , the 'common routine', or she can undertake the 'terrifying' journey we already realize to be the way of the saints. She opts for the latter, and goes to a 'sanatorium', presumably the headquarters of an austere missionary society.

The way Eliot presents the choice suggests he has mellowed somewhat towards the world since *The Family Reunion* and *Murder in the Cathedral*. Neither Celia nor Reilly has the contempt for the ordinary displayed by Harry; and Celia certainly displays more charity and compassion than Becket. It is recognized that there are two ways of fulfilling the divine plan, two ways of expressing that 'real love' which, said Eliot, is always 'ultimately the love of God'. There is the way of human relationships, the way represented (or misrepresented) by the Chamberlaynes, as well as the lonely and intense way chosen by Celia. 'Neither way is better,' says Reilly. 'Both ways are necessary'; and he seems to mean it. Yet we still feel that in Eliot's view the second is much the higher. The first, though 'a good life' in 'a world of lunacy, violence, stupidity, greed', consists of making 'the best of a bad job'. It is the way of easy and rather empty contentment: 'Two people who know they do not understand each other, / Breeding children whom they do not understand / And who will never understand them.' Offered this as an alternative to the 'terrifying journey', Celia understandably regards it as a 'betrayal'. It is, after all, a pretty patronizing view of the 'good life' in the world.

The result of her journey, like that of the Chamberlaynes, is revealed in a last act that occurs two years later and was regarded by Eliot himself as barely more than an epilogue to an action already completed. Edward and Lavinia are throwing another cocktail party, and the tone, as often before, reminds us that the play was subtitled 'a comedy'. The tale told by Alex of the monkey-worshippers of Kinkanja is at first funny and absurd, then disagreeable but still remote, and then, quite suddenly, immediate and very shocking indeed. Celia has been crucified beside an anthill. Edward's first reaction is that this was mere waste – the plague-stricken natives she insisted on tending died anyway – and feels some personal guilt for it. But Reilly, as befits Eliot's mouthpiece, has the last word. He had, he said, a pre-vision of Celia's death when he first met her. It was her 'destiny' and 'part of the design', yet its specific form was chosen by her. His words come closer than some will like to endorsing a belief in predestination, but the element of will, or at least of consent, is surely sufficient to justify his conclusion. Celia's martyrdom was 'triumphant'.

It is also interesting for its impact on the other characters. Peter Quilpe, who is making what he admits to be 'a second-rate film' in California, at first laments the time he has wasted dreaming of Celia; but then agrees he has been living on an 'image' of her and that such self-absorption isn't 'good enough' for her. Her death is evidently something of a spiritual awakening for him. Meanwhile, the sensitivity and altruism of both Edward's and Lavinia's reactions to it show how far they themselves have advanced. In fact, throughout the third act they demonstrate maturity, perception, and consideration and affection for each other. Lavinia is going to have a baby, a prospect not very apparent in the text, but emphasized elsewhere by Eliot; Edward looks forward to taking her away on holiday to the kind of remote hideaway they could never have tolerated before. The existence of love has been demonstrated, in marriage as in martyrdom. Both ways have been justified, and the play can end with a celebratory party.

Not all critics admire it without reservation. Many have pointed to the verse which, though never less than spare and lucid, has little of the metaphoric life to be found in *The Family Reunion*. It is worth noting that at the one point at which it irrefutably 'intensifies' into poetry, the poetry is actually a quotation from Shelley's *Prometheus Unbound* and not by Eliot at all. Indeed, Eliot himself admitted that his reliance on criteria of strict dramatic utility left it 'perhaps an open question whether there is any poetry in the play at all'. And while the original text was being revised (and, it seems, reduced) for the stage, he complained that 'every step in simplification brings me nearer to Frederick Lonsdale'.

This is precisely the destination some accuse him of having reached. Raymond Williams, for instance, believes that the play's over-conventional style and West End tone reduce a savage death into 'a story at a cocktail party': a potentially rewarding play becomes 'a theatrical compromise'. Eliot, he thinks, should have followed his 'bright angel' to the 'agony in the desert'. But even if he had possessed the kind of dramatic talent that would have allowed this, which is uncertain, such a decision would surely have tilted the play's sympathies too far towards the 'negative' or ascetic way of expressing love. It would have exaggerated Eliot's tendency to belittle the 'affirmative' way, of human relationships. As it is, his choice of London settings allows him to emphasize that God is at work, not only in distant climes and times, but in places we can all recognize now; and he surely does so much more forcefully and plausibly than in *The Confidential Clerk*, by comparison a painless, frivolous piece. The girl to whom we once chatted over a cocktail may (suggests Eliot) actually have become a Christian martyr. The silly old woman who is boring us, the traveller who is regaling us with unlikely ancedotes, may be fulfilling spiritual purposes of which we know nothing.

This brings us to the vexed questions of the 'guardians': Julia, Alex, and the man to whom they direct those in spiritual need, Reilly. Why, and who are they? Ordinary people, doing good by stealth? Guardian angels in human dress? Men and women symbolizing the love and care of the Church? Simply an unconventional means of manipulating a tricky plot? The evidence is mixed. They are not by any means omnipotent: Alex seems to have achieved little or nothing in Kinkanja; Reilly admits to having had his failures, and also to failing to understand what he him-self actually means when he dismisses his patients in words akin to those of the dying Buddha, 'Work out your salvation with diligence.' Nor does he impose solutions on those patients: he shows them the logic of the case, and asks them to choose for themselves. On the other hand, he clearly has a more than usually efficient system for gathering infor-mation, more than usual wisdom, and much more than usual authority.

Again, the guardians' second-act ritual takes the form of an ancient Greek libation, includes pagan imagery ('may the Moon herself influence the bed'), and makes no explicit mention of anything or anyone Christian. Yet, of course, Celia dies working for a Christian organization, in a Christ-ian village, and in the manner of Christ himself. Perhaps we are not meant to know. Perhaps the real message simply is that there is much more in heaven and earth than is dreamt of in the world of the West End play.

J. B. Priestley
(born 1894)

John Boynton Priestley was born in 1894 in Bradford, the shabby industrial city that was to be translated into 'Bur-manley', microcosm of run-down Britain, in *The Linden Tree*. His father was a teacher, but the boy Priestley left school young and worked in a wool merchant's office, where he began to write the articles that took him, after prolonged front-line service in the Great War, to London as a freelance journalist. He prospered, publishing reviews, essays, short stories and novels, the most successful of which, *The Good Companions*, he co-adapted for the stage. His first original play was *Dangerous Corner* (1932), ill-received by most critics but acclaimed by James Agate as 'a brilliant device' and liked by the public.

It is the earliest of Priestley's so-called 'time' plays, the others being *Time and the Conways* and *I Have Been Here Before*, both dating from 1937. These two were designed to illustrate the chronological theses of, respectively, Dunne and Ouspensky, but need no such abstract justification. *The Conways*, showing a family in 1919, 1937, and then again in 1919, is actually about the fragility and pathos of hope, about disappointment and decay. *I Have Been Here Before* uses a marriage in crisis to dramatize the power of the will over a seemingly predetermined fate, an idea implicit in many of Priestley's later plays. *Dangerous Corner*, rather similarly, suggests that there are moments in our lives when we either embrace or avoid disaster, an unexceptionable point illustrated by two alternative realities, in one of which a chance remark leads to revelations and suicide, and in the other illusion and a kind of brittle content is preserved.

These plays are not as unconventional as they seemed at the time, but they did proclaim the arrival of a playwright less afraid of ideas and of technical experiment than any of his English contemporaries. Then and since, his work has shown rare scope and variety. There have been moral thrillers, notably *Dangerous Corner* and *An Inspector Calls*. There have been such agreeable comedies as *Laburnum Grove* (1933), about an archetypally 'dull' suburbanite who is actually a master-forger, and *When We Are Married* (1938), in which some sanctimonious Yorkshire bigwigs suddenly find their marriages invalid and themselves 'living in sin'. There have been the quasi-Chekhovian *Eden End* (1934), in which a failed actress tries to replant her roots in the Yorkshire countryside; the allegorical 'farcical tragedy', *Bees on the Boat Deck* (1936), which reduces England to a stranded ship threatened with destruction; the stream-of-consciousness *Music at Night* (1938), in which a group of people reveal their fears, hopes, pains and loves while listening to a concert; the expressionistic *Johnson Over Jordan* (1939), in which the protagonist is confronted after death with the many failures and few achievements of his life; the barely dramatized debate *Dragon's Mouth* (1952); even a collaboration with Iris Murdoch on the stage version of her satire on sexual manners, *A Severed Head* (1963).

It has been a stylistically diverse career, but also a philosophically consistent one. A key concept is 'responsibility', something Priestley conscientiously displays himself and constantly recommends to his audiences. Man should not live for himself alone. Society can be improved, indeed made infinitely fulfilling to the individuals within it. Human nature is not unalterable, nor perfection an impossibility. A kind of universal togetherness, rich, mysterious and smacking of the divine, is the ideal and goal. There are glimpses of this near the end of *Johnson Over Jordan*, where Priestley's small-time Everyman is surrounded by those he loved and helped, and in *Music At Night*, when the characters feel themselves serenely subsumed into a collective consciousness, intoning such lines as 'There cannot be you and I, or any separate selves, and we are walled in no longer, but are free' and 'The guilt of one is the guilt of all, and one cannot suffer without all suffering.' We are members of one another, responsible in our smallest acts for humanity as a whole.

This is a visionary socialism, at its most attractive, if also naïve, in *They Came to a City* (1943). The characters are confronted with a utopia in which all is cooperation, sharing and communal fulfilment. Some love it and remain; others, embittered or ossified by their previous lives, choose to return to earth and Earth; the two main characters make the same trip home planning to work for the transformation of our civilization into the 'city'. Priestley, writing without knowledge of Auschwitz and Belsen, or even of the random violence of our own society, certainly tends to underrate the intensity, the subtlety, some would say the invincibility, of human evil. Indeed, one does not find adequate recognition of horror, terror or anguish in any of his plays, and sombre and resonant emotion only in *I Have Been Here Before*. He has never, for instance, come to terms dramatically with his own traumatic experiences in a war that 'sliced my generation into sausage-meat held above a swill bucket'. On the other hand, he consistently acknowledges the existence of cynicism, callousness, bigotry, hypocrisy and greed, and not always in the predictable guises. If a pet target is the businessman, neurotically obsessed with making money in order to make more money, another is the kind of socialist who thinks of people as units or numbers. His favourite characters are usually young, vibrant and female: Carol in *The Conways*, who dies, or Dinah in *The Linden Tree* (1947), who represents the future, 'a new race'. She finds positive excitement in the prospect of living with her professor-father in Burmanley and working to transform that dispiriting place into a new Jerusalem.

The period in which the plays are set is often significant. The optimism of the Conways in 1919 reflects a post-war feeling; their disillusion in 1937 smacks similarly of the period. The Edwardian era particularly fascinates Priestley. Many characters hark back to it with a nostalgia that he partly shares and partly regards as an escape from their essential responsibility, which is to the present and future. In the pointedly titled *Eden End*, set in 1912, there is much ironic illustration of the period's false security, its feeling that its own political confusions could get no worse. There'll be no war, says a main character, 'the world's got a lot more sense than it's given credit for in the newspapers. And it's got science now to help it.' This is also clearly intended as a warning to complacent audiences in the Decade of the Dictators, for Priestley's plays, whenever their action occurs, are nothing if not responsive to the temper of the times of their performance. *They Came to a City* reflected the feeling, prevalent as the Second World War turned the allies' way, that a shining new Britain could be built; in *The Linden Tree* the mood was still enthusiastic, but dourer, more realistic, as befitted the age of Crippsian austerity.

Priestley's sense of responsibility, paradoxically enough, may explain some of his artistic inadequacies. His characters usually represent social attitudes, political stances, verbal examples of which tend to be repetitively and over-deliberately fed into plots which themselves are rather obviously schematic. A few have size and power: Ormund, for instance, the melancholy businessman in *I Have Been Here Before*. A few, such as Ormanroyd, the drunken photographer in *When We Are Married*, have a Dickensian energy. But they do not display the idiosyncrasies, the oddities, the consistent inconsistencies of life itself. They are the creations of a dramatist of ideas, though that is a label Priestley dislikes; a dramatist for whom a man's social attitudes, function and purpose are more important than his private essence; a dramatist who prefers the explicit to the implicit, who tends to state or debate rather than to enact. It is entirely logical that the plays in which they appear should often have become expressionistic or even abstract.

Possibly this makes Priestley sound a cold and forbidding dramatist. Not so. His unwilling nostalgia, his affection for the family, his love of the English hearth and countryside all prove otherwise. His common sense, his Yorkshire shrewdness coexists with a warm heart; his prosaic style of dialogue ('that familiar flat thin idiom', as he ruefully called it) with a romantic temperament. His socialism is a matter of caring, even loving. His achievement is to have kept the theatre alive and thinking at times when it was threatening to expire of frivolity, smugness and commercialism. That it is nowadays easier to discuss the large questions in dramatic form – Is man bad or good? What, if any, is the future of the race? – is largely due to his perseverance, his insistence in the teeth of fashion that they were important and had to be asked.

An Inspector Calls

Everything in the dining room of the Birlings' house in Brumley is complacency and superficiality. Even the furniture is ostentatious, creating an effect that is 'substantial and comfortable' but not 'home-like'. The family is celebrating the engagement of the daughter, Sheila, to Gerald

Croft, whose father, like her own, is a wealthy manufac-
turer. It is a relationship Birling himself sees largely as a
business transaction, which may eventually allow the two
firms to work together 'for lower costs and higher prices':
that's to say, against the interests of worker, consumer and
community. Indeed, he generalizes his optimism, declaring
that employers are coming together to protect the interests
of capital and that the nation will enjoy a period of 'steadily
increasing prosperity'. This, in 1912, two years before the
outbreak of the war to end wars.

The irony is obvious and strongly underlined by Priestley. 'There will be no war,' promises Birling. 'Scientific
progress makes it impossible. Why, look at the new liner,
the *Titanic* – unsinkable, absolutely unsinkable!' In twenty
or thirty years' time, 'say in 1940', industrial conflict will
be forgotten, as will 'all these silly little war-scares'. This
is, of course, Priestley's sardonic nod at the audiences of
1946, when the play was first performed.

The effect is of blind hubris, as well as egoism and greed.
Birling expects a knighthood soon, but only because he
received Royalty when he was Lord Mayor and is a 'sound
party man'. He attacks the 'cranks' who speak of 'community and all that nonsense'. His advice to the young is
that 'a man has to mind his own business and look after
himself and his own'. By the time the doorbell rings, some
ten minutes into the play, Birling has shown himself to be
badly in need of enlightenment and correction. So have his
compliant family and guest, if to a lesser extent.

They are not disappointed. The visitor announces himself as a police inspector and reveals that a young woman
has died 'in great agony', having swallowed disinfectant.
And then, and for most of the rest of the play, we get the
revelations, each artfully following the other. Birling sacked
the girl for helping to organize a strike for higher wages.
Sheila calls this 'a rotten shame', only to discover that the
girl was fired from her next job, assistant in a fashionable
store, for no reason except Sheila's pique. Then Croft found
her, desperate, in a shady bar, set her up as his mistress,

and left her. The Birlings' son, Eric, drunkenly picked her up in the same place, and impregnated her. Finally, she was grandly rejected as undeserving by Mrs Birling's charitable committee, which she approached for help. The verdict that emerges, in whodunnit style, is that all five of these self-satisfied celebrants are guilty. They form a chain which, it seems, led logically to a death.

Priestley makes it apparent – notably by invoking one of Birling's more sottish, ruttish colleagues, Alderman Meggarty – that the family is not uniquely destructive. Theirs is the offence of the powerful and privileged against the under-privileged and powerless, and it is one that is actually sanctioned by the law. There is, of course, no question of any of the cast appearing in the dock for the wrongs they did Eva Smith, Daisy Renton, or whatever identity their victim was obliged by her declining circumstances to adopt. Yet Priestley's inspector behaves as if their moral and social faults were the crimes they perhaps should be. He treats the Birlings' pretensions and veiled threats with professional contempt. Again and again he rubs in the horror of the girl's death and the family's culpability. He tells Birling, magistrate and friend of the Chief Constable, not to 'stammer and yammer', and the rest that he is 'losing all patience' with them. In fact, he underlines his stated belief that there isn't much difference between 'respectable citizens' and 'criminals' by treating them all like suspect felons. As the repentant Sheila says, he isn't like an ordinary policeman at all. He is, however, what inspectors 'ought to be' – 'a real one at last'.

His name is Goole, which those who wish may read as 'ghoul' or even an embryonic 'god', but it is his purpose that really matters. Perhaps he is true justice; perhaps, as Gareth Lloyd-Evans argues in his *J. B. Priestley: The Dramatist*, the embodiment of a collective conscience; perhaps simply the outraged socialist, Priestley himself. Certainly, the playwright uses this 'massive, solid' figure to express his essential beliefs about responsibility and community.

It would do us all a bit of good if sometimes we tried to put ourselves in the place of these young women counting their pennies in their dingy back bedrooms . . . This world being what it is, a battlefield rather than a home, this desire of women to love is a weakness: in another kind of world it might be a source of strength . . . We don't live alone. We are members of one body. We are responsible for each other. And I tell you that the time will soon come when, if men will not learn that lesson, then they will be taught it in fire and blood and anguish.

On that note Goole exits; but Priestley's moral thriller is not yet over. The stunned Birlings contemplate the fragments, not only of their moral self-respect, but of their family solidity. Sheila's engagement to Gerald is off, at least temporarily. Eric has been revealed as a drunkard and thief, who stole from the family firm to help the girl. In turn, he has accused both parents of inadequacy. But then they all begin to ask some questions. Phone calls establish that there is no Goole in the local force, no dead girl in the local hospital. It was a hoax, worked by flashing photographs of different girls at different members of the family. The household begins to return to normal, that is, to blindness and self-satisfaction. True, Sheila and Eric join forces to draw the correct conclusion, which is that, if they have not literally caused a suicide, they have all acted in ways that might easily have done so. The younger generation, it seems, has learned something. But Birling, whose main anxiety has been that a scandal might cost him his knighthood, is amused by what he now regards as a politically motivated prank. So is his wife, the most unapologetic and intractable of the Birlings, in spite of what could have been the death of her first grandchild.

Perhaps Priestley should have ended here. The older Birlings' immutable imperviousness to anyone but themselves is, after all, the real horror of the play. Instead, there is another twist. The phone rings. A girl has died after swallowing disinfectant, and a police inspector is on his way. The curtain falls as the characters 'stare guiltily and dumbfounded'. Priestley has enigmatically suggested that the identity of this second inspector is important, but nothing here helps us discover it. Could Goole be an import from the 'time' plays, a warning messenger who offers the Birlings an opportunity to repent, one they have now lost by their blinkered callousness? Is his successor the bearer of 'blood and fire and anguish' or, as seems more probable on a literal level, an ordinary policeman likely to cover up the indiscretions of leading citizens? Given uncertainties as sweeping as this, one must ask if the twist is necessary, helpful, or (indeed) anything but an excuse for a sensational close.

But the play as a whole remains an impressive achievement, notwithstanding the obvious objections, namely implausibility and heavy-handedness. It is true that, even if the Birlings' victims were all different girls, it is highly unlikely they would link together so neatly. It is also true that Priestley seems unafraid of emphasis, re-emphasis, overstatement. There is a relentlessness about some of his ironies, for instance Mrs Birling's prolonged condemnation of the 'idler' who wronged the girl and is, of course, her own son. The girl herself emerges, not as a fallible individual, but a capsule version of those qualities Priestley particularly admires in young women: energy, vivaciousness, pluck, affection, and the sheer goodness that can refuse Eric's money, on the grounds that it is stolen, and refrain from exposing him, even though destitution and death is the alternative. But any such criticism rests on the assumption that this is a naturalistic play, which in essence it isn't.

Rather, it is a lesson in civics invested with tension and cleverly manipulated into the form, not merely of a well-made play, but a play so well made that each of its theatrical surprises extends and deepens the lesson. Alternatively, or additionally, it may be seen as an updated morality play, with Birling perhaps representing avarice, Mrs Birling pride, Sheila envy and anger, Croft lust, and

Eric lust, gluttony and sloth. It is emblematic and didactic and unashamed of being either. In other words, its 'weak-nesses' are deliberate and may even be its strengths; and the answer to those who resist such a notion is simply, try and see it in the theatre, because it proves that, in Pries-tley's hands, a sense of responsibility can generate gripping drama.

Christopher Fry
(born 1907)

Fashion, having raised Christopher Fry in the 1940s, dashed him down in the 1950s, partly because his panth-eistic leanings and optimistic tenor seemed escapist in a climate of rigorous social responsibility, partly because of a reaction against a poetic style that had been unwisely compared to the Elizabethans. To Denis Donoghue, writing in 1959, his philosophy is naïve, his verse often 'the wanton prancing of words', his plays marked by 'mere whimsy' and 'spurious joviality', and he himself guilty of a 'verbal flip-pancy' that points to 'a really fundamental triviality'. But how adequate a summary is this twenty-odd years later?

It would be presumptuous to patronize Fry's religious faith. He was born Christopher Harris in 1907, son of an architect turned Church of England lay preacher, but eventually assumed the name of his mother's Quaker fam-ily; and he served in a non-combatant unit in the Second World War. One of his most striking plays, *A Sleep of Prisoners* (1951), was written for performance in a church, and uses biblical tales, dreamed by modern POWs, to ask why and how men justify violence and evil, to advocate a crusading pacifism, and to proclaim the possibility of spiri-tual renewal: 'The human heart can go to the lengths of God.'

God is a living if bewildering presence in his work. He leads St Cuthman to Sussex in *The Boy With a Cart* (1938), written after Fry had worked as a teacher, a sometime producer and performer, and the founding director of a Kent repertory company. He converts the Jute warrior, Cymen, to Christianity in *Thor, With Angels* (1948). He uses Moses to liberate the captive Israelites in the impressive *Firstborn* (1948). Miracles occur in all these plays. All evoke, in Fry's words, 'a world in which we are poised on the edge of eternity, a world which has deeps and shadows of mystery, in which God is anything but a sleeping partner'. A world, we may add, of contradiction and paradox: of a God capable of horrifying Moses by destroying, not the selected evil, but the humane and far-sighted son of the recalcitrant Pharoah.

The paradoxes and conflicts are handled more playfully in his comedies, but not, Fry would claim, less seriously. To him, comedy is an escape from 'despair' into 'faith'. It is an intuition of a 'universal cause of delight', offering 'an angle of experience where the dark is distilled into light'. It stands for spirit over materialism, joy over desolation, good over evil, life over death: its characters 'unmortify themselves' and 'persevere in joy', and, since it invariably begins as a potential tragedy, it ends by communicating not a 'vulnerable optimism' but a 'hardwon maturity of delight'. This is the theory. The achievement of his four 'seasonal' comedies is more modest.

A Phoenix Too Frequent (1946), representing spring, is a charming anecdote describing how the forces of negation, a near-nihilistic soldier and a young woman proposing to entomb herself with her dead husband, are defeated by the love that inevitably blooms between them. The autumnal *Venus Observed* (1950) is more elaborate, the tale of an elderly duke brought to accept the loss of youth and romance, to recognize the selfishness of his habitual detachment, and to marry the mistress who has burned down his astronomical observatory in protest against his preoccupation with abstract spaces rather than subluminary reality.

The 'winter' *Dark is Light Enough* (1954) shows how the even-handed altruism, the near-divine serenity of a countess caught between armies in 1848 converts the cowardly wastrel she has protected into someone as responsible and self-denying as herself. All three plays involve search and discovery, reconciliation and commitment: the key characters end wiser, completer, than they began. New levels of being must be embraced; life lived more abundantly.

That isn't to say these comedies are equally successful. The last is disconcertingly static, partly because of the countess's undeviating perfection, partly because the characters spend even more time opining and less doing than in Fry's other plays, none of which are remarkable for their momentum. His poetic effects are, however, generally less elaborate in his later than in his earlier work, where they sometimes hold up the action without offering compensating advantages. This brings us to the nub of the critical argument over Fry: how effective a poet is he?

His view is that we have 'domesticated the enormous miracle', and failed to notice that the reality around us is 'wildly, perilously, incomprehensibly fantastic'. Poetry is the best way of discovering and expressing the unrecognized wonder of it all, 'the language in which man explores his own amazement'. It expresses hidden truths that deepen under our eyes without ever becoming fixed or absolute, according to a logic 'felt along the heart'; and it must be as 'fully charged and as pliant' as the poet can make it, reflecting life experienced 'at full pressure'. Once again, however, the achievement seems smaller than the aspiration.

Many of Fry's verbal effects are merely frolicsome. He delights in puns, archaic insults, wordplay, not always in appropriate contexts: 'all sin and bone' and 'amor vincit insomnia' in the sombre *Sleep of Prisoners*, for instance. Someone can take another 'by the scruff of the heart', or accuse someone else of being a 'spigoted, bigoted, operculated prig'. Speeches skip airily from metaphor to metaphor, then wryly send themselves up with a banal colloquialism. One sentence in *Venus Observed* continues for forty-four lines, invoking rivers, lime flowers, bells, death-watch beetles, dragons and much else in a cheerfully narcissistic discussion of language; and all for fun and show.

This element of show has exasperated many critics; and certainly Fry often seems to exploit metaphor for its own sake. The poetic effects appear unrelated to the character of the speaker, the nature of his feeling, the intensity of the action, or any other dramatic quality. They tend to be decorative rather than essential, external rather than organic; and rarely embody the 'full pressure' of living. However, they are sometimes good in themselves: a hawk, for instance, is 'a bright dash on the cheek of the wind'. Their wit, even their flippancy, is functional in so far as it reflects Fry's absorption with the world's incongruities and his parallel view of himself as both metaphysician and clown. And they do sometimes succeed in communicating his 'amazement', especially his somewhat animistic view of nature. At his worst he can be affected, precious, and guilty of what Stephen Spender called a 'ruthless facetiousness', reducing robbery or murder to a gay verbal conceit. Yet he's also capable of an infectious exuberance that does, perhaps, successfully affirm his belief in the essential goodness of things.

Since the mid-fifties Fry has translated others, written original screenplays, notably for *Ben Hur*, but only twice been performed on the stage himself. *Curtmantle* (1961) is a sympathetic, somewhat prolix portrait of Henry II in conflict first with Becket, then with his unruly sons, and offers a characteristic moral in Queen Eleanor's 'Consider complexity, delight in difference . . . do you think you can draw lines on the living water?' Fry's ideal is always a world that embraces spirit, mind and matter, God and man, in creatively diverse conjunction. *A Yard of Sun* (1970) belatedly completes the 'seasonal' quartet with a summer story of revival and reconciliation in post-war Siena. The play's principal jobber and wheeler-dealer is sent packing, and integrity and love triumph in a conclusion unusually sunny, perhaps sentimental by contemporary standards. It is, however, yet more proof of its author's peculiar capacity for faith, hope and charity, his undiminished delight in creation.

The Lady's Not for Burning

We are in the house of Hebble Tyson, mayor of Cool Clary, in '1400 either more or less or exactly': a stage-direction that instantly prepares us for the light, bantering tone of Fry's 'spring' comedy. More explicit reminders of the season soon intrude. Love is 'an April anarchy'; the people are 'in the same April fit of exasperating nonsense'. A character inveighs against the false hope with which he feels spring tantalizes a meaningless world, and is mockingly answered by a 'canting cuckoo'.

He is Thomas Mendip, back from bloody wars abroad and disillusioned with every aspect of life. Indeed, he spends the play repetitively proclaiming his scepticism and disgust, his feeling that it is time for God to end 'the deadly human anecdote' with a 'cosmic yawn of boredom'. Logically enough, he wants to be hanged, a request regarded as eccentric by Tyson, who anyway is confronted with a more pressing matter, the arrival of a young woman accused by the populace of witchcraft. 'I am Jennet Jourdemayne,' she ringingly announces, 'and I believe in the human mind.' She is the enemy of superstition, a dabbler in science, the friend of fact and reason. Those who know their Fry will already appreciate the contrasts and their implications. He, who craves death, seems doomed to live: she, who wants life, seems fated to die. He must be saved from his despair; she, not only from the pyre, but from an exorbitant rationalism.

And so, of course, they both are. Fry may first conceive his comedies as tragedies; but we never believe that anything ugly or deadly can occur here. The play's title jauntily proclaims just that, and so does its style, which positively frolics with metaphoric wit. Somehow the deaths Thomas has caused in Flanders seem milder for being called the 'indefinite leave that needs no pass'. His very despair is contradicted by the verve with which he customarily expresses it. The plot requires that Thomas and Jennet be both tortured; that a mob rampages outside, howling for Jennet's death; that Tyson and the local justice, Tappercoom, prepare to have her killed, their minds partly on the property she will forfeit; that her death will be peculiarly horrible. In other words, Fry introduces evil into his comic universe, only to underrate it (the thumbscrew has been applied as 'the merest . . . the purest cajolery') or keep it safely offstage (a brick hits a minor character, nothing much more) or camouflage it in metaphor (the head-wound caused is 'a splash from the cherry-red river that drives my mill'). By the time Thomas talks of 'the howl of human jackals' in Cool Clary, we feel he's only indulging in another rhetorical image. Evil cannot triumph in the play, not merely because it's never been satisfactorily evoked, but because it has been patronized as quaint or droll.

The play's principal conflict is purportedly between death, or the death-wish, and the life-force. What it actually offers are contrasts between the dull, mundane, and the emotionally more exceptional. Tyson is no monster, but a man fussily 'afflicted with office' whose response to every difficulty is the bureaucrat's 'Have you filled in the necessary forms?' or 'It will have to be gone into at the proper time'; and the horizons of his sister, Margaret, are relentlessly domestic. But Jennet, in particular, disturbs their rut. Margaret mildly remarks that her heretic's charm 'makes orthodoxy seem irrelevant'. Tyson, with his belief that 'the standard soul must be mercilessly maintained', finds her attractive, bewildering and deeply troubling, 'too unusual not to be corrupt'. And Margaret's son, Humphrey, whose engagement to Tyson's ward Alizon explains the festivities of Act III, proves himself (in Fry's words) 'respectable on the surface and lustful below' by offering to use his influence on the town council to free Jennet in return for sex. Donoghue, though a hostile critic, has correctly defined Fry's fundamental conflict as life-as-norm versus life-as-miracle; and these people represent the 'norm' in all its pettiness and hypocrisy.

It should not seem odd to call what happens within and between Jennet and Thomas a miracle, because Fry's view always is that reality is charged with a wonder we too often fail to perceive. The point is explicitly made in the play by a kindly, bumbling chaplain who declares that 'everything astonishes me . . . when I think of myself, I can scarcely believe my senses'. That is also the reaction invited by the main characters' conversions. Jennet's determination to cling to 'the actual, the essential fact' (doubly strong for having seen her father succumb too deeply – though, a characteristically ironic touch, successfully – to the fascination of alchemy) is undermined both by Thomas's charisma and by his arguments. He may not believe in man, but he appears to believe in God, and certainly wants to convince her that the universe is infinitely complex and contradictory: 'We have wasted paradox and mystery on you, when all you ask us for is cause and effect.' Before long she is coming 'suddenly upon my heart', feeling 'my life increasing', and even talking of dying a Christian. By the end she has recognized the strength of her feelings, and wants to 'fill the curled shell of the world with human deep-sea sound, and hold it to the ear of God'. She has renounced two dimensions for three.

And so, very unwillingly, has Thomas. His emotional destination is evident from the extravagantly theatrical curtain-line to Act I, 'For God's sake hang me, before I love that woman.' While he teaches and deepens Jennet, she teaches and deepens him: 'You are making yourself a breeding-ground for love and must take the consequences.' By Act III he is unwillingly admitting to feeling that 'something condones the world, incorrigibly', a sentiment Fry himself sees as the conclusion of his comedies; and soon afterwards he admits 'the disastrous truth – I love you'. The rag-and-bone merchant whom he claims to have murdered, and Jennet is accused of bewitching, conveniently materializes; Tappercoom advises the lovers to escape; and off they slip, Thomas feebly protesting that the world is no less bad for his personal regeneration. They will now look for 'love, though neither of us knows where on earth it is'. The lost, as often in Fry, have discovered part of themselves, and may find more.

The play begins with the word 'soul', and ends with the prayer, 'God have mercy on our souls'. Body has been infused with soul, matter with spirit, defeatism with hope, winter with spring, the ordinary with the miraculous: all has been made whole by the power of a love that Alizon, who elopes with the mayor's secretary in a parallel sub-plot, sees as evidence of the perplexing 'kindness of God'. The exuberance of this vision explains the exuberance of the language, even if it doesn't justify its more whimsical excesses. The mood of the 1980s isn't friendly to puns like 'longitude with no platitude', or the sort of conceit that transforms a shooting star into 'phlegm' on its way to 'a heavenly spittoon', or the description of tears as 'two little wandering Jews' and tear-stained faces as 'dripping like newly weighted anchors'. Much of the verbal decoration seems exasperatingly self-regarding.

Yet much is more functional, and, to the austere post-war Britain of 1948, seemed refreshingly colourful and up-beat: fun, and fun capable of touching both the feelings and the mind, if not of greatly extending either. Fry recommends audiences to think of *The Lady* 'in terms of light, of inconstant April sunshine, of sunset, twilight and full moon; of human intelligences in a dance together'. Today it may be most interesting as a poetic experiment and a period romance; but it contains moments when that light does glitter, that dance allure.

John Whiting

(1917–63)

In 1961 the critic Kenneth Tynan proclaimed the demise of tragedy, arguing that its place was a world where man had little control over his environment, not one where politics, psychology and psychiatry could offer at least a tentative solution to nearly every variety of suffering. This sentiment drew a passionate rejoinder from John Whiting, who called himself 'one of that disappearing species, a private individual' and disliked much of the socialist drama Tynan admired. 'The tragedy of men is that they are men,' he wrote, 'and when there is food and drink, houses and clothing, health, security and sanity for all, we will still be scared to death of death. The germ of tragedy will still be there.'

Whiting did not write anything easily dignified as a 'tragedy'; but much of his slim *oeuvre* reflects the melancholy and somewhat fatalistic tenor of these words. It is sceptical about man's nature, which is normally far from altruistic or constructive. It is also greatly preoccupied with death, tending to regard life itself primarily as preparation for a conclusion that carries with it little hope of any hereafter. And as such it has a prophetic aptness, because cancer killed Whiting himself in 1963, when he was only forty-five and his considerable promise remained largely unfulfilled.

He was the son of a soldier-turned-lawyer, trained at RADA, and acted in repertory before enlisting, and eventually being commissioned, in the war-time artillery. In 1944, after illness forced his discharge, he returned to the provincial theatre, and began to write: an unremarkable triangle-comedy called *No More A-Roving*, and then, in 1948, *Conditions of Agreement*, in which two overgrown children, one a cripple, the other a retired clown, destroy the sentimental memories and peace of mind of a harmless, rather stupid neighbour. When this sardonic comedy was presented in 1965, critics commented on its affinity with Pinter's *Birthday Party*; but it remained unperformed in Whiting's lifetime. Instead, he made it the basis of a television play, *A Walk in the Desert* (1960), in which the persecutor is a still more malicious cripple, his victim a young unmarried mother. Whiting's moral universe is, on the whole, a cruel one, rarely friendly to innocence or illusion.

Yet the play that followed *Saint's Day*, which shows this world at its worst, was the mellow, amusing *Penny for a Song* (1951), about the preparations of the south-coast gentry for Napoleon's expected invasion. It is a good-natured, even cosy celebration of English eccentricity and the national reliance on 'muddling through', affectionately indebted to the Home Guard of 1940; but it is not without darker touches. An ex-soldier, blinded in battle, passes through *en route* to London, where he hopes to convert the King to pacifism: a reminder of what war really means and also an example, scarcely less naïve than the rural patriots he meets, of that habit of self-deception which continued to fascinate Whiting. But this is a comedy, and its innocents are disenchanted either painlessly or offstage, after the action is over.

Love plays a part in the scheme, as in most of Whiting's plays, and is more positively and perhaps sentimentally presented than in any other; but it has no more lasting power. The soldier leaves the daughter-of-the-house for good, warning her he'll 'discard himself', 'fall apart', once his political ends are achieved. Rather similar, though for more elaborate reasons, the protagonist of *Marching Song* (1954) feels obliged to reject the emotional opportunities offered him. He is General Rupert Forster, imprisoned by his nation's conquerors and, though now free, in disgrace with his countrymen. He committed an atrocity, the slaughter of children, in order to accelerate a vital advance, only to find himself emotionally and physically immobilized, his inadequacies as a man clear to him, his military pretensions meaningless. His love for his mistress has not survived incarceration, and the pull exerted by a younger, more vital woman fails to prevent him making the logical choice: he commits suicide.

The action, as often in Whiting, consists of the re-examination of the past, the removal of such illusions as remain from it, and the re-evaluation of the present. In short, it is a somewhat inactive action, and tends to justify the accusation sometimes thrown at the dramatist, that his work is cold, static, 'literary'. He himself thought the play suffered from 'intellectual elephantiasis'. On the other hand, it is intellectually stimulating, provocative. It suggests that a Nazi general and war criminal – Whiting, though he doesn't name it, had Germany in mind – may deserve sympathy, respect, even admiration. It certainly reflects Whiting's detestation both of 'simplicity' and of 'knitted woollen morality'.

His next play, *The Gates of Summer* (1956) never reached London, perhaps because, like *Marching Song*, it combines moral complexity with a lack of dramatic momentum. It is set in Edwardian times, and concerns a disgraced politician, John Hogarth, who is looking for personal fulfilment and, perhaps, a Byronic death in what he believes to be an anti-imperialist uprising in Greece. But Whiting called this supposed comedy 'the harshest play I have ever written', and the 'revolution' is actually an attempt by decayed aristocrats to recover their power. Indeed, the play deflates all aspirations, all pretensions, reducing love itself to something of a travesty. As in the previous two, a girl attempts to deflect the protagonist from the path dictated by his principles, but this time she is a capricious, dangerous, even murderous creature. Whiting's attitude to women, as to love, grew more cynical with time.

This is certainly apparent in his last and commercially most successful play, *The Devils* (1961). The only words that the tortured and mutilated priest, Grandier, addresses to the hunchback abbess, Jeanne, whose sexual hysteria has doomed him to the pyre, are: 'Look at this thing which I am, and learn the meaning of love.' The piece itself contains some remarkably vivid writing, and is unusually eventful for Whiting, but is generally agreed to lack the complexity and depth of his best work. To some extent this is inevitable, since the play concerns an entire seventeenth-century community; yet one still feels something cursory in Whiting's analysis of Jeanne's agonies and even of Grandier's struggles, as he seeks to find significance, first in sensual love, then in renunciation, self-disgust and humiliation.

All the same, Grandier is a characteristic Whiting protagonist. He may not be an actual exile, like Southman and Hogarth, but he is a natural loner in a world that seems, not only ugly and violent, but too trivial and shallow to satisfy his profounder needs. He is, if you like, evidence of Whiting's elitism, his mistrust of people in the mass, his fascination with the man of more than usual honesty, insight and spiritual ambition. Whether or not he may be summed up, in Eric Salmon's nice description of the archetypal Whiting hero, as a 'self-immolating romantic in search of an absolute', his spiritual search certainly propels him towards death. Not only do others need to destroy him, as they do the main characters in *Saint's Day* and *Marching Song*. He himself seems bent on self-destruction, like Forster and, to a lesser extent, Hogarth. 'I am,' he says, 'a dead man, compelled to live.' Death is his 'meaning and purpose'. Like Stella in *Saint's Day*, he would seem to regard the purpose of experience as 'to give foundation to the state of death'.

This is to simplify, for Whiting's mind was an odd and intricate one, and would no doubt have produced many more odd and intricate plays, perhaps even the 'masterpiece' on which he said he was working as he neared the death that, ironically, coincided with his recognition as a seminal contemporary dramatist. As it was, he left us, not with anything easily encapsulated as an overriding 'view of life', but with a series of questions of more than usual scope. What justifies a man, what gives him nobility? To what extent can he rise above his animal nature, to what extent resist compromise? Is death preferable to moral and spiritual failure? Does it have value in itself, and, if so, what? Just what kind of moral universe are we doomed to inhabit?

Saint's Day

The critical reception of *Saint's Day* in 1951 is a theatrical scandal. The play was attacked, sometimes violently, from all sides for its oddness and obscurity; and it took letters to *The Times* from Tyrone Guthrie and Peter Brook (who praised its 'passion and unbroken tension'), and then from John Gielgud and Peggy Ashcroft (who found it 'moving, beautiful and fascinating'), to restore some semblance of balance.

Thirty years later, it's possible to spot pre-echoes of Pinter, Arden and others in the play, and tempting to conclude that its ill-fortune was to appear too soon to be properly appreciated. After all, we have come to expect to make more mental and emotional effort when we visit the theatre. We are prepared to tolerate long, difficult speeches. We are no longer discountenanced by a sardonic, serio-comic tone, nor surprised by violence or the threat of it. We are used to greater variety in subject-matter and style than those whose sensibilities were moulded by the drama of the thirties and forties.

Yet *Saint's Day* would never have slid easily into any climate of taste. It is too original, too idiosyncratic. Whiting himself did not expect it to be performed, regarding it primarily as an exercise in technical self-discovery, 'a sort of anthology of what you can do', complete with 'all sorts of literary devices and tests such as parody and memories'. At one point foreboding takes the form of a pastiche of T. S. Eliot ('Careful! We are approaching the point of deviation . . .'); the last act may be seen as a prolonged classical reference, with a postman as messenger, a watching chorus of village women, and retributive killings offstage; and one critic has actually found a hint of the medieval *Sir Gawain and the Green Knight* in a green scarf given the protagonist. More importantly, neither the characters nor the play as a whole can easily be pinned down, summed up, given moral definition or meaning. In 1961 Whiting agreed with an interviewer that *Saint's Day* was best approached 'as an imaginative statement rather than a logical argument'. It may even be wise for the audience, as he himself suggested, to 'leave the intellect in the cloakroom and bring the emotions into the theatre'.

Certainly, the play's contemporary critics sometimes seem to approach it too analytically, and miss its emotional force, its power to disorient and disturb. From the start, we feel there's something uncomfortably askew about the place and the family with which we're presented. No one knows the time. It is very cold. The room in which the action occurs is filthy in places. It is also 'an architectural freak', with touches of stylish grandeur, and dominated by a large painting, 'harsh in texture, garish in colour', which represents five people and a dog grouped round a sixth, blank figure. It was, incidentally, the accidental discovery of a similar mural in a derelict Victorian–Gothic house during the war that gave Whiting his first idea for the play.

The situation gradually becomes apparent. It is the eighty-third birthday of the poet Paul Southman, and he is about to go to London to be formally reconciled with the literary world that sanctimoniously rejected his 'blasphemous, bawdy, scraggy limericks' and sent him into exile twenty-five years ago. Stella, his granddaughter, wants him to go. Her young husband, Charles Heberden, a painter who himself became a voluntary exile after precocious success as an adolescent, thinks the celebration a 'stunt'. He wants to perpetuate an isolation which seems as total as it could be nowadays. Cars cannot approach the house. There is no train near by. The family does not take newspapers or buy new books. It knows little of the world beyond, and is profoundly hostile even to the local villagers, against whose peace of mind Paul turned his satiric anger when he first arrived and who responded by mounting a half-hearted attack on the house. The family's only contact with its community is through its one retainer, who cadges credit from shopkeepers who, he says, hate and despise him.

The first news we're given of Paul is, appropriately enough, that he is cleaning a pistol; and soon after his appearance he is wondering whether his servant is betraying him with 'the enemy', the villagers, or loyally spying on them. He is an old man with more than his quota of bitterness and malice, qualities encouraged in him by Charles, himself a contemptuous, laughing cynic. Together, they make scurrilous fun of the 'fashionable' poet and critic, Robert Procathren, who is to pick up Paul and take him to London, and successfully enrage Stella, the least reclusive member of the family. Her aim is to have old Southman restored to greatness, as a sort of birthright for the child she is carrying. This hope and her pregnancy are the only positive elements in a milieu upon whose barrenness Whiting insists, perhaps to excess. The date is 25 January, and the servant's name is seasonal, John Winter. Much is heard of two trees outside the house, once places for Stella to play, now 'ugly and old and dead'. Stella's father, mother and sister are dead, too; and Paul's dog, itself old and smelly, dies during the play. Even the village is a community without young men.

It is a bleak landscape, and the family festering inside it seems likely to become still crankier and crazier the longer it withholds itself from everyday reality. Then in comes Procathren, very much the 'clean, temperate, respectable, responsible, restrained, realistic, reasonable' young lion at whom Charles sneered, to offer his somewhat glib salutations to Southman. He is promptly manipulated into situations that bewilder and trouble him. Stella begs him to 'get us away from this place', and Southman, who has concluded the villagers poisoned his dog, asks him to help answer this atrocity 'by as direct and cruel an act'. Before he knows it, he has been mocked, browbeaten and goaded by Charles and Paul, by now playing soldiers with the malicious zest of the over-age children of *Conditions of Agreement*, into learning to use Paul's pistol – which goes off in his hand, killing the offstage Stella.

This is the 'point of deviation' forecast in the Eliot parody. Not for nothing is the play's date that of the conversion of St Paul; and one of the main effects of Stella's death is to change, perhaps redeem, Paul Southman. We have seen his paranoia at its worst. Specifically, we've seen him behave with astonishing vindictiveness to the local vicar, Giles Aldus, a bookish recluse who has come asking the family to help deal with three army deserters, who are marauding through the village, terrorizing the people. Paul's response has been to humiliate Aldus and promise to ally himself with the soldiers 'against your impudent mob'. The crusading satirist who once 'lifted the skirts of the old whore', society, thereby 'destroying the illusions of youth and the wisdom of age', has (we feel) succumbed to illusion himself and become pettishly, pointlessly destructive. But his one positive trait is a capacity for love, notably for Stella; and from her casual slaughter comes grief, madness, what looks like reconciliation with his species, and what conceivably may be a new Pauline faith. Whiting being Whiting, this 'conversion' is not straightforward. Looked at from one point of view, Southman abandons his twisted, paranoid 'reality' for a deeper unreality in which he imagines Stella to be alive and expects his birthday celebrations to go ahead. Yet just before his death, we find him welcoming frightened village women to the safety of his house and dancing, singing and playing gently with one of their children: 'I'd like pretty things and children around me again,' he announces, all rancour gone.

His murderer, if that's the word, is Robert Procathren, whose spiritual progress after the 'point of deviation' has been equal but opposite. The shock of Stella's death robs him of innocence, and his rationalist, humanist faith suddenly seems to him a bland illusion. Death is now his one reality and obsession. Life he sees as a journey 'from darkness to darkness to darkness', which he should have spent 'learning how to die': a nihilist's version of an idea which, as we've seen, underlies much of Whiting's work. It is an insight which leaves him bitter, vengeful. He teams up with the deserters; so successfully deprives Aldus of his faith that the broken old man burns his unique collection of religious books, thus firing and eventually destroying the village itself; and ends the play hanging Southman and Charles on the dead trees outside the house. For some critics his loss of faith, if not perhaps the reprisals he takes, represents the disillusion of the generation which had just won the Second World War: as Christopher Fry remarked, the play 'shudders with the fact' of the A-bomb. Perhaps. Like much of the play, Procathren's behaviour is open to conflicting interpretations. He reacts with the same aggrieved fury as society itself when Southman deprived it, too, of its pet illusions; he also exacts retribution upon men whom for much of the action it would not be fanciful to call evil.

Can we say, then, that Charles and Paul bring their deaths on themselves? What *is* the moral universe they inhabit? Certainly, the word 'responsibility' is much invoked, and it is Paul himself who says that Stella's death isn't a mere accident: 'There is always the responsibility – it must rest with someone.' The play tends to justify this claim. A sort of malign chance, expression perhaps of some baleful supernal power, plays its part in the scheme, allowing Paul's beloved dog to die, killing Stella with a stray bullet, bringing three murderous soldiers into the village, all on the same day. Yet it is human perversity that fashions these elements into a still more destructive pattern: Paul's malevolent paranoia that misinterprets the evidence, Charles's malice that encourages Paul to act on that interpretation, and a combination of the two that puts a gun into Procathren's inexperienced hands and teaches him ugly truths 'in such a dreadful way'. The irony, however, is that Paul goes to a death he may to some extent merit at the very moment he is relearning to live. Charles's end is a rather different matter. Unlike Paul, he expects it, and accepts it without protest, using his last minutes to paint the blank figure on the mural from the dead face of the wife with whom he had shared a callous, loveless marriage. For him, physical death seems only to formalize a spiritual death that has occurred already.

By the laws of naturalistic probability the play is severely wanting. It is hard to accept that Robert would involve himself in Paul's private war, still harder that he could persuade the army deserters to become his personal hangmen. Though their leader, the suggestively named Christian Melrose, is well characterized in himself, his attempt to explain and justify his obedience is weak, and would be better cut. Yet the play is likely to carry all but the irredeemably literal-minded with it in performance, thanks to its dramatic momentum and nightmarish logic. Like the plays of Pinter, himself one of its admirers, it gives theatrical shape to suspicions, fears and horrors likely to be found in many more subconsciouses than that of its author.

It is a paranoid vision as well as an intricate play about, among other things, paranoia itself, and yet it doesn't leave an altogether negative impression. We may possibly feel that the deaths at the end represent a necessary cleansing. We are certainly likely to sense a degree of light and hope, not only in Pauls regeneration but in the more symbolic figure of the child with whom he plays. At the last moment her name is revealed as the same of that of the most positive and sympathetic character the play offers. As the last members of the doomed Southman family are hanged outside, she 'performs a grave dance', Carroll's *Alice* in her hand. Life goes on; Stella lives, and may fare better this time.

Terence Rattigan
(1911–77)

There were at least two Terence Rattigans. One was the urbane celebrity and great commercial success, who admitted pandering to an archetypal middlebrow theatregoer he called Aunt Edna. The other wrote plays in which his fellow-dramatist, David Rudkin, detected 'a deep personal, surely sexual pain': he was 'someone peculiarly haunting and oblique who speaks to me with resonance of existential bleakness and irresoluble carnal solitude'. The first fell into critical disfavour with the coming of Osborne, Wesker and Arden; increasing recognition of the second's existence was already restoring Rattigan's reputation at the time of his death in 1977.

He was born in 1911, son of a diplomat, and educated at Harrow and Oxford, though he left the latter without taking a degree, having already decided to become a professional playwright. Three years later, in 1936, came the triumph of *French Without Tears*, a comedy set in a language school: funny, but not altogether frivolous, and in some ways auspicious. It offers early examples of Rattigan's fairness to characters others might deride or condemn. More importantly, its theme is obsessional desire, deliberately provoked in the play's captive males by the unscrupulous Diana. At the end this irresistible but destructive being seems likely to pursue the play's hero, an embryo playwright, back to London: 'It's a bloody tragedy,' he wails, as the others laugh and the curtain falls. Prophetic words, perhaps.

It is always dangerous to read a man's life into his work, but tempting to do so in this case, particularly now we have the excellent biography, *Terence Rattigan*, by Michael Darlow and Gillian Hodson. The playwright's childhood appears to have been a lonely one, made no easier by his father's persistent infidelity to his somewhat frigid mother. Echoes of this marriage may be found in his Nelson play, *Bequest to the Nation* (1970), his Ruritanian frolic *A Sleeping Prince* (1953), and, most explicitly, in *Who is Sylvia?* (1950), in which a diplomat spends a lifetime trying to rediscover an old flame in other women, tolerated by a wife who recognizes her own inadequacy. Several plays involve troubled relationships between sons and fathers or father-figures: *A Sleeping Prince*, *In Praise of Love* (1973), *Bequest to the Nation*; *Love in Idleness* (1944), a comic modern treatment of Hamlet and Claudius; and *Man and Boy* (1963), an interesting play about a financier on the brink of ruin and his ambivalent attitude to the son who has rebelled against him, yet abjectly worships him, in spite of misuse. Even Alexander the Great, hero of *Adventure Story* (1949), turns out to be maniacally proving himself to his dead father.

This last play also suggests that the conquest of the self must precede the conquest of anything else, let alone the world. Rattigan is always more interested in the inner man than in his public self, and, though he liked to talk of himself as a liberal socialist, has little to say about politics or 'society' as such. *After the Dance* (1939) takes a jaundiced view of the bright young things of the 1920s in later life, drinking and partying themselves to death; but it is essentially about individuals in their struggles with love, the bottle, and feelings of waste and emptiness. *Love in Idleness*, five years later, suggests a growing conservatism in the successful young playwright. Indeed, it may be accused of pandering to the privileged, since it defines its purportedly left-wing Hamlet as a prig and a self-deceiving humbug and its right-wing Claudius as a tolerant man of the world. But the point is that both characters come to recognize that emotional involvement is more important than political commitment or achievement.

The Winslow Boy (1946) is about a father's fight to clear his naval-cadet son of the accusation of petty theft; and it, too, concentrates on events within the family, leaving potentially exciting scenes in Parliament and the courts to occur offstage. The questions raised are, however, wide-ranging – how pure are the motives of those fighting for justice, how acceptable are the damaging side-effects of their battle, and does it all matter very much anyway? – and some of them are unavoidably public. There are, it seems, enough people of goodwill in all parties to ensure that right will eventually prevail. It's a conclusion that seems complacent nowadays, but it's characteristic of Rattigan. Indeed, his 'politics' comes down to a general faith, expressed in plays as diverse as *Separate Tables* (1954), *Cause Célèbre* (1977) and *Heart to Heart* (1962), in the slow and painful triumph of British decency and fairmindedness over mob-thinking, bigotry and vindictiveness.

His plays, at root, are pleas for understanding and tolerance, commodities for which he undoubtedly felt personal need. He was a homosexual, in his view because of his failed relationship with his father, disliked his own homo-sexuality, and lived at a time when the practice was not just taboo but criminal. His most sympathetically and dee-ply drawn characters are often loners, sometimes failures, always misfits: the phoney major in *Separate Tables*, whose vice is furtively accosting women in cinemas, and the neu-rotic spinster who has befriended him; Alma Rattenbury in *Cause Célèbre*, who scandalizes the nation when her boy-lover kills her husband, but whose vices 'add up to some kind of affirmation'; T. E. Lawrence in *Ross* (1960), so devastated by the discovery of his own homosexuality that he tries to reduce himself to an anonymous number in the air force; Crocker-Harris, the dessicated schoolmaster in that small masterpiece, *The Browning Version* (1948).

Crocker-Harris, suddenly and surprisingly restored to the semblance of life by a schoolboy's gift, is one of many characters who have learned to repress or conceal their emotions. Here, Rattigan succeeds in defining a national habit, though perhaps one less prevalent now than in his heyday. As the writer-protagonist of *In Praise of Love* sug-gests, the *vice anglais* may be 'our refusal to admit to our emotions: we think they demean us'. This character is keeping from his wife his knowledge that she is dying, not realizing she is withholding precisely the same knowledge from him, and touchingly conceals his new-found devotion under the grouchy, selfish front he has always shown her. In *Flare Path* (1942), Rattigan's tribute to his fellow-fliers in the war-time air force, the conflict arises from two confes-sions, both painfully made to a young wife: her ex-lover declares he needs her, adding that this is 'all very shy-making: I am sorry'; her pilot-husband, no less apologet-ically, reveals that his breezy manner hides a shameful fear and desire for comfort. Her view, expressed to the latter, is that openness and honesty are imperative. It is also Rattigan's view.

He sees the difficulties, though. Some of his people don't reveal what they feel because they dare not, some because they don't want to feel it in the first place. Obsessive passion is a recurring theme in Rattigan, as is the humiliation that often accompanies it. It is something his characters find virtually impossible to resist or control. Nelson can see that Lady Hamilton is a crude, vulgar sot, and is appalled by what he has done to his dull, forgiving wife; but he has come to feel that sexual ecstasy is 'the very purpose of man's existence on earth . . . I am obsessed and I want her absolutely'. In *Variations on a Theme* (1958), Rattigan's heroine rejects the millionaire who wants to become her fifth husband for an unprepossessing and sexually ambiguous ballet dancer, a compulsive choice which, it is clear, will lead directly to her death.

Passion exerts its pull in defiance of reason and even liking. In the TV play *Heart to Heart* a cabinet minister's former secretary gives a television interviewer – himself, incidentally, emotionally in thrall to a cold, brittle wife he despises – evidence of his corruption. She loves him, yet thinks him 'dreadful'. Asked how these admissions can be reconciled, her answer is quick: 'What on earth has what you think of a man to do with what you feel for him?' Similarly, *Separate Tables* reconciles a drunken journalist and the socialite wife he has been imprisoned for battering. The only thing worse than being with each other, it seems, is being without each other. Passion is destructive, but so is the rejection of passion.

It is a troubled yet humane vision, and one that is strengthened, not weakened, by the craftsmanship that was once so admired and came eventually to be regarded with suspicion. To be sure, Rattigan's deftly shaped, precisely paced plots sometimes tend to manipulate life into patterns Aunt Edna would regard as theatrically effective. We are no longer so impressed by neat expositions, the artful creation of tension, well-timed revelations, calculated pathos, or even such a famous curtain-line and *coup-de-théâtre* as that in which the Winslow Boy's would-be barrister, having seemingly destroyed him by venomous cross-examination, blithely announces he is innocent and accepts his brief. Yet it is arguable that the peculiar nature of Rattigan's vision, so often involving repressed or thwarted passion, finds its appropriate expression in the old-fashioned form he chooses. The one reflects the other. Unruly emotion is thrust underneath by the disciplines of the 'well-made play', by the flat and sometimes insipid language, and, not least, by the refusal of the censor of Rattigan's heyday to countenance the explicit portrayal of sexual desire; and underneath, as we've seen, is where his characters strive to keep it. Consequently, when it *does* come to the surface, it has considerable impact.

Does this mean that Rattigan has dated? In a social sense, perhaps. As Darlow and Hodson put it, he was 'better as a subversive in an occupied country than as . . . an effective leader after liberation'. Yet even in the most permissive of nations, which Britain hardly is anyway, people's superegos will always be struggling with their ids. They will be trying and failing to reconcile reason and feeling, to achieve a unity within; and that's precisely the moral search that is Rattigan's true subject.

The Deep Blue Sea

In the 1940s Rattigan fell deeply in love with an actor who, Darlow and Hodson report, was unable fully to return his devotion. Eventually the young man started another homosexual affair, which also failed, causing him to overdose himself with sleeping tablets and gas himself to death. Rattigan, seriously upset, almost immediately began work on *The Deep Blue Sea*. In its first form it actually involved a relationship between men; but by 1952, when it opened, its origins had been camouflaged, in most people's view successfully. It was a woman who was discovered by the gas fire as the curtain rose, unconscious, but saved from death by an underfed meter.

She is Hester Collyer, wife of a judge, whom she deserted ten months ago for a former test-pilot, Freddie Page. Their shabby flat is in an area that has 'come down in the world', as she herself manifestly has, too. As the play proceeds, we gradually learn what has happened. Freddie is off playing golf, having forgotten Hester's birthday, an omission which is obviously symptomatic. He wants her to divorce her husband and marry him, because by his lights he loves her. The trouble is that his lights aren't hers. He is a breezy, amiable young man, who 'can't be a ruddy Romeo all the time' and believes in 'moderation in all things', including love. To her, however, Freddie is 'the whole of life – and of death, too, it seems'.

It isn't a romantic love. Rattigan makes it evident, to a degree unusual in the early fifties, that Hester's feelings are substantially, even overwhelmingly physical, though not so simply so that they can be summed up as 'lust'. When Freddie, not yet knowing of her suicide attempt, kisses her, she responds 'with an intensity of emotion that is almost ugly'. When a neighbour, generalizing from an obviously shallower experience, tells her that the 'physical side' is 'awfully unimportant' beside the 'spiritual', she is almost openly contemptuous. And when Freddie concludes he must leave her, she acts with unrestrained anguish, howling 'Don't leave me alone tonight' for all the house to hear.

Yet she also has the clear-sightedness to see how abject her position is. She is described as having 'a thoughtful, remote face', and she fully recognizes the inadequacies of a lover who admits himself her emotional and intellectual inferior. Indeed, she evidently struggled against her passion at first, but the battle was 'unequal'. Her reason has had to watch her will succumbing to a love it finds irresistible and knows to be inadequately reciprocated.

The play's subject, according to Kenneth Tynan, is 'two incompatible kinds of passion', 'the failure of two people to agree on a definition of love'. Hester feels that her husband saw her as a 'prized possession', and certainly didn't have the same idea of love as herself: 'I had more to give you – far more than you ever asked from me.' Now the pattern recurs more dangerously. As her suicide note to Freddie declares, 'You can't help being as you are, I can't help being as I am.' Their affinity may even be 'evil', and is certainly destructive. Her demands have turned him increasingly to drink, as a consequence of which he lost his last flying job; his inability to respond to them has brought her to the brink of the grave. How is the impasse to be resolved?

Clearly she cannot return to her husband, though he wants her back. Rattigan would never countenance so glib an ending, and, indeed, seems unconventional enough to sanction the continuance of the affair with Freddie, if only it worked. But he thought a second, successful suicide attempt would be pat and predictable. He wanted to show, in Darlow and Hodson's paraphrase, 'the necessity, difficulty and courage of facing oneself and one's life as it really is', even if that life has no apparent purpose. So he introduces what is generally agreed to be a rather unsatisfactory character, a struck-off doctor turned bookmaker's runner and part-time hospital volunteer, to point out that 'to live without hope can mean to live without despair'. Beyond hope, he says, is life: 'it's true – I know'. Thus fortified, Hester manages to bid adieu to a man whom shortly before she would have done absolutely anything to keep, even though he himself now shows signs of weakening and wanting her to ask him to stay. He will once more become a test pilot, this time in South America. She may go to an art school and 'start from the beginning again'. The play closes with her again at the fire, turning on the gas, then lighting it. Reason has at least temporarily triumphed over destructive instinct.

This ending has been much criticized. Tynan thought that the case for suicide had been so well stated that Rattigan forfeited respect by arguing Hester out of it. Specifically, he objected to her insistence to the 'doctor' that she does not *deserve* to live, feeling that the point was she could not *bear* to live: 'When, finally, she chooses survival, it is for all the wrong reasons.' This isn't quite fair, since her feelings of valuelessness were made apparent, though not as emphatically as they might, earlier in the play. Indeed, it was a combination of anger, self-hatred and shame that

led her originally to opt for the 'deep blue sea', meaning
death. Not 'deserving' and not 'bearing' were both part of
a 'great tide of illogical emotions'. On the other hand, it's
true that by using the 'doctor' to accentuate her moral
feelings ('You're dying because you feel unworthy to live')
Rattigan does deflect our attention somewhat from the destructive intensity of her love. Tynan's word for this was
'dishonest': it seems kinder to suggest that Rattigan, who
believed strongly in the primacy of people over ideas in
drama, for once allowed what he wanted a character to
mean to determine what she became and did.

Yet for nearly all the play she is abundantly enough alive
for us to be able to debate her qualities. John Russell Taylor
can call her 'really a silly woman with no internal resources
whatever, asking no less than that she should be able to
centre her life entirely on a man whose life will be entirely
centred on her': others have seen her as a modern Phèdre,
a woman whose capacity for emotion makes others seem
stunted, failed. Both points of view are perhaps partly true.
And if she is no straightforward heroine, Freddie is certainly no glib villain. It's true that his reaction to her
suicide attempt is egoistic and self-pitying; but then he has
something to pity himself for. Demands are being made on
him that, as he himself regrets, he just can't fulfil without
pretending, cheating. He is a 'perfectly ordinary bloke,
kind, well-meaning', but unable to cope with feelings that
confuse and frighten him. He is as much a victim of his
dispassion as Hester of her passion. Moreover, as a war-
hero increasingly lost in a changing world, he also has his
own serious problems. It's altogether characteristic of Rattigan that someone he might condemn as the emotional
enemy is allowed to justify himself, amply and
convincingly.

The other characters are less interesting, partly because
they are subsidiary, partly because they are functional,
representative. The young couple next door have had their
sexual troubles, but these are clearly the manageable ones
of average, 'normal' people, without undue capacity for

emotion. The landlady, Mrs Elton, is there to demonstrate the decency, generosity and broad-mindedness which Rattigan persisted in believing characteristics of his fellow-citizens. Yet everyone and everything is slotted into the plot with his usual unobtrusive skill. The only creak in the play's mechanism comes when the suicide note is somewhat implausibly read aloud, so we can hear its contents.

But it isn't just skill that keeps an audience in the state of keyed-up tension observed and shared by Tynan: we want to know what happened to Hester because her emotions are sufficiently authentic and formidable for us to care about her fate. Rattigan may look thin beside Racine, genteel next to Strindberg; but he, too, knows the pit into which heart and gland can sometimes hurl us.

Samuel Beckett
(born 1906)

Samuel Beckett is very reserved, both as man and as writer. He dislikes discussing his work, insisting always that 'I meant what I said', and he keeps his life, too, from prying eyes, saying only that it is too dull to interest anyone. Certainly, the basic facts may be quickly stated. Born near Dublin in 1906, son of a prosperous quantity surveyor. Brought up a strict Protestant, but soon abandoned all religious belief. Educated at a minor public school, where he shone in sport, and at Trinity College, Dublin. Went to Paris, first to teach, then to eke a precarious living as a writer, and became a friend and acolyte of the exiled James Joyce. Published a critique of Proust, poems, short stories and the novel *Murphy* before the Second World War, during which he worked (and with conspicuous courage) for the French Resistance. Wrote *Molloy*, *Malone Dies* and *The Unnameable*, and then, as a relaxation from the more arduous and important calling of novelist, the play *Waiting for Godot*, which was presented in Paris in 1953 and London in 1955. Over the next two decades produced some twenty-one works for the theatre, radio, TV and the cinema, none as long as *Godot* and some spectacularly terse. Married his long-time friend, Suzanne Dumesnil, in 1961. Was awarded the Nobel Prize for Literature in 1969.

Until 1978 a commentator would necessarily have left the story at that, perhaps adding something about Beckett's celebrated generosity to what, given his work's scepticism about such relationships, seems a surprising number of friends. But that year Deirdre Bair published a biography which, characteristically, he did nothing to assist and nothing to impede. This has been severely criticized, both for supposed inaccuracies and for alleged presumption; and this is certainly not the place to relay its more lurid findings. What it does make clear, however, is that Beckett's bleak philosophy was not detachedly pieced together in an ivory tower. Much of his life has been spent in agony of body and mind. He has, as he reportedly said in 1946, been obliged to accept that 'I shall always be depressed'. The 'dark side' is 'the commanding side of my personality'; and he has learned to 'make it work for me'. His *oeuvre* is about people's strategies for survival, and precisely that for him too. It is pain confronted, distanced, concentrated, crystallized.

Its emotional impact has certainly been underrated by some critics. Indeed, Beckett himself is apparently unsympathetic not only to those who seek to deduce a metaphysical 'system' from his plays, but to those who admire his formal skills. The only form to his work, he once observed, is the continual screaming of a man he heard in hospital, dying of throat cancer. This is obviously an exaggeration; but it needs to be borne in mind as a corrective when we praise him, as some have done, for patterning his effects with the mathematical precision of Haydn or Beethoven, or when, as we must, we look for some intellectual or spiritual consistency in his plays.

In their view, man has been dumped for reasons unknown on to a world seemingly designed to frustrate, disappoint and hurt him. The mime, *Act Without Words 1*

(1957), sums it up: a figure flung violently on stage, tantalized with a carafe of water, maliciously thwarted in his most ingenious efforts to get it, and finally left in a state of near-catatonic apathy. His persecutor is invisible, represented only by an offstage whistle. In *Act Without Words 2* (1960) a goad appears, provoking two men to clamber out of sacks and perform rituals which, though different, are felt to be equally futile and meaningless. If the world is controlled by any supernal power, which it probably isn't, it is a decidedly unfriendly one, with a mentality akin to the schoolboy who enjoys tearing wings off flies.

And there is no escape except death, which comes with cruel arbitrariness: too late for the anguished protagonist of *Footfalls* (1976), whose response to the reminder that she is in her forties is 'so little?'; too soon and suddenly for the child crushed by the railway train in *All That Fall* (1957). Suicide is a possibility raised in several plays, and in *Embers* (1959) and *Eh Joe* (1956) has actually occurred in the past; but only in the little-known *Theatre 2* (1958), in which an unnamed figure stands ready to defenestrate himself while two contemptuous bureaucrats examine his 'unpardonable past', does it seem a practical expedient for any character we meet. They are trapped, and they must endure. They are trapped in rooms, dustbins, urns, or, in the case of Winnie in *Happy Days* (1961), first up to the waist and then up to the neck in a mound of sand under a blazing sun: the immobility of Beckett's characters, and the metaphoric daring with which he expresses an incarceration much more than physical, are by now legendary. They must endure bodies often racked with sickness and pain, and endure the unceasing protest of the minds which nature's caprice has attached to them. Endure lives that seem interminable while being, paradoxically, the merest flicker in the infinity of time and space. Endure having none of the meaning, the significance, for which they crave.

There are no solutions, and few if any consolations. Love is at best elusive, evanescent: a commodity half-recollected, and possibly invented, by the old tramp of *That Time* (1976);

a commodity that makes a tantalizingly beautiful appearance on the recording machine with whose help the protagonist of *Krapp's Last Tape* (1958) is scanning a past that promised much and led to nothing. To both these characters love is a distant memory that now serves only to obsess them in sad and cynical old age; and to others it is a word given to hypocrisy, habit, or selfish need. *Play* (1963) is a triangle-drama in which husband, wife and mistress, trapped in funeral urns, endlessly re-enact the drab and sordid encounters which have so absorbed them. The propinquity of her husband, Willie, is one of several factors that give Winnie the false comfort with which she sustains life and the illusion of contentment in *Happy Days*; yet he provokes her bitterness and disgust as well as the kind of mechanical affection to be found in many analogous marriages. This disgust, incidentally, may also reflect Beckett's own disgust at man's 'animal nature'. Willie has a 'tail', 'crawls', lives in a 'hole', on 'straw', eats his own snot, and seems supposed to be identified with the 'castrated male swine' with whose bristles Winnie brushes her teeth. Similarly, Krapp is as dirty and coarse as his name implies, lives in a 'den', and stuffs himself with bananas that constipate him. The metaphors are not those of someone reconciled to the body.

Nec te, nec sine te: neither with you nor without you. The tag Beckett himself applied to *Godot* seems equally relevant to *Endgame* (1957), *Happy Days*, *All That Fall*, in which a complaining cripple meets her blind and cantankerous husband at a railway station, and *Theatre 1* (1956), in which the cripple is male and cannot check the hostility he feels towards the blind fiddler he wishes to befriend him. In Beckett's world relationships range from the painful to the baleful. Moreover, no two people bring precisely the same associations to the same words, and therefore communication is practically as well as emotionally difficult: 'One cannot,' as Beckett himself puts it, 'listen to a conversation for five minutes without being acutely aware of the confusion.' Nevertheless, many of his characters do need each other, if only to give them pain-killer or to convince them of their own reality. It is essential to Winnie to keep talking, and essential to her that Willie should be there, listening, witnessing, validating her increasingly desperate existence, and, of course, allowing her to distract herself from the awfulness of her predicament.

In fact, she deceives herself, because his attention is intermittent and erratic, to say the least. Solitude is the natural condition of Beckett's characters, whether or not they are actually alone: the mind is their retreat, and the only place that seems real to many of them. *Cogito ergo sum* in a world of illusions. Yet the mind, as many discover, is often more trap than refuge. Voices may follow the fugitive, hounding him with guilty memories, as in *Eh Joe*. Strange fixations may overpower him, as in *Embers*, whose main character cannot escape the sound of the sea in which his father drowned himself, or *Footfalls*, whose protagonist spends her life pacing up and down, agonizedly 'revolving it all'. Here and elsewhere Beckett insists on the complexity of the consciousness, with its disjointed memories, its inconsequentialities, its confusions and its fantasies, and makes it clear that the concept of identity, self or 'I' is no static or tidy one: he also, and more dramatically, shows the pain of consciousness, the torment of being 'I'. *Cogito ergo crucior*.

The strategies for coping with this pain are various. Some characters try to externalize it by telling stories about third-person suffering, an expedient obviously analogous to that employed by the artist or writer, including (one presumes) Beckett himself. There is a suggestion that if only the narrator could get his fiction absolutely and unanswerably *right* he might at last find rest, peace. But truth inevitably refuses to be pinned down, and the stories tend to tail away inconclusively, unsatisfactorily. This is the case in *Endgame* and *Embers*. It is also the case in the interesting *Cascando* (1963), which, like the aptly titled *Words and Music* (1962), uses both words and music to represent the creative consciousness; but still remains tantalizingly short of finding the perfect expression for the story of Woburn, the

derelict who ends drifting out to his death at sea. A somewhat similar point is made from a different angle in *Radio
2* (1962), in which an importunate and callous Animator
(representing, perhaps, the critic) persecutes the captive
Fox (perhaps, the writer) to dig up intimate revelations
which, as reformulated by him, are clearly a distortion of
an unfathomable truth. This little parable should be read
as a caveat by all those tempted to analyse Beckett's work
too confidently. Nothing in it is ever wholly certain. As he
himself has said, 'The key word in my plays is "perhaps".'
He is 'a non-knower, a non-can-er'. Again, 'to be an artist
is to fail as no other dare fail.'

Simply telling stories is, then, no solution for Beckett's
more anguished characters. The lonely tramp, whose fragmented autobiography *That Time* is, has invented 'old tales'
in order to 'keep the void out'. Like the protagonist of *Not
I* (1972), he has tried to think of himself as someone else,
a stranger: 'not knowing who you were from Adam, trying
how that would work for a change . . . no notion who it
was saying what you were saying whose skull you were
clapped up in whose moan had you'. Always, he talks of
himself as 'you', never 'I'. Finally, he tries to avoid selfhood
and suffering by imagining 'never having been', non-
existence. That none of these strategies fully works is shown
by the last words of the play, in which he laments that his
life has 'come and gone in no time'; but their logic and
tenor is evident. Alienation from the self becomes an
attempt to escape from the self by increasingly radical
efforts of imagination: in short, to become the very 'void'
the character was struggling to 'keep out'.

Beckett has quoted two tags that might help those approaching his work. One is from the seventeenth-century
Belgian philosopher Geulincx: 'Ubi nihil vales, ibi nihil
velis', 'Where you are worth nothing, you should want
nothing'. The other is from the Greek philosopher Demo-
critus: 'Nothing is more real than nothing'. In a transient
and insubstantial world the best defence is to renounce the
desires, abandon the delusion of free will, and try to achieve

a new reality by becoming, as near as possible, nothing. But this nirvana is not, of course, attained by any of Beckett's characters. Winnie dreams of floating up 'into the blue, like gossamer'; yet her interminable chatter shows that the prospect of any release into the void frightens her, and her graphically emphasized incarceration in the physical obviously makes it a practical impossibility. The main character of *Film* (1965) does rather better in what Beckett calls his 'search of non-being', his 'flight from extraneous perception'. He is able to escape other people's eyes: he cannot, however, evade the 'agony' of being watched by his own intent, ceaseless self. You can cut yourself off from your 'fellow bastards', as the derelict in *That Time* describes humanity, but never from your own excruciating consciousness, the 'penny-farthing hell' of the mind.

Clearly, it would have been better never to have been born, a thought implicit in Hamm's resentment of his father ('accursed progenitor') in *Endgame*, and explicit in the bedridden mother's reiterated apology to the distraught daughter of *Footfalls* for having given her birth. It is a point of view few will share, yet many must admit has a certain logic to it, given the vast, uncaring universe which Beckett postulates as our momentary habitat. He has the honesty and the courage to look full-square at that universe and its implications, and to do so with compassion and even humour. As many have observed, there is a tension between the resilience of several of his characters and their dour predicament, and between his own bleak conclusions and the admittedly harsh and sardonic laughter with which he sometimes reaches them. He may live in Paris, and may have first written many of his plays in French, thus painstakingly avoiding what he regards as the richness and excessive allusiveness of his native tongue: he remains to a large degree in an Irish tradition.

This is, however, more true of his earlier work than of his later, which has little of the ebullience of, say, *All That Fall*, a play which sometimes seems to send up its characters' self-pity and whose humour occasionally becomes broad and even bawdy. Though his general attitudes have changed little over the years, their expression has become starker, more concentrated, in several cases more difficult to comprehend, and in many more grimly beautiful. Examples include the exquisite *Come and Go* (1966), which evokes with extraordinary concision the hopeful childhoods and barren, hopeless old ages of three women; . . . *but the clouds* (1977), in which one of Beckett's lonely wanderers pursues his obsession, the memory of a woman; and the celebrated *Breath* (1969), which reduces the world to a heap of rubble and life to a single inspiration and expiration of breath bounded by two faint cries, the whole lasting perhaps one minute of stage time. The finest of the later plays, however, are *Not I*, *That Time* and *Footfalls*, all of which leave one with the impression of having seen, heard, thought, felt and generally learned far more about the emotional down-and-outs they involve than chronology would seem to permit.

Beckett is perhaps best seen as a theatrical poet, meditating upon universals and transforming them into succinct yet dense parables of desolation and despair. For all his scepticism about language, the words are invariably precise yet resonant, and the visual images arresting and suggestive. *That Time*: an aged face with long flowing hair, listening as his life story is free-associated by his own voice from three sides. *Footfalls*: a spectral Miss Havisham, traipsing ceaselessly to and fro. *Not I*: an unstoppable mouth. *Ghost Trio* (1977): a silent figure in a grey room, looking down a grey corridor to a small boy in a black oilskin, who faintly shakes his head. And here, perhaps, in the nutshell of the later Beckett's imagination, we have an image that takes us back to its theatrical beginnings, to *Waiting for Godot* itself.

Waiting for Godot

The first point to be made about Beckett's best-known play is that it tells us far less about Godot than about waiting, passing time that would, of course, pass anyway. Two derelict old men spend consecutive evenings on a country road whose sole landmark is a tree that remains totally bare in Act I and in Act II, as if to parody spring and hope, sprouts four or five leaves. It seems that they have been here yesterday, and it seems likely they will be here tomorrow, the day after, and every day until their not-too-distant deaths. They bicker, make up, meander from subject to subject, chat of the past, philosophize inconsequentially, play, abuse each other, make up, wonder what they are doing, contemplate suicide, communicate as best they can with two passers-by. They talk to each other 'so we won't think', that is think too hard, realistically and despairingly; and they interest themselves in those who intrude on their limbo in order to 'see the evening out' and avoid being 'bored to death'. The prospect of silence or solitude strikes them as appalling, yet so does the prospect of spinning out words *ad infinitum*: 'I can't go on like this', 'That's what you think'. The only escape from either predicament would seem to be the arrival of the being with whom they supposedly have an appointment, Godot; but twice in the play he breaks his undertaking to come, and the inference is that he will go on doing so, tomorrow and tomorrow and tomorrow.

The two old men are markedly different in character. Vladimir is resilient, and as hopeful as anyone can be in Beckett's grim universe: Estragon is sceptical, pessimistic, bitter, sullen. Vladimir has expectations of Godot, and is instrumental in dealing with his messenger: Estragon is waiting less for Godot than for death, and regularly talks of accelerating its arrival. Estragon attempted suicide in the remote past, and Vladimir rescued him from it. Estragon is grouchy, self-absorbed, self-pitying, and considers himself unluckier than Christ, who lived in a comfortable climate and was 'crucified quick': Vladimir tries to keep up Estragon's spirits, constantly fussing and nagging at him like a wife or, like a mother, singing him lullabies and placing his own coat over his prone body. Estragon snoozes:

Vladimir is wakeful, watchful. Estragon forgets: Vladimir remembers. Estragon eats: Vladimir abstains. Estragon cadges alms: Vladimir disapproves of that. Estragon is constantly getting himself into fights offstage, and takes an aggressive, bullying attitude towards the boy who announces Godot's non-arrival: Vladimir is gentler, kinder, more upset by injustice and oppression. Estragon is more taciturn, placid, phlegmatic, Vladimir more excitable, neurotic, intellectual, and questioning. It is Vladimir who raises the story that has always fascinated Beckett, that of the thieves crucified with Christ, and thinks the salvation of one out of two 'a reasonable percentage' and cause for optimism: Estragon feels that people should believe so poorly documented a tale proves only that they are 'bloody ignorant apes' or, in the original French, 'cons'. Vladimir seems to believe in salvation, Estragon only in the relief of extinction.

We can, if we like, sum them up as superego and id, or point out that 'Vladimir' means ruler of peace, establisher of order, and *estrago* destruction or devastation in Spanish; but it is always dangerous to simplify Beckett. It is evident, however, that they are temperamentally, not just different, but opposite, and therefore perhaps complementary. On several occasions Estragon moots the possibility of separation, but it never actually happens, partly because 'it's not worthwhile', partly because he obviously needs Vladimir at least as much as Vladimir needs him. 'Don't touch me, don't question me, don't speak to me!' he snaps, finishing his outburst with, 'Stay with me!' Quarrels invariably and touchingly end in a mutual embrace. Beckett told the actor Jack MacGowran that their relationship was an irresistible force meeting an immovable object – 'but they are interdependent'.

Interdependence also marks the relationship of their visitors, though this is perhaps more sadomasochistic in character. On the face of it, one is the other's slave. Lucky is driven on stage carrying the luggage of Pozzo, who cracks a whip and painfully jerks the rope tied round Lucky's scuffed neck, calling him 'pig' and 'scum'. The cruelty of the situation outrages Vladimir and even offends Estragon; and yet it is hardly straightforward. Lucky weeps when Pozzo announces he proposes to sell him. The reason he performs his duties as porter with gratuitous conscientiousness may be to dissuade him from doing so. Pozzo, too, is briefly reduced to tears when he thinks of the way Lucky 'goes on', referring presumably to the kind of long, fragmented, quasi-metaphysical tirade that the latter delivers a little later. The contradictions of their relationship are even more evident in Act II, in which Pozzo enters blind, almost helpless, less leader than led, yet still directs imperious insults at Lucky, who is now dumb but still roped, encumbered with baggage, and obedient. Whether from tradition, habit or some more pressing need, these men, too, appear to be more than literally tied to one another.

Their relationship, like everything else in the play, has been incessantly debated by the critics, who have seen them as capitalist and proletarian, bloated body and frayed mind, and much else besides. However, all we can say with confidence is that Pozzo, at least on his first appearance, has a more strongly social identity than protagonists who exist in dual isolation from a world that manifests itself only in the regular beatings Estragon endures offstage. He lives in a 'manor', owns 'slaves', describes the stage as 'my land', and is very sure of his importance and superiority. But this complacency does not survive the loss of his sight. Affliction changes him from a man primarily concerned with wealth, status, power and the other obsessions of social beings into one who exists on an altogether deeper level of awareness. In the first act he talked of his 'schedule', and consulted a watch which, perhaps prophetically, vanished just before his exit. In the second, chronology has the same significance for him it was to have for the Beckett of *Breath*: 'One day we were born, one day we shall die, the same day, the same second . . . they give birth astride of a grave, the light glimmers an instant, and then it's night once more.' Pozzo, in short, sees that his old strengths and comforts were illusions, and ends his spiritual journey in a plight not so different from that of Lucky, whose tirade, albeit a confused and even crazed parody of academic pedantry, does have substance to it. Notwithstanding the alleged existence of a loving if wayward God, and in spite of human progress, man continues to 'waste and pine', 'shrink and dwindle', and the world itself to revert to chaos.

That this is also the conclusion of Beckett himself is given added plausibility by his reported comment that Lucky may be lucky because he has no more false expectations. Yet is it wise to use the word 'conclusion' of a play that, as he has also said, is 'striving all the time to avoid definition'? The predominant note is interrogative. Indeed, it has been estimated that a quarter of the dialogue consists of questions, few of which receive satisfactory answers. Nothing seems certain or consistent. One day Estragon's boots are too small, the next too big. Or maybe they are not the same boots at all. 'Let us do something while we have the chance', says Vladimir, confronted with Pozzo's cries for help, 'let us not waste our time in idle discourse'; and then proceeds to do precisely that. And both acts end in the identical way. Vladimir: 'Well, shall we go?' Estragon: 'Yes, let's go.' Stage direction: 'They do not move'.

This demonstrates not only their indecisiveness, or (rather) the impossibility of making decisions that matter or change anything, but the gap between intention and action, cause and effect, perception and truth. Indeed, there may not be such a commodity as truth at all. Estragon is almost pathologically forgetful, and Vladimir's grasp of reality, or what may be reality, is not as sure as he likes to believe. Where were they yesterday? Is this the day of their appointment? What day of the week is it? What time of the day? And have they met Pozzo and Lucky before the first act? Estragon says not; but then he only 'supposes' he has seen them a moment after their exit, has forgotten them by the second act, and even mistakes (if it is a mistake) Pozzo for Godot. Vladimir confidently declares he knows them, although he has hitherto shown no sign of doing so, only to add 'unless they're not the same'. And is Estragon's name Estragon or, as he tells Pozzo, Adam? Is Vladimir really Mr Albert, the name with which Godot's boy addresses him? Why does the boy claim never to have seen him before, the very day (if it *is* only a day) after we have seen them talk? Is Estragon speaking more aptly than he seems to know when he answers Vladimir's 'There you are' with an 'Am I?'? And why is Vladimir so anxious – in a production directed by Beckett apparently very anxious indeed – to be reassured by the boy that 'you saw me, you won't come and tell me tomorrow that you never saw me'? In a world as confusing and deceptive as this, the very concept of identity is at risk. 'I' may not exist.

One of Vladimir's hopes of Godot is clearly that he will validate his existence, and conceivably even give him significance and point. But then who, or what, is Godot? Beckett apparently toyed with the possibility that he was, in fact, Pozzo unrecognized, but changed his mind. He admits only that he based the name on the French slang words for boot, *godillot* and *godasse*, and says that if he had known who Godot was, he would have revealed it in the play. It is, however, difficult to believe that the English translation of *dieu* wasn't somewhere at the back of his mind when he punned irreverently on footwear. Indeed, Godot sounds like a cheeky diminutive of God, akin to 'Charlot', the French nickname for Chaplin, the very comedian Beckett reportedly wants directors to bear in mind when they mount the play. Moreover, Godot is described as having the 'white beard' Lucky mentions as an attribute of God; and when Vladimir hears this his response is suggestive, 'Christ have mercy!' Does he react with terror because the image evoked is that of the grim, punitive deity of the Old Testament? Or should we pay due attention to Beckett's own comment, that the beard shows that Godot is very old and that 'if he were less experienced there might be some hope'? The two interpretations are not perhaps mutually exclusive.

Altogether, there is much about Godot to suggest a sceptically resurrected version of the God Beckett rejected as a young man. People pray to him without definite answer. He feeds humanity incomplete information and tantalizing promises through chosen spokesmen. His ways are inscrutable to the point of perversity. We are told, in one of the play's many invocations of the Bible or biblical imagery, that he beats the boy who looks after his sheep and shows kindness to the one in charge of the goats. In other words, he distributes suffering inequitably. Alternatively, he remains aloof to it, 'does nothing'. Vladimir and Estragon can claim, as 'billions' of us can apparently claim, to have 'kept our appointment' with Godot, and received no reward for doing so; and yet if they 'dropped' him, as Estragon suggests, 'he'd punish us'. He is a figure who inspires both fear and teasing hope: which is presumably why Vladimir is terrified on the first occasion he thinks he is approaching, and on the second triumphant. 'We're saved!' he cries then, and at the very end repeats the word: if he comes, 'we'll be saved'. Godot, it seems, is as powerful and unpredictable as the God who saved one thief and damned the other, apparently because of a few words gasped *in extremis*.

And, of course, he may not exist at all. Vladimir calls Godot 'a kind of acquaintance', but clearly has never met him. He knows nothing either of his appearance or of his moral practice. In reply to his 'vague supplication' he has received an equally vague 'he'd have to think it over', and even that comes, not directly from Godot, but from an intermediary who is not to be trusted, a boy who denies a meeting we ourselves have witnessed and delivers absolute promises that are invariably broken. The giving of these promises, perhaps even the giver, could be a mischievous if alluring invention. God *may* be real and *may* one day save us. On the other hand, Christ and the prophets may have been bamboozling us.

It is a suggestion unlikely to impress committed Christians, whose views on suffering, prayer and the experience of God would be very different from Beckett's; but those who adhere to any other faith or system will find him little more sympathetic. Beckett reduced the information given about Godot when he translated the play from French into English, and the impression deliberately left is even vaguer, more general, than at first. If Godot is primarily the 'god' of an agnostic strongly drawn towards atheism, he may also be seen as anything or everything that promises without delivering, attracts without satisfying. He is what side-tracks us, helps us postpone despair, gives us the illusion of purpose and importance in a world which offers us little, if anything, more than the certainty of death. Even the optimistic Vladimir comes to some such conclusion towards the end of the play: 'Astride of the grave a difficult birth. Down in the hole, lingeringly, the gravedigger puts on the forceps. We have time to grow old. The air is full of our cries.' The words are markedly similar to those of the disillusioned Pozzo, but there is a crucial addition: 'habit is a great deadener'. If we keep talking, keep distracting ourselves, keep slogging through the interminable moment of time inexplicably allotted us, keep waiting for our own pet Godot, we may be able to avoid facing the fact that he will never come.

Can we call *this* Beckett's own conclusion? The same qualifications apply as before, with one important addition. *Godot* is a play likely to make its audiences laugh as well as puzzle and wince. Vladimir and Estragon were conceived as shabby clowns, and there are elements of vaudeville as well as of autumnal poetry in their crosstalk. Pozzo variously reminds us of a ringmaster, a master of ceremonies, and a ham actor, pompous and sententious; and even Lucky, with his long white hair and (usually) eccentric dress, seems to have wandered in from circus or music-hall. There are pratfalls, misunderstandings, comically prolonged farewells, rather a good gag about Estragon's lungs, and much funny business with the Laurel-and-Hardy bowlers the characters wear.

To be sure, there is much about the humour to remind us that one of the clown's functions is to mock values and belittle effort. It is not a kindly or comfortable laughter that the play provokes. Beckett himself apparently said that the falls are 'related to the threat in the play of everything falling', a point apparent enough when Vladimir tumbles as he tries to pull the blind Pozzo to his feet, and Estragon tumbles pulling up Vladimir. Again, it is far from simply comic when Estragon once again decides to hang himself and takes off the cord that holds up his trousers, causing them to fall down and, a moment later, himself and Estragon to stumble as they test the cord's strength. The worst of their despair is thus made to look as absurd as the best of their hope. As Beckett has said, the play's spirit is that 'nothing is more grotesque than the tragic'.

And yet, paradoxically, the characters have dignity even when dignity eludes them. There are many reasons why *Godot*, for all its difficulties and apparent inaccessibility, continues to be regarded as an important play. It is technically audacious, using two tramps and a bare stage to explore the great abstractions. It is written, one might say scored, with a poet's sensitivity and a musician's skill. Its tragi-comic tone is the tone of our age. As Martin Esslin remarks of Beckett's work in general, it confronts us 'with concrete projections of the deepest fears and anxieties, which have been only vaguely expressed at a half-conscious level' and thus perhaps constitutes 'a process of catharsis and liberation analogous to the therapeutic effect in psycho-analysis of confronting the subconscious contents of the mind'. Not least, it shows that the hideous uncertainties of existence can be faced with pluck, resilience and humour. Sean O'Casey called it 'a rotting and remarkable play' with a 'lust for despair'. That is only partly true. The lust is also for life.

Endgame

The people of *Godot* sometimes seem to recognize that they are really actors, playing in a theatre. 'End of the corridor, on the left,' says Estragon incongruously when Vladimir leaves the 'country road' to urinate. The effect is to add to the general sense of metaphysical insecurity, because it suggests that the humanity these tramps represent may itself be performing on a 'board' for invisible spectators beyond. Reality, or what the two main characters take for reality, is similarly undermined in Beckett's next important play, *Endgame*. 'I see a multitude in transports of joy,' says Clov sarcastically as he turns his telescope on to the audience, 'that's what I call a magnifier.' 'What is there to keep me here?' he asks Hamm, and gets the reply, 'The dialogue.' 'Aside', 'soliloquy', 'underplot', 'making an exit': again and again the two of them talk in terms which variously imply that there may be something deceptive about the world with which Beckett presents us, that nothing can be taken at its face value, that at least some of the anguish on show has its histrionic side, and that the characters are trapped in an ontological situation analogous to that of performers, who must come onstage and subordinate free will to the roles foisted upon them.

The theatrical metaphor is resonant, but it is not the only one the play offers. The name of Hamm, his lordly manner, his tendency to posture and parade his suffering ('Can there be misery loftier than mine?'), and the relish with which he narrates a melodramatic tale in which he himself is protagonist and villain, all suggest a thespian of the old school: a 'ham' actor. Hamm may also be the hammer, abusing characters each of whose names is similar to the word 'nail' in some language or other. The post-diluvian desolation of the world outside the room in which the play occurs, combined with the fact that in his original draft Beckett actually made Clov read the biblical story of the Flood, evokes Ham, son of Noah. Finally, Hamm's blindness and impotence, his immobility in his wheelchair centre-stage, some of his words ('me to play'), and the title of the play itself, suggest a game of chess about to end with the destruction of an isolated king; and this interpretation actually receives support from Beckett himself.

He reportedly told the Hamm in a German production directed by himself that he was 'a king in a chess game lost from the start. From the start he knows he is making loud senseless moves . . . Now at the end he makes a few senseless moves as only a bad player would. A good one would have given up long ago. He is only trying to delay the inevitable end.' On the other hand, several critics have pointed out that the play as a whole defiantly refuses to be summed up in any single way; and in this, too, they would seem to have Beckett's support. 'We're not beginning to . . . to . . . mean something?' asks Hamm, and Clov replies, 'Mean something! You and I, mean something! Ah, that's a good one!' The exchange has obvious metaphysical import: it is also a warning to any over-zealous analysts in the audience. Explication must proceed very cautiously.

'Finished, it's finished, nearly finished' are the play's opening words. They are spoken by Clov, who may be Hamm's son or may simply be his slave, just after he has removed the dustsheet under which the old man has spent the night; and the period of time that follows does indeed seem to be more conclusive than what Clov calls 'that bloody awful day, long ago, before this bloody awful day', meaning yesterday. 'Something is taking its course': something, perhaps, is coming to an end. 'Moment upon moment, pattering down . . . and all life long you wait for that to mount up to a life,' says Hamm; and maybe, at last, that accumulation of monotonous moments is complete. 'Grain upon grain, one by one,' says Clov, 'and one day, suddenly, there's a heap, a little heap, the impossible heap.' The reference here is to the Greek philosopher Zeno, who argued that if you divided a pile of millet in two, and then continued dividing one pile and adding it to the other, the operation could never end, because the smaller pile must always remain in at least infinitesimal existence. But now the 'impossible' may be about to happen. The heap may achieve totality in death.

Beckett himself has compared Hamm and Clov to Estragon and Vladimir at the end of their lives, but they are even more likely to remind us of Pozzo and Lucky. Hamm's appeal to Clov to 'forgive me' for having caused him suffering suggests that, unlike Pozzo, he has a capacity for guilt; but he has, it seems, 'owned paupers' and behaved with sadistic arrogance to those who have called upon his charity. Now, in his helplessness, he remains imperious, demanding, self-pitying, and brutally cynical: 'Lick your neighbour as yourself' and, at the very end, 'peace to our . . . arses' are his contemptuous travesties of Christian injunctions. He treats Clov's touching complaint that his 'light' is 'dying' with derision and relishes the thought of him suffering in the future. He has nothing but hatred for his father, Nagg, who, like his mother Nell, he keeps 'bottled' in a dustbin, encouraging him to emerge only when (again like Pozzo) he wants an audience for his rhetorical confidences. His love, such as it is, is reserved for a dilapidated toy dog, which he anyway likes to imagine 'begging me for a bone, imploring me'. At one point his words seem meant to remind us of Shakespeare's Richard III; at others, of the Prospero whose 'revels now are ended' and whose slave uses 'the words you taught me' in order to curse.

Though Clov doesn't share Caliban's brutishness, he is hardly more able to resist his master's orders and insults. Once this wretched creature (he talks of himself as having been 'whelped') may have 'loved' Hamm, but now he refuses to kiss or even touch him. Indeed, he intermittently itches to kill him, and might already have done so if only Hamm had revealed his big secret, which is 'the combination to the larder'; but now so definitive an act seems beyond him. His life has not contained 'an instant of happiness'. All has, it seems, been obedient attention to Hamm's endless wants, for reasons he cannot explain but we possibly can. Their relationship is symbiotic. The two of them are interdependent, complementary. Perhaps they even add up to a single human whole.

Specifically, Hamm can't move, let alone stand: Clov can't sit, but hobbles about with scarcely a pause. Hamm asks, Clov provides. Hamm needs: Clov, perhaps, needs to be needed. They are 'obliged to each other'. Hamm, it has been suggested, is the clamorous body, Clov the tormented mind, or Hamm the mind and Clov a sort of shattered superego. We are watching someone's disintegrating self, or maybe a schizophrenic consciousness. The continuous presence of physically helpless but still troublesome parents – rather literally, Nagging their offspring – tends to support this interpretation. Alternatively, or additionally, we are seeing the inside of a dying man's skull. This interpretation is supported by the setting, a bare room filled with 'grey light' and, high up, two 'small windows', not unlike eyes.

Yet Beckett himself told Jack MacGowran, who played Clov, that it wasn't all happening within the mind of one man. Just to make things more confusing, he has apparently denied that Hamm covers his face with his bloodstained handkerchief at the end in order to die. We are not absolutely bound to believe an author so insistent on the elusiveness of truth, but his words should make us doubly cautious when we are tempted to be categorical. We cannot even be sure that the day we witness is markedly different from any other, though this certainly seems the case. Nagg and Nell act out their hideous parody of a marriage in its senility, she asking if it's 'time for love' and resurrecting tantalizing memories, he sucking on a dog-biscuit and clamouring for candy, both trying and failing to kiss; but today Nell's pulse appears to have stopped, and soon it 'looks' as if she is dead. Meanwhile, Hamm seems to be growing less assertive, feebler, Clov more insubordinate and independent, until what feels like a dénouement is reached. Hamm resigns himself to 'the end', and tells Clov he doesn't need him any more. Clov appears ready for a journey, and stands silently watching as Hamm throws away all his props and disappears beneath his handkerchief.

Is it really the end, or is this monstrous travesty of a family, if family it is, doing what it did yesterday and may do tomorrow, acting out a separation, a disintegration, it half-desires and half-fears? And what of the world outside this claustrophobic little hell? That, too, seems to be at or near its end. From one window can be seen dead land, from the other dead sea. There are, we are variously told, no more bicycle-wheels, nature, spring, sugar-plums, tides, navigators, rugs, coffins and (worst) pain-killer. The doctor is dead; so is Mother Pegg, a neighbour killed by 'darkness'; and so it seems is everyone 'at Kov, beyond the gulf'. Everything is 'zero', as if laid waste (a thought even more likely to have struck an audience in 1958 than now) by the nuclear Armageddon. The only living creatures, apart from those we see, are: first, a flea that tickles Clov; second, a rat supposedly lurking in the kitchen; third, a small boy Clov claims, truthfully or untruthfully, to be able to see through the window towards the close.

All this raises several questions. For instance, is this blasted world objectively observed by the characters, or is it their subjective impression of a quite different environment? In one passage, inadequately explained by most critics, Hamm tells of a 'madman' who looked at all the 'loveliness' outside and saw only 'ashes': he adds that his case 'is . . . was not so . . . so unusual'. And Clov recalls being asked to 'raise your head and look at all that beauty, that order', adding that he can see only 'a little trail of black dust': 'I say to myself that the earth is extinguished, though I never saw it lit.' The version of external reality offered us may be a metaphoric one, an expression of the characters' depression and nihilism. Twice they talk as if things might actually be different, better, somewhere out there. It could be 'still green' beyond their 'hole'. They could possibly make a raft and be carried far away to other 'mammals'. And Clov, though he doesn't leave, and may not be going to leave, is dressed at the end as if he's going *somewhere*. Perhaps there is an escape. And perhaps, fundamentally, it is an escape from one's own distorted and distorting consciousness.

Yet the play leaves no such hopeful impression. Hope, it suggests, is probably just another snare and distraction; and 'escape' – well, escape to what? Hamm's 'madman' was actually fortunate. Indeed, he was 'spared', because he hadn't been deluded into thinking the world better than it is. Whether the version of reality beyond the room we're given is real or metaphorical finally makes no difference: either way, it tells a basic truth. The world is worthless. And 'mammals' would be better not found, because 'mammals' would do better not to exist at all.

Thus the flea must be killed, lest evolution starts again from it. So must the rat. In the play's first French version, Hamm begs Clov to exterminate the small boy, invoking images of Christ, Moses and Buddha, in other words all those who brought mankind its supposedly illusory hopes. In the English one he is satisfied that this 'potential pro-creator' will die outside or 'come here', presumably to share the family's collective fate. Those anxious to find a chink in Beckett's pessimism have suggested that this boy *may* exist and *may* survive; but they are surely missing the point. Survival is a disaster, *the* disaster. Hamm must overcome his propensity to, as Beckett puts it, 'say "no" to nothing-ness'. Clov, wiser, declares that he'll 'weep for happiness' when his end comes.

Endgame is as despairing a play as even Beckett has written. God, in Hamm's self-contradiction, is a 'bastard' who 'doesn't exist'. Meanwhile, 'the end is in the beginning, and yet you go on': go on, deluding yourself that you have significance and purpose, that 'perhaps it won't all have been for nothing'. The bleak truth, as Beckett sees it, may be contained in Hamm's remembered or imagined advice to the petitioner who begs him to take in the child he hopes will solace him in his old age. The man's 'responsibilities' lie, not in saving the boy, but in abandoning him to death. 'Use your head, can't you?' he repeats violently. 'You're on earth, there's no cure for that.'

In short, hope, meaning and even life itself are absurdi-ties, a point of view emphasized both by the sardonic, funny-glum tone of much of the play, and by what Beckett himself apparently calls its most important sentence: Nell's 'nothing is funnier than unhappiness'. Suffering, too, is a joke, but a joke we know too well, still funny 'but we don't laugh any more'. The solution, if any, is perhaps to consent to the void. At one point Hamm says that his narrative tale, though incomplete, is 'better than nothing', and Clov's reply is archetypal Beckett: 'Better than nothing! Is it possible?' It is nothingness that Nell seems to have attained and Nagg will soon attain in their dustbins, to nothingness that Hamm finally resigns himself, and in nothingness that Clov will presumably find himself should he actually venture out of the house and into the deadness beyond.

Not I

Not I is the most striking of Beckett's exercises in dramatic minimalism. A whole life, so it seems, is reduced to a seventeen-minute gabble emerging from a bizarre and unsettling visual image. Near a tall 'auditor' of indeterminate sex, who stands in the murk dressed in a 'loose black djellaba, with hood', is an actress totally invisible except for her mouth, which is lit with a spot. The effect is of a writhing sea-creature, or maybe someone's palpitating pudenda, isolated in limbo; and yet it expresses the desperation and bewilderment of one of those tormented conciousnesses that have preoccupied the later Beckett.

'Mouth', as she is called, tells a story we may tentatively piece together from the onslaught of breathless, disjointed phrases. Its subject is a woman casually begotten, born prematurely in some 'godforsaken hole', abandoned by her mother, and raised in an orphanage run by a religious order which has left her with a sense of sin and guilt much more potent than any truth contained in the talismanic phrases she obsessively repeats, 'God is love', 'tender mercies'. Indeed, the idea of a merciful God reduces the narrator to the only outbursts of laughter in the play; and that is not surprising, since Mouth's adult life has been one long desert.

Beckett apparently regards her as a capsule version of the crazed old crones he used to see stumbling down lanes in his native Ireland, and that is certainly the picture likely to be evoked in the hearer's head. We see her drifting about, stopping every few steps, staring into space; wandering through fields, looking aimlessly for cowslips to make into a ball; standing speechlessly in a supermarket, 'mouth half-open as usual', waiting for the assistant to put the goods on her shopping list into an old black bag; and once making an appearance in court, saying nothing when brusquely (and, given her character, pertinently) asked 'guilty or not guilty?', and glad when they led her away. The reason for this brush with the law isn't given, but it may have resulted from one of the occasions she broke her almost permanent silence. Once or twice a year, usually in winter, she would get a sudden urge to 'tell', and start pouring out a 'steady stream' of 'mad stuff' in the nearest lavatory, only to 'die of shame' at the inevitable stares.

This sounds very much like the 'steady stream' we are hearing now; but there is a crucial difference. Something new has happened. At the age of seventy or thereabouts this 'old hag' had a quasi-mystical experience. One April morning in a field everything went dark except for a single ray of moon-like light which first remained still, then began to 'move around'. Her first reaction was typical of Beckett's more wounded characters. She thought she was being punished; and the fact that she was not suffering, indeed could not remember 'when she had suffered less', did not prove this was not so, since this abject old woman had always found comfort and relief in punishment deliberately inflicted and none whatever in what were supposed to be pleasures. She considered groaning and writhing in pretended agony in order to propitiate this mysterious force, but could not do so, partly because she was unluckily 'incapable of deceit' and partly because she found herself unable to make any sound. But then, without her willing, wanting or even understanding it, her mouth was suddenly 'on fire'. It poured out words unstoppably, as if there was something 'she had to . . . had to . . . tell'. But what? How it was, how she had lived? It seemed not. What, then?

If we may indeed identify Mouth with the old woman's mouth, and think of the whole monologue as autobiographical, we may reasonably conclude that what we are hearing is *this* outpouring, *these* questions, *this* search for understanding. The fact that the narrative is in the third person, so far from disproving this, tends to support it. Just as the old tramp in *That Time* talks of himself as 'you', so Mouth is 'she' or 'her' to herself. Partly, this is a way of dramatizing the split between mind and body upon which Beckett so often insists. The old woman thinks of her body, including the mouth itself, as a 'machine', and this time a machine that has become 'disconnected' from the brain. One part of herself is out of the other part's control, even of its comprehension. Her mind is 'begging' her mouth to stop, but it is like a tape-recorder run amok: as Beckett himself has said, it is purely 'an organ of emission, not intellect'.

But this is an insufficient explanation. Five times the monologue rises to a crescendo: 'What? . . . Who? . . . No! . . . She! . . .', the last time with a capitalized 'SHE!' added. Why? Why should the mind not just feel, but *need* to feel, disconnected from the body in the first place? If the mouth may indeed be seen as a demented tape-recording machine, only the intellect can have originally dictated the words it now automatically emits: why, then, should both intellect and mouth refuse to acknowledge that the subject of their narrative is, in fact, 'I'? The principal reason for this 'vehement refusal to relinquish third person', as Beckett calls it, is surely that thinking of herself in the third person is one of the old woman's strategies for avoiding yet more pain. It is a way of putting a distance between consciousness and experience. These agonies belong to someone else, not to me. I am the fly on the ceiling, watching someone else squirm. This life has been wasted by someone else, not by me. Such things happen to other people: *Not I*!

The day-time moonbeam may therefore be somewhat akin to the spotlight in *Play*, which hits each of the three characters in an almost inquisitorial manner, demanding confessions. What it surely demands by 'poking around', 'ferreting around', is that Mouth does indeed acknowledge herself, does use the word 'I'. But she cannot do so, and so her autobiography is doomed to meander frantically and repetitively on, never reaching fulfilment. Her situation is thus analogous to that of the artist or writer, whose fate it is always to fail. As we've seen, the characters in *Cascando* might find peace, if only they could pin down the truth that always eludes and frustrates them. Similarly, though Beckett nowhere says so, Mouth might acquire *something* if only she would face and accept herself as she was and is. She herself sees the potential reward as feeling 'forgiven' her unnamed (and probably non-existent) sins. Perhaps she is wrong, and self-recognition would bring only fresh suffering, and not peace; perhaps not. Perhaps it would give her some identity, integrity, even dignity in what some critics have suggested may be a review of her life at or near her death.

The question is incapable of certain answer, but at least it brings us face to face with another of the play's tantalizing problems, the role of the auditor, standing there dressed like a father-confessor. He does nothing whatever except to make the same movement after the first four times Mouth refuses to 'relinquish third person': it is a 'simple sideways raising of arms from sides and their falling back, in a gesture of helpless compassion'. This 'lessens with each recurrence till scarcely perceptible at third', and does not occur at all at the fifth and most climactic refusal. According to Martin Esslin (whose seminal *Theatre of the Absurd*, incidentally, is still an excellent introduction to Beckett as a whole) the figure incarnates the mind, watching the body as represented by the mouth; but, if so, its presence is surely redundant, since the split between body and mind is more than adequately aired in Mouth's words. More likely, he (or she) is you, I or Beckett himself: filled with compassion for the broken old woman, yet helpless to do anything about it, especially as she herself cannot make the leap from 'she' to 'I'. Whether the gradual reduction of his gesture means that he feels increasingly helpless or decreasingly compassionate, more resigned and bored, is not apparent. Either way, the point surely is that in this cruel world we are essentially alone: others may listen, and by listening perhaps even validate our existence for us, but they cannot ultimately change us from what we are into what we might be.

The artistry of the Beckett of *Not I*, his succinctness, precision, yet resonance, is surely remarkable. The single expletive 'Home!' tells us all we need to know about Mouth's life when she is not out, trudging the countryside. Yet the play refuses simply to be admired aesthetically or analysed intellectually. Beckett himself told his New York director that he was 'not unduly concerned with intelligibility: I hoped the piece would work on the necessary emotions of the audience rather than appealing to their intellect'. And that, surely, is what it does. No one could possibly comprehend this babble at a single sitting. At first confrontation, it lures us into sharing the confusion, the disorientation of the protagonist as she struggles to make sense of things. It is also designed to appal us, the more strongly the more familiar with it we become.

Here is a woman who counts herself fortunate if she can avoid all sensation except an inevitable 'buzzing', a 'dull roar in the skull'. Love is a threat which she has been 'spared'; feeling of any kind a danger which she dreads, but, to her relief, is again 'spared' during her experience in the April field. She remembers weeping just once in her life, but only for a moment, and so detachedly, so numbly that she only knew the tears in her lap were her own because no one else was near. She has, in short, consented to the reduction of herself to a 'she', almost an it, a thing. *Not I* is pain and grief distilled, a concentrated lament for lives without happiness, meaning or hope: Beckett in agonized miniature.

Brendan Behan
(1923–64)

Republicanism was bred into Brendan Behan from the very start. Indeed, his father, a Dublin housepainter, was actually in prison for political 'crimes' at the time of the boy's birth, in 1923. At the age of eight he joined the Fianna, a Republican youth organization, and was only with difficulty dissuaded by his Catholic mother from going to Spain to join the small Irish contingent fighting Franco. In 1939, an unsuccessful bombing mission to Liverpool on behalf of the IRA led to the sixteen-year-old Behan's arrest and the incarceration he entertainingly describes in his autobiographical *Borstal Boy*. In 1942, not long after his return to Ireland, he was sentenced to fourteen years for attempting to murder a Special Branch detective, only to be released under a general amnesty in 1946. He began to write poetry and short stories, and in 1952 was commissioned by Radio Eireann to write what was planned as a comedy series but turned out to be two short plays, *Moving Out* and *The Garden Party*.

One describes how a mother moves her family from a Dublin slum to a suburban housing estate without the knowledge of her husband; the other, how the paterfamilias and his next-door neighbour, nagged by their wives to dig a vegetable patch, get the local police to do the job by pretending that stolen loot is buried in their gardens. Both are very slight, offering only occasional flashes of the extravagant humour that was to light up much of Behan's later work. 'It's a class of high treason,' declares the lazy husband, earnestly explaining his refusal to touch his municipally owned garden, 'come under the Abatement of Polygamy Act, I believe.' But such ebullient minutiae do not prepare one for the measured excellence of *The Quare Fellow*, or even for the energetic comedy of his next (and best) radio play: *The Big House* (1957), which deals with the plundering of an old mansion owned by a fragile Anglo-Irish couple named Ananias and Boedicea Baldcock.

In 1958 came the production, first in Gaelic and then in English, of *The Hostage*, about a young English soldier threatened with execution by the IRA in retaliation for the forthcoming hanging of a Republican in Belfast. From the start, it's apparent that Behan's political convictions have changed vastly since his activist youth. 'As the curtain rises,' says the first stage direction, 'pimps, prostitutes, decayed gentlemen and their visiting "friends" are dancing a wild Irish jig': this, in the lodging-house the IRA regards as a safe gaol for its hostage. It is, in fact, a brothel, owned by a wildly eccentric patriot who believes he is still fighting in the 'Troubles' of 1916, and run by a superannuated hero who has mythicized his own past exploits, but tends to be contemptuous of the nationalists who have replaced him. The IRA is 'as dead as the charleston', he says, 'out of date' in the age of the H-bomb.

This appears to be the view of Behan himself, who was, of course, writing before that organization's 'provisional' wing had begun to demonstrate its effectiveness as a guerilla army in Ulster. In the play, the IRA is represented only by an 'officer' and a 'volunteer', the first a 'thin-faced fanatic' who flaunts a puritanism absolutely alien to his author's Falstaffian temperament, the second an incompetent torn between his duty as guard and the demands of his bursting bladder. Neither are remotely as sympathetic as their English hostage, an eighteen-year-old orphan who has no understanding of Irish politics, religion or any of the other matters that exercise his captors. A love affair, tenderly if somewhat sentimentally conceived by Behan, burgeons between him and the equally innocent house skivvy. All is ended by a police raid in which, ironically, the boy-soldier is accidentally shot.

It's a sprawling, disorderly play, given some tension and a semblance of dramatic unity by this character's predicament. But it would be foolish to condemn it for untidiness, because untidiness is precisely what Behan celebrates. His heart is with the homosexual navvy Rio Rita, his coloured boyfriend Princess Grace, the coy royalist Miss Gilchrist, the lecherous civil servant Mulleady, the rough-tongued brothel madam, her girls, and the rest of the human flotsam and jetsam that make the house the agreeably chaotic place he believes it to be. The combination of this comical mess and the sudden, sad death of the hostage may at first glimpse seem reminiscent of the O'Casey of *The Plough and the Stars*. But Behan's sense of pain is much less acute, his attitudes towards the mess and chaos far less critical, and, not least, his characterization considerably less discriminating. Indeed, the play might almost have been written by Fluther Good or some other of O'Casey's more feckless tenement dwellers.

The Hostage, like *The Quare Fellow*, was first directed in Britain by Joan Littlewood, who always encouraged her actors to improvise and invent during rehearsals. Consequently, it is impossible to be sure that every word in the play is 'by' Behan. A similar caveat must be made about *Richard's Cork Leg*, which was put together by his friend (and sometime director) Alan Simpson from the drafts Behan left behind at the time of his premature death from alcoholism and diabetes, in 1964. It cannot be confidently asserted that it is the play as he would have finished it. On the other hand, it does develop logically from *The Hostage*, both for good and ill.

Ill first. It is seriously lacking in tension and coherence. It opens in a cemetery, where the Hero Hogan is waiting to disrupt a fascist meeting. These 'blueshirts' do not, however, arrive until late in the play, by which time we have been distracted from the threat they supposedly represent by some random, rambling exchanges involving the Hero, two prostitutes camouflaged as nuns, the sanctimonious and puritanical Mrs Mallarkey, her desirable daughter, and a layabout, lecher, dispenser of good-humoured common sense and (so Mr Simpson tells us) Behan self-portrait, named Cronin. Then there is a brief rumpus; and we find ourselves in the Mallarkey household, which is surreptitiously invaded by disguised blueshirts and policemen. As Hero Hogan tries to escape, Cronin is accidentally shot dead, like the 'hostage' before him.

But if Behan's control of plot and shape declined with time and drink, his humour became more pointed. *Richard's Cork Leg* is packed with mischievous, teasing and sometimes subversive lines, often put into the mouths of the ignorantly

assertive and aimed at patriotism, factionalism, religious
bigotry, authority, class, anything that leads people to
strike attitudes the author finds pretentious or intolerant.
'Other people have a nationality,' we're told, 'the Irish and
the Jews have a psychosis.' The Blessed Evelyn Waugh
'was a young girl that wouldn't marry Henry the Eighth
because he turned Protestant'. According to one devoutly
Catholic prostitute, a convert is when a Protestant becomes
a Catholic, a pervert when a Catholic becomes a Protestant.
According to the ultra-Protestant Mrs Mallarkey, hers 'is
a Christian house, and we don't want Roman Catholics
here'. The Holy Family were not poor, this status-conscious
woman later insists. 'They had a little carpenter's shop,
and they probably did a bit in the hardware line as well,
like father.'

Behan's verbal play could be sharp: his thinking was
often soft-centred. Most of the time, he scarcely acknowledges the existence of suffering, still less of extinction. The
corpses at the end of *The Hostage* and *Richard's Cork Leg* both
return to life and join the rest of the cast in a sardonic,
death-defying chorus. Behan's basic philosophy was one of
live and let live, preferably with a glass in the hand and a
bawdy or blasphemous toast on the lips. 'Pity is my vice
and my downfall,' declares Cronin in as near to a
summing-up as the plays give us. 'I pity every sort and size
of sinner, even the ones who don't fall into any officially
approved category of pityees. I've become one myself. I
stand by the damned anywhere – if they are people put out
of heaven, put me out with them.' Even at the cost of going
to hell? asks someone. 'Sure,' comes the reply. 'It can't be
much worse than Liverpool prison.' A thought that brings
us, logically enough, to *The Quare Fellow*.

The Quare Fellow

The Quare Fellow is the least self-indulgent, the most tense
and pointed of Behan's plays, thanks partly to Joan Littlewood's tightening of the original text during rehearsals,

partly to its sobering subject. As in *The Hostage*, the action
consists of a period of waiting, but this time for an event
whose grim certainty casts a shadow across the whole play.
The place is an Irish prison, and tomorrow morning a man
is to be hanged.

There is little of the music-hall extravagance of the later
plays. Even a scene in which an old lag surreptitiously sips
the meths a warder is rubbing into his rheumatic leg has
a documentary purpose. Everywhere, Behan chronicles the
atmosphere of a prison as accurately as he can, so that we
can have no excuse for disbelieving what he tells us about
capital punishment. He has been there himself, and he
knows. He knows about the early-morning rituals, the obsession with cigarettes, the body searches, the use of
water-pipes for the passing of messages, the dislike of sexual
offenders, the exchange of professional information about
locks and explosives, the terrible boredom. And he introduces us to a reasonably representative spread of inmates:
from the 'hard case' known only as Prisoner A to the
wayward old alcoholics, Dunlavin and Neighbour; from
'Silver Top', who attempts to hang himself shortly after
being reprieved from the gallows, to Prisoner D, an em-
bezzler apt to intone self-importantly against any unorthodoxy or inefficiency in the prison regime.

But the conversation, entertaining in itself and illuminating about prison life though it often is, never ventures
too far or long from the main subject of interest, the approaching hanging. The prisoners vividly imagine the condemned man's last night on earth, and speculate about
whether death is instantaneous: 'Who's to know what happens in the hour your man is swinging there, maybe wrig-
gling to himself in the pit.' For them it is an excuse for
lurid, but not always uninformed gossip. Neighbour, for
instance, remembers once seeing the black face and fearful
rabbit-eyes of a hanged victim. And plenty of information
comes from more authoritative sources.

We hear this mainly in the second and third acts, which
move us from the prison interior into its yard, where a

half-dug grave awaits completion – a constant visual reminder of the execution ahead. We hear of the importance
of assessing a victim's weight correctly. A slip either way,
and he will slowly strangle or his head will snap clean off.
Apparently, there have been times when the warders have
had to jump on his back or swing on his legs, the better to
break his neck. Indeed, we actually meet 'himself', as everyone calls the convivial, rather vulgar publican brought from
England to perform the hanging. We see him slip off disguised in a warder's cap to look at the 'quare fellow', as
everyone calls his victim, and then hear him making his
calculations. We also meet the chief warder, who worries
in case the condemned man sees his grave, and the prison
governor, who checks that he is to get a good last breakfast.
And off the warders go to the death-cell for the final stint,
carefully removing their wrist-watches and reminding each
other of official instructions, according to which 'an air of
cheerful decorum is indicated, as is a readiness to play such
games as draughts, ludo, or snakes and ladders'.

The impression we are gradually given is of a macabre
ritual, somehow made worse by everybody's attempts to
carry it out with a humane efficiency: an ugly happening
that means 'a bad night', not only for the victim, but for
those entrusted with dispatching him, men we feel to be as
trapped by their situation as any prisoner. Yet virtually
everyone takes the inevitability of it all absolutely for
granted. Indeed, the only character in the play who appears
to have a principled objection to capital punishment is one
of the warders who is to sit up with the 'quare fellow'. He
has, he says, seen rather a lot of 'neck breaking and throt-
tling', and 'they say familiarity breeds contempt'.

His name is Regan, and he is certainly a most original
creation: a warder in whose compassionate view all men
are sinners and some of the executioners 'bigger bloody
ruffians' than their victims. He is notorious among his
colleagues – represented mainly by an ambitious, hypocritical and vindictive officer named Donelly – for asking mur-

derers to pray for him. If Behan has a mouthpiece in the play, this is him. Not only does he express a well-informed disgust: he also makes the important point that capital punishment cannot exist without the consent of taxpayers and voters. They, not the hangman, are truly responsible. Perhaps the 'whole show' should be presented in a public park, so they should know precisely what they are getting for their money.

This last suggestion was, of course, Behan's challenge to his audiences at a time when capital punishment still existed both in Britain and Eire. How could they tolerate what was being done in their names? This is the question the play asks, though not in any overt or hectoring way. True, Behan cannot altogether avoid accusations of weighting his scales. It is arguable that, by making a senior officer his main opponent of hanging, he has tilted the debate unfairly in favour of the abolitionists. On the other hand, this character, like everyone and everything in the play, seems perfectly plausible. We feel we are confronted with authentic people, experiences and reactions, adding up to serious evidence. And Behan never attempts to manipulate our sympathies by showing us the pathetic plight of the 'quare fellow' himself. On the contrary, he keeps him off-stage throughout, and even emphasizes that his was a particularly horrible crime, the dismemberment of his own brother. If judicial strangulation is deserved, such a one would deserve it. But is it ever deserved?

The play is serious, but not exactly sombre. There is more than enough humour in Behan's observation to justify his claim to have written a 'comedy-drama'. This has two main effects. One is to emphasize his detachment, his distance from his material, thus paradoxically strengthening its persuasiveness. Even the fateful trip from condemned cell to gallows is described in the coolest possible way, with a prisoner providing a breezy commentary from his window, as if it was a horse-race. Where Behan might have wallowed in the horror of the event, he sardonically understates it. Here, we feel, is a man who is deliberately refusing to whip up our feelings of indignation. Here, consequently, is a man to trust.

The other effect of the humour is to emphasize that, in spite of everything, life goes on and, in spite of everything, is of value. A man may be done to death, and anonymously buried under a headstone with the wrong number on it. This may be a depressing and disturbing experience for everyone. Yet the warders will continue to talk about promotion, the young convicts about women, the older ones about food and drink. The two ancient alcoholics, who should by now be dulled by imprisonment, are still capable of outwitting the warders, playing practical jokes on a fellow-prisoner, and taking bets on whether or not the 'quare fellow' will get a last-minute reprieve. And at the moment of execution all the prisoners howl from their cells in ferocious protest. The human spirit survives, resilient and defiant, even in the house of death: *The Quare Fellow*, from whatever angle one regards it, is Behan's affirmation of life.

John Osborne
(born 1929)

John Osborne has said his aim is to give 'lessons in feeling', meaning in love, friendship, hate, outrage and, perhaps, despair. In his work these commodities are normally represented by one dominant character in conflict with apathy, triviality, stupidity, cupidity or some other manifestation of an uncaring society. His are the plays of an instinctive and sometimes irrational rebel: of the adolescent expelled from school for striking a headmaster who objected to his mockery of the Royal Family; of the 'angry young man' who, soon after the success of *Look Back in Anger*, achieved notoriety with an epistle called *Damn you, England* ('You're rotting now – quite soon you'll disappear'); of the tetchy reactionary into whom Osborne has perversely transformed himself in recent years. The complaints and targets have changed, but the essential message has remained consistent. Be true to yourself; respond, feel, or die.

Emotional death threatens Archie Rice, the failed comedian who gives *The Entertainer* (1957) its title, and actually overtakes the hero of *Epitaph to George Dillon*, written in collaboration with Anthony Creighton in the early 1950s and first performed in 1958. This is a callow piece, but of obvious interest to the student of Osborne. He had been born in London in 1929, son of a commercial artist who died prematurely, and brought up by his mother, who herself came from a boisterous, quarrelsome clan of publicans; he had worked on a trade paper as a journalist, taught school, become an actor; he had made the first of his five marriages; and, not surprisingly, his first play expresses the insecurity and exasperation of a young man who expects society to reject, or, worse, pervert his talent. The protagonist, a slyer, more cowardly version of Jimmy Porter, is absorbed into the dim-witted lower-middle-class family off which he has been battening, and buys commercial success by vulgarizing the plays he's written. Those who dislike Osborne's later work will see warning-signs in his uncritical faith in the priggish George's emotional superiority and in the scorn with which he dismisses as mediocre 'caricatures' characters a better dramatist might have attempted to explore. But even they must concede that *Dillon* introduced a fresh talent into a mainly moribund theatre: articulate, restless, irreverent, dissatisfied, a natural misfit in terms of class, family, culture and society itself.

It was *Look Back in Anger*, however, which established Osborne's reputation, and *The Entertainer*, with Laurence Olivier in the lead, which consolidated it. All his plays are to some extent reflections or reports on the state and prospects of an England that continues to excite his infuriated love, but this more specifically than most. Archie's mock-patriotic songs, his advice to audiences not to clap too loud ('it's a very old building'), and the nude Britannia in the background, all indicate that the decline of the music-hall is to be identified with a national decline. At the same time, Archie himself is a character of some resonance, a posturing philanderer and emotional derelict who nevertheless has the honesty to recognize his dishonesty and face his loss of self-respect. But warning-signs are to be found here, too: the sentimentality of the climax at which Archie laments his son, killed by Cypriot terrorists, in the style of a black blues-singer who once moved him; the nostalgia implicit in the play's affection for Archie's father, a gentlemanly left-over from vaudeville's better days. Increasingly, Osborne's disenchantment with the present was to lead him to romanticize a vaguely conceived past.

There were still more ill-omens in the musical, *The World of Paul Slickey* (1959), Osborne's first commercial failure. Artistically, it was undisciplined; and the laboriousness of its attack on yellow journalism and the aristocracy suggested that, while Osborne might be the master of invective, his talent was ill-suited to satire or parody. Roughly the same point may be made about both *The Blood of the Bambergs* (1962), whose mockery of idolatry of the Royal Family lacks wit, and whose story tails ineffectively away, and the much later *End of Me Old Cigar* (1975), which is set in a brothel catering for the rich, successful and crass, and dwindles into sentimentality when a girl and her client outrage the militant feminists in charge by falling in love. Osborne's dramatic strength does not consist in constructing and sustaining plausible and dynamic plots, especially plots involving the interaction of several people. Even the well-received *Under Plain Cover* (1962), about a couple who maintain an affectionate relationship by sadomasochistic and fetishistic games, collapses with the introduction of a prying journalist and the unnecessarily sensational revelation that the married pair are really brother and sister. No, he is at his most confident when one character dominates the proceedings and shapes the play, as in *Look Back in Anger*, *Inadmissible Evidence* and *Luther*.

Luther (1961) tackles a subject that demands a more psychologically and spiritually trenchant dramatist than

Osborne; but it is an energetic and far from crude picture of a rebel in conflict with his father, his God, his own anguished mind and intransigent body, and the corruption, smugness and superficiality of his world. Clearly, we are meant to see parallels with the decadence of our own society, as we are in *A Patriot for Me* (1965). That play's critics have complained that Osborne pays insufficient attention to its main character, Redl, the bourgeois officer who rises to importance and trust in the Austro-Hungarian army, fights a losing battle with his sexual inversion, allows himself to be blackmailed by the Russians, and, after his exposure and suicide, leaves the imperial nabobs even more determined to rely on their own caste and class; but, reticent though he is by Osborne's rhetorical standards, his character is well observed and his appalling loneliness treated with sensitivity and sympathy. The play demonstrates the ambivalence – one that can veer from contempt to respect in the course of an evening – of Osborne's attitude towards homosexuality, a recurring interest in his work.

Apart from *Very Like a Whale* (1970), a television play about an industrialist in a state of depressive collapse somewhat akin to Maitland's in *Inadmissible Evidence*, he has written little worth remembering since *Patriot*. His adaptation of Lope de Vega, *A Bond Honoured* (1966), presented the Osborne rebel at his most melodramatic, raping and murdering his mother, repeatedly raping the sister who turns out to be his daughter, blinding his father, renouncing the God of his forefathers, and finally accepting his own destruction as the logic of his embittered, defiant life; *A Place Calling Itself Rome* (1973), a clumsily updated *Coriolanus* that tells us little more about our own class-riven society than Shakespeare's original, is still awaiting its first production; and *Time Present* (1968) and *The Hotel in Amsterdam* (1968) must have strained the faith of many who felt, with Ronald Bryden, that in *Look Back in Anger* and *Inadmissible Evidence* Osborne had been 'the voice of our generation'.

The turning-point may have been Maitland's long, big-oted denunciation of his daughter for the crime of being young and Osborne's failure to allow her one word in rebuttal. Increasingly, his plays have become thinly disguised excuses for him to mount indiscriminate attacks on targets both large and small, none of which is permitted to defend itself. Pamela, the actress-heroine of *Time Present*, admittedly has a generosity which counteracts what would otherwise be unrelieved bitchiness and gives her some substance as a character; but her identity is mainly rhetorical, her function to be a combination of obituary and scathing editorial. For her father, an old-school actor dying offstage, she has a nostalgic regard; for the world around her, little but distaste. Her verbal hit-list becomes an encyclopedia of the 1960s: hippies, drugs, 'trendy' clothes, boutiques, underground papers and bookshops, women writers, women politicians, the Labour Party, the nation's technological pretensions, 'committed' actresses, American drama, Americans, 'faggots' and 'pooves', and the critics, with their 'frigid little minds'. The duty of the other members of the cast is either to listen admiringly or by their very existence to justify her complaints.

The Hotel in Amsterdam is less easily accused of being a vicarious ego trip, because the character most likely to dominate the evening, a voracious film director, is kept offstage. In fact, he commits suicide back in England while his associates spend the weekend escaping him in Holland. The result is, it seems, supposed to be a celebration of friendship in action: the trouble, apart from inadequacies of plot, is that one character, a scriptwriter with some of Osborne's characteristic wit and several of the familiar prejudices, still thrusts himself to the fore, and everyone else has astonishingly little solidity or life. Again, they listen while he holds forth: the archetypal Osborne situation, but one of diminishing interest when the speaker has nothing fresh or provocative to say.

Back in 1958 Osborne announced his intention of asking questions about ordinary people's lives:

What are the things that are important to them, that make
them care, give them hope and anxiety? What kind of
language do they use to one another? What is the meaning of
the work they do? Where does the pain lie? What are their
expectations? What moves them, brings them together, makes
them speak out? Where is the weakness, the loneliness?
Where are the things that are unrealized? Where is the
strength?

As several critics have pointed out, these are precisely the
questions he does not ask. He displays no sympathy for
any but a gifted, or supposedly gifted, minority of characters; he doesn't seem to see drama in terms of search or
discovery. He came nearer to prophesying the course of his
work when, in the same manifesto, he promised to 'fling
down a few statements – you can take your pick' and
indicated that those statements would be 'sweeping'. Indeed, his recent 'lessons in feeling' demonstrate what happens when 'feeling' loses contact with an observing eye and
an appraising intellect, and increasingly becomes yearning
for a golden yesteryear. Osborne seems to have meant it
when he declared that 'one prejudice is worth twenty principles', and also that he would like 'to see the whole hideous, headlong rush into the twentieth century halted a
bit'. On the brink of the twenty-first century that sounds
dangerously close to opting out of reality altogether.

Certainly, it is hard to see what *A Sense of Detachment*
(1972) – at once a desultory satire on *avant-garde* theatre
and an exploitation of its techniques – proves by juxtapos-
ing snippets of Shakespeare, Yeats and other poets with
extracts from modern pornography. That our generation
uniquely lacks the capacity for love? This idea comes to the
surface when a character goes on to denounce technical
innovation, industrial progress and economic union:
'People don't fall in love: that idea is no longer effective in
the context of modern techniques.' The interesting questions, of course, are why people need pornography and
whether and how the Common Market will subtract more

than it adds; but Osborne's characters are not there to investigate or debate, rather to buttonhole and pronounce.

What makes this more irritating is his tendency to divide the world into Us, who for all our faults safeguard honest feeling and honourable values, and Them, the enemies of such things. This is so in *West of Suez* (1971), at the end of which an eminent writer, centre of a group of expatriates representing post-colonial England, is first harangued by an American yippie who conveniently incarnates much that Osborne finds mindlessly destructive in the young, and is then killed by rampaging blacks. 'They've shot the fox,' intones someone over his body, implying, with scant justification, that all that is cultivated and decent has been desecrated. The tendency is even more marked in *Watch It Come Down* (1976), at the end of which a commune of writers and artists is violently attacked by country 'yobbos'. 'We all, *the few of us*, need one another,' wails a wife to her dying husband. The italics are Osborne's; but nothing he has shown, as opposed to stated, proves that this is a cultural élite worth preserving or that those outside are as philistine as we are meant to believe.

His recent work represents the triumph of vague feeling over hard thought, impression over fact, notions over ideas, paranoia over anger, prejudice over conviction, and perhaps clutter over art. To this list *Watch It Come Down* adds the triumph of an often precious and sentimental diction over the blistering rhetoric that was once Osborne's trade-mark. Meanwhile, the man himself has transformed his public image from that of social critic, crusader for a world at once more caring and responsive to the individual, to that of an aggressive eccentric, working off his petulance on frankly minor issues: hence his British Playwrights Mafia, an organization supposedly dedicated to harassing theatre critics, and his suggestion that it's a patriotic duty to misdirect the foreign tourists allegedly cluttering the London streets. It is sad, because the same mind once diagnosed our fears and furies, expressed our despair, and changed the British theatre. But, whatever the future does or doesn't hold for him, Osborne has at least written one play of historical importance, another of excellence, and two or three others worth rediscovering. Very few playwrights can claim as much.

Look Back In Anger

The historically important play was, of course, *Look Back in Anger*. Indeed, its arrival in London in May 1956 is still generally regarded as the point at which the theatrical climate began to change into one in which serious, provocative and socially broader drama could at last expect to flourish. In Jimmy Porter's rasping rhetoric the voice of a new class and generation made itself heard on an English stage that was, as Arthur Miller had complained, often 'hermetically sealed off from reality'; and many shared the feeling of liberation. Kenneth Tynan, its most enthusiastic reviewer, doubted he could love anyone who did not wish to see the play; John Arden remarked that it supplied 'passion and contemporary relevance' at a time when their absence was no longer even noticed; and Tom Stoppard has said that it was the excitement it generated that made him first think of writing drama.

If it is looked at dispassionately, as a play rather than an event, the claims made for *Look Back in Anger* may now seem as surprising as those made a century earlier for T. W. Robertson's *Caste*. Technically it is, as Osborne himself concedes, a 'formal, rather old-fashioned' piece, and the plot involves the hoariest of subjects, a misalliance and the eternal triangle. The upper-middle-class Alison shares an uncomfortable room and an even more uncomfortable marriage with Jimmy Porter, who comes mainly 'from working people'. Alison's friend, the actress Helena Charles, persuades her to leave Jimmy, only to fall into his arms and bed herself. Alison has a miscarriage, and returns to Jimmy, whom Helena nobly renounces. Osborne's debt to the tradition of the 'well-made play' is everywhere to be seen. It is there in the convenient coincidence, an appointment about a job, that allows Helena to remain in the same house as the man whose wife she has just helped to sneak away, and there in the calculated curtains that end several scenes: Helena strikes Jimmy, sees the anguish in his face, passionately kisses him; Alison unexpectedly returns and Jimmy exits, snapping 'friend of yours' to Helena; and, last of all, there's a reconciliation that even Tynan found marked by 'painful whimsy'.

Moreover, the supporting characters lack life, as often in Osborne. Helena's inconsistencies may be explained as those of a basically conventional girl briefly seduced by an unfamiliar passion; but some of her lines verge on cliché ('When I saw you stand there tonight, I knew that it was all utterly wrong') and she herself often seems to be the more-or-less mechanical agent of a predetermined plot. Again, the Porters' friend and neighbour, Cliff, is little more than that useful and traditional figure, the confidant. It could be argued that by his amiability and resignation he balances Jimmy's bile. Rightly or wrongly, not all those low in the social hierarchy feel at odds with the world. But such a point would be stronger if he were more enterprisingly individualized.

Curiously enough, Alison's father does more in his brief appearance to interest us and deepen the play. Colonel Redfern is, in Jimmy's not-unsympathetic words, 'a sturdy old plant left over from the Edwardian wilderness that can't understand why the sun isn't shining any more'; but he has the honesty to admit as much himself, the decency to concede that he and his wife were to blame for trying to prevent his daughter's marriage. Cumulatively, he gives the impression of being what the stage directions claim, an 'essentially gentle, kindly man'. Osborne's respect for him may be seen as an early example of his nostalgia for a simpler, more orderly yesteryear. The generosity of the characterization does, however, also add a dimension to a play always in danger of being overwhelmed by its main character. Indeed we may feel that Redfern, though perhaps for better reasons, is hardly less the victim of a hard, uncaring society than Jimmy.

And what of the daughter he comes to fetch home? Alison has displayed will and determination in the past, notably by marrying an 'unsuitable' man in spite (indeed, because) of her family's active opposition; but there is little of that to be seen now in a woman who seems mainly to want peace, quiet, a cessation of marital hostilities. Yet before we criticize Osborne for creating a dull, passive character, we should note that passivity is with her almost a positive quality, unresponsiveness the weapon with which she resists and fights Jimmy. She concedes as much when she recalls pretending not to listen, 'because I knew that would hurt him'. It would have been easy, she adds, to have said 'Yes, darling, I know what you're feeling'; but she didn't do so, partly because of an undemonstrative temperament, partly because she knows it is her strength. In fact, she is more observant and acute than she lets Jimmy recognize: witness her tart comment when Helena accuses him of having a chip on his shoulder, 'Don't try and take his suffering away from him – he'd be lost without it.' She is also less conventional than Jimmy supposes or Helena is: witness her willingness to abandon 'the book of rules' and, so far from blaming her best friend for stealing her husband, to surrender him to her.

Jimmy, too, seems to have married for somewhat romantic reasons, in his case a combination of love, chivalry and revenge. He was the dilapidated anti-hero on the off-white charger who liberated the fair maiden from her privileged prison, only to find that she would or could not give him whatever it was he wanted. Again and again, he insists on the virtues of feeling, caring, responding: 'Oh heavens, how I long for a little ordinary enthusiasm.' His objection to institutionalized religion, the reason he regards Helena's and Alison's churchgoing as treachery, seems to be that it is against 'passion and kindliness'. Cliff has 'a big heart – you can forgive somebody almost anything for that'. His one-time mistress, Madeline, excelled in 'animation . . . the delight of being awake and watching'. The only friend of Alison he likes, Webster, has 'guts and sensitivity'. When he showed Alison's photo to the mother of his own best friend, Hugh, her lachrymose joy was 'pure gold'. And, conversely, what most enrages him is emotional sterility, and more specifically the failure to react to him. His case against Alison is that she is a 'monument to non-attachment'. He would rather wage a sentient war than endure a moribund peace.

In his diagnosis of this troubled marriage, this collision of apparent opposites, Osborne by no means sides wholly with Jimmy. The first stage directions are substantially critical: 'He is a disconcerting mixture of sincerity and cheerful malice, of tenderness and freebooting cruelty; restless, importunate, full of pride . . . To be as vehement as he is is to be almost non-committal.' Certainly, there is felt to be importunacy and pride in his insistence on the primacy of emotion. 'He thinks,' says Alison, 'he's got a sort of genius for love and friendship'; and yet he actually makes 'few friends'. He tends to believe that only he has the capacity for strong and honest feeling; and that, too, is demonstrably false. 'What I endured to get you out!' he wails apropos Alison's family, apparently oblivious to what *she* endured then and afterwards. He will write a book about their life together, 'remembered in blood and fire: *my* blood'. Alison is 'devouring' him; he is the 'indigestible mess' in her 'tripes'. Soon there'll be 'nothing left of me'. 'Only *I* cared,' he declares characteristically, remembering his father's death. At times his self-absorption and self-importance seem tantamount to emotional fascism. Not to feel as he feels is to betray him: 'Either you're with me or against me.'

These emotional claims, Osborne suggests, are suspect in several respects. According to Cliff, it may be significant that Madeline was 'nearly old enough to be his mother', and according to Alison, Jimmy is 'like a child'. Perhaps the misogyny he displays, the fear that women will 'bleed

him to death', reflects his own sexual and emotional im-
maturity, itself an explanation for his ailing marriage.
Again, his contention that pain is an inevitable concomitant
of being fully alive comes across partly as an excuse for
enthusiastically inflicting it himself. He likes to believe he's
conducting a conscientious crusade to increase the world's
supply of emotional energy: in fact, there's gratuitous
cruelty in his attacks on Alison's mother ('My God, the
worms will need a good dose of salts the day they get
through her!') and, of course, on Alison herself. If only she
could have a child die, 'if only I could watch you face that!'
Even so, adds Jimmy, he doubts if she'd become 'a recognizable human being'. And yet the sadist is capable of
tenderness, too. When Alison *does* lose her child, and
actually 'grovels' in the way he wanted, he doesn't splash
and sing in her tears, as he'd promised. Instead, he cradles
and gently soothes her.

Add a gift for withering and sometimes witty invective,
and we've a character of some complexity, and certainly a
much more interesting one than in other triangle-dramas
of the day. But that does not, of course, explain Jimmy's
special significance for the younger generation of 1956. A
war had been won, the beginnings of a welfare state established, some redistribution of wealth and eradication of
privilege attempted, equality of opportunity for all promised. Then, in 1951, Labour had been defeated, and the
Conservatives elected to office. A few months after the
opening of *Look Back in Anger* their leader was to plunge the
nation into an imperialist débâcle at Suez. Britain was
supposed to have changed, and yet it remained madden-
ingly the same. People like Alison's brother Nigel, the
bowler-hatted 'platitude from outer space', were still in
Parliament. According to Jimmy's newspaper, bishops
could still proclaim it a Christian duty to help make H-
bombs and describe class distinction as a lie 'wickedly
fostered by the working classes'. According to Jimmy himself, reason and progress were selling out, and the old
traditions, the old beliefs rising in the stock market. The

'old gang' still had most of the money and the power, and was ready to close ranks against intruders, especially one like Jimmy, a social upstart educated not at Oxbridge, nor even at 'redbrick', but at a university he himself wryly calls 'white-tile'.

The play does not explain Jimmy's frustration and anger primarily in terms of social alienation. There is no doubt something in his temperament that has made him a drifter, who has tried job after job and is now squandering his talent and education on a sweet stall in a Midlands town. There is also something in Alison's temperament, as there might be in many women of lowlier origins, designed to exacerbate his frustration and anger. To some extent, the play involves individuals and relationships that might exist in any clime or time. And yet Alison's sang-froid and Jimmy's indignation are also the result of, respectively, social conditioning and a sense of social grievance. The world outside the room into which they have retreated does indeed seem unfriendly, both to their relationship and to Jimmy's almost religious belief in emotional self-expression. Certainly, there's no obvious place for him in the fabric of a stagnant, inert society.

But does it follow, as he suggests, that there are no 'good, brave causes left' for him to fight? This is the play's most quoted sentiment, and also its most misused. First, it needs to be seen in its context, which subordinates it to Jimmy's familiar paranoia about women and the difficulty of avoiding being 'butchered' by them. Second, it clearly isn't altogether true. What of Oxfam, CND, British colonialism, and the Russian oppression of Eastern Europe, soon to show its ugliest face in Hungary? Or if all that seemed too remote, what of the class privilege represented by Alison's family? No, the line reflects Jimmy's own inadequacies at least as much as Osborne's own beliefs. According to the latter, it is the sound of 'ordinary despair'. And yet its very fame suggests that it did also touch some more general nerve in the disaffected young of the day.

That was no less true of Jimmy as a whole. He was not

Osborne's political or social loud-hailer; and yet many of his comments on his environment seemed pertinent to those of his peers who, for one reason or another, shared his confusion, ennui, impotent rage, and defeatism. He was too individual to be the spokesman of any group; yet his very idiosyncrasy and oddity encouraged those who felt out of joint with the times to identify with him. He was, to extend Tynan's comparison, our local Hamlet, and left us thinking not only about his own contradictions of character but also about the nature of the Elsinore that had helped make him the puzzled, vindictive, defiant creature that he was: a psychological case-study with sociopolitical reverberations that have dated but by no means disappeared.

The criticism, often expressed in the early days, that Jimmy is not 'constructive', and does not seek or provide 'solutions', is surely misconceived, because it ignores the essential helplessness of his character. He will 'never do anything and never amount to anything' in the world; he has turned to personal relationships for fulfilment, and there made demands that have not been and perhaps cannot be satisfied; people seem to him to need him only on their deathbeds; he is, by his own admission, a 'lost cause', verbally energetic yet practically futile, a loudmouth howling in the dark. The play ends, as it must, with him and Alison finding what solace and sanctuary they can in the place of last resort, namely each other: huddling together for warmth like animals, in what Alison has called 'a silly symphony for people who couldn't bear the pain of being human beings any longer'. The game of bears and squirrels they ruefully play is now less sentimental and more ironic than perhaps it once was. They are both well aware of the failure it represents. They see their own absurdity. But what else can they do, where else go, how else cope?

Inadmissible Evidence

Inadmissible Evidence is commonly agreed to be the last play of incontrovertible merit Osborne wrote. Certainly, it is the last one in which he turned his limitations into a positive advantage. As often, one character dominates the stage. Everyone is unimportant – indeed, barely exists – except in his or her relationship to the solicitor, Bill Maitland. Again, this character spends much of his sustained monologue railing and complaining. Yet we do not feel, as we do in some of the later plays, that the protagonist is simply a cracked trumpet through which the dramatist is blazoning his own prejudices. In 1964, when the piece was first performed, Osborne still retained some sense of detachment, and Maitland is a character he saw with scathing clarity, in the round, from outside as well as inside. Indeed, *Inadmissible Evidence* may be seen as a carefully chronicled journey into the head of a man on the brink of mental, emotional and spiritual breakdown, an arena that naturally limits the reality of the supporting characters. It is an objective picture of a subjective experience.

This reading is reinforced by the stage directions, several of which suggest that the play is about a man who progressively loses touch with the world outside. We are told that a 'feeling of dream and unreality' grows stronger during the second of the two acts, so much so that we cannot always be sure there's a listener at the other end of the telephone into which Maitland obsessively talks; and the first act begins in the very centre of his troubled mind, with an authentic, unambiguous nightmare. The solicitor is in a lawcourt, accused of having published an obscenity, namely his life. Prodded by the judge, who is his managing clerk, Hudson, and grimly watched by his junior clerk, Jones, Maitland flounders and rambles. We gather he's a heavy drinker, a hypochondriac, forever dosing himself with pills; a self-made man, envious of those with more social advantages than himself; self-disgusted, to the extent that he feels 'irredeemably mediocre' and wonders if he's ever made a decision that wasn't shabby or wrong; capable of sympathy for his 'poor, bloody, agonized' clients; overdependent on others; friendless, and, though not loveless, inclined to think he has inflicted more pain than pleasure in love. And the litany of self-accusation rises to a tormented climax: 'I can't escape it, I can't forget it, and I can't begin again.'

Already, the character is becoming an archetype of middle-aged ennui: what more can Osborne do, how can he build a play out of him? Well, Maitland's principal fear, even greater than his fear of internal disintegration, is his fear of the rejection that his behaviour tends to court. He betrays his wife, offends her friends, seduces the office girls and then drops them, insults his daughter, bends his mistress's ear with a torrent of self-doubt and self-pity, and gives every indication both to his subordinates and to his clients that he is losing control of himself and his business. And, inevitably enough, there is a mass exodus from his life. People *do* reject him, a process that allows Osborne to fill out his character and to shape and pattern a plot.

At first, the fear of rejection sounds like paranoia. The taxis, Maitland says, won't stop for him. The caretaker at his apartment house has snubbed him. But before long people are giving more serious signs that, as far as they're concerned, he is ceasing to exist. His secretary, proclaiming herself 'sick at the sight' of her ex-lover, slams off in tears. The barrister he principally provides with work won't speak to him on the phone, nor will his managing clerk. The long-suffering Hudson, offered a partnership by the now desperate Maitland, leaves for a rival firm. Clients abandon him. His daughter, denounced for being a member of the younger generation he simultaneously hates, fears and envies, walks out without saying a word to him. His latest conquest, a sexy telephonist, announces 'I don't like you either' and, in what's been justly criticized as the least motivated instance of rejection, leaves the office, presumably for good. Finally, his longer-term mistress, Liz, makes it apparent that she, too, has had enough. Left alone, Bill swallows yet another pill and phones his wife, telling her he sees no point in coming home. He will sit in his empty office and wait until he's found by someone, most probably by an official of the Law Society, which has been investigating his dubious professional ethics.

At the end, then, he is rejected and ruined and (it seems) past resisting. He has accepted his guilt of the moral charges thrown at him in his dream, and is resigned to his own dissolution. Why did it happen? What was there in him to bring about such a fate? When the play was new, critics drew special attention to his alienation from the Britain of the 1960s. He was an over-age Jimmy Porter, sickened by the power of science and sociology, by the computers that will make even lawyers redundant, by all-concrete redevelopment schemes, by the politician who 'turns us out into a lot of little technology dogs turning his wheelspit of endless bloody consumption and production', and by a new generation he sees as 'all cool, dreamy, young, cool, and not a proper blemish, forthright, unimpressed, contemptuous of ambition but good and . pushy all the same'. These and other targets Maitland attacks with articulate scorn, to some extent creating the impression of a man, like Porter, born out of his time.

But note that most of his pet hates have a common denominator, whether they are inanimate or, like Jones, the go-getting 'child of the jet age', animate. They are cold, soulless, lacking in humanity. And here is the answer to those who find Maitland's aspirations vague as well as his motivation obscure. He is almost childlike in his need for others, in his desperation to keep talking, keep communicating, if not in person then through the telephone. Bluntly, he craves love. He has maudlin visions of himself with his daughter: going out to dinner, and looking at each other 'with such, such oh, pleasure – we'd hardly be able to eat'. Liz, he 'loved more than anyone'. Yet there is something in his personality which makes it inevitable that they will hurt him and he them. When love is offered him, he is doomed to find it unsatisfying and seek to destroy it.

And he seems to know it. For all his alcohol-induced bleariness, he is clear-sighted and self-aware. He recognizes his weakness, accuses himself before others accuse him, and sees reflections of his predicament in the husbands of the women who visit him as clients, seeking divorces: the one who is being rejected by everyone, including his girlfriends; the one with the allegedly excessive sexual appetite; the one who shuts himself up in his room and weeps. There is even a parallel between him and his one male client, Maples, who has been accused of a homosexual offence. He, too, is a misfit, an unhappy outsider, self-destructive and about to be ruined. The stage directions insist that this last character be performed by the actor playing Jones, though the reasons for this are not clear. It is easier to explain why all three female visitors are to be performed by the same actress. To Maitland, who sinks into self-absorbed reverie when they recite their married histories, all the faces are beginning to look alike, all the miseries to sound alike. More importantly, they all remind him of his own failure in marriage. We can speculate that the character they resemble is actually his own wife, Anne, who never appears in the play.

After the first production, high claims were made for the play. It was, suggested Ronald Bryden, a modern tragedy – 'Osborne has gathered our English terrors in Maitland's image, and purged them pitiably and terribly.' These claims were repeated fourteen years later when the play was revived in London, but this time with a shift of emphasis. The play, it now appeared, was not so specifically about the generation that was hitting forty in 1964 and felt increasingly alienated from its society. It was not, or not mainly, a social tragedy. It was less particular and yet more intimate than that. If it was a tragedy at all, it was a personal tragedy: the tragedy of a man whose fatal flaw was the inability to sustain or receive the love that to him was nevertheless the highest good. And if so, it is of all Osborne's plays the one most likely to last.

Arnold Wesker

(born 1932)

Arnold Wesker, like Pinter, was born in the East End of London in the 1930s and, like Pinter, was the son of an immigrant Jewish tailor. There the similarities stop, because Pinter is the least politically involved of contemporary dramatists and Wesker one of the most. The fulfilled and virtuous life his characters are so often striving to achieve cannot, in his view, be a private and reclusive one; and the one play of his which exclusively concerns a personal relationship, *The Four Seasons* (1965), is arguably his most disillusioned and disillusioning. Man was not meant for woman alone.

Wesker has drawn more directly than most dramatists on his experience. His mother was a communist, like Sarah in *Chicken Soup with Barley* (1958). His sister and brother withdrew from London to Norfolk, like the protagonists of *I'm Talking About Jerusalem* (1960), and he himself married a Norfolk girl who, like Beatie in *Roots* (1959), had been a waitress in a hotel. His national service, like that of the recruits in *Chips with Everything* (1962), was spent in the RAF and, afterwards, he became a professional pastry-cook, like Ronnie in *Chicken Soup*. And his first play, written in 1957, when he was twenty-five, and finally performed in 1959, actually evokes a typical day in the life of a number of overworked chefs, waitresses and kitchen porters.

The Kitchen, as it's called, makes a good introduction to Wesker. Here's the vivid documentary quality of which he was sometimes to prove himself capable, notably in *Chips*. But here, too, is a determination to be 'significant', and significant about matters of size and moment. 'This stinking kitchen,' says a porter in a meditative interlude between the frantic activity of the first and second acts, 'is like the world. It's too fast to know what happens. People come and go, big excitement, big noise. What for? In the end who do you know?' And here's the first evidence of Wesker's much-criticized didacticism, his habit of making the implicit explicit, his eagerness to permit general issues to be openly debated. The kitchen, filled as it is with babbling, wrangling people of various nations, is a microcosm of Western industrial society. It is a place of brief, loveless attachments, of hard, unfulfilling work done by the many for the benefit of the few, and of vague, hopeless dreams of escape. 'He works, he eats, I give him money,' cries the restaurant proprietor after a cook has run amok with an axe and smashed the gas lead. 'That is life, isn't it? What more do you want? What is there more?' The point (of course) is that there could indeed be much more. So the final stage direction states, so the play tends to demonstrate, so the rest of Wesker's work was to reiterate.

More – but precisely what, and how is it to be achieved? Wesker's most complete discussion of the question is, as we'll see, his celebrated 'trilogy'; but his susbsequent plays all have some bearing on it. All confront the possible with the actual, the ideal with reality. Man seeks to soar, only to be grounded by pressures outside and limitations within. Even in *Chips with Everything*, the play in which Wesker most successfully controls his urge to leap precipitously from the specific and implicit to the general and overt, the conflict is perfectly apparent.

The basic training of a group of RAF recruits, carefully and often humorously recorded, becomes a study of the way the English élite absorbs rebellious instincts and deflects revolutionary ones. An upper-class boy, Pip, cannot sustain his revolt against the hierarchy. Partly this is because his motivation is suspect – he is sublimating his hatred of his father, he enjoys exercising power over the 'yobs' with whom he has identified and whom he basically despises. Partly it is because his comrades have been, and still are being, intimidated and crushed by a slippery but ruthless establishment. Pip admits defeat, and himself becomes an officer. It is a deliberately glum conclusion, but we're still meant to leave the play feeling that there are untapped qualities in the serf classes: one boy suddenly begs for education, knowledge, sacrosanct qualities in Wesker's world; he and others demonstrate an angry solidarity when one of their number is persecuted; invited by a contemptuous wing commander to perform 'a dirty recitation or a pop song' at a Christmas party, a Scots recruit recites a poem by Burns and the rest join in an 'old peasant revolt song', 'The Cutty Wren', 'menacing the officers' with it. This last incident has been much criticized, as well it might be, since it is hardly the way twentieth-century British youth expresses its social indignation. Wesker's faith in the potential of the working classes can, as it suggests, lead him into wishful thinking. Reacting against the cynicism which sees ignorance and apathy as unalterable, he occasionally succumbs to sentimentality, and makes claims for human creativity which aren't plausible or temperate. But then temperance, discretion, restraint aren't virtues that greatly impress Wesker: which may be one reason why commonsensical critics sometimes find him exasperating.

The history of Wesker's Centre 42 may be revealing. Just how imaginative and ambitious this exercise in offering culture to the masses was to be may be seen from his essays, *Fears of Fragmentation*. Unluckily, the trades unions did not provide all the hoped-for support, the people remained largely unresponsive to the festivals that were experimentally mounted, and the movement's London centre, the Round House, fell so far short of Wesker's original vision that he eventually dissociated himself from it. Others might have compromised that vision, arguing that setbacks were to be expected and that, anyway, something was better than nothing. Wesker, characteristically, would not do so. Compromise, with cynicism, is perhaps the ugliest word in his vocabulary.

Their Very Own and Golden City (1965), which bears some of the scars left by Centre 42, makes this doubly clear. The architect Andrew Cobham hopes to build six model communities, planned, owned and run by the residents themselves. But trades union support is minimal, and Cobham is obliged to turn to a Tory government and private industry for help. One flawed and unsatisfactory city is built, and Cobham ends up a social success but a moral and spiritual failure, irredeemably contaminated by the compromise he once tried to resist. One seems meant to feel that it might have been better if, like Wesker, he had conserved his ideals by withdrawing from practical reality.

After this, Wesker's work, though still usually with a public dimension to it, does become more private in its emphases. There is one exception to this rule, and it is an impressive one: *The Wedding Feast* (1977), adapted from a story by Dostoevsky. The main character is the owner of a Norfolk shoe-factory whose rather ostentatious enlightenment and generosity to his employees doesn't prevent them humiliating him when they get the chance; and the conclusion is that gestures of reconciliation are not enough, and that genuine cooperation between management and worker can only come when genuine power is genuinely shared. Wesker himself regards it as a minor piece, 'very funny and intellectually undemanding'. In fact, it has qualities of dramatic tension, wit, mental rigour and (above all) contemporary relevance not often apparent in his recent work.

It is certainly not in the mainstream of his later development, the coming character of which is hinted at in *Their Very Own and Golden City*. Would people be happy and fulfilled, asks Wesker, even in a perfectly planned community? Andrew gives the honest if cynical answer: 'You can't leave misery behind, it comes with you.' Indeed, part of his general deterioration is the withering of his relationship with his wife, whom he comes increasingly to treat as a convenient housekeeper. It is one of Wesker's axioms that a man's personal life must have emotional substance before he can be publicly effective. It is, however, one of his fears that true personal fulfilment, like true public effectiveness, is a practical impossibility.

The Four Seasons, in so far as its two characters may be regarded as representative, suggests so. It is true that Wesker specifically says that they are not simply 'man and woman', and makes it clear that they bring to their year-old affair distinctive pasts, with distinctive failures. But what reduces them to wrangling and finally to an awful indifference is something almost archetypal: her instinctive possessiveness, his unwillingness to be possessed. Much of the emotional observation that precedes this (for Wesker) unusually pessimistic conclusion is penetrating, and one emotionally charged event, the making of an apple strudel, is a justly celebrated example of Wesker's joy in creative skill. There are, however, two main worries. When Beatrice declares that 'nothing should be held back, ever', she is, it seems, speaking for her author. According to the play, love is absolute giving, unerring mutuality, a constant ecstasy, or it is not properly love. It does not consist of the give-and-take, the ups and downs, the long-term hard work, that a less romantic writer might suppose. It is not surprising that Adam's and Beatrice's relationship does not survive so demanding a definition. Indeed, all its failure may prove is that, once again, Wesker's vision is too uncompromising for everyday life on an everyday planet.

The other trouble is language. Wesker often sounds unconvincing when he moves away from the Anglo-Jewish rhythms he handles so well; and his attempts to achieve a stylized lyricism here are not always successful. 'We'll paint ourselves a white temple. Do you hear that? A white temple, and I'll worship you in it' . . . 'I have a golden eagle for a lover' . . . 'I'm a flower, see me? See me opening, watch me, I'm blossoming.' Critics must always ask themselves if their resistance to Wesker's more high-flown moments doesn't come from unworthy traits, from emotional parsimony or mere embarrassment. But it is a sad truth that in real life people do not often find it as easy to feel or express uncomplicated, upbeat passions as his plays sometimes suggest. There is certainly something overblown here.

The Old Ones (1972) and the short *Love Letters on Blue Paper* (1977) are also substantially about private pain, but they both introduce a grim new factor into the ontological argument, namely death. It is possible to debate endlessly about the value and meaning of life, as the brothers Emanuel and Boomy do in the former play, one emphasizing all that is good and hopeful, rather as Wesker himself tends to do, the other all that is bad and disillusioning, like his more cynical antagonists. But what's the point of bothering when everything is soon coming to an end? *The Old Ones*, as this suggests, is one of Wesker's harsher plays, in some ways his harshest. Age brings loneliness, senility, and the awful feeling of having misused one's life. Youth tends to be stupid, apathetic and even violent, or well-intentioned, bewildered and helpless. The conclusion comes from Emanuel: 'If all action seems vain, must we cease all action?' In Wesker's view there is a positive virtue in carrying on the moral and spiritual fight even if defeat is all but inevitable. He has been accused of a naïve optimism: a brave and lonely defiance would sometimes be nearer the mark.

There is no need to dwell over the remaining plays. *Love Letters* is spoiled by a tendency to idealize the wise and cultivated trades-union leader who spends the action slowly dying; yet Wesker's handling of his wife, who can express her devotion only by writing to him through the post, is sensitive and touching. For once, he concedes that it is difficult for the English to communicate passion, and, having made that admission and established a living relationship, he is able to rise to an emotional climax both intense and true. On the other hand, *The Friends* (1970), about a group of designers coming to terms with their working-class origins and revaluing their cultural aspirations after the death of one of their number, hardly seems to justify the resounding claims recently made for it by Glenda Leeming and Simon Trussler in their helpful *Plays of Arnold Wesker*. It brings together several of Wesker's worst traits: affected language, sententiousness, a tendency to idealize without good reason, and to move prematurely from the specific to the general, discussing issues and even coming to conclusions on the basis of characters who have yet to be established as real. On the other hand, it does contain one speech always to be borne in mind by critics inclined to shrug off aspects of Wesker they dislike.

> I despise the Englishman. His beliefs embarrass him. Belief
> demands passion and passion exposes him so he believes in
> nothing . . . Passion invites ridicule; men wither from that.
> Listen to an Englishman talk, there's no real sweetness there,
> is there? No simplicity, only sneers. The love sneer, the
> political sneer, the religious sneer – sad.

Wesker may not always have communicated his passionate
beliefs effectively. He may sometimes have mistaken realism for cynicism, and clung to ideals that had no hope of
fulfilment. But at least he has felt that passion, held those
beliefs, and kept those ideals alive, if only as distant mar-
kers for people tempted to be satisfied with the here and
now. Again and again he has resisted human practice and
reminded us of human potential. It is an honourable
achievement.

TRILOGY

Chicken Soup with Barley

Roots has made Wesker familiar to successive generations
of students, and one can see why the examination boards
have thought it a good choice. It does, after all, dramatize
a perennial problem of adolescence: the newly awakened,
increasingly critical consciousness in conflict with an apathetic, unchanging family. But in other ways the emphasis
on the play is a pity. It is dramatically the least satisfying
of the trilogy whose second episode it constitutes. More to
the point, it is very essentially part of that trilogy, and not
to be read in isolation. Roughly speaking, Part 1 is about
the failure of the socialist ideal to translate itself into political practice in Britain, and consequently about the disillusion of most of the original idealists. Parts 2 and 3 turn
from macrocosm to microcosm, describing and assessing
two potential answers to that disillusion. How is a humane

socialism to survive and progress? Through the evangelizing efforts of cultural missionaries? Through exemplary attempts to get back to basics, rejecting the city, twentieth-century industry and the cash-nexus in favour of the country, craftsmanship and fulfilment 'on an individual level'?

Let us begin at the beginning, which is *Chicken Soup with Barley*. In 1958 it seemed an uniquely ambitious undertaking in itself, and, even now we're much more used to political drama, remains impressive in its size and scope. It opens in 1936, on the day the East End blockaded the streets against the parading fascists of Sir Oswald Mosley, and it ends in late 1956, after the Soviet invasion of Hungary: two key events, the one bringing hope and the other despair to those who espoused communism as a moral creed and a spiritual faith in the middle years of the century.

Wesker, wrote Kenneth Tynan, 'thinks internationally, but feels domestically; and it is this combination of attributes that enables him to bring gigantic events and ordinary people into the same sharp focus'. The deterioration of socialist hopes is at once observed, shared and paralleled by characters who are all instinctively public in their interests yet mostly very responsive to one another on the personal level. They are aware of themselves as part of history and of a community, a circle of friends and a family. You might say they lead double lives, each integral to the health of the other. Fulfilment in both is clearly essential to their wellbeing. But fulfilment is precisely what they fail to find in either.

In the first act the Kahn family and their friends are excited and optimistic. They set out to overcome Mosley's supporters, and in a limited way they succeed. 'There is no turning back now, nothing can stop the workers now,' declares Prince Silver, and Monty Blatt looks forward to 'a revolution soon'. Dave Simmonds is actually carrying the struggle to Spain, where he is clearly confident of a communist success. 'There's only one difference between them and us,' he says, 'we know what we're fighting for. It's almost an unfair battle.'

But the seeds of disillusion are already present. Prince is reminded that many of the anti-fascist demonstrators were 'just sightseers'. Monty is accused of 'only enjoying the battle' and 'forgetting the ideal'. Dave is warned that it won't be 'all glory' in Spain, and that a bigger war is coming. And things are clearly not well between the matriarch Sarah Kahn, who is all 'energy' and 'vitality', and her husband Harry, who is 'amiable, but weak'. His interest in politics is too bookish for her activitist taste. He reads Upton Sinclair and talks intelligently of Spain and socialism; but when events get hot outside he escapes to the house of his mother, to whom he's still emotionally enslaved. He also steals money from Sarah and lies to her about it, lapses that infuriate her. 'Weakling, you! *Weakling!*' she yells, and pitches crockery at him.

Act II, which occurs in 1946 and 1947, introduces us to their son, Ronnie, who is to figure so substantially in the rest of the trilogy. He enthusiastically distributes May Day leaflets, insists that with Labour in office 'the whole country is going to be organized to cooperate instead of tear at each other's throats', and claims to be 'a socialist poet'. But elsewhere deterioration is apparent. Ronnie's sister Ada is 'weary of spirit'. She has come to believe that the real problem is the proletariat's subservience to machines, not its failure to own them. With her husband Dave Simmonds, whose army experiences have left him profoundly disillusioned with the working class, she proposes to leave London for the country. And Harry, though still able to rouse himself sufficiently to remind her that 'it *is* an industrial age, let's face facts', succumbs to his first stroke, and sinks deeper than ever into hypochondria, apathy and helplessness, all attributes designed to madden Sarah.

And so to the by now inevitable conclusion, which is set in 1955 and 1956. Monty, unseen in the second act, reappears with a wife in the third, and turns out to be a successful Manchester shopkeeper embarrassed by his communist past. Harry, now close to being a vegetable, accidentally excretes in front of these guests, and Ronnie, who is working in a kitchen in Paris, returns home in a state of despair. He has lost his political faith and his personal ambition. The family has disintegrated, and so has their socialist idealism. Only Sarah remains unflinching in her beliefs. 'You're a pathological case, Mother – you are still a communist,' shouts Ronnie, to which her reply is simple, 'If the electrician who comes to mend my fuse blows it instead, so I should stop having electricity?' If Stalin executes the leaders of the Jewish Anti-Fascist League, and Kruschev invades Hungary, so socialism is meaningless?

As a London revival in 1978 proved, the play is lively, humorous and gripping. The rhythms of Jewish speech are lovingly recorded, many of the people observantly and vividly portrayed. Perhaps they sometimes sound like aspects of an argument, mouthpieces for the debate between hope and disillusion occurring in Wesker's mind. Yet, as we've seen, political involvement is part of their very identities. It is absolutely natural for Ronnie to initiate a conversation with a visiting aunt with 'What price partition in Palestine?' If the climactic confrontation between mother and son is not, as it would be in almost every other play of the period, about the personal and particular, but about the abstract and general, it is because they genuinely feel the abstract to be personal and the general to be particular. The effect is not damagingly didactic, even at this point, when Wesker is arriving at a provisional conclusion.

The nature of this conclusion has much to do with his (and our) assessment of Sarah, not a simple matter. To her, communism is primarily an expression of love, not of economic theory. She dismisses her sister-in-law Cissie, a trades-union organizer, as cold. 'What's the good of being a socialist if you're not warm?' she asks. 'People like that can't teach love and brotherhood.' She insists, in a crucial speech that Wesker has admitted represents his own views, that 'love comes now. You have to start with love. How can you talk about socialism otherwise?' But how can she make this claim when she is so intolerant of her husband's weaknesses, so quick to nag at him and complain about him to others before his face?

There are two answers to this. First, that her nagging is purposeful, a series of attempts, though more and more weary as the years go by, to browbeat him into becoming a good man, husband and comrade. For her, love is active, challenging, even aggressive. She does not share Harry's very passive view, that you 'can't change people – you can only give them some love and hope they'll take it'. Second, one personal failure should not anyway vitiate the value of the personal testament she presents to the wretched Ronnie. The point of life, she tells him, is to keep on fighting, believing and (above all) caring, no matter how disillusioning the results. 'You've got to care, or you'll die,' she cries as the curtain begins to fall, and repeats more or less the same words twice. It is Wesker's own defiant motto, put into the mouth of this turbulent, majestic emblem of endurance: an affirmation of faith in the possibility and power of love, not altogether convincing, nor meant to be altogether convincing, at the end of what without it would be a profoundly defeatist play.

Roots

Ronnie Kahn, present in spirit though absent in person, is the character who links *Chicken Soup* with *Roots*, itself set in 1959. Judging by his abundantly quoted opinions, he has recovered much of his resilience and optimism between the two. He has also become engaged to Beatie Bryant, a waitress in the hotel where he was working. She comes home to visit her mother, sisters and brother. He is to follow sixteen days later, to be introduced to the family.

Wesker works long and laboriously to establish a not-very-complicated situation. It is said that George Devine, the director of the Royal Court, wanted him to fuse the first two acts into one; and it is still tempting to question the wisdom of his refusal, because they do 'cover much the same ground. Romantic preconceptions about the country are persistently exposed as foolish. These people find life a hard slog. Unemployment is always a threat for the farm labourer, sickness a commonplace, some degree of poverty an everyday reality; and they can imagine no possibility of change. Beatie's father, about to be laid off from his job as a pigman, takes no interest whatever in the union magazine when it arrives. Her brother-in-law Jimmy Beales, a member of the Territorial Army, talks enthusiastically about the prospect of strike-breaking. They have no political consciousness, no awareness of themselves as members of a victim class, no desire to assume more control over their own lives. They do not question the *status quo*. They accept it.

They do not think very much, nor feel very strongly. They are emotionally undemonstrative. Beatie's sister, Jenny Beales, greets her 'with reserve' instead of any hug and kiss, and later describes love as 'squit', meaning nonsense. Beatie's mother's first reaction to seeing her daughter is 'Blust, you made me jump,' followed by 'Well, you've arrived then.' But these people, if not easily delighted, are easily offended. Beatie's mother is 'not speaking' to at least two members of her family, in each case for a trivial reason. And when they do talk, their conversation consists largely of random observation and lazy gossip, with neither speaker fully listening to the other. There is much that is petty and apathetic about these country folk.

Of course, it would be wrong to imply that there are not individual differences, and individual virtues, behind these general traits. Jenny, for instance, is much more kindly and friendly than her mother, who can quickly become angry and aggressive. Jimmy, who married Jenny after she gave birth to another man's illegitimate child, is a decent man with some sense of humour. But the only true individualist in this glum society is Stan Mann, a puckish old farmer said to have drunk away a fortune. He is, however, generally regarded as the last of his kind, and dies suddenly in

Act II. The reaction of the Bryant parents is characteristically phlegmatic: 'Rum ent it?' . . . 'He were a good ole
bor . . . a good ole stick.' After the spritely language of the
Kahns in *Chicken Soup*, the very rhythms of these Norfolk
people seem numb and dead, incapable of expressing the
least enthusiasm or excitement. Theirs is, in the most unromantic possible way, the voice of the earth.

Beatie, as Wesker insists throughout the first two acts,
is part and not part of this little world. Back in Jenny's
house she begins to read a comic, remarking that 'Soon
ever I'm home again I'm like I always was . . . I do the
same lazy things an' I talk the same.' Her reaction to one
of her mother's confused anecdotes, in this case about a
supposedly incompetent doctor, is the same automatic, un-
thinking 'Yearp' with which her mother reacts to her own
conversation. But there are differences, some of them innate
and some acquired. She has much more natural spirit and
energy than the others. She enjoys cooking food and cleaning houses and, when she does the latter, she is 'gurgling
with sort of animal noises signifying excitement'. She responds to Stan Mann's death with instinctive horror: 'Oh
hell, I hate dying . . . seem like the whole world gone
suddenly dead, don't it?' Again, it is difficult to imagine
any other member of her family suddenly and vividly describing a nightmare: 'I dreamt I died last night and heaven
were at the bottom of a pond.' To them, that would be
high-flown 'squit'. But if she has more emotional capacity
than anyone else, and therefore more potential for development, she is still in some ways immature. Confronted
with a wasp, she reverts to the 'voice of her childhood':
'Mammy, mammy, take them ole things away!' It isn't
surprising to learn that she was the spoiled baby of the
family, envied by her brothers and sisters.

So much for the innate Beatie. There is also the Beatie
that is being built upon it, the one who has not yet assim-
ilated the humanist-socialist wisdom Ronnie has been
trying to teach her. At times she quotes him directly, at
times simply parrots him, leaving one with the feeling that,

though her heart may be with him, it isn't altogether with what he says. Indeed, she admits as much when she says that she has been 'pretending' to be interested in his views, that 'learning was at school and that's finished with', and that 'once we're married and I got babies I won't need to be interested in half the things I got to be interested in now': lines that go a long way towards explaining Ronnie's eventual conduct. But, from the first, there are also signs of authentic change and growth. Her cross-examination of Jimmy about the Territorials, for instance, suggests that she is able to think for herself and think quickly. It is as if she were testing mental muscles she still hardly knows she possesses.

But Wesker is not, of course, interested in Beatie only as a developing individual. Through her, or (rather) through Ronnie as she relays him, he offers a critique of the aspects of modern British society her family represents. In response to their persistent failure to communicate, we get the idea that words are 'bridges, so that you can get safely from one place to another – and the more bridges you know about, the more places you can see'. In response to their small-mindedness, we're told that it doesn't matter if people are ill-educated, 'as long as their minds are large and inquisitive, as long as they are generous'. And, in two of the play's most celebrated, or notorious, scenes, Wesker mounts an attack on plastic culture. Mrs Bryant has been so crass as to enjoy what does, admittedly, appear to be a pretty feeble pop song. Beatie tells her it is 'sloshy and sickly'. She recites the lyrics, and declares them meaningless and lacking in 'passion'. Rather later, she berates her mother for describing Mendelssohn as 'squit' – 'God in heaven, you live in the country but you've got no, no, no majesty . . . your mind's cluttered up with nothing and you shut out the world' – and invites her to appreciate Bizet's 'L'Arlésienne' Suite. 'Socialism,' she announces, quoting Ronnie, 'isn't talking all the time, it's living, it's singing, it's dancing, it's being interested in what goes on around you, it's being concerned about people and the world.'

Add creativity, respect for the artistic achievements of the past, and (of course) dramatic changes in the ownership of production and distribution, and you have something close to a dictionary definition of Wesker's socialism. But the emphasis is *Wesker's*. It is difficult to avoid the impression that his characters are too often the incidental medium between him in the pulpit and ourselves in the congregation. If the weakness of the first two acts is lack of compression, the weakness of the play as a whole is an over-obvious didacticism. Even Stan Mann is found rather implausibly putting across Wesker's opinions: 'The young 'uns is all right though. Long as they don't let no one fool them, long as they think it out themselves.' And Beatie-cum-Ronnie are often mouthpieces. What makes a pop song third-rate? asks Mrs Bryant. Beatie tries to remember what Ronnie said: 'Something about registers, something about commercial world blunting our responses.' The reason for her awkwardness is only too transparent. It is Wesker's attempt, surely unsuccessful, to make it credible that Beatie might put over the intellectually sophisticated point he himself feels obliged to communicate to the audience.

The sermon, if such it be, rises to its climax at the end of the last act. The family gathers to await Ronnie, and he doesn't come. In fact, he breaks off the engagement by letter, a turn of events that leaves Beatie's mother triumphant and vindictive and Beatie herself strangely eloquent. She delivers herself of a long homily about the working class's lack of 'roots', meaning a nourishing culture, capable of stimulating the mind, developing the feelings, and generally promoting responsiveness. 'The whole stinking commercial world insults us and we don't care a damn,' she cries. 'Well, Ronnie's right – it's our own bloody fault. We want the third-rate – we got it!' At this point an 'ecstatic smile' lights up her face. 'I'm not quoting no more,' she tells her by now impervious family. 'Ronnie, it does work, it's happening to me, I'm beginning, on my own two feet – I'm beginning.'

Beatie is, as the final stage direction says, 'articulate at last'. Ronnie's thinking has become her own. Though her family will, as the same stage direction admits, 'continue to live as before', she has, in Wesker's words, been 'saved from the fire', and may in time help to save others. It is hardly a natural response to being jilted. But then Beatie has an exemplary function, which ends by diminishing the natural life in her. She has been transformed from a woman into a spokesperson for the Wesker virtues. There is something most implausible about her affirmation of life: implausible, and patronizing. One cannot altogether blame her family when they refuse to listen to her ringing evangelism. Why should they respond to the presumptuous challenges of a boy they don't know, why concur with a girl who sounds much more sententious than Wesker seems to realize?

But this may be a harsh view. Tynan, not a sentimental critic, thought Wesker had written 'the most affecting last act in contemporary English drama'; and by most accounts Joan Plowright, who created the character of Beatie, made the closing speeches emotionally credible. With the right actress, the scene can perhaps work in the theatre. With the wrong one, indeed with no more than an average one, it must seem pretty meretricious stuff.

I'm Talking About Jerusalem

Beatie is mentioned by Ronnie in *I'm Talking About Jerusalem*. 'She could have become a poem,' he says. 'I gave her words, and maybe she did.' But that is only an aside. What brings us to rural Norfolk this time is the experiment in pre-industrial living that Ada Simmonds announced in *Chicken Soup with Barley* that she and her husband, Dave, were to undertake. Can it succeed, should it succeed?

The answer to both questions turns out to be no; but the second no is much more qualified and complex than the first. Dave is clearly right to denounce the city factory – 'Morning after morning they come in with cold hatred in their eyes, brutalized.' He is right to insist that 'a man is made to work and that when he works he is giving away something of himself, something very precious'. He is right to find something inadequate in the kind of 'socialism' whose sole aim is to make the worker owner of a machine that would sap his spirit under any economic system. But is the logical conclusion of all this that Dave and Ada should withdraw completely from the city and, indeed, from the century, scratching a living by selling hand-made furniture? Sarah Kahn, whose instinctive wisdom seems as much a touchstone as it was in *Chicken Soup*, thinks not. 'Why you want to go back to the Middle Ages?' she asks. 'What's wrong with socialism that you have to run away to an ivory tower?' A stage direction tells us that this last is 'the real question'. After all, as Sarah proceeds to point out, 'the city is human beings – and what's socialism without human beings?'

In the first act the Kahns may be somewhat apprehensive, and Sarah somewhat discouraging, but the mood is still hopeful. This is 1946. The Labour Party has recently been returned to power. 'It's right [Dave and Ada] should be pioneers,' Ronnie tells his mother. 'Everybody is building. Out go the slums, and the National Health Service comes in. The millennium's come and you're still grumbling.' He is over-excited, and meant to sound exaggerated, naïve and a little absurd. But we're still left feeling that his sister and brother-in-law, in spite of all the doubts, are attempting something brave, worthwhile and potentially fruitful.

As in *Chicken Soup*, optimism is systematically defeated. Act II introduces us to an old friend of Dave's, Libby Dobson, whose own failure to translate his ergonomic ideals into successful practice has left him hopelessly soured. Part of his attack on the Simmonds' chosen life is merely malicious, but part has substance: 'Would you have the world do without cars, planes, electricity, houses, roads? Because *that's* the logical conclusion. If no man should be tied to turning out screws all his life, then that's what it means.' A few months later, there is another blow, this time not merely verbal. Dave has been preparing for the leap into self-employment by working for a local farmer. He has brought home some old, discarded lino belonging to this gentleman and, when challenged, denies having done so. He is sacked, leaving Ada to conclude that 'your ideals have got some pretty big leaks in places'. Is it possible to live in a capitalist–industrial society without using at least some of its products and thus implicitly condoning it? Is the Simmonds' life-style an illogical evasion of reality, as well as of responsibility? Have they themselves the moral resources to sustain it? Is the real threat outer or inner?

Pondering such questions, we're plunged into the act's second scene, which occurs six years later, in 1953. Dave hasn't exactly prospered, but he has a workshop and an apprentice, Sammy. But it is from precisely this source that the new attack comes. The boy enjoys making furniture with Dave, but he wants money and advancement, and feels he can get them only in a factory. Then Ada appears in numb misery, back from seeing her father, Harry Kahn, insane from his stroke. She tells Dave that a client has cancelled his order for a chair, thinking the price too high, and it is clear from Dave's indignation that this is a regular occurrence. How can they possibly continue?

They can't. There is one more scene, however, before they confess failure, and here the criticism comes from Ada's aunt Esther who, with her aunt Cissie, has come to stay with the Simmonds. Dave plans to buy machinery to help him with the hack work, thus, of course, becoming increasingly dependent on those mass-manufactured implements Dobson accused him of disingenuously forgetting. 'He'll be like a factory,' remarks Esther, 'only not big enough to make their turnover. So where's the ideals gone all of a sudden?' And the scene ends with a row between her and Dave. He accuses her of having no 'vision', she retorts by satirically calling him a 'prophet', and the pent-up feelings of persecution come pouring from him. All along, he and Ada have insisted that they have not been making any grand symbolic gestures. They are not trying to 'change the world'. Their experiment is 'on an individual level', done for and by themselves. But now Dave changes his tune: 'No one's ever heard of me and no one wants to buy my furniture, but I'm a bleeding prophet and don't anyone forget that.'

But by the final act, even the claim to be a 'spokesman' has been abandoned. It is now enough for him to make a living for his wife and children, and he has come to believe he can do that more successfully in London. He will set up his carpentry shop in some basement. 'Who knows, maybe people will buy furniture in town,' he says. 'They say you can sell them anything in London.' That last sentence shows, as clearly as any could, the distance Dave's hopes and ideals have travelled since the first act.

So the pattern of *Chicken Soup* has been paralleled. It is 1959 and a Tory government has just been elected, adding to the depression of the Simmonds' departure. What began in ingenuous optimism has ended in disillusion, and, once again, it is Ronnie's voice that most eloquently chronicles the decline. Ada and Dave are calm and accepting, but he 'sinks to his knees in utter despair', unable to take the knock to his beliefs their failure represents. To some extent, this demonstrates his naïvety. He put Dave on a pedestal, and, more to the point, he overrated the significance of his experiment. Kenneth Tynan, reviewing the play, suggested that Wesker's mistake was to 'equate the failure of a privately owned furniture business with the failure of socialism'. In view of the qualifications already introduced into the text, the accusation would be more aptly directed at Ronnie.

On the other hand, Ronnie's response is close to his author's. His 'desperate' defence of ideals and visions – 'They *do* work, and even if they don't work then for God's sake let's try to behave as if they do' – is quintessential Wesker. Dave's dismissive rejoinder only shows the extent to which he has succumbed to defeatism and even to cynicism, both commodities detested by Wesker. And Wesker considers Ronnie sufficiently important to give him the play's last, emphatic line: 'We must be bloody mad to cry.' He repeats it, as Sarah did the closing words of *Chicken Soup*, 'If you don't care you'll die'; and the connection between the two lines is obvious. The first play in the trilogy ends with 'You *must* care', the third with 'I *do* care'. And Beatie's eloquence at the conclusion of *Roots* may be seen as a positive and optimistic blend of the two: I care, and you must care.

I'm Talking About Jerusalem has had a worse press than the two preceding plays. Even the sympathetic Tynan found Ronnie's last cry 'an empty gesture, utterly devoid of intellectual substance'. But much of the characterization, for instance that of the old aunts, is vivid, and the process of Dave's failure is dissected with precision. For once, the gulf between specific experience and the general debate derived from it does not seem too great. The experience justifies the debate rather than being a mere excuse for it, and the debate itself surely has some weight and interest. No doubt there are unsatisfactory moments. I myself find that the scene in which the Simmonds' parents and their children play a game symbolizing and celebrating human growth rings no truer than the singing of 'The Cutty Wren' in *Chips with Everything*. But the conclusion, however intellectually wanting in itself, does arise from a play worthy of intellectual respect. It is an emotional response to a problem intelligently tackled, and it goes some way towards summing up the feeling of the trilogy as a whole. However great the discouragement, however improbable the gain, virtue consists in continuing to care and continuing to try.

John Arden
(born 1930)

John Arden was born in 1930 in Barnsley, was educated at private schools and Cambridge University, and briefly practised as an architect. He had, however, wanted to become a professional writer from the age of sixteen, when he composed a play about Hitler in the style of *Sweeney Agonistes*. This ambition became reality in 1957, thanks to the financial support of the Royal Court, which had given a production without décor to *The Waters of Babylon*, a quirky, original piece whose main character seemed to be everything an audience ought to hate: a pimp and slum-landlord who has served as a guard at Buchenwald and is presently organizing a corrupt municipal lottery. The critics were disconcerted by the broad, farcical style, the elaborate, sprawling plot, the mixture of colloquial prose, verse and song, and, not least, the apparent sympathy with which the protagonist was treated. As they soon discovered, all these qualities were characteristic of Arden.

If there's an overriding theme to his earlier plays, it is the difficulty of coercing, constraining or otherwise controlling the human animal. From folk-song and ballad Arden has acquired much of direct use to his work, including the belief that the British always were an 'extraordinarily passionate people, as violent as they are amorous, and quite astonishingly hostile to good government and order'. This is apparent even in the minor *Happy Haven* (1960), in which a group of old people rebel against their patronizing doctor, reducing him to infancy with the elixir of youth he plans to use experimentally on them; and his masterpiece, *Armstrong's Last Goodnight* (1964), demonstrates it perfectly. This is set in Border country in the 1520s, a time when free-booters were putting Scotland in danger of war by their raids on England. The poet and diplomat Lindsay dedicates himself to bringing the worst, John Armstrong, into 'the king's peace and order' and saving the realm 'through my craft and my humanity'. But this attempt fails, owing partly to the intricacies of feudal politics, partly to unforeseen mischance, partly to Armstrong's own unpredictability and capacity for violence. Armstrong's unruly impulses prove too much for the man of intellect; and he is hanged.

This is a rich, complex piece which always seems more interested in demonstrating the incompatibility of its protagonists than in judging them. Similar mutual misunderstandings, and the same moral openness on Arden's part, also mark the excellent *Live Like Pigs* (1958). A 'respectable' housing estate, represented by the conventional Jackson family, cannot assimilate the Sawneys, a rough, disorderly family recently evicted from a derelict tramcar. Nor can the Sawneys cope with the still wilder group of travellers that invades their new house. The result is violence and riot, the latter instigated by the Jacksons' friends and neighbours. One of Arden's recurring ideas is that a capacity for fierce feeling lies repressed in the most 'orderly' people, and can prove their undoing.

This is certainly the case with Colonel Feng in *The Workhouse Donkey* (1963), the police-chief who discovers in himself 'improbable longings' and falls embarrassingly in love with the daughter of one of the more corrupt citizens of the town he is attempting to purify 'according to the rigid statutes'. The principal reason for his failure to fulfil his aim is, however, the resistance of local political interests, prime among them one Alderman Butterthwaite, a Lord of Misrule on a scale even his party colleagues eventually find outrageous. The conflict between order and anarchy ends in defeat for both extremes, as in *Armstrong's Last Goodnight*. Reason is insufficient to tame instinct; but instinct, recklessly indulged, may destroy itself.

Arden's earlier work may be seen as a series of modern variations on Euripides's *Bacchae*, with Pentheus constantly striving and failing to curb Dionysus. Indeed, he explicitly invokes that god in his preface to *The Workhouse Donkey*, declaring that the theatre must grant pride of place to 'noise, disorder, drunkenness, lasciviousness, nudity, generosity, corruption, fertility and ease'. In both subject and style, his earlier plays tend to celebrate such attributes, while simultaneously recognizing what is destructive, bestial or simply anachronistic about them. At best, the result is a rare blend of exuberance and intricacy, energy and intelligence, strong theatrical colouring and complete resistance to moral blacks and whites.

This last trait is particularly noteworthy in view of the

more set attitudes propagated by Arden's recent work. In 1961 we find him ruefully acknowledging his 'disgracefully complex temperament', and proclaiming his 'grave' objections to any character that was evidently its author's mouthpiece. In 1963 he could declare that he tried to write a scene from the stance of every character in it, never so that the audience could identify with any particular one. He was committed to understanding all sides of the argument: 'If you dramatize a conflict and you say, one side in my opinion is white, the other black, and you underrate the strength, integrity and common sense of the black side, then you will give your side an easy walkover. Well, you wouldn't be writing a play if your side had an easy walkover . . . therefore, why not be fair?'

The reference here is to Butterthwaite and Feng, but could as well be Herod in *The Business of Good Government* (1960) or King John in *Left-Handed Liberty* (1965). Arden is at pains to discover what these much-abused figures have to say for themselves, and in each case it is a surprising amount. Again, in 1966 he was reiterating his dislike of 'tidily packaged plays', and insisting he always tried to find out what was of value in a character, however low. His job as playwright was to demonstrate the sheer complexity of today's problems, and try to elucidate them without, however, presumptuously deciding for the audience what viewpoint it should adopt. He was not, he specifically insisted, a politician himself. His function was 'dramatizing the raw material from which the politicians work'.

Arden would now regard much of this as the self-justification of a 'hedger and a fence-sitter and a contemptible poltroon'. The words come from his autobiographical *Bagman* (1970), in which the dreaming playwright finds even his supposedly subversive work tolerated as 'educational' and 'stimulating' by the leaders of an evil society and dismissed as irrelevant by those trying to overthrow it. At the end, 'John Arden' concludes that he is doomed to be a detached observer only; but this is an attitude which John Arden's preface attacks as 'reprehensible, cowardly and not to be imitated', explaining that events in Ulster and contact with Naxalite revolutionaries in India had finally radicalized him. The 'enemy' was now 'the fed man, the clothed man, the sheltered man, whose food, clothes and house are obtained at the expense of the hunger, the nakedness, and the exposure of so many millions of others, and who will allow anything to be *said*, in books or on the stage, so long as the food, clothes and house remain undiminished in his possession'. It was apparent that Arden was suffering from a kind of artistic schizophrenia. Should he continue to write balanced, 'fair' plays, and risk compromising his Marxist beliefs? Or should he be more directly polemical, whatever the artistic cost? Increasingly, he has opted for the second alternative.

Only one of his recent plays displays the imaginative abundance, the intellectual distinction, the love of irony, ambiguity, paradox of his early works; and that is *The Island of the Mighty* (1972), which shows, among much else, how a pagan upsurge prevented Arthur and Merlin maintaining order in post-Roman Britain. It is actually an adaptation of three television plays long before put aside by their author, and, significantly, it was classified by him as a throwback to a style of drama he had renounced. Significantly, too, he disowned the Royal Shakespeare Company's production of the play, apparently because its anti-imperialist thrust was insufficiently obvious. Indeed, he actually picketed the theatre with his wife and co-adapter, Margaretta D'Arcy.

Miss D'Arcy has shared the credit for all Arden's recent work, with the sole exception of the radio play *Pearl* (1978), which deals again with the potential power of the writer, in this case a seventeenth-century dramatist who tries (and fails) to help forge links between parliamentarians, puritans and Irish nationalists. It is, however, questionable whether this collaboration has been either artistically fruitful or as politically effective as Miss D'Arcy, herself a fervent socialist and Irish patriot, would presumably hope. Arden has said that he writes plays simply by taking a story and putting it into dialogue: Miss D'Arcy, however, thinks of the theme first, the story second. The latter method is clearly more likely to lead to didactic, even propagandist drama; and that, on the whole, is what the collaboration has produced.

Their *Hero Rises Up* (1968) concerns Nelson, who is seen as a passionate or 'curvilinear' man who squandered his energy on the aspirations of a 'rectilinear' order; but he lacks complexity and hence interest, as indeed does the play as a whole, with its cartoon style and crude ironies – 'He smacked them all to smithereens, all for to make 'em free.' *The Ballygombeen Bequest* (1972), too, has plenty of melodramatic-cum-farcical energy, but little of the old intellectual sophistication. It is about that Irish curse, the absentee landlord, here represented by a stupid, arrogant, hypocritical and greedy Englishman whose face, at one climax in the original production, was actually bathed in a sinister green light. Significantly, Arden has said that it is in such a style that he wishes his work to be performed in future.

He and his wife have also become increasingly dissatisfied with the professional theatre, especially the state-subsidized sector, which they tend to see as part of a conspiracy by which the government perpetuates the illusion that Britain is a free society and is hence able to fulfil its oppressive aims more easily. They have organized plays with and for the communities in which they have lived; they created a day-long 'event' about Vietnam at New York University; and, recently, they put on *The Non-Stop Connolly Show*, a night-long cartoon-play about the Irish socialist leader, in Liberty Hall, Dublin. Their future work seems likely to be written for 'fringe' companies of revolutionary socialist cast, or for politically committed amateurs.

Arden has defended his development with vigour, declaring that he was 'at last affirming from his own hard experience the need for revolution and a socialistic society, and moreover convinced that his artistic independence and integrity will be strengthened rather than weakened by so doctrinaire a stance'. He will, he says, now write less as an onlooker, more as a participant. That this is a principled decision cannot be doubted. Whether it is also naïve, in so far as it expects the theatre to have more practical influence than perhaps it can in the short term, is open to debate. Either way, it is difficult not to feel a twinge of regret at the passing of a playwright who, judged by admittedly old-fashioned criteria, seemed as important as any in the 1950s and 1960s: one whose work had no obvious impact on the march of events, but whose trenchant and searching questions helped shape the consciousness of a generation.

Sergeant Musgrave's Dance

The origins of the play that moved Raymond Williams to call Arden 'the most genuinely innovatory of the young English dramatists of the 1950s' are threefold: John Whiting's *Saint's Day*, which he much admired; an American film called *The Raid*, in which Confederate soldiers seize a Yankee town; and a specific atrocity in British-governed Cyprus, in which the murder of a soldier's wife was followed by the killing of five people, one a little girl. It is an incident markedly similar to this last one – though Arden has been unsentimental enough to transform the wife into a private soldier, Billy Hicks, and the little girl into a young woman with a 'known record as an associate for terrorists' – which brings Sergeant Musgrave and his three co-deserters from the Victorian army to the embattled British colliery-town where the play is set. They pretend to be seeking recruits; but what Musgrave is really recruiting is a sufficient number of victims for an act of exemplary reprisal. If one death deserved five, then five deserves twenty-five. And where else but in Hicks's home-town to find those who are, perhaps, ultimately responsible for his murder?

This is what Musgrave repeatedly calls the 'logic' of the situation, and logic, order, discipline are supremely important to him. He was 'the hardest sergeant of the line', and is still one who 'works his life to bugle and drum'.

Indeed, he brings the same relentless single-mindedness, the same intolerance of human failing, to the task of subversion as he did to his colonial duties. He deserted precisely because he felt those duties 'got scrawled and mucked about and I could not think straight'; and now he uses a similar image to warn his subordinates against the town's distractions, and specifically against any dealings with Hicks's former mistress, the barmaid and part-time prostitute Annie. His plan is straight, black, and clear, he tells her: 'If you come to us with what you call your life and love – I call it your indulgence – and you scribble all over that plan, you make it crooked, dirty, idle, untidy, *bad* – that's anarchy.' Love to him is scribble, and life itself almost seems to be equated with anarchy.

Annie unsurprisingly sees Musgrave as grim, cold, created 'by the north wind in a pair of millstones'. He's a man who can imagine the end of the world in terms of a steady, well-dressed military parade; and, as this suggests, he is also 'a religious man', with a strong belief in the punitive Jehovah of the Old Testament. With the help of God's 'mechanism', his logic, he will uncover and expunge the 'corruption' in this town, end the cycle of murder and guilt, make men aware of 'the cruelty and greed of armies', turn them against the 'war of sin and unjust blood' that killed Hicks, cure the 'madness' Britain is exporting to its colonies, and 'change all soldiers' duties': all by one 'terrible' deed that will be remembered for ever.

But Musgrave's plan fails. He assembles the townspeople for what they think is a recruiting meeting, having already mentally selected some victims: the mayor and colliery owner, who has cut his men's wages and locked them out, and now tries to bribe Musgrave to enlist their leaders; the constable, who offers him a list of 'agitators'; and the parson, who couches essentially the same request in moral and patriotic language, talking of the 'fine, strong men' of the colonial army and the 'skulkers and shirkers' at home. The skeleton of the murdered Hicks is hoisted high, and a Gatling machine-gun trained on those Musgrave blames for the 'corruption' abroad. But then things begin to go wrong, and the scene ends with the arrival of dragoons, come to prevent industrial violence, arrest Musgrave and restore law and order.

The reasons for Musgrave's failure are crucial and various. Consider, for instance, his fellow-deserters. Attercliffe, the oldest, joined the army when his wife rejected him for a more prosperous man, seems to have been responsible for the death of the 'girl', and has now become a total pacifist: he wants to demonstrate the evil of all war, and to do so without more killing. Hurst is a dangerous thug, who deserted after murdering an officer and looks forward with relish to the prospect of vengeance. Sparky, the youngest, was inveigled by Musgrave into helping to 'pay for' the death of Hicks, his best friend; but he doesn't know how or even whether he should. Midway through the play he decides to desert the deserters to find freedom and love with Annie, is stopped by Hurst, and is unintentionally bayoneted by Attercliffe in the ensuing struggle. It is the news of Sparky's death, and the other soldiers' inability to explain it adequately, that eventually alienates the colliers, whom Musgrave tries to persuade to join him against those who rule and abuse them.

Thus Musgrave fails because he and his comrades have markedly different aims: so different, indeed, that Attercliffe actually presses himself against the Gatling's muzzle rather than allow Hurst, 'distorted with rage' behind it, to kill anybody. He fails because these differences result in a death, technically accidental though it may be. He fails because his 'logic' is undermined, as rigid logic often is, by unforeseen mischance. He fails, in short, because he does not appreciate the unpredictability and complexity of things, and he fails because his plan was misconceived in the first place. Arden has advised those seeking the play's 'moral' to pay particular attention to its two women, Annie and her employer, Mrs Hitchcock; and the latter's view is that Musgrave brought the problems of a 'different war' into a community with its own important battles. As Arden has recently said, Musgrave fails because he cannot 'understand the political implications of the labour movement'. Perhaps he should have given the colliers his Gatling, instead of preventing them stealing it, as he does. At the same time, as Attercliffe points out, he has tried to end war by its own rules – 'You can't cure the pox by further whoring.' Violence begets violence; and it isn't surprising that the end of Musgrave's efforts should be, not only the deaths of himself and his comrades, but the reinforcement of the corrupt and repressive hierarchy he had planned to destroy.

The conflict between mind and will and those human qualities that resist organization and order is, as we've seen, fundamental to Arden's work; but here it seems unusually elaborate, contradictory, paradoxical. To quote Mrs Hitchcock again, Musgrave's logic itself becomes 'scribble': an uninvited interference with whatever 'life and love' the community possessed and, as such, a kind of 'anarchy'. And his logic is flawed in a deeper sense still. At the play's spectacular and ironic climax, Hurst beats 'frantically' on a drum, up goes the skeleton, and Musgrave dances, 'waving his rifle, his face contorted with demoniac fury'. There's a wild, anarchic spirit somewhere inside the enemy of anarchy, unaware of it though he is. How can anyone accept, as the disciplined agent of divine law and order, a man who understands neither himself nor his species, and dismisses every human complication as 'not material'?

The play's intellectual difficulties seem enough in themselves to explain why many reacted against it at first. It is difficult to side either with or against Musgrave. He is both sympathetic and unsympathetic or, more precisely, his aims seem admirable but his methods abhorrent; and even at the beginning, before we know what his exact plans are, he is viewed ambiguously, as a man of flinty integrity and some absurdity. The function of one of the play's principal characters, Joe Bludgeon, the bargee who brings the soldiers to the town, is to parody Musgrave and bring out the respects in which he is naïve. This cynical, devious, malicious opportunist – 'crooked' in appearance where Musgrave is 'straight' – mimics the praying sergeant at one point. At others he seems designed to represent that waywardness and changeability, that spirit of misrule, which it is Musgrave's tragic flaw to underrate. It is characteristic that at the recruiting meeting Bludgeon should at one moment ally himself with the deserters, the next arrest Musgrave on behalf of the arriving dragoons, and end as the lord and master of the unruly feast that closes the scene: a disreputable Dionysus triumphant – mocking, illuminating, and exposing the protagonist's deficiencies.

Another reason for the play's initial unpopularity was resistance to its supposedly 'Brechtian' style, principally its interjection of verse and song into the dialogue. Arden has explained this device several times. He is, he says, opposed to a 'half-and-half' language that is neither prose nor poetry. The function of prose is to convey plot, character and relationships, that of verse to be 'a sort of comment on them'. Again, 'the dialogue can be naturalistic as long as the basic poetic issue has not been crystallized; but when that point has been reached, the language becomes formal'. Again, verse has only a limited place in the theatre, because it brings with it so many associations, becomes too much to understand, and also grows hypnotic; but it has a use at moments of 'emotional tension'. There are specific examples of all these claims in *Musgrave*, which, it should incidentally be noted, is mainly written in a quasi-Victorian variant of the 'knotty lyricism' that Ronald Bryden rightly felt to characterize Arden's stylish, rather self-conscious prose. The author himself has drawn particular attention to the moment when Annie, who bore Hicks a child which died, is asked what she thinks of soldiers, and answers in a sixteen-line ballad, describing how the military killer seduces girls and they 'send him weeping over the sea', knowing he'll soon be dead. It is, he says, 'a generalized comment on soldiers', an 'oracular pronouncement' on a subject that is 'actually the theme for the whole play': she is also 'speaking out of emotional pressure, and therefore can drop into verse without any difficulty at all'.

The play contains ballads, and in a sense is a ballad itself, packed with what Arden calls that form's 'primary' colours – 'black is for death and for the coalmines, red is for murder, and for the soldier's coat the collier puts on to escape from his black'. Visually and verbally, he insists repeatedly upon them. In the first scene alone, Musgrave is called Black Jack, the card-playing deserters talk ominously of black spades, the bargee refers to soldiers as 'blood-red roses'; and off they go, in their red uniforms, to the black town. The play aims to combine an archetypal simplicity of story with considerable moral intricacy; and the critical consensus today is that it succeeds.

Nevertheless, some qualifications continue to be expressed. Some object that the mayor and parson are mere caricatures, contradicting the early Arden's claim to present characters from their own points of view: his answer is that they are in a situation which brings out their public personalities only, that the result is caricature by omission and not by exaggeration, and that in another play they might become more rounded. Bryden felt that the 'melodramatic comings and goings' at Sparky's death dislocate the play's flow and sense of reality, and that the last scene 'peters out in discussion' as Mrs Hitchcock improbably offers her moral summing-up. Arden himself concedes that there is 'something wrong with the play I have never been able to put my finger on', and is particularly critical of the churchyard scene which ends the first act: it fails (he thinks) to balance the business of giving necessary information so that the audience understands the situation with that of withholding information so as to keep up tension. Perhaps the real trouble is that the play is just a little too conscious of its themes, too calculated in its construction of the plot and dialogue that parades them, and so, for all the passion of its parts, comes to seem somewhat dispassionate, dry and academic.

And yet one feels that a pacifist, which is what Arden

was when he wrote the play, is earnestly and honestly exploring his feelings about war, the responsibility for it, and the ways in which men may be turned from it. Musgrave's particular solution seems less surprising than twenty-five years ago, now that we have had so much experience of terrorism with moral pretensions; but those who still find it eccentric must admit that his story illuminates the subject as a whole while (or, rather, *by*) recognizing its sheer complexity. Even the play's closing words provoke, tease, send us away with questions. Attercliffe sings a song about a soldier who gives his love a 'blood-red rose-flower', and comes home to find it withered and her eating an apple, given her by a new 'darling dear'. The apple holds a seed that will raise a flowering tree; but what will grow when he and Musgrave are hanged? 'Do you reckon we can start an orchard?' he asks. The question may be ironic, indicating the sterility of what they have been and done; it may be hopeful, indicating that they may be remembered, and the seed they have planted one day bear fruit. Arden being Arden, it's more likely to be both at once.

Harold Pinter
(born 1930)

The world in which Harold Pinter's characters have their edgy, embattled being is, on the whole, a hostile, menacing, even rapacious one; and so was the world in which the sensibilities of the playwright-to-be were formed. He was born in 1930 in East London, the son of a Jewish tailor, and grew up at a time when fascism both in England and (of course) abroad was at its most dangerous. When the war started he was evacuated to the country, not an experience he found happy, and returned to London in time to see the first flying bomb pass over his house. Several times, he claims, he opened the back door to find the garden in flames.

Even peace did not resolve the tensions of an area where anti-Semitism had long been endemic. Pinter tells of walking to a Jewish club through an alley in which the resurgent fascists would regularly skulk with broken milk bottles:

> The best way [to get out] was to talk to them, you know, sort of 'Are you all right?' 'Yes, I'm all right.' 'Well, that's all right then, isn't it?' and all the time keep walking towards the lights of the main road.

In other words, the trick was to communicate obliquely, indirectly, in language that on the surface had no connection with the perils on hand, but in essence was soothing, appeasing, perhaps even submissive. It is a type of expedient that was to be much employed by his dramatic characters.

At seventeen he went to drama school, but dropped out, faking a nervous breakdown. About the same time he was called up for National Service, but pluckily. (and interestingly, given his later concern with people's potential for violence) risked prison by declaring himself a conscientious objector. He was already a published poet, and soon afterwards became a professional actor, working in a variety of regional reps. His first play, performed at Bristol University in 1957, was *The Room*: his next two were *The Dumb Waiter* and *The Birthday Party*, the second of which proved a critical and commercial disaster when it was presented in London in 1958.

It is now, however, recognized as a remarkably original play. Stanley, a young out-of-work pianist, is idling away his days in seaside lodgings, when two men appear from nowhere, reduce him to a speechless wreck, then spruce him up in bowler hat and striped trousers, and drive him away to an unnamed destination. His persecutors' motives are no clearer than his own sins. One, an Irishman, tends to accuse Stanley of public wrongs: 'Why did you leave the organization? . . . You betrayed our land.' The other, a Jew, emphasizes the personal: 'You verminate the sheet of your birth . . . You betray our breed.' But the vagueness of this increasingly odd and lengthy indictment is obviously deliberate. The play is about everyone's long-repressed guilts and unspoken fears, everyone's dim suspicion that one day his past may catch up with him and vengeance be exacted for what he has done or is thought by someone, somewhere to have done.

More precise interpretations are possible and have often been assayed. For instance, the references to parents and children are abundant, indeed obsessive. Perhaps the play is about the cruelty of growing up and being forced to face the world: hence the contrast between the untidy, irresponsible, perhaps rather infantile Stanley of the beginning and the Stanley of the end, who has been filled with a sense of sin, purged, scoured, and turned into an everyday robot, ready for office or grave. But, as often with Pinter, to define the play too closely is to limit it and lose something. What it primarily communicates is an insecurity the more unsettling for being unspecific. So, too, do *The Room*, set in what its main character wrongly supposes to be a safe haven against the mysterious and menacing forces lurking outside, and *The Dumb Waiter*, in which two assassins waiting beside an abandoned kitchen for an unknown victim are puzzled and alarmed by the eccentric instructions that intermittently rattle down to the serving-hatch. Out there danger lurks. And even if the refuge to which one has finally retreated seems as safe as the womb it somewhat resembles, this danger may one day strike and destroy. The woman-protagonist of *The Room* ends up blind, Stanley catatonic, one of the assassins a defenceless target himself.

It was Pinter himself who pointed out that the appearance of menacing, demanding strangers at the door had been a common experience in Europe for years past. Political inferences, as this remark suggests, may sometimes be extrapolated from his work, perhaps most obviously from *The Hothouse*, which he wrote in 1958, but did not allow to be performed until 1980. It is partly a grotesque satire on bureaucratic callousness and incompetence, occurring, as it does, in a government-run 'rest home' most of whose staff outrageously exploit the patients and are, it appears, eventually massacred by them. The only benignant employee is tormented with noise, light and bizarre questions, and ends as much a mental ruin as Stanley. Yet even here Pinter concentrates primarily on individuals in their personal relationships. More than any of his contemporaries, he is concerned with the primary drives and needs, for sex, love and friendship, for attention, respect and status, for a place to sleep, eat and be secure, for influence, power and dominance. His characters tend to be possessive, both of people and territory. They are obliged to be so, because they are in constant danger of being deprived of what matters to them, down to their very identities. Hence the jealousy, the competitiveness, the fear, the hostility and the anger that frequently characterizes their encounters. Many of them are, in Pinter's own words, 'at the extreme edge of their living, where they are living pretty much alone'. One slip, or one push, and who knows what horror may not overtake them? A man may begin the day in apparent control of himself, his marriage and his house, though a trifle disturbed by the beggar who haunts the road beyond his ample garden: he may end it with his inadequacies exposed, his confidence gone, his house and wife lost, a helpless beggar himself.

That is the pattern of *A Slight Ache* (1959), which in itself seems sufficient answer to those who have patronized Pinter as a 'miniaturist', meaning that he covers only a very limited area of experience. Miniaturists aren't usually concerned with matters of survival and destruction. To take a still more artistically satisfying example, they don't often produce plays like *Tea Party* (1965), which shows a seemingly confident but essentially insecure businessman driven insane by the paranoid imaginings provoked in him by his tantalizing secretary and by the over-close relationship between his wife and her brother. Even Pinter's less cataclysmic plays commonly have reverberations beyond themselves. *The Lover* (1963) concerns a husband and wife whose fantasies are that they are one another's lover and mistress, master and whore: it is also a remarkably neat and inventive synopsis of the English tendency to split sex and 'respectable' love into separate compartments. What seem to be miniatures often leave you feeling you've been contemplating murals.

The paradox is, of course, largely the result of Pinter's distinctive style, his habit of couching important transactions in commonplace, even banal language and, conversely, of investing the seemingly ordinary with extraordinary significance. His characters commonly say very little, or even nothing, when they mean very much. Often, too, they camouflage their real meaning, substituting a sort of code for direct statement. Arguments about whether it is correct to say 'light the kettle' or that wasps 'bite' are the outer and visible signs of inner and deeper discord in, respectively, *The Dumb Waiter* and *A Slight Ache*. In *The Birthday Party* the old riddle about why the chicken crossed the road becomes an assertion of dominance and a threat of violence. A request for olives is an expression of sexual jealousy and anger in *The Collection* (1961). In *No Man's Land* (1975) a story about the complexities of a one-way street system is actually a warning to an importunate intruder that he may be getting too deep into an intricate and perilous situation. Sometimes the metaphor is visual, not verbal. The businessman in *Tea Party* signals his uneasy involvement with his secretary by persuading her to play football with his cigarette lighter. The two men in *The Basement* (1967) express the sexual and territorial war they are waging by playing cricket with a recorder and, for ball, a marble which strikes one violently in the face. To Pinter, there may be great emotional weight in the most innocent game, the most trivial request, the most innocuous exchange of platitudes.

This isn't to say that his plays are about that commodity so fashionable in the 1960s and 1970s, 'failure of communication'. On the contrary, his people tend to communicate pretty effectively; but the level on which they communicate is not always the obvious, surface one. 'The speech we hear,' Pinter has said, 'is an indication of that which we don't hear. It is a necessary avoidance, a violent, sly, anguished or mocking smokescreen which keeps the other in its place.' Again: 'So often, below the word spoken, is the thing unknown and unspoken . . . Most of the time we're inexpressive, giving little away, unreliable, elusive, evasive, obstructive, unwilling. But it's out of these attributes that a language arises. A language, I repeat, where under what is said another thing is being said.' Yet again: 'I think that we communicate only too well, in our silence, in what is unsaid, and that what takes place is a continual evasion, desperate rearguard attempts to keep ourselves to ourselves.' Pinter's diagnosis has particular aptness in England, a country where social custom, embarrassment, and a belief in privacy tend to inhibit people from saying what they mean and meaning what they say. But the basic messages his characters relay are, of course, international: 'I hate you', 'Do this', 'Get out', 'Give me that', 'Give me yourself'. Years ago he said that his work was about 'the weasel under the cocktail cabinet', and then withdrew this uncharacteristic self-revelation, explaining it was tossed out thoughtlessly in response to an irritating question. But post-Freudian critics, familiar with the weight psychiatrists give free-association, aren't to be fobbed off so easily. The phrase nicely sums up both the obfuscating social pretence and the animal savagery beneath.

Much of Pinter's peculiar effect derives from just this, the combination of strong and sometimes deadly feelings and a palpable sense of mystery. His plays demand extraordinary alertness of an audience, because the manoeuvring that precedes and causes the basic human transactions is often extremely elaborate and the characters' relationships, and especially the power they exert over one another, may shift from speech to speech or even from sentence to sentence. And even the acutest of observing eyes is not always enough. Some of the motives on display may be clear enough: others are not. They must be sniffed out, surmised, or simply guessed at; and, as in life, no firm or finite answer may emerge. 'We're not quite sure of the author's intention here,' Pinter remarked when he was directing his own *Lover*; and there is no reason to suppose him disingenuous. He's still one of the few dramatists to admit what the serious novelist recognized sixty or seventy years ago, that an author isn't God and may not be able to explain his characters' every action. Indeed, he would argue that some of their acts are probably inexplicable: 'There can be no hard distinctions between what is real and what is unreal, nor between what is true and what is false. A thing is not necessarily either true or false; it can be both true and false.' His function is to create the characters, give them their freedom, and edit the result into a play: our function is to listen, interpret where we can, and confess to an educated uncertainty when the evidence is ambiguous or incomplete.

To take a relatively simple example, *The Collection* leaves us with a fascinating and suggestive puzzle. A woman, Stella, has told her husband, James, she slept with a stranger, Bill, at a provincial hotel. Menaced by James, Bill has at first denied the story, then confirmed it, quietly exulting in the sense of sexual superiority it gives him. James has punished Stella by pretending to have established a friendship with Bill. Finally Harry, who is Bill's homosexual (probably) protector, has made him admit to James that his encounter with Stella was not physical. But the play ends with Stella 'neither confirming nor denying' this supposed truth. James, like the audience, is left to wonder how much is fabrication, and why fabrication should have occurred in the first place; and the possible answers are not conducive to his peace of mind and self-esteem. This final mystery is absolutely plausible and also dramatically functional, since it gives Stella power over the wretched James. She is, incidentally, one of a line of Pinter women who bewilder, disturb and even overwhelm men with the sexual force-field they effortlessly project. They range from Sally in *Night School* (1960), the demure school-mistress who doubles as a night-club hostess, to Ruth in

The Homecoming and Kate in *Old Times*. They are tantalizing, elusive, powerful, dangerous.

Pinter has often been accused of needlessly withholding information from his audiences, of making a mannerism of mystery. A more precise criticism may be that he refuses to penetrate inside his people as far as might be allowed even by his own respect for their privacy. It is a curious fact that the two characters who reveal the most of their internal selves are mental cripples: Aston in *The Caretaker*, with his long description of his sickness, and the garrulous and possibly schizophrenic Len in *The Dwarfs* (1960). There have been times when one has felt that Pinter has, so to speak, taken us to the edge of a psychological well, made us aware of its depth, and even allowed us to hear the echoes reverberating from inside, yet has perversely refrained from venturing down and actually showing us the tin cans, used contraceptives, frogs, snakes and slime at the bottom.

But Pinter's primary justification, as we've seen, is the truth and honesty of his approach. To define is to limit, and to limit is to distort. It is also to deny the audience the opportunity for the kind of wary speculation that he would regard, not as an amusing diversion, but as an actual moral imperative, a means of survival in a subtle and threatening world (indeed, his very motto might be 'Be watchful'). A second and simpler justification is that Pinter's psychological reticence hasn't prevented him from creating some of the more memorable characters in modern drama, from the insecure blusterer Roote and the calculatedly insolent Lush in *The Hothouse* to Davies in *The Caretaker* to Spooner, the derelict poet in *No Man's Land*, fastidious, aloof, predatory. Even such minor pieces as *A Night Out* (1960) and *Night School* contain striking and vibrant creations: a querulous, domineering mother and a fake-genteel prostitute in the one, and two twittering, bickering aunts and a braggadocio wheeler-dealer in the other.

It would, however, be wrong to give the impression that Pinter's interests and methods have not changed during the twenty-odd years he has been a dramatist. Very roughly, we may say that the amorphous terrors of his early work gave way to more naturalistic plays with plots that were, if only on the surface, rather clearer. Then, in 1968, he began to explore ideas implicit in his previous work and explicit in some of Len's speeches in *The Dwarfs*, the subjectivity of perception, the shifting nature of reality, the relativity of truth and the impossibility of validating it. In short, he began to delve into the more elusive areas of the consciousness and, in particular, into those where memory has its sometimes shadowy, sometimes surprisingly sharp existence. At the same time, his language became more lyrical, as perhaps it had to be in order to reflect these concerns, and his situations more abstract and static.

In *Silence* (1969) three character sit on chairs, rehearsing the history of their relationships in fragmented monologues, relieved by very brief snatches of dialogue. *Landscape* (1968) is more realistic, since one character, himself plodding, unimaginative, and somewhat coarse, spends the play directly speaking to the other, his wife, about a walk with his dog, an encounter with a stranger in a pub, and similar minutiae. But she, like the people in *Silence*, is trapped inside her own head, where she endlessly remembers her romance with a man who may and may not have been her husband in his youth. The subject is perhaps the way time affects the sensibilities, numbing the man's and marooning the woman's. It is also one that had fascinated Pinter since the days of *The Room* and *The Birthday Party*, the power of the past over the present. The result, like *Silence*, has its beauties and insights, but is somewhat undramatic, since it inevitably lacks what was abundantly present in his previous work, namely conflict.

That commodity is rather cleverly restored in the two following plays, *Old Times* and *No Man's Land*, in which the intrusive Spooner exploits the confused memories of the rich, reclusive alcoholic, Hirst, in order to fulfil his own territorial ambitions. Specifically, he joins Hirst in his fantasy world to establish a hold over him and a secure place in his household. It is a plot that allows Pinter to develop his new interests, but also reconciles them with his old. Memory itself becomes an integral ingredient in one of those tugs-of-war he charts so trenchantly.

In the 1970s Pinter's output, both of first-hand work and of adaptations for the screen, was much sparser than in the 1960s. Meanwhile his second career, that of theatre director, grew and flourished. Indeed, he wrote no play at all between *No Man's Land* and *Betrayal*, which appeared in 1978 and turned out to be his most critically unsuccessful effort since *The Birthday Party* two decades before.

The capsule objection to this seemed to be that the plot was too clear and unambiguous: it was a triangle-drama, whose only unusual characteristic was that it was told backwards. It began after an affair between a literary agent and his best friend's wife had dwindled into apathy, and ended at the moment of its emotional conception. In fact, the relative simplicity of the situation and the extraordinary spareness of the dialogue conceal some of the most terse, fraught and elaborate encounters that Pinter has concocted. The lover studiously hides the truth from the husband, who comes to know about the affair, and knows his wife knows he knows, but does not know if the lover knows he knows or knows his wife knows he knows; and the husband does not reveal his knowledge, perhaps because he genuinely cares for the 'best friend' who is betraying him and whom he himself is betraying by withholding both that knowledge and the information that he, too, is having unconfessed affairs with other women. And so one might go on, chronicling states of mind and collisions of feeling that often seem too complex to be summed up at all.

The play has its connections with Pinter's previous work. There is the tantalizing, rather dangerous woman, who this time ends by rejecting both husband and literary agent for a third man. There is sexual competition and conflict, though of a much subtler kind than before. There is a suggestion that, despite the conflict, a powerful bond exists between the two men, itself arguably more important to them than their relationship with the woman. There is the pull of the past, the unease caused by memory, the sense that time is a destroyer. Above all, there is scarcely a line that does not express, however obliquely or mutedly, pain, regret, anger, jealousy, fear, desire, remorse, or some concatenation of dynamic emotions. Once again, the play says little and implies much. In short, it proves that the most original British dramatist of our time is still a vital and challenging creative force.

The Caretaker

Pinter has said that *The Caretaker* copes with 'a particular human situation, concerning three particular people'. It isn't a play of 'symbols'. But this characteristic lack of pretension has not deterred some of Pinter's admirers, who have found it difficult to believe that so seemingly simple a piece could prove so potent in the theatre, and have sought solace in one far-fetched interpretation after another. Davies, the elderly tramp, must be Dionysus, or perhaps the Wandering Jew, or maybe the tempter in a modern *Everyman* play, or conceivably Everyman himself, this time beset by a dark angel and a bright angel, namely the brothers Aston and Mick. Or is Aston the carpenter Christ, hoping to establish his Church in the form of a garden shed? Or could Mick represent a vicious and destructive social system? Or might the play involve, at some profound level, the Old Testament God, the New Testament God, and suffering humanity? The wisest course for the reader, disoriented by these conflicting claims, is to return to basics, that's to say to the play itself. How inadequate is it if no abstractions are deduced from it?

At this point it is obviously necessary to describe the plot, not such an easy matter when Pinter is the author. Indeed, one might say Pinter is challenging the audience to divine, on the basis of the evidence he discreetly feeds it, precisely what the plot is. We are to note the characters' shifting attitudes towards each other, unravel their motives, watch their manoeuvrings, and see if we can piece together cause and effect. We must explain why Davies is saved by Aston from a beating-up and brought to the flat that actually belongs to Mick, what Mick's reaction to this is, and why and how Davies ends up rejected by both brothers.

Very well. Why does Aston, a mentally damaged man lately released from what was evidently a singularly hellish asylum, take in Davies, a shabby, smelly drifter? The cluttered and chaotic room he inhabits may give a clue. Here is another piece of junk, different from those Aston has already accumulated in one obvious particular. This time, it is human. Aston still finds the inanimate world taxing enough (notice that he spends the play trying to mend the same electric plug) and the animate one even more so (he avoids places where he was known in his pre-hospital days, and describes what might have become a sexual encounter with numb bewilderment). But he has, it seems, made some progress. He is ready for a relationship, if only with someone as physically derelict as he is mentally so. He needs company and, perhaps, a friend.

Unluckily, he picks on Davies, who tends to see people either as threats or dupes, and has long spent his life evading the one and freeloading from the other. He is suspicious, mistrustful, and self-righteously indignant when the world fails to accord him his due. He rages at 'bastard' monks who refuse him free shoes and at 'Poles, Greeks, blacks' who presume to act as if they were his equals. It is important to him to cling on to such rags of superiority as he can still muster: he's 'eaten my dinner off the best of plates', he left his wife when she boiled her underclothes in the saucepan, he knows the man who runs the best public convenience in Shepherd's Bush. It is also important to him to remain anonymous or, rather, pseudonymous: if his real name and whereabouts are discovered, his enemies will be round to beat him up or clap him in prison. One day, he will get down to Sidcup and recover the identity papers he left there fifteen years ago, and all his problems will be magically solved. Until then, he will skulk and scrounge.

One can imagine few people so absolutely incapable of friendship; but that doesn't deter Aston. In all Pinter's *oeuvre* there is no character who behaves so generously. He gives Davies a bed, a key, and money. He offers him a job. He buys him a bag full of clothes, to replace those Davies lost in the pre-curtain fight. He does his best to satisfy the tramp's main want, for comfortable shoes. But from the first there are indications that Davies is not a man to feel genuine gratitude, still less reciprocate. His natural querulousness asserts itself as soon as he's invited to stay. It is a 'bit rough' that no cup of tea is available. Told by Aston that he has been talking in his sleep, he instantly becomes resentful and aggressive: 'You got hold of the wrong bloke, mate.' All this, before he has encountered the younger brother, Mick.

The part Mick plays in the destruction of Davies is open to dispute: how conscious, how unconscious is it? Let us tentatively piece together the evidence Pinter scatters about the play. Mick is a self-employed builder with ambitions, one of the most fanciful of which is the transforming of these run-down rooms into a palatial maisonette. His hope was that his convalescent brother would renovate it in return for house-room; but already he seems more likely to reduce it to a junkyard. And now he gives Mick's own bed to a tramp! It's probable that this energetic young man decides at once that Davies must go, and spends the play putting that decision into practice.

First, he tries bully-boy methods. He twists Davies' arm, forces him to the floor, and proceeds to intimidate him in a way characteristic of Pinter. The old man's limited intellect is bludgeoned by grotesque family reminiscences and bewildering personal memories, punctuated by repeated questions that the context makes distinctly menacing: 'What's your name?', 'Sleep well?' At the same time Mick makes his proprietorship brutally clear. It is 'my room', 'my bed'. He ends this phase of the attack with sarcastic contempt. If Davies can raise the money, he can rent the flat or even buy it: 'Who do you bank with?'

It seems a pretty straightforward attempt to frighten away an unwanted intruder – except for one tiny thing. Mick has grabbed Davies's trousers, thus effectively preventing him going. Perhaps he is taking sadistic pleasure in teasing the old man. Or perhaps he is biding his time. Perhaps it is enough now to show Davies that he is there only on sufferance, *his* sufferance. Conceivably, he wants to discover if this unlikely visitor will or won't make a friend for his troubled brother. But such speculation is halted by the entrance of Aston. After more aggressive horseplay, allowing Mick to re-emphasize that he is the real power in the house, the young man abruptly exits, to resume the attack in the middle of Act II.

This begins with more intimidation, more sarcasm. A vacuum cleaner lunges after the terrified tramp in a room plunged into darkness. 'I was going to suggest that we'd lower your rent, make it a nominal sum,' he is pointedly told after the light has been restored. But now Mick's strategy becomes subtler. The threat of violence isn't the ideal way to get rid of a man who is, after all, his brother's guest. How much better if Aston can be shown the real nature of his supposed friend, and thus be moved to get rid of him himself. Whether or not Mick's plan is wholly conscious from the start, it certainly works very nicely. It is morally and emotionally satisfying, too, because it means that Davies is made to show his own worst qualities and to bring about his own just punishment.

Affecting to be impressed by the knife the old man is feebly waving at him, Mick shares his worries about his brother with him and offers him the same job Aston has already mooted, that of caretaker. Davies's response is predictable. He quickly gives his allegiance to the dominant brother and begins to distance himself from the weaker one. The favours done him by Aston mean nothing. He 'done me no harm, but I wouldn't say he was any particular friend of mine'. Indeed, the once-deferential Davies becomes combative and demanding. Why doesn't Aston keep the window closed at night? Why hasn't he bought him any shoes? Then comes the long, painful speech in which Aston describes his sufferings in the asylum. To a friend, this would be a confidence to be appreciated and respected. To Davies, it becomes ammunition to use against Aston.

By the time he does use it, his grasping, feckless character has become only too apparent. Thinking himself secure in Mick's protection, Davies has come to regard Aston's favours as rights, duties inadequately performed. He hasn't provided him with cutlery, hasn't bought him a clock. He's 'no friend of mine'. He's 'got no feelings'. He 'doesn't care for me'. The play's title, as this last remark implies, is deliberately ambiguous. It is Aston who, a few moments later, brings Davies some comfortable shoes, only to be insulted because the laces are the wrong colour. It is Aston who, we're told in a marvellously suggestive passage, likes to stand beside his guest's bed in the morning smiling at him, a sign of warmth Davies regards with paranoid suspicion. Aston is prepared to offer care to someone most people would dismiss as a shiftless layabout. He, more than anyone else, is the 'caretaker'.

But Davies is too stupid, too impressed by proprietorship and power, to see who his true friend is. So he reacts to Aston's complaint that he is talking in his sleep in the ugliest possible way, telling him he is a lunatic who should be locked away, deriding the shed he plans to build, and finally menacing him with his knife. Told at last to leave, he tries to persuade Mick to throw Aston out of his own home. The strategy is almost complete. It only remains for Mick, having exposed Davies's treachery and brought about the important rift, to reject the old man too. He pounces on his unwise inference, made earlier in the third act, that he can help paint the flat. Davies has pretended to be a decorator, but is actually an 'impostor', a 'barbarian' who 'stinks from arsehole to breakfast-time'. Disillusioned, shattered, the wretched tramp creeps back to his original benefactor, hoping for a reconciliation; but it is too late. Some commentators have suggested that Aston may, after all, allow him to stay. My view is that they are wrong.

Pinter originally intended to end the play with Davies's murder, but came to realize that such sensationalism was unnecessary. The tramp has been destroyed, indeed has helped to destroy himself, in a much subtler way. He has no one to help him, nowhere to go, and no hope left except the increasingly absurd one of getting his papers from Sidcup. We all know that, in the unlikely event of his ever going there, he would find he had no identity at all.

Davies is the victim of his own inadequacies as well as of his perversity of character, and at the end he does command some sympathy. He is drawn and felt in the round, as vivid and plausible a character as may be found in modern drama. Those same adjectives could be applied to the play as a whole, too; and those who regard it as an abstract drama set in some emblematic limbo should see the film. With Pinter's approval, that showed the wood under the tarpaulin in the garden, streets and a second-hand clothes shop, and actually had Mick picking up Davies in his van and threatening to drive him to Sidcup, only to drop him back on the pavement after circling a traffic roundabout. But the most concrete of plays can, of course, have implications, reverberations. So it is with *The Caretaker*.

Martin Esslin's suggestion, based largely on an ingenious reading of Mick's first long speech, is that Davies is a sort of father-surrogate, one whose unreasonable demands the child must necessarily reject. That may be to take interpretation further than the evidence warrants. A more moderate claim is made by the playwright John Arden, that the play 'is a study of the unexpected strength of family ties against an intruder'. This is borne out by the strong bond that plainly exists between the brothers. Four times Davies mentions Aston's mental inadequacies, and four times he is firmly put down by Mick. When Davies asks who will live in the flat when Mick has converted it, the answer is 'My brother and me'. Again, the stage directions tell us that both men are 'smiling faintly' at each other after Davies has been rejected by Mick. It is entirely logical that the tramp's ham-fisted attempts to exploit the surface tensions in this deep and somewhat sinister relationship should redound on his own head.

Then again, Davies tries to oust Aston, not only from the family, but from the space in which he lives. This reflects Pinter's continuing preoccupation with both personal and territorial acquisitiveness. And yet *The Caretaker* does not need any such generalizations in order to justify its existence. Not many plays show such understanding of unspoken motivation. Not many succeed in chronicling the ebb and flow of relationships so intricately. Not many ask such watchfulness of the spectators, and not many reward it so handsomely. It seems positively ungrateful to ask for more.

The Homecoming

The first point to be made about *The Homecoming*, a necessary one since it is becoming institutionalized into a modern 'classic', is that it is actually a very shocking play. After all, what happens? Six years ago Teddy, eldest of the three sons of a north London butcher, surreptitiously married a photographic model called Ruth and left for America, where he has since taught philosophy at an unnamed but probably far-western university. Now he is breaking a European vacation to introduce his wife, who is also the mother of three children, to his father, brothers and uncle, who since his mother's death have lived an all-male existence in their big, shambling house. It is a curious homecoming. At their very first encounter one brother, Lenny, makes sexual overtures to Ruth. And the instant reaction of the father, Max, is to call her a 'filthy scrubber', a 'slopbucket' and 'bedpan'. Possibly he has recognized her from long ago, perhaps he has an instinctive sense of what she was and is to be, or perhaps he is simply expressing his ugly and erratic temper. At any rate, neither she nor Teddy take offence, and for a time all seems relatively serene, even 'normal'. But suddenly Lenny is dancing with Ruth and kissing her, and soon afterwards the other brother, Joey, is taking her to his bedroom. And Teddy returns to America and his children alone, leaving Ruth to remain with the rest of the family, who have decided, with her agreement, to make her a professional prostitute.

It *is* shocking, so much so that some critics have declared the story literally impossible and begun by considering it as an extreme metaphor for some much more general truth. That seems finicky and premature. The play may of course end as metaphor, but it is surely sensible to start by discovering if and to what extent the characters live, what their individual motives and reactions are, whether, how and why the 'impossible' might become possible.

From the opening it is clear that Jessie, Max's dead wife, is badly missed. The old man himself runs the kitchen and keeps the house clean, and resents it. He bickers with Lenny, who calls him a 'dog cook' and generally treats him derisively. He tells Joey, who feels hungry, to 'go and find yourself a mother', and shows some scorn for the young man's aspirations as a boxer. He reserves a special contempt for his chauffeur-brother, Sam, insidiously accusing him of a lack of virility. These men are, to put it mildly, getting on each other's nerves. This claustrophobic household needs a woman.

And what kind of woman do they need? Well, Jessie, whom the candidate would be replacing, was evidently not the pure wife and mother of domestic romance. Max's memories of her are sharply ambivalent. When he is in a good mood, which is not often, he talks of her as a woman with 'a will of iron, a heart of gold, and a mind'. More often she is a 'slutbitch'. Lenny's feelings about her also seem mixed. At any rate, he tells Ruth not to call him 'Leonard' since 'that's the name my mother gave me', and later displays a morbid interest in her sexuality, needling his father by asking him what 'it was like' the night he was begotten. And his mother's sexuality was evidently strong. Martin Esslin suggests that she herself might have been a prostitute, basing the idea on Sam's recollections of driving her around the West End, on Max's first reaction to Ruth's presence ('I've never had a whore under this roof before: ever since your mother died'), and, not least, on his sentimental but ironic remark that Jessie taught her sons 'every single bit of the moral code they live by'. As we later learn, Lenny is a professional pimp and Joey capable of rape. Esslin's case cannot be proved, but there is obviously truth in Sam's revelation at the end of the play, that Jessie had sex in the back of his limousine with Max's best friend, McGregor. Altogether, Ruth would seem well qualified for executive office in this ruttish and (perhaps) once-matriarchal household. Instead of the mother who was something of a whore, the men now have the whore who will be something of a mother.

As the play proceeds, Pinter establishes not only his male characters' need but their callousness. What Max was really like as a father we may judge from Lenny's parody of childhood terror: 'Don't use your stick on me, Daddy. No please. It wasn't my fault, it was one of the others.' And we have Max's own testimony for the image he hoped to create outside the house. He and McGregor, he boasts, were 'two of the worst-hated men in the West End of London'. To be sure, he has his mawkish moments, but most of the time he exudes dissatisfaction and hostility. The frequent violence of his language reflects what we feel to be his brutality: 'I'll chop your spine off' or, of the family in general, 'one cast-iron bunch of crap after another, one flow of stinking pus after another'.

Perhaps he was once a member of the underworld himself. He jumps at the idea of putting Ruth 'on the game' as if he knows about such things, and he has a son who owns several 'flats' in red-light Soho. Lenny, and to a lesser extent Joey, would seem to have inherited character traits from him, too, including a total amorality where the personal desires are concerned, a capacity for violence, and an apparent inability to care or love. Lenny greets Teddy as if he were a passing acquaintance, not a brother, and shows not the slightest respect for his marriage, which at first he insultingly refuses to credit at all. Within minutes he is telling Ruth two of those inconsequential, loaded stories in which Pinter specializes. In one he describes almost murdering a diseased prostitute, and in the other assaulting an old lady. This is his attempt to impress and dominate his brother's wife. It also tells us something about his own ruthlessness and that of the world in which he moves. We don't feel that this mocking, braggardly young man has any more scruples than his 'lousy, filthy father', as he dementedly calls himself.

How then could Ruth, the American professor's wife, conceivably consent to their squalid plans for her? Well, she has made it clear from the beginning that she has a will of her own and is, perhaps, interested in exercising it upon others. She demonstrates as much by coolly withstanding Lenny's first attempts to dominate her and, to his confusion, somewhat dominating him instead. This also indicates that she is practised in the wiles of sex, a suggestion reinforced as the play proceeds. For a time she seems content to play the virtuous daughter-in-law. But she dramatically interrupts a jaunty discussion on the nature of reality by pointing out that the sensuous movement of her lips may be more 'significant' than the words coming from them, the invisible rustling of her underwear more important than the overt shifting of her legs. It is a clear sexual invitation, and taken as such by her listeners. But their exploitation of her body is always on her own terms. Lenny is made to fulfil her minor whims and Joey somehow persuaded that he can be happy without going 'the whole hog' with her. Finally, she drives a hard and very professional bargain over her coming stint in Soho.

Now, this professionalism combines with other hints in the play to suggest what she has been in the past. We may speculate that Teddy made a last-minute, hole-in-the-corner marriage with her because he was ashamed of her and frightened by his family's possible reaction. She was, as she meaningfully says, 'different' then: a slut and, given six years of wedlock and three children, possibly a pregnant slut. This is perhaps to venture further than the play's evidence permits. We do, however, know that she posed naked beside a lake, and made a nostalgic trip back there just before leaving for America. Altogether, she does not sound a woman likely to settle easily into a conventional married life with a rather narrow intellectual on a college campus. And, indeed, she herself says that America is 'all rock. And sand. It stretches so far . . . everywhere you look. And there's lots of insects there.' No wonder she craves to return to the place near where, as she tells us, she was born. She craves power, feeling, sweat, bodies, people, in short, involvement and reality, rather than the hygienic swimming pools, the 'stimulating' discussions and emotional aridity of the desert university. For her, it is a necessary homecoming.

Her decision to stay has more obvious logic than Teddy's to abandon her, though that, too, can be cautiously explained. At first she is the one who wants to leave, and he the one anxious to present her to a father he speaks of with inexplicable warmth. But the way he 'clenches his knuckles' when alone suggests that even then he is apprehensive. And before long he is suggesting to Ruth they should 'cut short' their visit, and she is indicating, in the most spectacular way, how very congenial she finds this house of males. By then it is apparent that his hold over her is tenuous. We may, if we like, conclude from Teddy's announcement that 'she's not well', that she has been seriously depressed, and perhaps, with Esslin, that the holiday in Italy has been an attempt to repair their ailing marriage; but that, once again, may be to take speculation too far.

What is abundantly clear, however, is that she cannot be an ideal wife for an aspiring academic on a small campus, especially for one as imaginatively limited as Teddy's discussion about philosophy with Lenny suggests he is. He puts up a rather feeble fight for her, hurrying off to pack when danger looms and pathetically assuring her she can 'help me with my lectures when we get back'. But he is much more exercised and emphatic when it comes to bolstering his own self-esteem, as he does in a long speech in which he accuses his family of lacking detachment and praises himself for his cool equilibrium: precisely the qualities which, ironically enough, have lost him Ruth. And soon he has given up the battle in what one imagines to be a mixture of hopelessness and relief. He joins a family discussion about Ruth's sexual abilities and even prepares her for the family's sinister invitation. 'Eddie,' she says, using what's presumably his pet-name as he departs without acknowledging her, 'don't become a stranger'; but he is already a stranger and, we feel, has long been one. An open rift is by now inevitable.

The characters' conduct is plausible and, of course, deeply unprepossessing. Moral norms count for nothing in this house. Indeed, the only resident whose attitude to wives and children is at all conventional, Sam, is ignored and sometimes insulted by the others, nowhere more so than when he reveals his knowledge of Jessie's infidelity and promptly collapses with a heart attack. Even Teddy, his favourite nephew, coolly steps past his prone body, offhandedly remarking that this means he has lost his ride to London Airport. It is a family whose members, at least on the surface, treat each other with appalling indifference, a family incapable of altruism, grief or even friendly communication. Teddy has written to his father, but never, it seems, told him of his wife and children. When he meets Lenny, he does not reveal Ruth's presence offstage. And Lenny, when his father comes downstairs, says nothing of the arrival of Teddy and Ruth. All that is characteristic.

And yet these people communicate only too effectively on a more basic level. Their surface indifference, we feel, conceals a strange and frightening closeness. The sexual sharing which Lenny and Joey seem to find natural is one indication of this. There is also an obvious bond between Max and both sons: as Lenny claims to Teddy, the family is a 'unit'. This does not mean its members love or even like each other. It does mean that they are symbiotically linked, and that their joint needs and greeds override those of any individual component, as Teddy discovers when he comes home hoping, one imagines, to display his independence. The family absorbs, overwhelms. In its inescapability and amorality it is, as Ronald Bryden has observed, more easily recognized and described by the zoologist than by the psychologist. Somewhere beneath the clothes and the words raw animal instincts are on display. A battle is being waged for dominance, power, possession and sex, and it is one that Teddy indisputably loses but his brothers do not unequivocally win. At the end Ruth is left sitting serenely in a chair, with Lenny watching, Joey's head in her lap, and Max crawling across the floor towards her, whimpering for attention: the spider at the centre of her web, the queen bee in command of the hive, the human animal who will be at once mother and mistress to her subject brood.

No wonder the play shocked its audiences. If such dark and anarchic drives could be found in one particular family, as Pinter was at pains to prove, might they not be found in others too? Of what sexual transactions might we not be capable? *The Homecoming* hangs together on a naturalistic level, which is disturbing enough. It also gives flesh to subcutaneous fantasy, and expresses those fears and desires that we customarily force ourselves to keep hidden. Those who wish to ransack the text for a more allegorical significance may do so: the achievement already seems more than sufficient.

It remains to say something both for and against Pinter's use of language in the play. Sometimes the idiom seems a little mannered, notably when Lenny is berating Teddy, whose wife he has just stolen, for eating his cheese roll. The tiny quarrel, as so often in Pinter, disguises a much larger one, but in this case it does so too obviously. There is also something rather laboured about the irony, both here and later in the play, when Max calls Teddy a "lousy stinkpig" for refusing to contribute to the unfaithful Ruth's upkeep and Lenny suggests that he should be her American procurer. It rubs in the outrageousness of Teddy's treatment too strongly. But most of the time Pinter's words, rhythms, even pauses will stand up to the closest examination. To take a tiny example. Ruth has, it seems, been on the point of revealing something about her past. Teddy senses danger, and covers up, emphasizing what a good life they lead together and how much the children love her. Then:

> *Lenny* Your cigar's gone out.
> *Teddy* Oh, yes.
> *Lenny* Want a light?
> *Teddy* No. No.

If there were just one 'No', Teddy's inattention to his cigar and curious unwillingness to relight it might have little impact. But the second 'No' shows how edgy he is. For him, the situation is packed with possibilities of disaster. It is a subtlety of language and emotion apparent everywhere in the play. The words may be terse, inconsequential, flat: there are always great fissures of feeling somewhere just beneath.

Old Times

Old Times is a play of conflict, and sometimes nasty, painful conflict. This is a necessary first emphasis, because it has been seen as primarily 'about' perception, consciousness and, especially, memory. Now, it is true that we are never sure precisely what occurred in the past, immensely potent though that past obviously remains. It is also evident that the play is not absolutely naturalistic. On at least two occasions the characters briefly re-enact what appear to be events long ago. There are even times when one wonders if it isn't all happening in the confused, suspicious imagination of the male in the case. In short, it is taken for granted throughout that recollection can be misleading, perception unreliable, consciousness misty and truth impossible to uncover. It is an *a priori* assumption, as in *Landscape* and *Silence*. But Pinter draws on his old preoccupations, his more vivid concerns, to add a tension missing in those two plays, and does so, ingeniously enough, by making recollection, perception and consciousness part of the conflict. The past is the battleground on which the play is fought: memories are the combatants' weapons.

Specifically, Deeley is a film-maker, married to Kate. They live in an isolated farmhouse near the sea. A visitor, Anna, is expected. She was Kate's 'one and only' friend years ago. Indeed, they lived together. She also had the quaint habit of 'stealing' Kate's underwear. Deeley at this juncture is unaggressive, but tells Kate he will be 'watching her', to see by her reaction if Anna is 'the same person' who attracted her years ago. There is just a hint of danger in the air.

Anna arrives, and begins chatting excitedly about the full and fulfilling cultural life she and Kate shared in London, a place Deeley and Kate rarely visit. She then patronizingly compliments them on their 'sensible and courageous' decision to live in 'such a silence'. One does not need a Pinter codebook to see that Anna is implying that Kate leads a far duller existence with Deeley than she once led with herself, and the impression is reinforced when she suddenly makes a Freudian slip, congratulating him on having 'a wonderful casserole . . . I mean, wife'. In other words, Kate is simply a housewife and cook, or maybe even a passive dish, whose purpose is to be guzzled. Up to this point Deeley has confined any hostility he feels towards Anna to remarking on her use of the word 'lest', implying that she is a little precious. From now onwards the battle is on, and it is for nothing less than the emotional ownership of Kate.

The skirmishes vary in subtlety and intensity. The two compete over the degree of intimacy each has had with Kate, Anna talking with romantic relish of gazing at her while she sat 'flicking her hair', Deeley emphasizing his physical mastery of her. They compete over the correct interpretation of Kate's character, Deeley accusing her of lacking 'any sense of fixedness, any sense of decisiveness', Anna countering with an anecdote which implies that she, Anna, recognizes a profound decisiveness in her which he has failed to comprehend. They even fight with pointed snatches from nostalgic songs: 'Oh but you're lovely, with your smile so warm' from Anna, 'I've got a woman crazy for me, she's funny that way' from Deeley. At one point Deeley, speaking (as he often does) with the calculatedly unromantic aggressiveness that Anna's quavering sensibilities provoke, describes how he met Kate in a deserted fleapit. He picked her up after seeing the movie *Odd Man Out* and, rather later, their 'naked bodies met, hers cool, warm, highly agreeable'. Anna ripostes by declaring that memory is deceptive, implying that this encounter never happened and, not long afterwards, describing how she and Kate capped weeks of cultural junketing by seeing 'almost alone' *Odd Man Out*. At this blow (for such it is) Deeley changes tack, asserting his male ego by boasting about his worldly accomplishments and subtly denigrating Anna herself, whom he implies is neglecting the husband she left at home in Sicily and anyway lives a rich, spoilt life out there.

The first act ends with Anna inveigling Kate into a re-enactment of their life together, one in which Anna is eager to pander to her slightest need and from which Deeley is obviously excluded. By this time he has directly protested only once against what he clearly suspects is an attempt to humiliate him and steal his wife. When Anna has spoken of Kate being 'shyly poised over me', a phrase characteristic of her arch, rather cloying speech, he has snapped out, 'Stop that.' Everywhere else, the social niceties have just, if only just, been observed. A frigid politeness has characterized the combatants. When the Italian director Visconti presented a performance of the play in which Anna and Kate salaciously fondled one another, Pinter organized a protest of the English critics, an unusual action for so reticent a writer and one which indicates how strongly he felt that subtexts should remain subtexts and surfaces be respected. In the play the feelings are strong, but they tend to express themselves obliquely, in the guise of after-dinner small talk or casual reverie. It is, once again, a very English battle.

Even when Deeley's disgust erupts towards the end, he swiftly becomes oblique, indirect again. To explain. Kate has taken a bath, and Deeley, left with Anna, has produced some insulting memories to counteract her idealized ones. Indeed, he claims to remember Anna herself, 'squealing and hissing' with a girlfriend at a party and surrounded by grotesquely unattractive men. He spent the evening staring up her skirt. This is, perhaps, his way of telling her he thinks of her as a superannuated sex-object and isn't impressed by her cultural pretension. Whatever the message, their duel becomes increasingly unpleasant from now on. A discussion of Kate's bathing, drying and powdering habits ensues, allowing Anna subtly and Deeley emphatically to display their familiarity with her body. Anna reminisces about borrowing Kate's underwear, about watching Kate blush when she described how an unknown man at a party persistently stared at it, about telling Kate intimate tales in the dark of night. She was, says Anna, 'shy as a fawn'. There was 'a good deal of Brontë' about her, not 'in passion but only in secrecy'.

This provokes an obvious question from Deeley: what was she in passion? 'I feel that is your province,' says Anna. At last he speaks directly: 'Of course it's my bloody province. I'm her husband . . . am I alone in beginning to find all this distasteful?' Yet when Anna challenges him to explain, he does not make the honest answer, that the battle for Kate has passed all bounds of decency: instead, he makes another, somewhat frantic attack on Anna's supposed neglect of her husband and on her Mediterranean lifestyle. A moment later Anna speaks as directly as she ever does: 'I came here not to disrupt but to celebrate.' And this may indeed be what she believes she is doing. But the friendship she is celebrating and the way she celebrates it have both already (and with reason) proved too disturbing for Deeley to believe her. To him, the celebration is *ipso facto* disruptive; and battle promptly recommences, to end in the only way it can.

This ending is satisfying, yet somewhat surprising, since

Pinter has lured us into sharing the basically crass assumption of both Anna and Deeley. They have bickered over which has had the deeper experience and understanding of Kate, each with an eye to claiming possession of what was and is the most vital in her. But what they miss is that people are not objects and can only be possessed with their own consent. Kate quietly implied this in Act I, remarking that they are speaking of her as if she were dead. Now she makes the truth as she sees it brutally clear in a long, metaphoric speech, the last words we hear. She talks of seeing Anna dead and scrawled with dirt, of importing Deeley into her bed and of his resisting when she tried to dirty his face too: 'He suggested a wedding instead and a change of environment . . . neither mattered.' What Kate means precisely is open to dispute. In my view, she is saying that Anna, having in effect allowed herself to become Kate's slave, is emotionally dead to her: Deeley, who refused to submit, was a refreshing alternative. And yet marriage and a move to the country made no real difference: 'Neither mattered'.

It is a cruel rejection, yet we recognize its logic. All along it has been Kate's elusiveness that has provoked the others to dance round her, the very fact she can never be possessed that has incited them to desperate displays of possessiveness. She is the Pinter woman at her most disconcerting: withdrawn, self-contained, inscrutable, tantalizing, unreachable. She watches the increasingly ugly battle raging round her with great serenity, speaking little and, before the dénouement, only once at length, when she talks of the countryside almost narcissistically, describing her private enjoyment of its softness and blurred evanescence. You feel she luxuriates in her status as the prize for which the others are fighting. But she is a kind of prize that can only award itself, and that she will not do. Her strength is her detachment, her privacy, her untouchability even when touched. She is, of course, far the most powerful character in the play, the one that holds absolute sway over those trying to dominate her: those whose weakness is that they *want* to dominate her.

No doubt this is painful enough to Anna, whose emotional hunger we can (if we must) call lesbian, though the word seems too glib a label to apply to the complex sexuality of a character created by Pinter, the enemy of all glibness and labelling. It is positive anguish to Deeley, as the play's close appears to demonstrate. Earlier Anna had countered Deeley's sensual memories by describing an odd incident long ago. She spoke of a man sobbing in her and Kate's room, going away and then returning to lie on Kate's lap. We suspected then that the unidentified intruder was actually Deeley, and we end by knowing it, because the three characters re-enact the identical scene. Up to this point he has made light of the frustration Kate's character clearly causes him. He has spoken of her just a little waspishly, as a passive girl whose only virtue was silence. Now, in this frozen ritual, he reveals both his dependence on her and his despair. And the repetition of the scene makes us realize that the situation will never essentially change.

The play is written with an economy, a precision unmatched by any of Pinter's longer plays except *Betrayal*. The most unobtrusive words demand attention. Why, for instance, does Kate claim Anna 'stole' the underwear she clearly only borrowed? Does the hostile emphasis of the verb indicate the lack of connection Kate now feels with Anna? Is it a reflection on Anna's importunate intimacy, the presumption with which she pushed herself on Kate and sucked her emotionally? Again, note the eloquent offhandedness of Kate's reply when she's asked if Deeley is ever away for long periods: 'I think, sometimes.' Wives usually *know*. Yet again, consider the marvellous ambiguity of her 'You talk of me as if I were dead.' Actually, the 'were' is a subjunctive, and Kate means 'as if I *am* dead'. But Anna interprets it as an imperfect – 'No, no, you weren't dead' – and thus manages to imply that Kate is dead now. Only a writer of extraordinary sharpness could give so tiny a detail such weight.

It is also a play which, specific though the situation is, becomes unusually suggestive and resonant. As the surreal beginning and ending both indicate, Anna is present even when she is literally absent, because she is part and parcel of Kate's internal history. So the play is about those aspects of the people we love from which we are excluded, those that others may own, those we can only guess at and try not to mistrust. In other words, it is about the pain of not really knowing someone. More obviously, it shows how an intruder can bring out the doubts and tensions inherent in a seemingly stable situation. It shows how the past merges into the present, defines and threatens it. It shows how the past can be exploited, and memories used for people's present emotional purposes. It shows how subjective and how utilitarian we are with 'truth'. Not least, it presents us with two female archetypes, one remote and teasing, the other emotional and grasping, both equally threatening to men. And, through the character of Deeley, it expresses dreads and wounds that others, too, will have felt, though not perhaps so concentratedly. It is a play in which subliminal insecurities are made flesh, one of Pinter's very best.

Robert Bolt
(born 1924)

Robert Bolt was born in 1924, son of a shopkeeper, and was educated in Manchester. He worked in an insurance office, was commissioned in the wartime army, went to Manchester University, and became a schoolmaster, first in a Devon village, then at Millfield; and he was at the latter in 1957, when his first stage play, *The Critic and the Heart*, was produced at Oxford. While still in his teens he joined the Communist Party, an affiliation he later rejected, feeling it had 'nothing to do with democracy or freedom'. Thereafter his main political commitment was to the antinuclear-weapon lobby, and in the early sixties he was briefly imprisoned for refusing to renounce civil disobedience.

'Commitment' of more sweeping kinds is the prime concern of his work. What is a man's duty to himself, what to his society? Where, how, can he expect to fulfil his heart, mind and conscience? Is human wholeness a possibility, given our own inadequacies and the pressures of the world? Or are we doomed either to be mutilated or mutilate ourselves? Even the domestic *Flowering Cherry* (1957), Bolt's first success, has some relevance to these questions. The protagonist, a dissatisfied insurance salesman, talks interminably of owning an apple orchard; but when the possibility presents itself, he refuses it. He is, in Bolt's words, 'a man who substitutes violent words for action': as with many, his commitment is to a dream, a saving lie.

The protagonist of *The Tiger and the Horse* (1960), a senior university don, seems at first to be no less emotionally barren, having committed himself to a philosophy of withdrawal, lack of 'involvement'. His benign neglect of his more passionate wife, combined with his passive opposition to an anti-H-bomb petition she wants to sign, drives her violently insane, causing him in turn to renounce his beliefs and worldly ambitions. He dedicates himself to her, associates himself with her convictions, and even announces he will reapply himself to astronomy, the subject in which he apparently did his most original work. Bolt intended to suggest that those who commit themselves on a personal level will find they have committed themselves on a social and political level, too: 'Someone who is really engaged with another human will find willy-nilly that he is interested in the Bomb.' Unluckily, the play is too schematic to be persuasive. The characters are sometimes attitudes rather than individuals, and the conclusion (if not as implausible as the florid death that ends *Flowering Cherry*) seems distinctly pat.

Bolt himself shares the general dissatisfaction with these plays, thinking them awkwardly straddled between naturalism and non-naturalism, and summing them up as 'fourth wall drama with puzzling, uncomfortable, and, if you are uncharitable, pretentious overtones'. Since then he has mainly turned to historical subjects, hoping thereby to avoid the limitations of an absolute naturalism, achieve distance and plausibly give his characters more stature, and his themes greater size. The one exception to this practice is the curious *Gentle Jack* (1963), in which a cerebral young man is given emotional power by Pan, only to discover that this must include destructiveness as well as tenderness. It is, as Bolt says, a 'pessimistic' play, since it suggests that human wholeness, in the unlikely event of being achieved, must contain much that is ugly and evil. It is also (as he admits) too 'diagrammatic', too interested in ideas rather than people, and, in spite of well-written passages, dramatically scattered and somewhat confusing: 'as a theatrical event, it simply failed to happen.'

Vivat, Vivat Regina (1970) and *State of Revolution* (1977) both indisputably 'happened'. During the 1960s Bolt became an accomplished screen-writer, and the effect of this is perhaps to be seen in these plays' pace, fluency, and bold cuts between time and time and place and place. The first graphically shows how Mary Queen of Scots subordinated political wisdom to emotion, thus shortening a personally fulfilling life, and how Elizabeth I subordinated emotion to public duty, with the result that the nation thrived and she survived, but at immense cost to herself. The second is recognizably the work both of an apostate communist with a powerful belief in the primacy of the individual and of a dramatist who refuses to classify anyone as a villain and once claimed never to have created a character he disliked. It shows the idealistic aspirations of the Bolsheviks, the compromises forced upon them, and the degree to which they came to subordinate means to probably illusory ends. It shows men handing over all personal responsibility to a 'scientific' view of history upon whose validity their own individual conduct tended to cast doubt. Above all, it shows the unyielding commitment of Lenin, a naturally humane man prepared to deform himself and destroy others for the sake of his convictions. The result is arresting, but might be more satisfying if Bolt had brought more trenchancy to the moral-cum-political debate or more depth to the characters instead of offering only a modicum of either.

This criticism may also be directed at *Vivat* and perhaps even *A Man for All Seasons*. Bolt believes strongly in catering for his audiences' 'straightforward, childlike, primitive desire to know', and thinks they should not have to apply themselves 'with conscious effort' to understanding a play; but this attitude, though refreshing in some ways, may explain why his work sometimes seems excessively undemanding. His aim is to produce drama that combines simplicity of plot with moral subtlety and emotional complexity; but subtlety and complexity are relative terms, and Bolt could perhaps be more generous with both. The impression he persistently gives is of an intelligent, able craftsman writing somewhat 'down', consciously catering for a middlebrow audience that does not care to think too hard, deeply, originally or dangerously.

A Man for All Seasons

Bolt has been called the most Brechtian of British dramatists bar Arden; but, though he himself has said that 'Brecht is the writer I most wish to resemble' and described the style of *A Man for All Seasons* as a 'bastardized version' of Brecht's own, his claim is superficial. Ideologically, they are poles apart. Brecht would doubtless have seen Thomas More as an example of superstitious individualism. Even stylistically, their aims are opposite. Brecht's 'alienation-effect' was calculated to prevent audiences succumbing to illusion and indulging their sympathetic emotions, to encourage them coolly to ponder his social truths. Bolt brings onstage what he calls 'the common man', and uses him partly as narrator and commentator, talking directly to the audience from outside the action. On two occasions he actually reads extracts from modern histories. But this seemingly 'Brechtian' device does more to increase the plot's comprehensibility and fluency than to detach us from it. In any case, the proceedings themselves are mainly conducted in a conventionally naturalistic manner, and almost everything about the protagonist invites, rather than repels, the sympathy we traditionally offer heroes. And Bolt himself concedes that he wants to 'draw the audience into the play, not thrust them off it'.

Many have felt so drawn. His More is an unrelievedly attractive man: humorous even in adversity, warm to his family, a considerate enough friend deliberately to alienate someone to whom his friendship might prove embarrassing, kind to his servants, tolerant and forgiving yet clean and clear in his moral judgements, loyal to the king, conscious of his public duty, formidably intelligent yet sufficiently innocent persistently to underrate his own danger, unpretentiously pious and, of course, a man of unflinching integrity. He is 'the only judge since Cato who didn't accept bribes'. He is also the only Lord Chancellor in English history to lose office, property, freedom and (finally) head for the sake of his convictions.

All this Bolt shows, and manages to give an unobtrusive history lesson at the same time. Henry VIII is determined to divorce the ageing and now-barren Catherine on the somewhat specious grounds that she is his brother's widow and the Pope should never have given him a dispensation to marry her. The Pope demurs, being under the influence of Catherine's nephew, the Emperor Charles V. The row escalates. Divorce and remarriage to Anne Boleyn becomes wholesale rejection of the 'Bishop of Rome'. When the British bishops submit to this, More resigns as Lord Chancellor; but this isn't enough for the king and his minister Thomas Cromwell, who find the silence into which he then retreats only too eloquent. It becomes obligatory to swear to an Act of Succession, which not only recognizes Anne's male children as heirs to the throne, something More is willing to accept, but denies the spiritual authority of the Pope, something More cannot. He is imprisoned, but cannot legally be executed as a traitor, because he refuses to reveal the grounds of his objections. A lawyer himself, he exploits the letter of the law in order to survive; but it is no good. Perjured evidence is brought against him, and More is convicted and beheaded, proclaiming both his loyalty to Henry and his conviction that the king's spiritual claims are 'directly repugnant to the law of God'.

It is an accurate enough record, presented with no more dramatic licence than a limited cast makes inevitable. The problem is that the end of the story is so well known that it is difficult to inject tension into it. But Bolt does what can be done, presenting every argument and pressure that might have persuaded More to change his mind. There are the inadequacies of the Roman Church and of the Pope, generally agreed to be a 'strikingly corrupt old person'. There is the determination of a young, vigorous Henry, offering honours and veiled threats, culminating in promises of pardon or death. There is public duty: More is, after all, Lord Chancellor, enjoined not only to obey the king but to consider the kingdom, which remembers the recent civil wars and has good reason to fear that the absence of a male heir will mean their recurrence. Should he really place his personal salvation above the safety of the state?

Then there are private pressures: his wife's pain, anger and failure to understand him; the poverty and misery of his family; and, more subtly, his beloved daughter's suggestions that he has done all God could have expected, that he could swear an oath with (as it were) his fingers crossed, and that he is elevating himself into a hero. But even for this last temptation, reminiscent of the one that most troubled Eliot's Thomas à Becket, he has his answer. He will make every accommodation he possibly can, being 'not the stuff of which martyrs are made'; but there is a part of himself which he variously defines as his self, his soul, and God's love, from which he proves not merely unwilling but actually unable to retreat. When he finds he cannot live without ceding this ultimate integrity, he dies as blithely as a man can. As Bolt has said, he was someone with a great capacity for life and a 'splendid social adjustment', who nevertheless 'found something in himself without which life was valueless and when that was denied him was able to grasp his death': a man for all seasons, spring to winter.

The other characters are important as much for the moral contrast they make with him as for their contribution to his story. His son-in-law Roper, for instance, is also capable of standing against the tide, but out of rebellious temperament rather than unswerving principle: in spite of his grandiloquence, he tends to see right conduct in terms of public 'gesture' rather than substance. More's friend Norfolk represents traditional English decency, with all its limitations and lacunae, and his commonsensical wife the domestic virtues and the domestic moral horizons. Wolsey and Cromwell stand for pragmatism. They are men who will sacrifice any personal scruple to making things work: a thankless task, as the former finds during the play and the latter correctly foresees that he, too, will discover. And Rich is the opportunist, a disciple of Machiavelli who gives pattern to the play by gradually rising as More's star gradually falls.

Finally, there's the 'common man' who slips into various roles during the play: More's servant, accepting money from both Cromwell and the Spanish ambassador for information about him; a boatman, worried about the rising cost of rope; a pub landlord, More's gaoler and, finally, his executioner. Sir Thomas's lofty worries mean nothing to him. What matters is simply managing to make a living, in whatever way he must. Bolt has been criticized by the Left for putting the name of 'common man' to (Kenneth Tynan's words) 'the essence of boorish corruption': his answer is that the character represents, not the proletariat, but 'that which is common to us all'. Moreover, 'I had meant him to be attractive, and his philosophy impregnable.' This claim does, however, seem somewhat disingenuous, since his philosophy is only a rueful self-interest, combined with a care not to 'make trouble – or if you must make trouble, make the sort of trouble that's expected'. This is the advice with which the common man actually ended the play in its original London production, and its relevance both to More and to us is obvious.

The inference is that we are content to be 'common men', passively accepting our lot, when, if circumstances demanded, we could be Mores. At any rate, Bolt's view is that Sir Thomas gave a 'breathtaking performance as a human being', yet 'didn't do anything that you or I couldn't have done'. This seems dubious, and may also help explain why it is difficult to designate the play a tragedy. Its More is in some way disappointingly ordinary, even flat. We see little of the passion for life that attracted Bolt to him. Apart from the odd flash of temper, and a moment of pain in prison, we see little strong feeling of any kind. We do not see deeply into his soul or even into his motives. We see no internal struggle between passion and conscience, and even the play's external struggles lack size and bite, because the conflict often seems to be not so much between truth and compromise, or integrity and pragmatism, as between a canny legalism and the forces seeking to outwit it: between society and a man using, in Bolt's own words, 'society's weapons, tact, favour and, above all, the letter of the law'. More's serenity and secrecy both increasingly become dramatic liabilities, and Bolt's language, though it contains a little authentic quotation, a little historical pastiche and a great many supposedly resonant metaphors relating to the sea and ships, is generally too colloquial, too lacking in poetry to increase his stature or the play's temperature. Altogether, it is easier to identify with More than perhaps it should be.

Some critics have also been disappointed by Bolt's failure to examine More's historical context in any depth or detail. Had he done so, the result would certainly be a more complicated play, perhaps even an unmanageably complicated one, since the objective rights and wrongs of More's views are still obviously open to dispute. However mixed the king's motives in wanting a divorce, however inconsistent and corrupt his conduct, his severance of the links with Rome was welcomed by many of the enlightened men of his day, and not without reason. What would have been the history of England, the course of English learning, had it not happened? Only modern Roman Catholics will presumably be able to share both More's subjective and objective attitudes, and then probably with reservations. This does not invalidate the play. A character who crusades for a belief or faith cannot nowadays expect all the audience to share his views, since they live in a pluralist society. Provided his belief or faith is not outrageous, he may, however, win respect for his single-mindedness, honesty, courage and spirit of self-sacrifice; and that is what the agnostic Bolt would expect us to accord More, whatever our own convictions. 'All men who are able to give up life for something which they love, something not concrete or material or even personal . . . are subscribing to the same reverence for life.' If we like, we can see him as a saint; if, not, as a 'hero of selfhood'.

Is Martin Esslin right when he sums up the play as 'in the last resort no more, and no less, than the traditional English history play with moral uplift and patriotic afterglow'? Or Robert Brustein when he praises its 'remarkable intelligence, historicity, theatrical ingenuity and good taste'? Both, probably. Bolt tells his story sparely and paces it well, justifying his claim that it's the only one of his early plays not to suffer from an excess of plot. It is intelligent, but not as provocative as it might be; tasteful, not emotionally searching or taxing. It proclaims the supremacy of individual values with plenty of theatrical verve; but since it fails to look very far into the individual, or into the society he rejects, it cannot be counted more than an extremely competent dramatic chronicle.

Joe Orton

(1933–67)

Joe Orton was born in Leicester in 1933, the son of a cowed and inarticulate Corporation gardener and an aggressive, socially ambitious mother. The wretchedness of his up-bringing is finely chronicled in John Lahr's biography, *Prick Up Your Ears*, and it certainly helps explain his later fasci-nation with hypocrisy, with the contrast between genteel pretension and brutal truth. The nearest he came to writing directly about it is probably the short *Good and Faithful Servant* (1967), which laments the wasted life of an elderly wage-slave not unlike his father and is, interestingly enough, the only play in which indignation and grief are directly discernible. Mostly, he keeps such positive emo-tions so firmly concealed under a hard, nonchalant surface that we sometimes wonder if he has lost the capacity to feel them.

His first stage success was *Entertaining Mr Sloane* (1964). Kath and Ed, brother and sister, both have carnal designs on their lodger, Sloane, but they camouflage them, conceal them in euphemism, sometimes hiding their greed even from themselves. They have an extraordinary capacity for explaining away anything that might undermine their self-regard: so much so that Sloane can kick to death their father, who has recognized him as the perpetrator of an earlier, unsolved murder; Kath and Ed can politely black-mail him into becoming their sexual slave for six months a year each; and Ed can end the play with a breezy 'Well, it's been a pleasant morning,' without the least conscious-ness of behaving unnaturally. Indeed, he hasn't done so, because 'nature' to Orton is always acquisitive, never altruistic.

In *Loot* (1965) and, especially, in the posthumously pro-duced *What the Butler Saw* (1969) the tone is less 'natural-istic' and more farcical, the events more far-fetched, the satiric methods markedly different. The characters still make social and moral conventions look foolish, but they tend to do so, not by pretending an allegiance to them while actually following their own instincts, but by openly, brazenly ignoring them. 'Your sleep won't be disturbed tonight, dear', someone promises a psychiatrist's wife in *The Butler*. 'Life is full of disappointments,' is her answer. She flaunts her near-nymphomania unashamedly, one unfortunate result of which is, however, to compromise the play's success as a farce. To explain. The frenzied confusions of its plot begin when the psychiatrist tries to hide the secretary he is seducing, first from his wife, then from a government panandrum, inspecting his asylum. But the increasingly elaborate disguises and subterfuges that follow have no real logic to them because neither of these characters is shockable. One cannot easily laugh at someone's flouting of convention, or desperate attempts to recover respectability, when no one onstage is conventional or respectable. Farce cannot breathe in an atmosphere of amorality and permissiveness.

Is 'amoral' an adequate word to sum up Orton's particular attitudes? He himself was a promiscuous homosexual whose frequent forays into public lavatories, coolly detailed in his diaries, put him in consequent danger of arrest. Indeed, he was imprisoned for six months, though in fact for defacing library books so as to mock their contents and annoy the prurient. He was an outsider, profoundly alienated from a society he regarded as an 'old whore' under whose skirts was a 'pretty foul stench'. Any form of authority was automatically suspect to him; all totems, all taboos, were to be challenged; and any show of virtue was sure to be sham. The short *Funeral Games* (1968), for instance, defines the Christian Church as 'a bird of prey carrying an olive branch'. At one climax the main character, the greedy and vindictive leader of a pious sect, screams 'I'll teach you to strike a man of admitted charity,' and attempts to throttle his mortal enemy, a defrocked priest who has murdered his own wife.

That is characteristic. In the whole of Orton's *oeuvre* there isn't a single person with a capacity for unselfishness or love. All are actuated by avarice, whether for power, applause, respectability, money, sex, or some concatenation of gain. And, interestingly enough, this is not a matter for rancour or regret. On the contrary, Orton is more inclined to grin and gloat. He once claimed that he 'developed a mocking, cynical way of treating events because it prevented them being too painful'. But what he more frequently communicates is an indiscriminate scorn for human institutions and values, and a scathing glee in exposing them as corrupt, hypocritical or both. His is not a constructive, reformist drama. Rather, he celebrates a world he regarded as 'profoundly bad and irresistibly funny'. He wanted to remind the genteel that they, too, had tripes, glands, and genitalia, camouflage them though they might. As Mr Lahr puts it, he wanted to 'goose' his bourgeois audiences.

There may be something juvenile in this aspiration, but it can produce entertaining, anarchic drama: for instance, the exuberance of *The Erpingham Camp* (1967), a modern *Bacchae* in which the tyrant of a seaside fun-prison is punished for his hubris by rampaging holiday-makers. It helps explain many of his particular effects, too. Orton is constantly contrasting the outrageous with the mundane, the grotesque with the banalities of a plastic civilization. The revellers in *Erpingham* rip up the owner's 'Canvatex Van Gogh'; the priest of *Funeral Games* keeps his wife's body beneath the pile of 'smokeless' he has bought from the National Coal Board 'at the reduced summer rate'. 'Do you want to wash your hands before tea?' someone asks a character in this last play, and he obediently lathers not only his own but one he has lopped off from the corpse. It is then tidied away in a Dundee cake tin.

Ronald Bryden dubbed Orton 'the Oscar Wilde of Welfare State gentility', a phrase that nicely sums up his particular brand of cynicism and style of comic subversion. One of his favourite methods is to cap a statement or event that would expect a strongly emotional reaction with one that wildly underreacts to it. Thus one character kills another in the short *Ruffian on the Stair* (1964), incidentally smashing a goldfish bowl with a stray bullet, and the murderer's wife bursts into tears over the tiny corpses, 'They're dead, poor things, and I reared them so carefully.' Again, the psychiatrist's wife in *The Butler* reports that a pageboy has tried and failed to rape her. 'The service in these hotels is dreadful' is the reply. 'Try not to break his arms or legs,' she later tells the man deputed to restrain her supposedly insane husband. Why not? 'It makes the job of adjusting the straitjacket doubly difficult.' Line after line begins by suggesting that values may exist and ends by asserting that they don't.

The Butler may fail as farce, but it reveals much about Orton's mind. In it, sane people are certified as mad, males dressed in female clothes and females in male. It is as if Orton, who despised rigid categories, was insisting that there was no clear divide, not only between the normal and abnormal, but between the two sexes. No less interestingly, the stage directions become pretty extreme at a hectic dénouement in which two of the characters draw revolvers and start shooting. People are 'screaming with terror', 'white with shock', 'anguished, fainting'; a wound 'streams with blood', blood 'pours' down a leg. Suddenly, all is violent nightmare, as if Orton had suddenly realized, right at the end of his career, that the anarchy he celebrated could cause pain and that pain hurt.

It was an ominous insight. Before he had revised *The Butler* he was dead, his skull smashed open by his long-term flatmate and lover, by now demented with envy and sexual jealousy; and we shall never know to what extent that odd, flawed, intriguing play betokened some deepening of his witty, mocking, callous talent.

Loot

Loot, said Orton, took 'a farcical view of things normally treated as tragic'; and by 'things' he presumably meant death and bereavement. Mrs McLeavy is about to be buried in (a characteristic touch) her WVS uniform and beneath a wreath sent by the Friends of Bingo. But her son Hal, with his friend and lover Dennis, has plundered the local bank – and where better than her coffin to hide the booty? So his mother is planted upside down in a cupboard, then taken out, stripped and disguised as a sewing-dummy, in a continuing effort to outwit the detective on the case, Truscott. Unluckily, a traffic accident on the way to the funeral brings the loot back to the house, where it is transferred to the casket that held Mrs McLeavy's viscera, which have exploded. Truscott discovers it there, and the play moves to an ironic dénouement.

Part of Orton's purpose was to tease his audiences, mischievously tempt them to be shocked and simultaneously to ask them precisely what was shocking them. As he himself said, a coffin was only a box, and a corpse, as Hal says in the play, is 'dust . . . a little dust'. Accordingly, he went out of his way to cock snooks at a taboo he thought worthless. Much is made of the dead woman's glass eyes and her teeth, which Hal actually clicks like castanets while she is being undressed, in tribute to the Spanish prostitute he imagines employing in a brothel named the Consummatum Est. Later, he casually passes Dennis the same macabre objects, provoking the hardened Truscott to pronounce his 'sense of detachment . . . terrifying.' The same comment might have been made of Orton himself, who actually brought back his mother's false teeth after her funeral in order to amuse the cast of *Loot*. He seems to have found it easier than most people to distinguish love for the living from love for the recently dead, perhaps because he didn't feel much love in the first place.

The play's calculated irreverence is increased by Orton's insistence on the McLeavys' Roman Catholicism, a faith he chose, he said, because it provided more outward trappings than others and thus allowed him to emphasize the family's purported piety. At one point a picture of Pius XII is placed over the money-filled coffin. At another, Hal, having just wiped the remains of his mother's entrails from the casket, announces his intention to go, first to confession, then to a brothel run by Pakistani children. Mrs McLeavy's nurse, Fay, is an ardent co-religionist, too: 'three parts papal nuncio'. Yet she begins by trying to inveigle the lately bereaved widower into becoming her eighth husband, later admits that she has murdered all seven previous ones, and ends by advocating the 'accidental death' of the wretched McLeavy, now rejected for Dennis, whose attractions include his share of the loot.

Here is Orton's familiar point of view, encapsulated even more extravagantly than usual. People are motivated by greed, whether sexual or financial or some subtler variety. There is no altruism. No one mourns Mrs McLeavy, not even her husband, though he mouths conventional sentiments – 'Good-bye old girl, you've had a lot of suffering, I shall miss you' – and appears to believe them. When he is told (falsely) that she had accused him of murder, his reply is eloquently honest: 'Complete extinction has done nothing to silence her slanderous tongue.' The main object of his affection is, not her, but his own moral status: 'Me, a good man by any lights, moving among such people!' is his reaction to the news of the bank robbery. He is hardly less selfish than anyone else. Indeed, the only character more interested than he in the form of morality and religion, as opposed to the substance, is the spectacularly hypocritical Fay. It is, as it should be, her line that ends the play and sums up much of its thrust. Dennis and she, once married, must move out of Hal's house. And why? 'People would talk: we must keep up appearances,' she says, and continues to pray over the coffin of Mrs McLeavy, who has turned out to be yet another of her murder victims.

Everywhere, Orton draws attention to the unlovely truths concealed by reputation, image and pretension, nowhere more gleefully than when he comes to that English totem, the integrity of the police. Truscott is exorbitantly, outrageously corrupt. He lies, bullies, threatens and uses physical violence in his efforts to perpetuate his legend as a great detective. Having unmasked the robbers, he then

allows his silence to be bought with one-fourth of the booty.
When the pietistic McLeavy talks of exposing this knavery,
Truscott promptly handcuffs him with a cry of 'You're
fucking nicked, my old beauty,' words actually used at an
arrest by the notorious Inspector Challenor, a London detective suspended in 1965 for planting evidence on suspects.
'The police are for the protection of ordinary people,' com-
plains his victim, who has spent much of the play proclaiming his belief in that 'fine body of men'. 'I don't know
where you pick up these slogans, sir,' replies Truscott. 'You
must read them on hoardings.' At the play's end, its only
law-abiding character is on his way to prison, where he
will be punished for his credulity by being quietly killed.
Lawlessness triumphs, abetted by the right arm of the law.

Orton hoped *Loot* would amuse its audiences, yet declared that 'it shouldn't be one long giggle – there should
be depths'. Presumably he was referring to the play's
sweeping exposure of avarice and corruption. Perhaps he
also hoped to communicate his distaste for the world in
general. 'Think of your mum,' says Dennis, as Hal begins
unscrewing her coffin, 'she gave you birth.' 'I should thank
anybody for that?' is the reply of one who is, perhaps, as
near to an Orton-surrogate as the play offers. 'Is the world
mad?' cries McLeavy. 'Tell me it's not.' 'I am not paid to
quarrel with accepted fact,' answers Truscott. But these
are, of course, the merest hints, and the tone and style of
the play anyway tends to undermine Orton's more sombre
aspirations. Its characters are gaudy grotesques, mouthing
outrageous repartee as they swagger from one improbable
situation to another. They are not people who can possibly
engage any but our most superficial emotions. They are,
however, often wickedly funny.

However misanthropic its author may have tried to be,
the impression *Loot* leaves is rather one of bubbling *joie de
vivre*. Orton delights in comic invention both wild and
Wilde. Where does Dennis beget his illegitimate children?
'On crowded dance floors doing the rumba'. 'If I come
back,' Dennis tells Hal, whose Catholic upbringing has left

him a criminal unable to tell lies, 'and find you've been telling the truth all afternoon, we're through.' 'Your explanation had the ring of truth,' says Fay on learning where the loot is. 'Naturally I disbelieved every word.' Platitudes and clichés are constantly refashioned, inverted, or simply sent up.

> *Truscott* You have before you a man who is quite a personage in his way – Truscott of the Yard. Have you never heard of Truscott? The man who tracked down the limbless girl killer? Or was that sensation before your time?
>
> *Hal* Who would kill a limbless girl?
>
> *Truscott* She was the killer.
>
> *Hal* How did she do it if she was limbless?
>
> *Truscott* I'm not prepared to answer that question to anyone outside the profession. We don't want a carbon-copy murder on our hands.

Everywhere there is the spirit of satire and sometimes its substance. Truscott is now a parody Sherlock Holmes, deducing Fay's murky past from her wedding ring, and now a parody theatre critic, congratulating Fay on a parody confession of guilt with 'Very good: your style was simple and direct: it's a theme which less skilfully handled could have given offence.'

Offence is, of course, precisely what Orton himself meant to give. The irony perhaps is that the very way he chose to do so – that is, by treating supposedly serious, sacred and painful matters lightly, frivolously – also tended to extract the seriousness, the pain and the offence. In the end, *Loot* is not a lot more than a display of clever prankishness, entertaining mischief, very characteristic of the obsessively youthful decade in which it was written. But it *is* clever and entertaining. The playwright who wrote it was a loss.

Edward Bond

(born 1934)

Edward Bond is probably the most controversial figure in this book, the dramatist who has alienated more people, and yet had higher claims made on his behalf, than any now living. The original debate, about his preoccupation with violence, has now lost its steam, partly because his plays have come to make less use of obviously violent imagery, and partly because it is increasingly accepted that his interest in the subject, so far from being morbid, is actually responsible, constructive, and logical, given his attitudes to contemporary society. The argument has become more general and fundamental. Is his analysis of the problems of society correct, and are the solutions he proposes acceptable? To what extent is the ideologue, the propagandist for change, in conflict with the artist in Bond's work? One of the functions of drama is to test theory by confronting it with observation, practice, experience: does Bond ever distort reality in order to reinforce preconception?

He was born in 1934 into a North London milieu very like (he says) the South London of *Saved*, son of a labourer who had moved from East Anglia in search of work. During the war he was evacuated to Cornwall, an event he thinks important because it 'created a division between feeling and the experience of things' and made him more aware and questioning. School was secondary modern, a prolonged exercise in 'obedience and conformity'. He left at fifteen with no qualifications and one good memory, of a visit to *Macbeth* that so stirred him he couldn't understand how anyone could live the same way after seeing it. It was a reaction that will surprise no one who knows his plays. At best he responds with a Blakean outrage to truths most people prefer to ignore or avoid. Again and again, he looks with embarrassing directness at cruelty and pain, and asks us, in a manner analogous to those advertisements which depict starving children in India, how we can bear to live in a world which permits such things.

Dead-end jobs were followed by National Service in the army, after which he began to write plays, one of which, *The Pope's Wedding*, was given a production without décor in London in 1962. It is an interesting piece, set in an East Anglia whose labouring classes are seen as only a little less deprived and debased than their urban equivalents in *Saved*. Mainly, it involves a young man, somewhat similar to Len in the later play, whose attempts to reach and comprehend the local hermit become obsessive and finally destructive. He kills the old man, who is actually rather stupid and empty, in what appears to be an agony of frustration, having failed to achieve something whose extreme rarity the title wryly recognizes. Fulfilling relationships occur as often as Popes' weddings nowadays.

Saved followed in 1965, offering a picture of cultural impoverishment so bleak that many simply refused to believe it. Was British 'civilization' as bad as that, at any level? According to Bond, it was, and worse. He has always claimed to understate his uglier effects, and never to have introduced any violence without knowing of some worse example. More to the point, he has emphasized that such things are only the more lurid symptoms of a society that itself is a sustained atrocity perpetrated by the strong upon the weak. You cannot ride on a bus or strike a match, he has said, without committing cannibalism: 'You don't eat anybody physically, but you eat their despair, you eat the waste of their lives . . . we clothe the sides of our cars with human skin, because people have been abused to make them.'

This demonstrates both Bond's sensitivity to others' suffering and his fondness for arresting rhetoric. He is the most accomplished composer of polemical prefaces since Shaw, and from them a coherent, if contentious, philosophy may be extrapolated. According to this, human nature is a vacuum filled, almost always for the worse, by social and cultural circumstance. We could learn to love, protect, create, share, enjoy. Such things are acquired more easily than hatred or cruelty. However, we are usually brutalized by the combined efforts of a capitalist system which thrives on avarice, competitiveness and waste, and of a 'ruling class' whose educational system, factories, law-and-order, morality and religion are all forms of coercion. We become apathetic, or cynical and self-hating. Sometimes we become violent.

Violence, Bond insists, is a capacity rather than a driving need. To him, the idea that we have an instinct for destruction is one of those pessimistic myths perpetuated by a malign power-élite to keep others 'slaves'. It's here that many will part company with him; and, certainly, he has yet to explain adequately how innocent beings made their society as evil as he thinks it. The speed of our intellectual evolution, he suggests, has faced us with challenges for which we are not otherwise ready. Consider nuclear fission. We have precipitately created a world for which we are not biologically suited. Consider modern industry. Precisely how and why is not so apparent.

It is an essentially optimistic philosophy, and expressed with unfashionable confidence. Violence, says Bond, will disappear when the institutional violence that causes it is eradicated. A just society, governed from a broad base instead of from above, harnessing science and technology to the common good, releasing rather than repressing the creative imaginations of its citizenry, will gradually succeed in abolishing envy and fear and the defensiveness and aggression that result from them. It is the duty of the principled individual to avoid retreating into a decadent 'inner peace', and that of the artist, too, to remember that he is primarily a social being, with responsibilities to his community. There is no place for mysticism or obscurantism, absurdism or despair. Art must be 'the illustration, illumination, expression of rationality'. It must observe society, explain cause and effect, interpret change, monitor its consequences, criticize and, at the same time, reveal the standards by which it criticizes, the hopes it has of the future. It changes people's drugged consciousnesses by demonstrating how they might live. It makes them dissatisfied and determined to change themselves and their society.

Bond defines his own drama as 'rational theatre' and himself as a revolutionary socialist. Recently, he has written 'answer plays' from this stance; but most of his career to date has been spent provocatively scrutinizing the problems. *Narrow Road to the Deep North* (1968) is about varieties of power in ninteenth-century Japan. Which is worse, the tyrant Shogo, who rules by fear and open violence, or evangelical British imperialists, who rule by repressive morality and the inculcation of guilt? Only the last-moment appearance of a naked swimmer, presumably representing socially unconditioned man, suggests there might be a third way. *Early Morning* (1968) transports us to England at about the same period and is written in a satirical style that, helped by disorienting anachronisms, leaves an impression of farcical nightmare. Turmoil occurs in high places. Queen Victoria rapes Florence Nightingale, and uses her garter to strangle Albert, who has been plotting with Disraeli to kill her. Gladstone also appears, transformed into a murderous trades unionist; but the most important character is one of Victoria's Siamese-twin sons, Prince Arthur, a spiritual ancestor of the protagonist of *Saved*.

When his brother dies, he will not cut himself free from him: a refusal that dramatizes both his own instinctive virtue and the fact that he is still somewhat encumbered with a dead social self. For a time he falls into destructive despair, and actually manages to kill most of the cast by inveigling them into a tug-of-war on Beachy Head. The scene moves to heaven, which presumably represents contemporary society's utopian vision of itself. Everyone spends eternity contentedly eating each other's limbs, which, once devoured, simply grow again. Only Arthur refuses to participate and continues to feel pain. At the end, he is symbolically transfigured while the cannibals, who believe him irretrievably dead, organize an eating rota.

'The events of this play are true,' declares Bond's epigraph, in case we miss his essential seriousness.

Black jocularity does not, however, altogether suit either truth or Bond. *The Sea* (1973) is less ambitious but more successful: a picture of a small Edwardian community filled with images and feelings of death, its main characters a tyrannical lady-of-the-manor, a tradesman turned paranoid by years of misuse, and two lovers representing a faint hope of a healthier future. Bond followed this with two striking plays about the artist's relationship with a corrupt society: *Bingo* (1973), which suggests that Shakespeare committed suicide in despair because he had allowed his natural humanity to be contaminated by the greed and callousness of his day; and *The Fool* (1975), in which John Clare is driven insane by the conflicts between his own instincts, poetic talent and working-class experience and the expectations of a reading public which is also his sometimes vicious class enemy.

The play contains some of his most moving writing and vivid encounters: a scene in which disaffected labourers strip an old clergyman and pluck at his well-fed flesh, weeping as they do so; one in a London park, with a violent (and symbolic) bare-fist boxing bout occurring behind Clare and some of his more bullying patrons; another between the distraught, helpless poet and his not-unsympathetically handled wife, who regards his 'scribble' only as a promise of poverty. At its best, Bond's work is epic in sweep, yet graphic in its portrayal of exemplary incidents, and written in a marvellously spare, to-the-point style. It is inventive, lucid and fast-moving.

The Woman (1978), though staged after *The Bundle*, may be seen as a bridge between his 'question' and 'answer' plays. Its first half describes how suspicion, bigotry, political calculation and bloodlust undo a principled attempt to end the Trojan War; its second, set on a remote island, shows Hecuba outwitting and destroying the mad Greek general, Heros, and Ismene settling down with a slave escaped from the Athenian silver mines. In all Bond's plays individuals are at odds with their world; but in the 'problem' plays they are not always conscious of being so, are rarely undefiled by it, and, even when responsible enough to try, scarcely have the power to improve it. The lovers of *The Sea*, for instance, go off to discover, learn and 'change the world', but how, where and whether they can is left open. *The Woman* seems to have something marginally more concrete to suggest, that we needn't be too scrupulous about the way we rid ourselves of the entrenched enemies of the particular community to which we should perhaps commit ourselves. What we achieve is likely to be precarious, because the world beyond remains dangerous and threatening; but we must act in defence of right, here and now.

The Bundle (1978), which takes us back to the Japan of *Narrow Road*, expands this thinking. Periodic floods keep the peasantry in fear, poverty and subjection, a situation exploited by the local landowner, but recognized, analysed, challenged and changed by the young revolutionary, Wang. There are some fine scenes, notably one in which Wang submits to slavery in order to buy the safety of his adoptive parents, trapped by rising waters in a cemetery; but the 'solution' seems suspect. The landowner cedes power after absurdly little resistance, most of it unshown in the play; and not even the accidental drowning of one of their number disturbs the confidence and happiness of the newly liberated peasants, as they at last fortify the banks of their unruly river. Bond has always carefully pre-planned his plays rather than allowed them to develop organically; but this is the first time plan seems to triumph over probability, wishful thinking over truth, the didact over the artist.

Bond has come some way since *Lear*, ideologically as well as artistically. In 1971 he declared that violence would only generate more violence, Lenin lead to Stalin, and 'violent revolution always destroy itself': in 1977, he was arguing that 'left-wing political violence is justified when it helps to create a more rational society, and when that help cannot be given in a more pacific form'. He has also changed since

Saved. The Bundle, as the poems published with it make doubly clear, is partly intended to be about the misuses of altruism, a commodity displayed in small matters by the governing classes in order to camouflage their real crimes, and shortsightedly practised by the oppressed themselves. In 1972, Bond said that 'the end can never justify the means in important matters, and certainly shouldn't for a writer': in one of *The Bundle* poems he insists that we must be 'hard' and 'unforgiving' now in order to be 'kind' and 'do good' later. Wang reinforces the point by actually throwing an abandoned baby into the river rather than be tempted to take it in and be diverted from his fight against a society that causes parents to abandon children.

The critics mostly missed the implications of this, for two reasons. First, the original production took the horror out of infanticide by presenting the baby non-realistically, as a scarf suddenly unfurled. Second, Bond was following what had become his usual practice of setting the action in some more-or-less remote period. It has been deliberate policy on his part to investigate key stages of our development: the rise of a mercenary middle class in the Jacobean England of *Bingo*; the beginnings of the industrial revolution in *The Fool*. But there and elsewhere he has also meant us to identify our own social predicament with those he dramatizes. Thus we should see the river of *The Bundle* as analogous to modern industry, the Japanese peasantry to our own proletariat. Unfortunately, it isn't easy to do so; and those who do try to make the imaginative jump can hardly avoid wondering if Bond isn't manipulating them to share his socialist vision, and endorse his solutions, by a kind of exemplary exaggeration. Should we really make violent revolution in contemporary Britain because we are horrified by extreme incidents of exploitation, oppression and poverty in pre-industrial Japan?

The Worlds (1979) is an answer to precisely this objection. For the first time since *Saved*, Bond explicitly confronts contemporary British society; and he goes on to ask the extent to which violence is justified in changing it. Industrial workers aren't intimidated when it's suggested they should abandon their strike in hopes of securing the release of their company chairman, captured by a radical cell and threatened with execution unless all their demands are met. He is, after all, a plundering criminal who 'depends on force as much as any terrorist'. But what should they do when an innocuous chauffeur is taken hostage in mistake for another board member, and promised precisely the same death? Bond gives no clear answer, and the workers' decision is anyway pre-empted when the captive is killed by the chairman, who has been rescued, eased from office, and has thereupon run mad; but the guarded suggestion is that a good revolutionary end may indeed justify, not just terrorism, but a terrorism somewhat reckless about its victims.

There are some arresting theatrical moments, for instance when the doomed chauffeur, swathed like a mummy from top to toe, totters across the stage, a living emblem of human helplessness. But the portrayal of the boss class is crudely farcical, and some of the workers' and terrorists' speeches suggest that Bond is getting less confident that action can embody argument, and is coming to prefer the explicit to the implicit. This, like his 'solutions', may be the result of a growing desperation, a feeling that society is so grotesquely corrupt and the planet so perilously near self-annihilation that there can be time for neither aesthetic niceties nor moral qualms. But for those who take a less apocalyptic view, it is a disturbing development. Isn't Bond in danger of letting ideology dictate observation, rather than vice versa? More importantly, how can his new politics be reconciled with the compassion he often displayed for even his less lovely characters? What's happened to his Blakean belief that what hurts one must diminish all?

Saved

The central event of *Saved* is what *The Times* critic originally called 'the ugliest scene I have ever seen on any stage', the murder by young hooligans of a baby in a London park. It is shocking, but purposefully shocking, since it compels those who don't self-indulgently wince away in disgust to ask whether such things could really occur and, if so, how, why, and with what result. What's happening in the darker reaches of the 'brick desert' that Bond claims to be the background of seventy-five per cent of British people, as well as his own?

The baby's mother is Pam, who brings home a casual pick-up, Len, and, when he has become the lodger, rejects him for Fred, the putative father. She lives with her parents, Harry and Mary, who for no clear reason haven't spoken to each other for years; Fred and, to a lesser extent, Len are friendly with a group of youths whose leader, Pete, spends his first appearance boasting of having deliberately killed a child with his lorry. These are the play's two halves, fatally linked by the baby.

Pam seems only technically mature. Her main interest, apart from Fred, who becomes her obsession, appears to be sweets. She tightly guards as unimportant a possession as the *Radio Times*, and resents it being borrowed by those who haven't paid for it. Sex to her is either being 'nice' or 'bothering' someone, and certainly isn't something she respects. When Len, who wants to marry her, wonders if he's made her pregnant, he is told he has got a 'dirty mind'. The baby itself she regards as a millstone, a 'racket'. She leaves it to cry, or drugs it with aspirins. Always she describes it as 'it'; but then so does everyone else. Only from one monosyllable casually dropped by Len, and easily missed by reader or audience, do we learn that 'it' is a boy.

Pam has no more affection for her parents than they for her. 'Spite' is the first motive she ascribes to either. She doesn't know why they aren't speaking – 'never arst . . . never listen', she characteristically explains – and feels she 'can't do nothin' ' about it anyway. She has no sense of being able to affect others, and no curiosity whatever. When Len first asks her name, he is 'nosy'. When he shows concern for her, he is 'pesterin' ' her. The nearest she gets to generosity is promising to knit Len a sweater. But even then he must pay for the wool.

Her parents are no less emotionally stingy. They can't talk *about*, let alone to, each other. Mary feels and does nothing for her grandson. As for Harry, he once left her, but returned because he didn't want to 'soil me 'ands washing and cookin' ', activities he barely seems to realize she actually obliges him to perform. When she is too old to find another man, he plans to desert her permanently. 'Getting your own back', a prospect with which he also comforts the rejected Len, is clearly as important to him as not 'getting involved'. He is against holding private conversations because they might cause 'trouble'. It is better not to speak to anyone: 'it saves a lot of misunderstandin' '.

These people feel no responsibility for each other, or even for their own actions. When Mary hits Harry with a teapot, badly scalding him, she blames him for cracking it. Pam blames her own erratic temper on Len, whose presence she finds increasingly irksome. She even manages to convince herself that he caused all her disasters: ' 'e's killed me baby, taken me friends, broken me 'ome.' She has conveniently forgotten that she abandoned the pram in a display of resentment, and that Len tried to find her and bring her back to it.

The mental processes of Fred, who *did* help kill the baby, are similar. Pam 'ruined me life' by having the baby, then bringing it into the park; the police are at fault for letting hooligans roam about. This is before he is imprisoned for manslaughter, the only one of the killers to be so. On his release he goes further, accusing Pam, by now distraught with desire for him, of ungratefully making a scene: 'All I done for 'er and she 'as the bloody nerve to start this.' Meanwhile, the prime mover in the murder, Pete, is quick to defend himself when Fred suggests he's owed the meal the gang grudgingly buys him. ' 'e can't swing that one on me,' he snaps, and leaves.

There is a lot of self-righteousness and self-pity on show, but no self-criticism at all. Indeed, it would seem that no one killed the baby. But of course he *was* killed, and by no less than five youths, including his likely father. However, it happens in a way that what we see of Pam's house helps to explain and, conceivably, excuse. These young men, too, inhabit a barren, loveless world. Work, when obtained at all, is clearly a menial misery. Sex is a series of dirty jokes. Women are objects, useful if they have the 'regulation 'oles'. And once again the baby is 'it': an 'animal', with 'no feelings'.

Boredom, frustration, *macho* swagger, and contempt for those even more powerless than themselves coalesce to cause the killing. The pram is pushed about, the baby pinched. The youths discover his nappy is dirty, and pinches become punches, stones are thrown. 'Might as well enjoy ourselves', 'Yer don't get a chance like this every day'. Not before time, the treat is over, and the killers run off, making what the script obscurely calls 'a curious buzzing'.

That may perhaps be explained by one of several odd comments Bond himself has made about the play. To him it has an 'Oedipal pattern' involving Harry and Len, whom Harry has caught in what he thinks a compromising situation with Mary. But that doesn't seem a very illuminating insight, because (as Bond himself points out) Len tries to help, not harm Harry in the ensuing row. This is *Oedipus* inverted, then forgotten. However, Bond goes on to claim that the baby's murder 'shows the Oedipus, atavistic fury fully unleashed'. There is indeed something primitive about the 'buzzing'. Maybe some tribes make such noises after the sacrifice of a scapegoat, which is maybe what the killing partly is. But *Oedipus* is still the wrong provenance.

Another of Bond's odder comments involves the characters' idiom. In South London, he has said, 'they talk a very virile and provocative and adequate language'; in *Saved*, he wanted to use working-class Londoners' 'exact language, because it's virile, poetic, expressive ... it still has the levels of function you find in Shakespeare – the sound of the word and its meaning'. Now, it's true that he creates a consistently terse, abrupt style of speech, a brutalist poetry that also persuades you it's absolutely authentic; but it is hardly 'adequate' or 'expressive'. On the contrary, it surely reflects and reinforces the deadened feelings and truncated lives of most of the characters. Again and again, they fall into cliché, often using it as a substitute for emotion, thought or argument. Harry can avoid facing the true ignominy of his big row with Mary by talking of 'clearing the air', 'sorting ourselves out', and 'a rough patch'. He can even sound vaguely right-minded when admitting that Mary knows he'll eventually desert her: 'We don't have secrets, they make trouble.' The effect, as here, is sometimes ironic. 'You wouldn't help a cryin' baby' is one way Pam expresses her irritation with Len, who, unlike her, would and did; 'People can't get away with murder,' Harry says of Pam's promiscuity, forgetting that people can and have.

These people haven't the intellectual, moral or linguistic tools to acknowledge reality, still less control or reshape it; and the obvious question resurfaces, why not? For Bond, the answer is clear. Even those who victimize are victims themselves. Their violence is a consequence of institutionalized violence. The murder is 'not done by thugs, but by people who like plays condemning thugs'. We should leave *Saved*, not saying 'oh, what dreadful people, they all ought to be locked up', but trying to 'understand all the pressures that went into the making of that tragedy' and, having understood, being 'so strongly moved as to want to take action'.

It may, however, be easier for someone who knows Bond's essays and later plays to accept this than for someone seeing *Saved* in isolation. To be sure, most people should still be able to come some of the way with him. They should recognize the 'cycle of deprivation' that links the baby with Pam, her with her parents, and no doubt them with some equally stultifying background. They should conclude from the presence of so many deprived characters that someone, something, has been depriving them. But this is all infer-

ence. There is no explicit internal support for Bond's attack
on the governing classes, and very little sense of any exploitative society beyond: a TV that rattles on unwatched,
a jukebox playing mindless love-songs, nothing much more.
Bond himself has pointed out that the killers mouth
'ruling-class slogans': by which he presumably means
Pete's appeal to Fred, 'Shirker, yer got a do yer duty', and
other characters' description of the baby, 'looks like a
yeller-nigger' and 'onk like a yid'. He would like us to see
the murder as an act of racism, or working-class fascism,
an example of the way the ruling class manipulates its
slaves' anger and aggression to its own ends. But how many
will do so on the basis of what they actually see?

To some extent, Bond is the victim of his own stylistic
integrity. With *The Pope's Wedding*, *Saved* is his most naturalistic play, and to insert even guarded comments or (let's
say) an exemplary policeman or magistrate would be to
spoil it. We are to be plunged into the social pit as it is,
nothing less and nothing more. By doing so, however, Bond
risks our overlooking or misinterpreting his deftly placed
evidence. Nearly all the play's original critics did precisely
that. And yet the risk may be worth taking. The play is
sufficiently plausible to suck most people into the reality it
presents, and sufficiently disturbing to nag at them afterwards. Perhaps plays that ask rather than answer questions
achieve more in the long run.

The final question is, what's the result of the baby's
death? On the face of it, nothing changes, except perhaps
for the worse. Fred emerges from prison 'a kid', likely to
end up an 'ole lag'. Pam mourns Fred, but not the baby,
and threatens suicide. She sells the pram to some ghoul for
£50, to the annoyance of Mary, who prices it at £200. The
pressures build up in Harry's house until the explosion
we've observed. Some commentators have found comfort
in the fact that he and Mary are at last exchanging words;
but since these vary from the ultra-acquisitive ('my teapot',
'my tea') to the vicious ('filth', ' 'ope yer die'), it is difficult
to concur. The next scene makes Harry's extreme vindic-

tiveness apparent, and the last suggests that mute hostility has re-established itself.

Yet Bond calls *Saved* 'almost irresponsibly optimistic', mainly because one character remains good, in spite of upbringing, environment and the pressures shown in the play. That is, of course, Len, whose instinct is always to help, no matter how badly he is used. He busies himself about the house for Mary, carries her shopping bags, fusses over the pram's brakes, brings Fred cigarettes in prison, loses his job looking after Pam when she is sick, tries to interest her in the baby, is ready to reconcile her with Fred in spite of his own thwarted desire for her, brings her home after Fred has rejected her, and prevents the row between Harry and Mary becoming murderous. At this point, he decides enough is enough, and prepares to leave the family, only to be dissuaded by Harry, who implicitly points out, in Bond's words, that 'you will find yourself in a house exactly like this'. There's no escape; but there is now what Bond calls 'the chance of friendship' with Harry himself, whose 'widow's mite' of kindness is 'in the context a victory, and a shared victory'.

Len has his faults. His curiosity, his questioning temperament, has its morbid as well as its constructive aspect. He likes to listen to Pam having sex with others, and wants to know 'wass it feel like' killing the baby. Indeed, he watched the murder from the nearby trees: 'I didn't know what to do. I should a stopped yer.' Yet he remains resilient and doesn't reject people even 'at their worst and most hopeless': 'I cannot,' continues Bond, 'imagine an optimism more tenacious, disciplined or honest than this.' We leave him mending a chair broken in the big row: a positive image and, for Bond himself, 'the scene that moves me most'.

Len's resilience is perhaps improbable under the circumstances, but it's unsentimentally presented and finally very impressive. Whether it's enough to make the play itself 'optimistic' is less certain. The effect he can have on the 'brick desert' and its brutalized populace is, after all, minimal. Even his own future looks remarkably bleak. We are bound to leave the play mainly remembering the ignorance, the helplessness, the violence and, of course, the murder. Bond himself provocatively calls this 'a typical English understatement', an atrocity negligible beside the 'strategic' bombing of German cities, and inconsequential beside the 'cultural and emotional deprivation of most of our children'; but that is hardly the way we experience it in the theatre. There, it horrifies, and seems to sum up very much of the world in which it occurs. It has been claimed that the title, *Saved*, refers to Len's ability to remain uncontaminated, and is not ironic. But that isn't the view of the author, who points out that 'when people say they're saved you know their troubles are really just beginning', nor is it likely to be that of most audiences. It would take little less than a miracle to 'save' those floundering in this pit.

Lear

Shakespeare's *King Lear* is a play Bond enormously admires, but one he thinks crucially flawed. In particular, he dislikes its stoicism. 'To endure till in time the world will be made right' is, he says, a dangerous moral, especially for a world whose time may be running out. Indeed, the play is a little comfortable: 'You don't have to question yourself or change your society'. His job, therefore, was to rewrite it 'for ourselves, for our own society, for our time, for our problems'.

The execution turned out to be as bold as the intention. We are shown a semi-mythic, semi-modern Britain ruled by Lear, a paternalist tyrant using slave labour to build a great wall which will keep his enemies out and guarantee eventual 'peace' and 'freedom' inside. His daughters, Bodice and Fontanelle, at first sound sensible, like their prototypes, Goneril and Regan. They will marry Lear's hereditary enemies, the Dukes of Cornwall and North, and raze the wall. Before long, however, they have overthrown their father and instituted a régime even more vicious than his. In time, they too are overthrown, by a revolutionary army led by one Cordelia, whose husband has been murdered for harbouring the fugitive Lear. But this, it appears, is only to substitute Stalinism for arbitrary Tsarism. Means are subordinated to ends; 'political officers' interrogate the prisoners of the old régime, and 'undesirables' are shot; Fontanelle and Bodice are killed without trial; a petty swindler is hanged because 'certain economic offences have been made capital with retrospective effect' and he is a 'social liability'; and people are once again press-ganged to build the selfsame wall. Many of the old atrocities are perpetrated, but this time more calculatedly and coldly. Lear himself is blinded in an attempt to make him politically ineffective, with what the horribly considerate doctor performing the operation calls 'not an instrument of torture, but a scientific device'. In 1971, when the play was first performed, Bond manifestly took a more sceptical view of violent revolution than now and, as we'll see, tended to regard the winning of hearts and minds as the prime way of achieving social change.

Shakespeare's Lear makes a spiritual journey, Bond's a more political one. In defeat, he's at first maddish, self-pitying, vindictive: he has been 'too trusting, too lenient'. But when he is captured by his daughters' soldiers, he shows a genuine altruism by trying, unsuccessfully, to protect those who have protected him. In captivity he begins to elaborate what's to become the play's central metaphor, that of an animal in a cage, clawing to escape. Like Shakespeare's Lear, he achieves sanity in apparent madness, and, like Gloucester, he sees clearly only when he is blind. He denounces evil, especially that done in the name of order, justice and good. He learns compassion, and eventually he learns that compassion is not enough.

Here's the relevance of one of the play's odder inventions, the ghost of the character who originally offered Lear sanctuary, the 'gravedigger's boy'. He attaches himself to the deposed king, and at first serves a similar function to Shakespeare's disguised Edgar. His presence helps instruct the old man in pity. But Bond, the first dramatist since the Jacobeans to make widespread use of them, has said that ghosts are 'always nasty and corrupt'; and this one becomes hardly less so than the spectral cannibals of *Early Morning*. He wants Lear to return to his old farm and withdraw with him into an essentially private world. As the play proceeds, he becomes more and more importunate, and also thinner, more wasted, more obviously representative of a kind of living death. Lear, explains Bond, 'has a clear vision of a golden age which his political activities have helped to destroy, but he has to recognize that its loss is irrecoverable, and there are great dangers in romanticizing and clinging to the impossible'. 'Some things are dead, but they die with difficulty,' he says, and adds elsewhere, 'When Lear tries to hug this image of the past, it becomes evil . . . So that if you have aspirations and do nothing to make them real, then you aren't really thinking of utopia, you're just wasting your time in some sort of daydream.'

So Lear learns he must act, and act now. At first he delivers social parables to pilgrims visiting the Tolstoyan homestead where he lives with his disciples. But the government finds his enthusiasm for disarmament dangerous, and prepares to execute him, whereupon he comes to a decision that coincides with the second and final death of the gravedigger's boy, who (significantly) is savaged by the pigs he wanted Lear to spend his old age serenely tending. He travels to the wall and is shot as he begins to dismantle it: his belief, his exemplary commitment, will presumably survive.

In his author's words, he 'makes a gesture in which he accepts responsibility for his life and commits himself to action'; and 'responsibility', as often in Bond's work, seems a key concept. We must learn to take our share of responsibility for the future, for the present that will determine it, and, hardly less importantly, for the past that has fashioned the present. There is a curious scene in which Lear rhapsodizes over Fontanelle's body, which is undergoing an autopsy: the point, as he recognizes, is that he himself irreparably damaged what might have been the outer expression of that inner order and beauty. He 'destroyed' her. One of the things that worries Bond about Shakespeare's original is its failure to recognize that Lear helped cause Goneril and Regan; and he attempts to fill this supposed gap both here, and by bringing on Bodice and Fontanelle as they were as children, to offer an impressionistic memory of dead soldiers and a 'terrible bell'. No wonder they turned into loveless, destructive adults.

Bond's less attractive characters are always corrupted rather than corrupt. Cordelia, too, is what she is because her father was a 'priest' who 'taught her everything'. At first, she strikes us as withdrawn, unfriendly, neurotic; later, she sacrifices all to an arrogant vision of what's right. For Bond, she is 'a moralized person, and moralized people are not good people . . . She always has the words "good" and "justice" on her lips. And she is an absolute disaster for any society. So I very much wanted to convey through that figure that the people who have manipulated and taken over the language of ethics in our society are in fact very violent and destructive people.' Indeed, the play is substantially about upbringing and education. Many have been irrevocably twisted by their backgrounds, and some go on to try to indoctrinate others. Suffering and the ability to identify with others' suffering enables Lear to break the cycle. 'I must become a child . . . I must open my eyes and see,' he declares over Fontanelle's entrails: he ditches his old intellectual luggage, re-educates himself, and becomes a seer, instructing eager acolytes in Bond's view of the world.

Of course, not everyone will endorse that view, and even those who do may feel the gap between our own world and the one shown here is too wide for his purposes. We can hardly disclaim the play's atrocities, which include, not only Lear's blinding, but a scene in which Bodice destroys the eardrums of a tongueless captive with her knitting needle while Fontanelle screeches, 'Kill his hands! Kill his feet . . . I want to sit on his lungs.' More sadistic things have been done on and off the world's battlefields in our own era. But it seems that Bond wants us to identify his overt violence with the more covert violence he believes to be institutionalized in a society in which, as Lear says, we 'send our children to school in the graveyard', 'jackals and wolves' rend the poor and hungry, and 'good, decent, honest, upright, lawful men who believe in order . . . devour the earth'. Indeed, he would specifically compare Cordelia with Mary Whitehouse, the celebrated propagandist for moral cleanliness. But doesn't it take an exorbitant effort of imagination and will to witness the play's savageries and detachedly extrapolate truths about our own predicament from them?

Still, the play remains an impressive achievement. Some bardophiles may feel that Bond unjustly patronizes Shakespeare for the crime of having lived before Marx; and they may reasonably attack him in turn for the relative thinness of those passages in which his chopped, exact style becomes metaphoric, 'poetic'. Compare, for instance, his Lear's 'Who shut that animal in a glass cage? O God, there's no pity in this world. You let it lick the blood from its hair in the corner of a cage with nowhere to hide from its tormentors' with 'Poor naked wretches, wheresoe'er you are, that bide the pelting of this pitiless storm . . .'. Yet the very fact we make such comparisons shows that Bond is writing with an audacity, ambition and scope too rare in the contemporary theatre. How many modern plays contain seventy speaking parts, involve the clash and collapse of civilizations, and force us to ask ourselves such large questions as how we should hope to be governed, how rightly to live in an unjust world? Very few; and most of them are by Edward Bond.

Tom Stoppard
(born 1937)

Tom Stoppard's origins are Czechoslovakian, a fact that has become increasingly difficult to ignore when considering his plays. He was born in Zlin in 1937, son of a company doctor, and was taken as an infant to Singapore, where his father was killed by the invading Japanese. The family was evacuated to India; his mother remarried, this time to a British soldier named Stoppard; and by 1947 he was being educated in England. Though he is often described as the most 'intellectual' of contemporary dramatists, he never went to university, but instead became a journalist, based in Bristol. Local theatre reviewing first whetted his interest in writing for the stage and the triumph of *Look Back in Anger* in 1956 increased it – 'The theatre was suddenly the place to be: it was receiving disproportionate attention.'

In 1960 he resigned from his job and wrote *Walk on the Water*, later rechristened *Enter a Free Man* and performed with success in 1968. What brought him to public attention, however, was a student production of *Rosencrantz and Guildenstern Are Dead* in 1966. Within a year it was in the repertoire of the National Theatre, the company·that was later to present *Jumpers*, the play that most nearly fulfils his aim as an artist, to achieve 'the perfect marriage between ideas and farce or high comedy'.

The first and obvious point to make about Stoppard's work is that it is almost always very amusing. Even the short *Where Are They Now?* (1970), which takes an unwontedly resentful view of its subject, British private education, has a good deal of fun at the expense of schoolmasters, school slang, and so on. He is a writer who delights in unexpected verbal connections, word-games, puns, conceits, pastiche, parody. The beginning of *Dirty Linen* (1976), about MPs investigating immorality in Parliament, is characteristic: dialogue consisting entirely of foreign phrases in familiar English use, capped by 'bloody awkward' and then the apology for the swear-word, 'Pardon my French'. So is the description offered by *Night and Day* (1978) of the occasion on which a journalist slept with a news-source: 'debriefing'. Committees, news reporting, sports reporting, linguistic philosophy, psychiatrists, theatre critics, whodunits, war memoir, political memoir, travelogue, even telex messages: all these, and more, have become butts of Stoppard's sly and ebullient wit.

He himself sees his principal weakness as facetiousness. A severe and conceivably humourless critic might add, ingenuity for its own sake. Stoppard enjoys setting himself bizarre dramatic puzzles, and then solving them with all possible bravura. *After Magritte* (1970) opens on a tableau in which an old woman in a bathing-cap is lying on an ironing board with a bowler hat on her belly: these and other visual oddities are then given a rational, logical explanation. *The Real Inspector Hound* (1968) begins with two reviewers watching a stage thriller that has already claimed its first victim, a prone body whose identity Stoppard claims not to have known when he started writing. It turns out to be the corpse of the first-string critic of one of the newspapers represented in the auditorium, and the killer is unmasked as the third-string critic. The play, as often for Stoppard, has been a series of unplanned discoveries.

The result, admittedly, is one of his slightest pieces, a work of comic whimsy rather than solid imagination; yet even it has serious implications. The two protagonists, like Rosencrantz and Guildenstern, are unable to sustain their detachment, but are insidiously drawn into a perilous situation outside their understanding or control. This moral resonance is characteristic even of the Stoppard of the short, seemingly unpretentious radio plays. The genesis of both *If You're Glad I'll be Frank* (1965) and *Albert's Bridge* (1968) would appear to be nothing more than playful speculation. What if the telephone clock were a person, not a recorded message? Why not write a play about the bridge that needs to be repainted at one end the moment the other is finished? The first, helped by intermittent interruptions from a bus driver as trapped by his timetable as his wife by her job as the speaking clock, becomes a little allegory about the human need to impose artificial order upon the flux of a vast, incomprehensible universe. In the second, the protagonist withdraws from the world, only to see his private obsession, his bridge, destroyed by society in the form of an overweight army of labourers with paintpots.

Detachment, withdrawal, attracts many of Stoppard's people, but they find it impossible to sustain. The protagonist of *A Separate Peace* (1966) enjoys a life of tranquil irresponsibility in hospital, though there is nothing physically wrong with him: the puzzled staff finally manages to unearth the relatives he had wanted to escape, and he promptly discharges himself. The world insists on engagement, involvement, responsibility – but (asks Stoppard) why, how, and to what end? The everyday rituals of ordinary life look more than a little absurd, given the great unanswered and perhaps unanswerable questions. Has the universe any pattern or design, or is it as arbitrarily destructive as it sometimes seems? Are we victims of chance or fate? Have we free will, and does it matter if we do? Is morality simply a desirable pretence? Can we rely on any absolutes, or are we doomed to endless relativity? Character after character explicitly or implicitly grapples with such anxieties as he tries to discover his true significance and fulfil his proper purpose. The attempt is, of course, invariably a failure: George Riley, protagonist of *Enter a Free Man*, squanders his energies on fatuous inventions and impotent dreams, and ends as pathetic and dissatisfied as he began; Rosencrantz and Guildenstern actually end up dead. But no one with the least imagination or intellect can avoid making it. Indeed, human value may be precisely and paradoxically this: the persistence with which we try and fail to make sense of ourselves.

Certainly, this is Stoppard's own value as a writer. He is sometimes accused of being two dramatists imperfectly integrated, the one a jokesmith and prankster, the other a philosopher and metaphysician; yet even the word-play is evidence of an inquisitive mind, eager to investigate the logic, or lack of logic, both of language and of life. The odd and unpredictable comedy, the sudden and eccentric jokes – these surely reflect a restless, questioning temperament, always anxious to shift the perspective and look at the subject in some new, surprising and potentially fruitful way. Stoppard himself has said that his distinguishing mark is 'an absolute lack of certainty about almost anything'; that he writes plays because 'dialogue is the most respectable way of contradicting myself'; that his statements tend to be 'firstly, A, secondly, minus A'; that there is 'no point of rest' in his works, and 'the dislocation of an audience's assumptions' a major part of his purpose; that he likes to play 'a sort of infinite leapfrog' with rebuttal following argument, and counter-rebuttal rebuttal, and no last word. Stoppard's imaginative diversity and stylistic variety is (in short) the expression of his continuing quest for elusive and probably provisional truths.

He has, as is inevitable in the present cultural climate, been accused of a lack of political and social concern, and he has sometimes given comfort to such attacks by justifying his work on aesthetic grounds, as 'carpentry' which he tries to put together 'with the exactitude and love of a first-class cabinet-maker'. As we have seen, it has a moral dimension, and, as we shall see, *Jumpers* has a political and social one too. His most considered reply to the accusation, however, made in a 1974 interview, was that drama could have little immediate political or social effect, but might help 'provide the moral matrix, the moral sensibility, from which we make our judgements about the world'. Even if it dealt with topical concerns, its usefulness was likely to be long- rather than short-term, and in any case its handling of those concerns must be judged by the same criteria of excellence as its handling of anything else. By this time the issue was manifestly a live one in his mind, because he had recently written two plays asking the question his work to date had made necessary. In a world in which each of us is trying to discover his personal significance, what is the particular purpose and justification of the artist? To put it more specifically still: why Stoppard?

Artist Descending (1973) is a complicated, clever piece about three painters, a dilettante lot with a knack for misinterpreting what they see and hear. The result is a debate about perception as well as art, one that provides a useful introduction to the more important *Travesties* (1974). Indeed, it bequeaths that play one of Stoppard's favourite apophthegms: 'For every thousand people there're 900 doing the work, 90 doing well, 9 doing good, and one lucky bastard who's the artist.' The speaker, the second time, is one Henry Carr, a consular official who actually sued James Joyce for the cost of a pair of trousers he had worn in an amateur production of Wilde's *Importance of Being Earnest* in the Zurich of 1917. Out of this historical oddity, and the simultaneous presence in the city both of Lenin and of the Dadaist Tristan Tzara, Stoppard manages to build an extraordinarily ambitious play: jokes, songs, limericks, doggerel, Wildean pastiche, a brief striptease, a political lecture, all somehow integrated into an intricate discussion of the place of that 'lucky bastard' in society.

To Joyce, the artist is the priest-magician who gives immortality to what would otherwise be the transitory doings of forgotten men. To Tzara, he is the rebel and iconoclast, exposing the random evils around him. To Carr, he is a privileged escapist: 'To be an artist *at all* is like living in Switzerland during a world war.' To Lenin, who dominates the second half, he is either a bourgeois individualist, a 'whining intellectual', or the willing tool of the party. Precisely where Stoppard stands is unclear. One is tempted to say, everywhere and nowhere. Even the play itself would appear to participate on at least two sides of what's surely meant to be an unfinished debate. Since most of it consists of the fragmented memories of Carr, who has become an erratic and confused old man, it tends to demonstrate the unreliability of art. Yet at the same time, of course, it demonstrates art's potency, its effectiveness in exploring ambiguities, if not of pressing them to conclusions.

However, Stoppard himself seems to have left the play, if not altogether convinced of his responsibility to society, at least believing that there were some contemporary issues it might not be unhelpful to tackle. They may be summed up in the capsule phrase, 'human rights'. *Every Good Boy Deserves Favour* (1977) involves a political dissident incarcerated in a Soviet psychiatric hospital; *Professional Foul* (1977) is about an English philosopher, on a visit to Prague, whose moral horizons are altered by the unjust arrest of one of his former students; *Night and Day* concerns what Stoppard sees as a threat to freedom in Britain itself, the growth of the 'closed shop' in journalism; and *Cahoot's Macbeth* (1979) takes us back to Prague, to show us oppressed and harassed actors able to perform only in private houses.

The slightest of these pieces is the last, though it contains several acidly funny moments, and the most imaginatively audacious the first. Indeed, *Every Good Boy* brings onstage an entire symphony orchestra, primarily to embody the delusions of the dissident's authentically insane room-mate, secondarily to exploit music as a metaphor for order and harmony. Unfortunately, the presence of all those instrumentalists tends to overshadow the play's political content. The result sometimes betrays that it is, in fact, two ideas for different plays forced together by Stoppard: an impression also left by *Night and Day*, which partly involves British journalists covering a civil war in Africa, partly the sexual fantasies of a lonely expatriate wife. Neither piece quite achieves that seamlessness which Stoppard regards as his aesthetic aim.

His most impressive foray into a more 'committed' art is probably *Professional Foul*. Characteristically, it extracts a certain amount of sheer fun from the coincidence in Prague of both a convention of philosophers and an English football team; yet the latter have some metaphoric function to fulfil and the former an explicitly moral and political one. As in *Jumpers*, Stoppard uses both parody and direct statement to attack what he sees as the triviality and cynicism of much contemporary philosophy, and ends with the idea, also mooted in *Jumpers*, that man has a natural, instinctive sense of good and evil. Systems of ethics, argues his protagonist, are 'the sum of individual acts of individual right': which means that a nation which attempts to impose a collective ethic on unwilling individuals is *ipso facto* acting illogically.

The conclusion is debatable and, Stoppard being Stoppard, must anyway be regarded as provisional only. What matters is that the drama, which by its nature tends to concentrate on practice, is for once being used to examine the principles upon which practice is, or might be, based. In *Professional Foul* Stoppard returns both to moral fundamentals and to his own Czechoslovakian roots in hopes of discovering a significance for us and an identity for himself. Who, where, what is he? Who, how, why are we?

Rosencrantz and Guildenstern Are Dead

Shakespeare's Rosencrantz and Guildenstern are fellow-students of Hamlet summoned by Claudius to Elsinore in the hope that they will discover the cause of the prince's evident melancholy and supposed madness. Their attempts to do so succeed only in alienating Hamlet, who sees them as the ambitious and sycophantic hirelings of his uncle. They never learn that the king has killed Hamlet's father, or that Hamlet plans to kill Claudius in revenge. They probably don't know that the letter they carry to England is Hamlet's death-warrant, and they are obviously unaware that Hamlet has secretly exchanged it for one ordering their own execution. The morality of their slaughter is still much debated by scholars, some of whom see it as just punishment for their disloyalty to Hamlet, some as evidence of the prince's recklessness with other people's lives.

Stoppard is not interested in the question of their innocence or guilt, and, indeed, omits evidence that shows them at their more fraudulent and untrustworthy. His chosen method allows him to move in and out of the original play, so that a conversation between Rosencrantz and Guildenstern in contemporary English will suddenly and seamlessly become an authentic encounter in Shakespearean verse; yet the celebrated 'recorder' scene between them and the contemptuous Hamlet is missing. Stoppard is, however, very interested in questions of innocence and knowledge. Until the end his two characters know as little as or even less than Shakespeare's prototypes. The play is their attempt to acquire some grasp, if only an intellectual one, of a world they find confusing and alarming.

From the start it is clear that this world is indeed 'out of joint'. Rosencrantz and Guildenstern, ordered to Elsinore on a matter of 'extreme urgency', are tossing coins, which proceed to come down heads over ninety consecutive times. Those laws of probability which make 'for a kind of harmony and a kind of confidence', and relate 'the fortuitous and the ordained into a reassuring union which we recognize as Nature', are being outrageously flouted. Anything may happen, and, of course, much that is inexplicable actually does. The encounter with the anguished Hamlet described by Ophelia in Shakespeare's Act II, Scene *i* is witnessed by Rosencrantz and Guildenstern. The prince puzzles and worries them with an obscure reference to hawks and handsaws. Ophelia totters onstage as Hamlet snaps 'to a nunnery, go'. The performance of a play before the king ends in confusion and anger. Hamlet drags the dead Polonius across the stage, and Rosencrantz and Guildenstern are instructed to apprehend him. Finally, they find themselves *en route* to England with a letter that one moment bodes Hamlet's death, the next their own.

The play may be seen simply as an amusing piece of dramatic speculation about the offstage behaviour of two Shakespearean characters, and Stoppard's own comments on it have been notably unpretentious. His protagonists, he says, are in a situation analogous to that of the playwright. Their need is to fill the time as entertainingly as possible: his need, when he wrote the piece, was to inject enough interest and colour into each passing line to retain the audience's attention from moment to moment. No overall 'message' was calculated. However, any interpretation that arises out of the text has validity: 'What is written over my door is, "No symbolism admitted and none denied".'

Nevertheless, Stoppard has acknowledged his debt to the Beckett of *Waiting for Godot*, and many critics have seen similarities between the predicament of Rosencrantz and Guildenstern and that of Vladimir and Estragon, a comparison that has not always worked to his advantage. Robert Brustein, for instance, sees Stoppard's play as ingenious but derivative. Its insights, he claims, are prefabricated, its pessimism unfelt, its philosophical implications spurious, its tone cute, and its main characters 'whimsical to the point of nausea'. It is a harsh indictment, and perhaps a perverse one, since it accuses Stoppard of borrowing from Beckett and then proceeds to lambast him for not actually being that sombre and despairing metaphysician. Stoppard's deft, inquiring wit is his own, and (unsurprisingly) it produces deft, witty, inquiring plays that have, however, proved their power to grip in the theatre and tantalize in the study afterwards. The least that can be said for *Rosencrantz and Guildenstern Are Dead* is that it teases the fancy and tickles the intellect, fulfilling Stoppard's very modest aims as an entertainer and provoking us to speculate in general terms about the subjects that preoccupy him: perception, truth, free will, design, the moral character of the universe.

Guildenstern and, to a lesser extent, Rosencrantz are perhaps analogous to Stoppard in a deeper sense than he suggests. They are inquisitive, questioning. They play with language and logic. They play Wittgenstein word-games, one of which actually consists entirely of questions. And they remain uncertain of everything. Though their characters are distinct – Guildenstern the sharper, the more aware, persistent and resilient; Rosencrantz, the slower, gentler, softer, weaker – they are comically inclined to forget which of them is called which. They seem unsure of the points of the compass, even of what season of the year it is. Rosencrantz can't remember how long he's suffered from a bad memory, and only 'thinks' he can think at all.

Not only are the clear truths that might enable them to interpret the situation unavailable: there may be no such commodity as 'truth' in the first place. There may be only working 'assumptions'. Yet when they use these to explain Hamlet's behaviour, they end in flat self-contradiction: he is 'stark raving sane'.

'I like to know where I am,' cries the disoriented Guildenstern. 'Even if I don't know where I am, I like to know that.' But events remain outside his comprehension and, of course, his control. Things happen to him and Rosencrantz: they do not happen to things. They appear to have no active existence outside the plot of *Hamlet* and no power to influence that in the slightest way. They are, as they recognize, trapped in a machine whose master, if he exists at all, is unknown, whose direction and purpose are unclear, and whose momentum is irresistible. All they can do is keep talking, talking, talking, in hopes of, at best, staying sane while events play themselves out. Choice seems non-existent, the exercise of free will impossible – or, almost worse, might actually have been anticipated, pre-ordained by mysterious external forces. How awful, says Guildenstern, if 'our spontaneity were part of their order'. Rosencrantz considers jumping over the side of the boat, arguing that this 'would put a spoke in their wheel', and then changes his mind, when Guildenstern suggests that his suicide may be part of 'their' plan.

One of the few things Shakespeare tells us about his attendant lords is that they met 'players' on the way to Elsinore, an encounter eagerly exploited by Stoppard. Indeed, the theatrical metaphor in general adds much to the complexity and suggestiveness of his play. The player-king is delighted to find ready-made spectators in Rosencrantz and Guildenstern, almost as if he and his fellow-actors needed an audience to validate their very existence, and proves understandably upset when the two courtiers steal silently away, leaving them spouting their melodrama to what they slowly realize is the empty air: 'The silence was unbreakable, it imposed itself upon us, it was obscene.'

And later their rehearsal of *The Murder of Gonzago* is allowed to run far further than *Hamlet* permits, right up to the departure to England of the king's nephew with two 'spies', who are killed on arrival. 'Events must play themselves out to their aesthetic, moral and logical conclusion,' says the player-king, who tends in general to take a resigned, stoical attitude to things. 'It is *written*.'

The relevance of all this to Rosencrantz and Guildenstern's predicament is evident enough. At times they seem to half-recognize the existence of an audience, namely us. Maybe they are being watched by the invisible and unknown spectators we presumably symbolize; or maybe they are simply performing in an empty universe. Maybe their whole story, down to their deaths, has been pre-planned by some supernal Shakespeare. Maybe *Hamlet* precedes and defines every aspect of their being. Maybe independent action is impossible, and the best they can do is swagger and posture inside the fixed limits of someone else's melodramatic imagination. Maybe everything is an illusion, down to death itself, a subject much debated and frequently mimed in the course of the evening.

Or maybe not. After all, destruction is both seen and reported. The play ends on a tableau of corpses and with the news, relayed by the English ambassadors, that Rosencrantz and Guildenstern are indeed dead. Whether death consists of weeping implausibly at the end of a rope, or clutching terrible-eyed at a wound in one's throat, or simply 'the absence of presence', they have succumbed to it. Moreover, they have succumbed, if not exactly willingly, at least compliantly. They know from the substitute letter that they will be killed, and they accept their doom with the passivity that has characterized them throughout. They have done nothing wrong, they don't understand why they must die, but resistance, they feel, can make no difference: 'Our movement is contained within a larger one that carries us along as inexorably as the wind or the currents.' Perhaps it is the logic of an incomprehensibly vengeful order; perhaps it is only the blind, mechanical drift of a meaningless universe. Either way, as C. W. E. Bigsby remarks, 'the world which exists indistinctly and threateningly just beyond the focus of their vision is a brutal and uncompassionate one'. Either way, the final blow is death, and either way the response might as well be submission.

'We move idly towards eternity, without possibility of reprieve or hope of an explanation,' remarks Guildenstern: the kind of portentous line to which Brustein objects, yet one that by the end is more than rhetoric. Here is an elaborate representation of that search for identity, significance, certainty, security which may be foredoomed to failure yet in itself lends the searcher a certain dignity: a plausible picture of man's cosmic predicament, rendered with intelligence, humour and a melancholy compassion.

Jumpers

Stoppard has a liking for what he calls 'the theatre of audacity', and *Jumpers* is probably his most imaginative contribution to it. It begins with a chanteuse breaking down as she tries to sign 'Shine on Harvest Moon', and a moment later there is a striptease by a girl hanging from a chandelier, followed by some dogged acrobatics by yellow-suited gymnasts, one of whom is shot dead as he piles into a human pyramid. There are very long speeches about philosophical issues, farcical misunderstandings, a spoof detective, puns, verbal games, much witty repartee, and, in the world beyond the bedroom and study in which the action is set, what may be a *coup d'état*; and it all ends with a dream sequence.

Yet the subject of the play is a sober one: whether, in Stoppard's words, 'social morality is simply a conditioned response to history and environment or whether moral sanctions obey an absolute intuitive God-given law'. The reason that the singer, Dottie Moore, has something akin to a nervous breakdown is that she feels the landing of men on the moon has changed all her (and our) perspectives. We are 'no longer the still centre of God's universe'. Our world is 'little, local', and so, of course, are its ethical pretensions. And the acrobatics turn out to symbolize the ingenious but sterile contortions of modern philosophy, the gymnasts themselves to be 'logical positivists, mainly, with a linguistic analyst or two, a couple of Benthamite utilitarians, lapsed Kantians and empiricists generally, and of course behaviourists'. Their materialist thinking not only dictates the character of the university around whose campus the play occurs: it is reflected in the aims and actions of the Radical–Liberal Party whose victory at the polls they open the plot by celebrating.

This party enters office with a show of power. There are military parades and fly-pasts; property-company tycoons and assorted other bigwigs are arrested; there is talk of reducing the police to 'a ceremonial front for the peace-keeping activities of the army'. What's more immediately relevant to the arguments of the play is that the Church is to be 'rationalized', in other words deprived of its buildings, by a new Archbishop of Canterbury, an agnostic government agriculturalist. He parades along outside 'attended by two chaplains in belted raincoats'.

This is the attack, not so much of a right-wing dramatist upon leftist extremism, rather of a principled writer upon a society whose standards seem to him increasingly pragmatic, expedient, amoral. Its 'orthodox mainstream' philosophers disapprove of murder, not because it is inherently wrong, but because it is anti-social. There are prohibitions against killing for the same reasons there are rules in tennis, because without them social intercourse and Wimbledon fortnight would be a shambles. The ethical practice of this brave new world is illustrated by two British astronauts who have, it seems, found that damage to their booster rockets means there isn't enough thrust to take both of them home from the moon. They are called Scott and Oates, in obvious and ironic reference to the incident in which a polar explorer sacrificed his life to give his companions greater chance of survival. This time, they struggle at the base of the rocket, Oates is dashed to the ground, and it is Scott who announces: 'I am going up now. I may be gone for some time.'

This spectacularly justifies Dottie's fear that the moon visits will promote moral relativism and ethical decline. It also gives added piquancy to the context in which her husband is working and against which he is battling. He is George Moore, Professor of Moral Philosophy, a post almost as low in the university hierarchy as the chair of divinity, which has been vacant since its last occupant became a West Midlands curate. He is due to appear at a debate on the question, 'Man: Good, Bad or Indifferent?', at which his opponent will be the Professor of Logic, McFee. Most of the play he spends preparing and dictating his address, not knowing that McFee is, in fact, the 'jumper' shot dead at its opening.

He resists the idea that 'good' and 'bad' are simply subjective, relative terms. He insists that 'my moral conscience is different from the rules of my tribe, that there is more to me than meets the microscope', and that he therefore feels obliged to believe in what he calls 'an incredible, indescribable and definitely shifty God'. Again and again he attempts to explore, justify and propagate these articles of faith, invariably in the most arresting and entertaining way, only to end in agonized inconclusiveness or flustered irrelevance. A reference to the 'late' Bertrand Russell dwindles into a parenthesis about his punctuality; contemplation of the notion of infinity leads him to the theory that God is 'so to speak, nought'; speculation about the 'limiting curve' ends in what Moore himself calls 'a mysticism of staggering banality'. The close of the play proper is characteristic: he discovers he has impaled his pet hare with the arrow with which he had planned to refute one of Zeno's celebrated paradoxes, and in his distress he steps on and crushes the tortoise with which he was to have illustrated another. All his proofs end in a parallel failure and frustration.

He cuts a brave but forlorn figure, as befits one who is patronized as 'our tame believer, pointed out to visitors in much the same spirit as the magnificent stained glass in what is now the gymnasium'. The words come from the university vice-chancellor, Sir Archie Jumpers, materialist philosopher, gymnast, doctor, psychiatrist, lawyer, coroner, opportunist extraordinary, and supreme guardian of Rad–Lib orthodoxy. He is confident where George is self-doubting, active and effective where George is passive and helpless. George's marriage to Dottie, one of his ex-students and much younger than himself, is sexually unsatisfactory. Archie, however, spends the play going in and out of the bedroom in which she is nervously sequestered, coolly if implausibly justifying his visits as 'professional'. George paces his ivory tower, impotently appalled by the world outside. Archie covers up the murder, bribes the investigating policeman with the offer of the chair of divinity, and generally represents that world in smooth and efficient overdrive.

Stoppard, characteristically, did not know when he began the play why McFee was killed; and his solution is characteristically pointed. Conceivably, the murderer was an outraged colleague. More likely, it was the secretary with whom he had been having an affair. Either way, it was because he had decided to go into a monastery, having reached the conclusion that he had been wrongly denying the existence of altruism and perversely 'giving philosophical respectability to a new pragmatism in public life'. Precisely the same pattern of repentance and retribution is repeated in the play's 'coda', which is George's dream-version of the symposium for which he has been preparing. The new archbishop is distressed that his chaplains have used tear-gas to disperse common people shouting 'Give us the blood of the Lamb, give us the bread of the body of Christ.' He has begun to wonder if 'belief in man could find room for man's beliefs', is menaced by the rationalist Archie, and is promptly shot dead.

Stoppard's point seems to be that even logicians and agnostics crave absolutes, not to say an Absolute. It is a natural craving, and perhaps also a realistic one. Stoppard's own mistrust of materialist philosophy is on record, as is his belief that there must always be 'a moral standard, a consistent idea of what constitutes good and bad in the way human beings treat each other'. From this came 'the conclusion, not reached all that willingly, that if our behaviour is open to absolute judgement, there must be an absolute judge'. Hence *Jumpers*, 'a theist play, written to combat the arrogant view that anyone who believes in God is some kind of cripple, using God as a crutch. I wanted to suggest that atheists may be the cripples, lacking the strength to live with the idea of God.'

The play makes this last thought explicit at one point, but does not quite succeed in demonstrating it in terms of plot or character. Weakness does not, after all, characterize the atheist Archie. However, there is no doubt that the weight of the play's sympathy is with George's critique of the 'jumpers', with his defence of the 'irrational, emotional and whimsical' without which the world would be 'one gigantic field of soya beans', and with his suspicion (to put it no higher) that some unidentifiable First Cause both created man and provided him with a capacity for, or at least a sense of, goodness. As he embarrassedly confesses, 'now and again, not necessarily in the contemplation of rainbows or newborn babies, nor in extremities of pain or joy, but more probably ambushed by some quite trivial moment', he *knows* that God exists. And, as he adds in his last speech, everyone *knows* that 'life is better than death, love better than hate, and the light shining through the east window of their bloody gymnasium more beautiful than a rotting corpse'. Yet of course none of this 'knowledge' can be scientifically validated, and the play actually ends, as perhaps it must, with Archie's glib and cynical optimism: 'Many are happy much of the time; more eat than starve, more are healthy than sick, more curable than dying, not so many dying as dead . . .' Why worry about absolutes? Let's be satisfied with, if not exactly the greatest

happiness of the greatest number, at least a fair amount of
content for a fair amount of the population. It is a stance
the play leaves looking distinctly tawdry.

This is the first play in which Stoppard's aim was to 'ask
a question, and then try to answer it, or at least put the
counter-question'. What he ends by providing is nothing as
conclusive as an 'answer', and his intellectual opponents
are unlikely to be converted by the 'counter-questions' of
what he admits to be his 'bathtub philosophy'. Humanists
will obviously reject the suggestion that morality depends
on religious faith. Nevertheless, *Jumpers* is a courageous
attempt to move beyond the social criticism that mainly
preoccupies the contemporary theatre into a realm of metaphysics almost entirely ignored by it, to relate the two,
and, doing so, to raise issues of rare size and import; and
this is achieved, not only with a theatrical extravagance
that verges on the outrageous, but with a nice sense of
individual character. One remembers the arguments and
the florid effects, but one also remembers George, a tiny,
defiant figure, helplessly brandishing his fist at a cold and
brutal society and at what he still partly fears may be a
mechanistic universe: Stoppard's archetypal man seeking,
and failing, to find his precise place in the scheme of things.

David Storey
(born 1933)

All art is to some extent the transmutation of personal
experience; but in the case of David Storey the connection
seems more than usually close. He was born in 1933, third
son of a Wakefield miner, was given a middle-class education, and moved south: *In Celebration* (1969) is about three
middle-class sons coming north to visit their Yorkshire
parents, a miner and his wife. He has been a schoolmaster,
like the protagonist of *The Restoration of Arnold Middleton*
(1966). His experience as a farm worker no doubt provided
background for *The Farm* (1973), and as an erector of

showground tents for *The Contractor* (1969). At what he describes as the unhappiest period of his life he was an art student in London and played professional rugby football in the north at weekends: hence *Life Class* (1974), which is set in an art college, and *The Changing Room* (1971), which occurs off the field during a rugby game. Hence perhaps also the feeling, often apparent in his work, of being pulled in two irreconcilable directions at once. Yet it would be wrong to call Storey's work subjective, or even autobiographical. He has the detachment to raise the personal to the general; and he has given us a series of plays about mutilation, disintegration, and the elusiveness of human wholeness. If the inner and outer man, the spiritual and social, the intellectual and instinctual, were somehow to be unified, we might find happiness: but how is that to be achieved?

These concerns are evident in *Arnold Middleton*, which was written some seven years before it was performed, between the first two of the novels for which Storey is probably still best known. Feelings of being 'disenfranchised, dispossessed' and of living in a world of spiritual 'pygmies', along with marital pressures and much else, lead the protagonist to escape first into burlesque role-playing and finally, after a sexual crisis with his mother-in-law, into psychosis. His deformities (he declares in what seems to be the sanity of madness) have become his natural features: he can be defined only by his limitations, 'which are limitless'. The ending of this dense, difficult, entertaining play is unclear, and probably meant to be so, since Storey doesn't find resolutions easy or honest. But perhaps Middleton must learn to accept things, including himself as he has become, and try to endure.

That certainly seems the conclusion of the excellent *In Celebration*, which tends to regard class mobility, its subject, as a form of 'disfigurement'. The father's menial job, though not sentimentalized, 'has significance for him, while the work he has educated us to do is nothing: at the best a pastime, at the worst a sort of soulless stirring of the pot'.

The most openly dissatisfied of his three sons (representing, roughly, worldly success, the intellectual and spiritual life, and the revolutionary urge) seeks revenge on their mother, partly because she rejected him as a child, partly because he regards her ambition as the basic cause of his rootlessness and dissatisfaction; but he draws back at the last moment. 'It really is a question of soldiering on, or of compromising, or forgiving,' Storey has declared apropos this play and perhaps others. These are the three 'solutions' the brothers achieve: since the past is irremediable, the traditional ways irrecoverable, and the old simplicities probably illusory anyway, there would seem to be no other choices open to them.

Storey's characters tend to be at odds with society, with those who should be nearest and dearest, and even with themselves. At worst, they are cut off from roots, families, satisfying work, fulfilling relationships, and the ability to comprehend and articulate what is wrong. Their hands are, so to speak, dissociated from their minds, their minds from their hearts, and both hearts and minds from their tongues. The extreme case is *Home* (1970), which occurs in a madhouse tentatively identified with a decayed Britain, and mainly concerns two elderly men whose conversation is all polite evasion. Only when they start embarrassedly, silently and apparently without reason to weep can they express their amorphous sense of dereliction and waste. There is, however, plenty of supporting evidence to be found in succeeding plays.

The Farm translates disharmony to a pastoral setting. The labourers are ignorant and passive, the farmer drunken and full of resentment at his gruelling work, at his barren daughters and (especially) at his son, an aspiring poet who has left home for the south. Even the farm is likely to be swept away for a six-lane highway, much as the art college of *Life Class* is to be replaced with an institute of engineering. This play specifically involves the collapse of creativity. The students seem mostly unruly and uninterested, and their teacher has come to believe that the only purpose left to the artist is to shape and savour the events around him. Accordingly, he precipitates and coldly observes an indecent assault on the class model, thus losing himself his job and prospects, as he has already lost his wife, his beliefs and his artistic reputation. There seems little hope for him, and none for the protagonist of *Early Days* (1980), an ex-politician looking back from extreme old age on achievements that are 'dust' and remembering a wife he 'destroyed'. He gropes for a sense of identity, importance and power, but he lacks spiritual resource, and so becomes little more than a malicious prankster, playing with roles, ideas and words and upsetting his family by his impotent manipulations. Again, but more cancerously, his deformities have become his features, his limitations define him; and it is too late to change.

Storey has found several forms for his pessimistic but not despairing vision. *In Celebration* is an Ibsenesque demonstration of the power of the past over the present, open and explicit about the issues it raises. *Home* is more Chekhovian in style, an oblique, understated piece that works by inference and suggestion. The curious *Cromwell* (1973) is, at least in its later stages, poetic and somewhat abstract, a secular *Pilgrim's Progress* whose main character seeks a purpose first in military action, then in withdrawal from the social world, and, after his farm and child have been destroyed, moves onto a plane of spiritual aspiration whose actual character seems as indefinite to him and Storey as to us. In *The Changing Room* there is, as Storey says of *Home*, 'nothing great going on on the surface'; but this time that is because the style is akin to a documentary, the effect a meticulous study of a team assembling for and recovering from a match. If we are watchful, we can see that Storey characterizes with some care and touches at least glancingly on familiar areas of experience: a bad marriage, class divisions, the decline of old ways, the extent to which group endeavour is possible and desirable. If we like, we can conclude that, cut off from each other though individuals may be, they can occasionally find a sense of community in play. But that is up to us. Storey has said that his work 'lives almost in the measure that it escapes and refuses definition', and that a play which he fully understands 'is dead'.

He continues to experiment, even at the risk of critical hostility. *Mother's Day* (1976) and *Sisters* (1978) were both written after *Early Days*, both involve sexual excess on public housing estates, and the first is positively Ortonesque, an anarchic farce involving incest, rape, robbery and attempted murder. It is, as it turns out, a style that doesn't altogether suit Storey; and there's also awkwardness of tone in the more successful *Sisters*, in which a woman absconds from a lunatic asylum in search of security and stability, and finds the family house transformed into a brothel. Yet Storey has claimed that *Mother's Day* is a 'microcosm of English domestic life with its delusions, illusions and fantasies', adding that 'English urban life is sexually rapacious, and the play embodies that. Everybody involved in it is screwing everybody else, which is a reflection of the world we live in.'

In other words the play, like its sequel, is Storey's latest way of exploring those concerns which have continued to preoccupy him throughout his career: why do we misuse, damage and scar ourselves and other people? Knowing his persistence and seriousness as an artist, one can safely prophesy that it, too, will lead to something new.

The Contractor

To all appearances, nothing much happens in *The Contractor*. Like *The Changing Room*, it seems to be presenting us with the sort of events that usually happen offstage. In Acts I and II a tent is slowly, painstakingly assembled and raised, and in Act III it is lowered. What might well be the central occurrence in another man's play, a wedding reception, takes place in the second interval. Yet audiences and critics have not usually felt bored or cheated. On the contrary, they have tended to feel that the play's little contains a lot and implies more.

There is always a fascination in seeing men at work, and this time the work is recorded with documentary precision. Most of the play it continues in a kind of bass counterpoint to the themes introduced by the various characters. The majority of these are the tent erectors themselves, a motley group of 'misfits' hired by the only local employer who will have them, Ewbank, the Yorkshire 'contractor' of the title. But since the wedding is his own daughter's, we see much of him, too. Moreover, bride, bridegroom, and Ewbank's wife, mother, father and son drift in and out, adding detail and texture to the composition.

The style is naturalistic in the extreme; yet if we listen for hints (we should expect no more) we can learn something about the most casually glimpsed characters. For instance, it's almost invisibly suggested that the bride tends to dominate the bridegroom, and that he is uneasy, not only about the 'fuss' that the tent implies, but about the marriage itself. Again, it's gently indicated that the relationship between Ewbank's wife and his son, Paul, is warmer and easier than between the boy and himself, each of whom becomes silent and awkward when alone together. She weeps 'bloody buckets' when Paul leaves after the wedding; Ewbank's feelings seem much more mixed. As often in Storey, a relationship between father and son is marked by tension, and for some of the usual reasons.

Social change has affected the Ewbanks as it has all else, down to the view from their house, which was once a farm and a mill and is now a town in the process of becoming even more characterless than it already is. The oldest of the three family generations we see is represented by a retired artisan with a contempt for everything modern and a somewhat senile nostalgia for a world where (he claims) he worked a daily thirty or forty hours for next to no pay, making rope by hand. He carries around a sample of his craftsmanship to show anyone who will or won't listen.

Meanwhile Paul, his restless, dissatisfied grandson, spends the play trying to help the workmen with the tent and hide the fact that he is a university man. Somewhere inside, he seems to hanker to become what old Ewbank was or pretends to have been. Like many of Storey's young men, he evidently feels deracinated, split by his education: he has become an obsessive traveller, wandering in search (at bottom) of an identity.

His father's trade, mock-casually proferred him at one point, is no solution for Paul. It does not fulfil the contractor himself. Ewbank calls himself an artisan, and retains some of his own father's craftsmanly pride: hence the commemorative inscription on the ceiling of a tent everyone agrees to be unusually beautiful; hence his angry distress ('damn near broke my heart') at the mauling his unruly wedding guests give it. But it's still a pride unsatisfied by what he calls the 'come today, gone tomorrow' of contracting out canvas. Ewbank's manner is direct, blunt, brusque, aggressive, rude; but, as his wife indicates, he is more complicated than he seems. He feels his age and a sense of emptiness and waste: 'I have lived all this time, and I know nowt about anything.' He drinks too much. Money hasn't brought him content, and even seems to him a burden, since he resents spending it, especially on Paul and Paul's education, whose purpose he cannot see. His son-in-law – 'a bloody aristocrat, so refined if it wasn't for his britches he'd be invisible' – might be an alien being. He even wears his suit like 'a man who has never really found his proper station in life', and, indeed, seems in most respects as much a social misfit as his men. Indeed, he identifies with them: 'You could put us all into a string bag, you know, and chuck us away, and none'd be the wiser.'

His employees generally he defines as 'miners who've coughed their lungs up, fitters who've lost their fingers, madmen who've run away from home'. Actually, this particular gang consists of the following: Kay, the taciturn foreman, who has been in prison for embezzlement; Ben-

nett, broken and soured because his wife left him for another man; Glendenning, 'a good-natured, stammering
half-wit'; and two garrulous, shiftless Irishmen, Fitzpatrick,
described as 'hard, shrewd', and his sidekick, Marshall,
who has three unsuccessful marriages behind him. This last
pair brings some tension and dynamism to what might be
a static human situation. Purposeless and bored themselves, they turn upon others for their desultory amusement. They interminably joke, mock, scratch at their
victims' weaknesses and sorrows, and wound, driving the
cuckold Bennett to impotent threats of violence and even
provoking the seemingly imperturbable ex-convict, Kay, to
sack the worst offender, Fitzpatrick: a decision promptly
countermanded by Ewbank, who makes as much of a fetish
of firing nobody as of hiring anyone.

Storey has said that the play deliberately eschews confrontations: it is directed towards 'withdrawal from drama'
rather than 'explosion and revelation'. So both crisis and
violence are avoided, and the characters' relationships at
the end are much what they were at the start. But if they
have learned only a little new about each other, we have
acquired rather more understanding of them. We know, for
instance, that Glendenning has touching fantasies of having
children of his own. We can see a paternal protectiveness
towards the 'half-wit' in Bennett; but we may also feel that
the latter deserves to be as cruelly teased as he is, since he
has exposed Kay's secrets and needled the Irishmen for
their failure with women. Even the wastrel Fitzpatrick,
whose life is spent 'between one bottle and another, one
bar-room and the next', at least has a pronounced aesthetic
sense. The chat can seem repetitious, enervating; yet in
every cranny extra information is slyly, deftly concealed.

And what does it all add up to? Storey leaves that for us
to decide, and would presumably expect our decisions to
vary from production to production. Each time, he says, he
himself sees it in a different light: now as about 'the decline
and fading-away of a capitalist society', now as a metaphor

for artistic creation – 'All the labour of putting up the tent, and when it's there what good is it? What's it there for?'

> I get letters from people who ask me, does it mean this, does it mean that, and I often see some justice in their suggestions. And still the play is not confined to any one of these definitions; it contains the possibility of them, but it still continues to make sense – and complete sense – as the story of these men who put up the tent, and that's that. I think it's very important for me to leave all the options open.

All the same, the play mainly consists of work, and is perhaps most naturally seen as being about it. The end of all that effort, care and trouble is something essentially impermanent and dubiously useful. (According to Marshall, admittedly a less than reliable witness, the marriage celebrated inside the tent is 'heading hard for trouble'.) Some may think this only too characteristic of a society that depends on ever-accelerating production, built-in obsolescence, disposability: indeed, by Act III the tent resembles something ready for the dustbin. It's a society, not just likely to frustrate those seeking to fulfil themselves through their hands, but designed for those unattached to and uninterested in what they do, and calculated to make anybody a 'misfit'. There is no going backwards: old Ewbank is an absurdly anachronistic figure, a comic spokesman for a past he unwittingly exposes as considerably less ideal than he claims. And what is the way forward? Paul's confusion and bewilderment is its own answer.

Yet it isn't as simple as that. There is skill, there is team-work, there can even be shared satisfaction. The 'misfits' do create something which pleases the eye, with what a stage direction calls its 'gentle radiance coming through the drapes'. And isn't all human achievement transitory anyway? The situation is ambiguous, and to insist on any single interpretation would, as Storey himself suggests, be to shrink a play that is moving, funny, humane and resonant.

Alan Ayckbourn

(born 1939)

Alan Ayckbourn was born in 1939, son of a musician. His writer-mother left his father when he was five, and her later marriage to a bank-manager also broke up, though not before the dramatist-to-be had spent his formative years living in flats above small-town branches of Barclays' in southern England: 'plumb centre of where I write now'. His childhood was not altogether happy or stable and, after education at a public school, he spent a difficult time trying to support a wife and child from his earnings as a stage manager and sometime performer. The marriage eventually collapsed.

It was the late Stephen Joseph, pioneer of theatre-in-the-round in Britain, who encouraged the failed actor to write. Indeed, he produced his first four plays at the seaside resort of Scarborough, where Ayckbourn himself now runs the repertory theatre and presents all his work before its eventual transfer to the metropolis. London's initial reaction was not, however, favourable. *Mr Whatnot* (1964), an amusing if whimsical mime about a piano-tuner run loose in a stately home, was condemned by most reviewers. But *Relatively Speaking* (1965) was justly admired in both London and New York for the hilarious ingenuity with which it sustains its tale of the young man who assumes his fiancée's elderly lover is her father. Most of the humour comes from obvious misunderstandings, incomprehension and mutual bewilderment, as it sometimes does in the later plays. The human collisions have, however, become generally subtler since then: now it tends to be mere incompatibility – of classes, life-styles, moral or social preconceptions, or temperaments – that generates laughter.

Ayckbourn's development has taken him from farce to a comedy of character, and from a relatively cheerful style of comedy to an increasingly sombre one. His people are rarely satisfied. Their marriages are commonly disastrous. Their best-laid plans rarely come to fruition. The material world, whether represented by cars, lights, do-it-yourself furniture or electric toothbrushes, is unerringly hostile to human effort. And both men and women are capable of surprising, though usually unmeant, cruelty to one another. Some seem doomed to be permanent victims: Annie, in *The Norman Conquests* (1973), whose disappearing youth is spent being exploited by everyone, from the inert admirer who wangles meals from her to her bedridden mother upstairs; or Leonard in the underrated *Time and Time Again* (1971), a helpless and somewhat fey young man born to be rejected by women and misused by his appallingly insensitive brother-in-law.

Insensitivity, self-absorption, lack of consideration for or understanding of others, are commodities that particularly interest Ayckbourn. It is they, rather than obvious malice, that usually cause the damage he chronicles. Trevor and Susannah, the neurotically wrangling couple at the centre of *Bedroom Farce* (1975), successfully exacerbate the tensions in their acquaintances' marriages, but they do so unintentionally, even apologetically. And some of Ayckbourn's most destructive characters are positively well-intentioned. Colin in *Absent Friends* (1974), whose fiancée has recently died, uses a reunion with old friends to congratulate them on their good fortune in having one another. The effect of his ceaseless sentimentality is to underscore their unhappiness and propel one abused wife into a nervous breakdown. It is the authentic generosity of Anthea and Richard, the blithe and successful couple at the nub of *Joking Apart* (1978), that reduces all around to agonies of self-doubt, impotence and despair. The lowest point of all is reached by Vera in *Just Between Ourselves* (1976). Insecure victim of a relentlessly cheerful but myopic husband and his jealous mother, she ends the play in a catatonic stupor, hardly more than a human vegetable.

'Funny' writers are not usually so harsh to their characters; but then Ayckbourn has always insisted on taking risks, with form as well as content. *The Norman Conquests* is actually three overlapping but self-sufficient plays, each covering the fraught events of the same weekend from the stance of a different room. In *Bedroom Farce* all of the three bedrooms in which the action occurs are seen at the same time; and in *How the Other Half Loves* (1969) two living rooms become a single set, so that a visiting couple have only to swivel their chairs to participate simultaneously in what are supposed to be consecutive dinner parties. *Sisterly Feelings* (1979), about two sisters competing for the same man, is a comedy of permutations, in which the toss of a coin and (later) an actress's choice lead the cast by four alternate routes to the identical last scene. At the time of writing, Ayckbourn was working on a two-hander for ten people, the size of his company at Scarborough. As he himself says, 'I thrive when working under a series of preconditions.'

Just occasionally, the preconditions are too tortuously demanding even for him. In *Family Circles* (1978) three sisters bring their men to celebrate the wedding anniversary of their parents, who may and may not be trying to murder each other and who would certainly agree that, in the father's words, 'Whoever you choose to share the rest of your life, it invariably turns out to be the worst choice you ever made.' The play then tests this cynical proposition by attaching each sister to a different male for the first three acts and turning the fourth into a free-for-all, in which marriages and (hence) personalities change with baffling frequency. Inevitably, the audience flounders, though not before it has enjoyed much pointed observation.

Altogether, it is surprising that Ayckbourn's plays succeed as comedies, given an intricacy of plot better fitted to farce, and themes sometimes more suited to tragedy. But somehow he is able to reconcile technical ingenuity with a firm belief that characters must be allowed 'to develop and therefore to a certain extent dictate how a play should run'. Indeed, his people have become more painfully plausible over the years, though he still notes their vanities, pretensions, follies and troubled encounters with a wry eye and still sometimes puts them into comic perspective with what he calls a 'twist' or 'slant'. In *The Norman Conquests*, for instance, an emotionally charged supper becomes hilarious simply because one guest is sitting on a much lower chair than anyone else; in one of the short plays that constitute *Confusions* (1974) the presence of a solicitous waiter has a similar effect on a quarrel between a wife and her adulterous husband.

Ayckbourn is sometimes called a callous writer. The accusation ignores his ability to win an audience's compassion for the misunderstood and oppressed. He is still much scorned for his commercial success. The answer to that is to be found in his positive distaste for mechanical effects, easy jokes and neat, happy dénouements, as well as in the seriousness of his subject-matter: envy in *Joking Apart*; bereavement in *Absent Friends*; class conflict in the somewhat disappointing *Ten Times Table* (1977); and, in these and elsewhere, the everyday inhumanity of people to each other, especially within marriage and the family. Not least, he has been accused of being insular, local, obsessed with the trivia of small-town life. It is true that his people's language, furniture, manners and interests tend to place them with great social precision, whether they are at, above or below bank-manager level. But at his not-infrequent best he transforms suburban problems into much more universal insecurities and anxieties.

Possibly he will never succeed in writing 'a completely serious play that makes people laugh all the time', or, as he more elaborately puts it, 'a totally effortless, totally truthful, unforced comedy shaped like a flawless diamond in which one may see a million reflections, both one's own and other people's'. But he may be expected to continue trying to darken his humour and deepen our laughter. For a playwright who could easily choose to sit back and enjoy the fruits of his triumphs to date, it is an enterprising aim.

Absurd Person Singular

Joking Apart is subtler, more morally challenging, and demands a finer discrimination of its audiences; *The Norman Conquests*, a more complex construct; *Just Between Ourselves*, blacker, glummer, more emotionally adventurous. But *Absurd Person Singular*, first performed in 1972, contains within it the promise of them all. It is eccentrically set in three kitchens on consecutive Christmas Eves. It has a serious theme, namely social mobility, and a middle act daringly poised between laughter and pain. It may still be Ayckbourn's most consistently successful play.

It was written when he was becoming 'increasingly fascinated by the dramatic possibilities of offstage action'; and in Acts I and II parties occur in adjoining rooms, both dominated by the 'jolly, hearty' Dick and Lottie, a couple we hear but never meet. The first of these is given by Sidney and Jane Hopcroft. He runs a general stores, but clearly has ambitions, both social and commercial. She is happiest when she is busy in her neat, gadget-crammed kitchen. Both are somewhat lacking in confidence when it comes to coping with their guests, who are all above them in status: Ronald, manager of the bank from which Sidney hopes to borrow; his wife Marion, who gushes extravagantly about the Hopcrofts' house to their faces, but displays an upper-crust contempt for it and boredom with them behind their backs; Geoffrey, an architect and (it seems) full-time philanderer; and his wife Eva, who neurotically swallows pills and informs the bewildered Sidney that she is simply 'an embarrassing smudge on a marriage licence'.

Some of the humour is broadish by Ayckbourn's later standards; yet it emerges from character and usually throws light upon it. When Jane discovers she has run out of tonic water, she goes off in the rain to buy some, but forgets her back-door key, and so is obliged to hurtle back through the living room looking like a lifeboat-woman, and out again into the garden, where she spends the rest of the act skulking, trying to avoid being seen, and getting soaked. It is very funny and it is all caused by her and Sidney's social insecurity, her lack of sophistication and *savoir-faire*, his desperate need to impress.

Sidney has grown in confidence by the second act. He is 'the up-and-coming Mr Hopcroft', engaged on property developments sneered at as 'squalid' by Geoffrey, who himself seems somewhat in decline. At any rate, he is clearly having great trouble with a shopping centre he has designed. He is also proposing to leave Eva, for whose mental state 'decline' is too weak a word. Though it is her kitchen and her party offstage, she does not open her mouth until the end of the act, when she drunkenly begins to sing a carol. By then she has attempted to defenestrate, knife, gas, hang, electrocute and (twice) poison herself.

This is not at all funny in itself, nor meant to be. The grim joke is that her guests misinterpret her every action. Jane sees her head in the oven, concludes it needs cleaning, and gratefully proceeds to do the job herself. Sidney finds her trying to retrieve the pills she has dropped down the sink, and starts helpfully mending her waste-pipe. Even the vague and indolent Ronald tries amateurishly to fix the damaged light-flex. Material objects being the unfriendly things they are in Ayckbourn's world, Sidney ends up doused with water and Ronald half-dead from electric shock. But such incidents do not, of course, explain the scene's uncomfortable effect. Mutual incomprehension, the source of so much of Ayckbourn's comedy, is here taken to extremes that a lesser writer might make simply tasteless or cruel. Suicidal despair on the one hand, a genial and kindly imperviousness on the other: the contrast produces a kind of grisly, unnerving hilarity. This is bravura writing.

Act III is, as it should be, quieter and less frenetic, at least until the end. Eva's 'trendy homespun' kitchen has been replaced by the shambling grandeur of Ronald's Victorian house. The couple visiting it is very changed. Geoffrey has been greatly chastened by the collapse of the roof in his shopping complex and, with it, of his career. The one-time Lothario even fails to react with interest when Ronald amusingly exposes his own inadequacy as a husband by speaking of women, a sex he perplexedly regards as 'an old sports jacket or something, continually beginning to come apart at the seams'. On the other hand, Eva has pulled herself together. She seems to be in control both of Geoffrey and his business, though he is still proud enough to resist when she presses him to ask Hopcroft for a commission. She also takes charge of Marion, who has retired to her bedroom in an alcoholic stupor.

Marion's ruin is a good illustration of the unobtrusive professionalism of Ayckbourn, who has been carefully preparing us for it throughout. At the Hopcrofts', she cuts an assured and 'well-groomed' figure, but she is also heard complaining about the size of her gin. Next, we find Ronald warning her to stop drinking, after which she blearily switches on the light that half-electrocutes him and then laughs sottishly at his glazed and shaky behaviour. Now she totters downstairs, weeps drunkenly about the loss of her beauty and makes an embarrassing pass at Geoffrey. But before he can react, the doorbell rings. Sidney and Jane are outside. Everyone pretends not to be at home, but that does not deter Hopcrofts, who make their own way inside, wearing party hats. They press unsuitable presents on their 'friends' and then browbeat them into playing undignified games. The play ends with them capering around the kitchen as Sidney screams, 'Dance, dance, dance.'

It is a pointed ending. Sidney, so unsure of himself in the first act, is now the most successful and commanding of them all. Ronald describes him as 'doing frightfully well' and 'the chap to keep in with', and dare not offend him, because of the size of his deposit account. Eva ignominiously asks him to give Geoffrey employment, not an idea that is enthusiastically received. Marion starts to empty the bottle of gin he has just given her. They are, metaphorically as well as literally, dancing to his tune.

Socially, *Absurd Person Singular* is an observant piece. The language, as well as the furniture, places the characters with some precision. Marion's use of the words 'enchanting', 'divine' and 'gorgeous' is nicely contrasted with the Hopcrofts' lower-middle-class gentility: 'beg pardon?' instead of 'sorry', 'the wife' instead of 'my wife', 'Ron' for 'Ronald' or 'Ronnie'. It is also very much a piece of its time. Sidney is that success-symbol of the 1960s and early 1970s, the property speculator, complete with a suitably ugly philosophy about dog-eats-dog and you-scratch-my-back-I'll-scratch-yours. His rise is accompanied by the fall of those representing more traditional status, wealth and power: Marion, the leisured gentlewoman, and Geoffrey, the educated professional who applies moral and aesthetic standards to his work.

But it is rather more than a period chronicle, and also rather more than a sceptical study of marriage and relationships. It is about the change and decay to which we are all eventually subject. The Hopcrofts may have their temporary triumphs and the Evas their respites. The Geoffreys, Marions and Ronalds demonstrate a wider, more general truth. Like everything else in Ayckbourn's bleak, funny world, time itself is deeply inimical to hope, effort, fulfilment and happiness.

Howard Brenton
(born 1942)

Howard Brenton's programme-note for *Weapons of Happiness* might be an embryonic manifesto for several of the younger playwrights of the Left. The 'real' world, by which he presumably means the public world, must be present onstage. It would, he says, 'be pleasant to write about great idylls, but it would be an almost criminal activity with the state of things as they are'. And he goes on: 'Writers of my group all sense the enormous upheaval that is going to come. It is difficult to define the nature of that upheaval, but if you write a scene set in London today – about any class – that future upheaval will be present in that scene.'

This 'group' includes David Hare, Howard Barker, David Edgar, Stephen Poliakoff and Tony Bicat, among other less important or, like Snoo Wilson, less easily categorized playwrights. Each obviously has his individual qualities and peculiar emphases, but they all share a conviction that Britain is in deep and possibly terminal decay. The last years of this century may see us precariously surviving alongside the child-prostitutes in a British Weimar, as in Poliakoff's *Heroes*; ruled in fact if not name by an increasingly ruthless secret police, as in Barker's *That Good Between Us*; or scavenging for dogs from the relative safety of underground car parks, as in Bicat's *Devil's Island*. Other plays worth the attention of those looking for completer understanding of this Theatre of Cataclysm are Hare's *Knuckle*, *Teeth 'n' Smiles* and *Plenty*, Barker's *Claw*, *Stripwell*, *Fair Slaughter* and *Hang of the Jail*, Poliakoff's *City Sugar* and *Strawberry Fields*, Edgar's *Destiny*, and perhaps Peter Flannery's *Savage Amusement*. It is invidious to pick out the 'best' of a group which would see its justification, not in aesthetic terms, but as lighters of (Brenton's words) 'bush fires' which will 'smoulder into public consciousness'. Brenton is, however, probably the most widely respected.

He was born in Portsmouth in 1942, son of a policeman who later became a Methodist minister; planned to become a painter, but instead went to read English at Cambridge, a university he 'passionately hated'; became a stage manager at various repertory theatres, then a writer and performer, and joined one of the most innovative 'fringe' companies, Portable Theatre, which specialized in socially and politically provocative drama played with the minimum of scenery and in a succinct, fast, visually and verbally inventive concatenation of theatrical styles. For this he wrote *Christie in Love* (1969), in which the notorious murderer, himself naturalistically presented, is confronted with a rag-doll victim and two near-caricature policemen. Some critics have seen the protagonist as an existential hero cour-

ageous enough to enact feelings others repress, and Brenton
has given comfort to this view by calling the murders 'acts
of love'; but the play itself suggests something less tendentious. Christie's love seems mainly to consist of disgust,
hatred and fear of castration, attitudes which are, however,
shared to some extent by the policemen. They sing limericks replete with contempt for sex, go on to sentimentalize
women, love and the family, and end describing Christie's
death as 'a blow struck for married life'. Christie, in short,
reflects and represents a hypocritical society's corruption
of a vital instinct.

Brenton's early work is rarely so striking as this. *Gum and
Goo* (1969) and *The Education of Spinny Spew* (1969) concern
the older generation's attempts to cope with the childhood
destructiveness that it has probably helped cause. *Heads*
(1969) extends Brenton's belief that 'the mutilation of sons
by their mothers is almost universal'. Here, it is their girlfriend who mutilates two men with her craving for a male
ideal in which intellect and physique are perfectly blended.
Revenge (1969) is about a superannuated master-criminal
and an equally outdated master-policeman, both played by
the same actor, who pursue a romantic vendetta in an
England that, we're told, is becoming 'one giant pinball
table'. Its view of the 1980s – 'the casino towns, the brothel
villages, the cities red with blood and pleasure: public life
the turn of a card, the fall of a dice' – is worth comparing
with the forecasts of *The Churchill Play*.

Stylistically, the earlier plays vary from a terse and
abrupt naturalism to sardonic caricature at its most marked
in *Scott of the Antarctic* (1971), which presents the famous
explorer as a blinkered idiot spouting public-school platitudes as he tries and fails to survive a lunatic imperialist
adventure. Their main theme is the place of the individual
in a complex and corrupt world, and especially that of the
'saint or hero who drives a straight line in a society that
has become very distorted'. Scott is one of these. So is the
founder of Methodism in *Wesley* (1970), a surprisingly sympathetic portrait given Brenton's proclaimed atheism. And

so is Violette Szabo, the Second World War agent in *Hitler Dances* (1972), with her awesome yearning for slaughter. The bulk of this play involves the ghost of one of her hated Germans, who has been reduced to cannibalism in defeat, has been hounded to death, and now, resurrected Frankenstein-style, perpetuates her philosophy of destruction by murdering a crippled child. Like much of Brenton's work, it is packed with images of disease and decay, themselves loaded comments on the world as he sees it. Another recurring image, with a similar function, is sexual perversion, which in his rather puritan view appears to include homosexuality.

Both images are to be found in the short *Fruit* (1970), in which a hideously deformed osteopath's attempts to blackmail a homosexual Tory prime minister are thwarted by a slippery system. This is the first of several plays dealing directly with British politics: *Magnificence* (1973), about a squatter who turns terrorist after a bailiff's violence causes his pregnant wife to miscarry; *Brassneck* (1973), about political corruption in a Midlands town, written in collaboration with David Hare; *The Churchill Play*; and *Weapons of Happiness* (1976), about the unsuccessful occupation of a potato-crisp factory. The lively *Epsom Downs* (1977) deals with the subject of England more metaphorically: it uses Derby Day to take a sweeping look at a society in which some destroy themselves with gambling and drink, and others succeed by exploiting those needs. *The Romans in Britain* (1980) deals with imperialism, somewhat speciously comparing the British military presence in Ulster with Caesar's savage oppression of the Celts. This contains Brenton's most lurid sexual image to date, the homosexual rape of a druid.

The style of these plays is fluent and cinematic, in Brenton's words 'epic, but not Brechtian'. They take little interest in individual psychology, tending always, and often arrestingly, to see people in terms of social role, function and action. They are not, however, overtly didactic. Brenton is on record as saying that he hates 'moral pressure' and is interested in inducing 'moral vertigo'. He is, for instance, often unexpectedly generous to characters whom he, as a 'revolutionary socialist', might be expected to dismiss with brusque contempt: the factory owner in *Weapons of Happiness*, pathetically bewildered by events that undermine his moral self-esteem; or the homosexual, diseased High Tory in *Magnificence*, cynically revolted both by himself and by the silicone men who have replaced him in power; even the bailiff in the same play. In Brenton's view, the ruling class has lost much of its conviction, confidence and control.

Change, he believes, is necessary, indeed unavoidable; but it will not come from inside the existing system. Labour Party potentates are as thickly involved in the intricate evils described in *Brassneck* as anyone else. *Weapons of Happiness* suggests that the trades-union establishment, too, is too chummy with capital and commerce. Meanwhile, the ruthless entrepreneur flourishes. At the end of *Brassneck*, one such successfully sells the assembled industrialists, bureaucrats, ex-socialists and local-government bigwigs the idea of marketing 'a product for our times, the perfect product, totally artificial, man-made, creating its own market, 100 per cent consumer identification, generating its own demand': Chinese heroin.

At times Brenton's plays convey a feeling of helplessness at a situation with its own momentum, seemingly beyond anyone's power to control. The protagonist of *Magnificence* ends by blowing up both himself and a Tory minister who has offered him a 'humane resolution' he despises, and is blamed for 'the waste of your anger'; but what should he have done instead? The suggestion of *Weapons of Happiness* – the one given the imprimatur of a somewhat sentimentally conceived Czech communist-in-exile, representing European experience and suffering – seems to be hard political work at ground level in the big cities. The striking workers end up *en route* to Manchester, where they will presumably form a radical cell. They will, in short, 'survive in the cracks' of a concrete world, and perhaps one day change it. The image is from *The Churchill Play*, which it is time to consider in detail.

The Churchill Play

It begins with an arresting image, four servicemen guarding a coffin, from which emerges none other than Winston Churchill, on his way to be buried at Blaydon. But hardly has he begun to speak than the lights go up, and we are faced with the aircraft hangar that now serves as the recreation area of what is, it appears, a British concentration camp. The year is the one invested with special dread by George Orwell, 1984; and the scene we have just witnessed is the detainees' back-handed tribute to Churchill himself. It is part of the play the inmates are to perform to a parliamentary committee about to inspect their camp.

Gradually, the political background is filled in. There has been industrial violence, including a bloody confrontation between miners and strike-breaking soldiers. Inflation has been rampant. A Conservative–Labour coalition government has come to power and passed Draconian laws. Churchill Camp, as this is called, is the twenty-eighth in a British gulag, which is now filled with 'industrial saboteurs' and other unruly elements. The guards are professional soldiers, capable of extreme violence. During the evening a detainee guilty of insubordination is 'dumped' on to the rubbish tip and dies in agony offstage. He is the third killed that month.

Yet the tone is not melodramatic, nor the characterization black and white. The colonel-in-charge worries about what history will say, but feels he must do his duty. The camp doctor and recreation officer, Captain Thompson, desperately tries to reconcile his liberal conscience with the realities of the situation. The NCOs, though tough, dangerous and fundamentally hostile to the prisoners, are still on superficially friendly terms with many of them. The prisoners themselves are a mixed bag: Jimmy, a half-crazed anarchist with Luddite tendencies; Joby, 'shifty, hangdog and sly', a conservatively inclined journalist whose misfortune was to lose his temper and hit a policeman; Mike, desperately trying to keep his flagging anger alight; and others. They are all British, and all victims, even the guards. Brenton's intention, he says, was to show those who run the camp at their best. No individual was to be blamed. It was the whole country that gradually involved itself in 'conspiracy of obedience', almost without knowing it; the whole country that allowed freedom to slip away.

But what freedom, and *was* it freedom? Here is the relevance of Churchill as the prisoners present him in their play. He emerges as a maudlin rhetorician, personally brutalized by a harsh upbringing and the violent adventures of his youth. As a politician in peacetime, he was the enemy of the working class and the virtual murderer of striking Welsh miners. As a war-leader, he was overrated: 'people won the war', not he. In all respects he was completely out of touch with ordinary life and ordinary people. To emphasize this, Brenton rewrites history. Blitzed Londoners did not, as the record says, shout to Churchill, 'We can take it, give it 'em back': their words were 'We can take it, but we just might give it back to you one day.' They promised revenge, not support.

It was, however, the working class which continued to suffer at the hands of Churchill's successors-in-office. His influence on Britain is symbolized by an image very characteristic of Brenton, that of the syphilis which putrified the mind of his father, Lord Randolph Churchill. Similarly, Winston poisoned the nation itself. As several critics have observed, it is not an altogether unsympathetic portrait of the man personally, but politically it is a remarkably sharp attack on a great English totem. Churchill's legacy, it suggests, is likely to be the Churchill Camp.

Unsurprisingly, these sentiments fail to make a favourable impression on the visiting parliamentary committee. Its chairman is a smooth Conservative, its vice-chairman a representative of that part of the Labour Party which has not, it seems, yet joined the coalition government. The

latter cuts the sorry figure we have come to expect when
Brenton writes about Britain's principal party of reform.
He is a left-winger, overtly hostile to what he calls the
'English Dachau', yet impotent to change it, and maddened
by the degree of acquiescence implied by his presence on
the government's committee of inspection. So he drinks and
drinks, and ends by mumbling sottish, maudlin things
about his responsibility, shame and sorrow, ignored by
everybody.

The committee's third member has no such self-doubt.
She is a civil servant, 'on loan from the Min. of Defence
Think Tank', where she has been dreaming up new devices
for dealing with troublemakers. In Brenton's original script,
these consisted of sensory deprivation in an all-white room
and the planting of 'electrode controls' in the brain. In his
revisions for the Royal Shakespeare Company's production
in 1979, they were reduced to a less explicit but still unsettling 'drugs, surgery, control – kinder than your prison
wire'. The point will be familiar to those who know the
work of Brenton's group, especially that of Howard Barker.
The British élite can be as ruthless as any in Cambodia or
Chile, and more insidiously evil, because it is likely to pass
off oppression and atrocity as 'humane'.

It is this oppression which Brenton accuses us of tacitly
condoning. 'Pleasant roads in southern suburbs are as
much the wire in Long Kesh as the wire itself,' he has
declared in reference to internment in Ulster. So when
Thompson's wife urges him to return to the South and
become 'a real doctor again' and (later) says she wants 'the
house, the lawn, the plants, the children playing', she is
evading a responsibility she should face. In what Brenton
would presumably regard as a justifiable response, the
neo-Luddite threatens to 'kick in your 3-D colour telly. And
paraffin on your fancy furniture. And burn you, burn you
bright.' What have I done to you? she asks. And back
comes the inevitable answer: 'You put me in 'ere.' In Brenton's world there is no such commodity as innocence. Those
who do not oppose an iniquitous system are consenting to it.

The same accusation can be levelled with yet more force at her husband, perhaps the least attractive member of the camp's hierarchy. He treats the prisoners with what's meant to be understanding and imagination, and ends up despised by them, hated by the NCOs, and denounced as 'ill-disciplined, selfish, self-regarding' by his commanding officer; and rightly so. His 'humanity' is ingratiating and dishonest. He is, in Brenton's view, the archetypal liberal, forever absorbed with his own moral health, unable to face harsh truths or act decisively, and hence conspiring in the general drift towards disaster.

At the end, however, he makes a decision of sorts. He offers his medical services to the inmates, who have seized the NCOs' guns, and are holding the officers, their wives and the parliamentary party as hostages before breaking out of the camp. They ignore him. It is too late for reconciliation. For these men it is probably too late for any solution.

There is, suggests their leader, 'nowhere to break out to – they'll concrete the whole world over any moment now'. Their hope is perhaps simply 'to survive, in the cracks, either side of the wire – be alive'; but a roar of motor cycles outside, blinding light from searchlights and the sound of loudspeakers leaves us wondering if any survival is a likely prospect. Brenton's first version ended at this bleak point. His second adds just one line, uttered by a prisoner: 'The Third World War'. The battle between society and its dissidents will continue, intensify, perhaps lead to something new.

The idea behind *The Churchill Play* is, on the face of it, extremely sensational; and some may think it altogether invalidated by the history of Britain since 1974, the year in which the play was first performed. Indeed, the 1979 revival obliged Brenton to cut references to a Special Powers Act 1977 and an Emergency Provisions Act 1981. Nothing like that had happened or looked like happening. A mention of an inflation rate that had taken the price of a bar of chocolate from 10p to £5.50 had similarly disappeared. Yet without them the play appeared increasingly implausible. A prophecy so explicit and alarmist as a British gulag by 1984 obviously needs justification by observation and facts, not by speculation based on a general feeling of insecurity and unease. The result is bound to seem somewhat paranoiac, an accusation that may, in fact, be levelled at much of the work of Brenton's group.

But this conclusion demands two qualifications. The first obviously is that prolonged recession and reactionary governments could make it a complacent one, if not by 1984, at least by the end of the century. The second may be made of a good deal of science fiction, namely that the subject is less the future than disturbing and potentially dangerous aspects of the present. For instance, Brenton suggests that the prolonged war with the IRA in Ulster may already be producing a much more professional, ruthless and politically aware British army, one that might take the initiative in crushing symptoms of revolution on the mainland itself. A more general moral is that we must work hard to safeguard those civil liberties we have. 'When did freedom go?' asks the journalist. 'One evening. Y'were in pub. Or local Odeon. Or in bed w' your Mrs. Or watching telly. An' freedom went.' It *could* happen, without vigilance, even in Britain. Brenton's play may not be a trenchant analysis, but it is an imaginative warning.

Trevor Griffiths
(born 1935)

Trevor Griffiths was born in 1935, son of a chemical process worker who earned a pittance for 'cleaning out great acid vats the size of a theatre and feeding moving hoppers with sulphur on a shovel the size of a railway track'. The quotation is from *Sam, Sam* (1972), a semi-autobiographical play involving two brothers, one of whom remains trapped in the working class while the other moves upwards. That is precisely Griffiths's own family history. His brother was born too soon to take advantage of the 1944 Education Act; he himself went to grammar school and university, became a teacher, lecturer and BBC education officer, and began to write seriously in the late 1960s.

Social mobility is one of his principal themes, and it is always felt to involve loss as well as gain. The elder brother in *Sam, Sam* is unemployed and married to a shrew, yet he has a resilience and capacity for joy lacking in the younger brother, a teacher with political ambitions, a cold and unfaithful wife, and upper-crust in-laws who detest him. The protagonist of *The Party* (1973) is a TV producer rather similar in his working-class origins and in sexual problems that, true to Reichian theory, are reflected in his evident political impotence, his failure to place his radical convictions above the lure of success, wealth and comfort. The problem with talented people on the British Left, in Griffiths's view, is lack of genuine commitment: they will bite the hand that feeds them, but be careful not to bite it off. It is, he thinks, a moral imperative to resist being bought off by, or absorbed into, a capitalist society he persists in believing unjust and exploitative.

Consequently, Griffiths's plays do not ask whether the political and economic *status quo* should be transformed. They take the necessity of that for granted. Rather, they ask how radical change is to occur, and what tends to make it more or less likely. *The Party* is a debate about exactly that. Are we to place our hopes in the revolutionary potential of the Third World and certain Western minorities? Or in the building of a disciplined revolutionary party within the metropolitan proletariat? Or are we to wait for a spontaneous revolution that will discover its identity as it progresses? Various speakers put forward these views in a British drawing room against the background of the Paris riots of 1968, reports of which appear in ironic counterpoint on a TV screen; but where Griffiths himself stands is left deliberately unclear. As he himself says, his plays are meant to provoke speculation and argument, not provide fixed solutions. Characters must not be glibly condemned or endorsed, but allowed their own heads; and audiences must be permitted to react freely to the points of view they represent.

Certainly, this freedom is amply offered by *Occupations* (1970), a much more exciting piece than *The Party*, because its arguments are not abstract, but derive from and influence immediate events. On the one hand, we have the passionate and caring Gramsci, who is leading the great Fiat strike of 1920. On the other, Kabak, a detached and ruthless Soviet agent, who tries to edge the strike into full-scale revolution but, when Gramsci cannot face the bloodshed involved, does a surreptitious business deal with Fiat on his government's behalf. To what extent does a good end justify a perilous means? Is Gramsci a sentimentalist, or are the results of a revolution in which there is no love between leaders and led indeed likely to be worthless, as he thinks? And may not capitalism turn out to be adaptable enough to smother the revolutionary impulse if decisive action is not taken at the right time? To those who accuse Griffiths of insufficient commitment in his handling of such questions, his reply is that his 'commitment is on both sides of the argument and as absolute as I can make it'. He is, he says, a Marxist involved in a continuing debate both with other Marxists and with himself. His plays are dialectic in action, works of discovery and reassessment, not theses or tracts.

The theatre attracts Griffiths because he thinks it an ideal forum for serious discussion and because it usually allows the writer control over his work's integrity. But he knows that only television can reach great numbers of the working-class audience he particularly wishes to influence and, perhaps, mobilize. Unsurprisingly, his plays have sometimes worried programme controllers, and one of the best of them, a vivid study of a 1911 strike and its leaders called *Such Impossibilities*, has yet to be shown, even though it was written under commission in 1971. On the other hand, *Bill Brand* (1976), his series about the vicissitudes of a Labour MP, was a great popular success, as was the short *Through the Night* (1975), the graphic story of a mastectomy patient in a hospital whose impersonality is clearly analogous to that of many other British organizations and institutions. Griffiths's other television plays are *Absolute Beginners* (1974), which shows a steely and uncompromising Lenin in conflict with softer comrades in Edwardian London, and *All Good Men* (1974), which uses the seventieth birthday of a socialist statesman to assess the achievements, compromises and failures of the British Labour Party. He has also written drama for radio, notably *The Big House* (1969), in which a reactionary personnel officer and a self-seeking shop steward are replaced by a new generation, younger, more idealistic, but potentially no less corrupt and corrupting.

Griffiths has been criticized by the Left for unorthodoxy and by the Right for perpetuating class warfare. Some have attacked him for excessive reliance on a naturalistic form, an accusation to some extent answered by the unconventional first act of *Sam, Sam*, and some for presenting his ideological contradictions in too explicit a way, one probably justified by *The Party*. Yet he still has the quality to leave Tom Stoppard, a playwright some way to his right, wondering if he isn't the most talented of all their contemporaries. Certainly, his sophistication, powers of analysis, and sheer intellectual trenchancy make almost every other dramatist on the Left look amateurish by comparison. He is also able to invest argument and debate with considerable vitality, product perhaps of the fundamental conviction that is never far behind his questionings and self-questionings.

'I can't accept that those who stay in the working class are stupid, idle or useless,' he has said, 'because I have had it all around me, I know how lively and vibrant it can be. There's skill, there's talent, there's enormous energy. It's a resource, and at the moment it's simply going to waste.' His plays, at their best, are intelligent and impassioned attempts to discover how that resource can be used and that waste prevented: they are tributes to, and examples of, that skill, talent and energy.

Comedians

The shape of Trevor Griffiths's most commercially and artistically successful play to date is simple and neat. In the first act, six apprentice comedians have a warming-up session with their teacher, Eddie Waters; in Act II they perform at a bingo club for the benefit of a London agent, Bert Challenor; and in Act III there is a post-mortem on their audition. Griffiths conceived the play after hearing of a retired comic who was giving precisely such lessons in Manchester, the city in which it is set. It would also allow him, he realized, 'to explore a part of myself unreconstructed since childhood', namely his sense of humour.

Actually, it allowed him to do more than that. Waters represents, in Griffiths's own words, 'an old tradition of liberal teaching, of loving people, of care, consideration, compassion, and he is essentially incorruptible'. He despises jokes which tend to exploit and perpetuate a stereotyped, prejudiced view of women, Jews, Irishmen or blacks. In his view, a comedian must always tell the truth, especially about what hurts, worries or frightens people; he must illuminate bigotry and fear, make it 'clearer to see, easier to deal with'; he must 'liberate the will and the desire, change the situation'. On the other hand, the cynical Challenor sees comedians as suppliers of easy escapism to 'thick' audiences: 'I'm not looking for philosophers, I'm looking for someone who sees what the people want and knows how to give it to them.' This is his last-minute message to the aspiring entertainers: a navvy, a van-driver, a docker, the owner of a sleazy night club, a milkman, an insurance agent, all anxious to escape stultifying, tedious jobs.

By the end of Act I, it is clear that integrity is a main issue. How many will remain true to their teacher's principles, how many sell out in hopes of eventual wealth and fame? Mick Connor tells a number of jokes about the Irish, which variously show them being oppressed by English landladies, grilled by prurient priests, and beset by sexual troubles. He is rejected by Challenor for insularity and 'earnestness'. Sammy Samuels starts with somewhat similar jokes about his fellow-Jews, then abruptly switches tack, and comes out with some much cruder cracks, notably about blacks with large penises and a propensity to cannibalism. He is told to 'ditch the first half of your act', but accepted. The double-act of Phil and Ged Murray collapses in confusion when one tries to ingratiate himself with Challenor by inserting a crack about a stupid Pakistani on a rape charge, and the other refuses to cooperate. George McBrain rattles out joke after joke about sluttish women and thick-witted Irishmen, and is acclaimed for being 'near the knuckle, but not halfway up the armpit'. Finally, there is Gethin Price, of whom more in a moment.

Some of the jokes told by the three who betray Waters are indeed nasty and offensive. Not many sensitive people would defend McBrain's gibes about his sexually voracious wife. On the other hand, his crack about her Ulster family – 'Ugly? Listen, they wore hoods *before* they joined the UVF' – seems unobjectionable and even funny. And his one about the old lady who sees a Belfast man with a bullet hole in his forehead, and says 'Thank God it missed his eye,' would seem to confront and even illuminate fear, according to Waters's prescription. Conversely, Samuels's joke about a Jewish momma and her bank manager tends to reinforce a racial stereotype, even though it comes before he is supposed to have 'sold out'. What this suggests is that humour may be a more slippery and complex subject than the play's scheme recognizes, and that the line between a life-enhancing and a life-denying joke is narrow, elusive and hard to define. Even O'Connor's gags, on the face of it genuine attempts to investigate victimization and oppression, depend on a stereotyped and prejudiced view of the Church.

But at least the play encourages this sort of speculation.

It wants us to ask ourselves what we are laughing at, and why. It invites us to go further, and look at humour in moral and even political terms; and, whatever our reservations about the tenor of some specific jokes, the evidence as a whole seems conclusive enough. On the one hand, we have the liberal humanists of laughter, mainly represented by Waters, and on the other its acquisitive opportunists, led by Challenor. And as in humour, so in life itself. Stand-up comedy becomes an emblem of people's conduct in capitalist society.

Yet anyone who knows Griffiths's work will quickly see that a vital element is missing. Hence the relevance of Gethin Price, who extends the conflict between integrity and commercialism, liberal humanism and greed, into one between liberal humanism and proletarian revolution. He is the most gifted of Waters's pupils, but also the most rebellious. At the last moment he has abandoned his original act, not for the slick nastiness of McBrain and Samuels, but for a display of fierce class aggression. He appears dressed as a blend between the Soviet clown Grock and a football hooligan, smashes a violin, and then proceeds to tease and abuse two dummies in evening dress. 'There's people'd call this envy,' he tells them, 'it's not, it's hate.' He pins a flower between the fake girl's breasts, causing a red stain to spread across her dress; and he cries 'National Unity? Up yours, sunshine'; and he plays the Red Flag on another violin.

There are two problems with this act. First, it is not particularly funny, and would seem to have little to do with the art of the comedian. Second, it exploits class stereotypes as unashamedly as others have exploited sexual or racial ones. People are not dummies, after all. But in the theatre it can be an extraordinarily forceful and disturbing scene, and its point is unmissable. Humour need not be tawdry and exploitative. It need not be kindly and healing. It can also be angry and bitter, a humour of protest and subversion. To the opportunists and liberals we must add a third category: the fiery radicals of laughter and life. Griffiths, as is his wont, divides his sympathies, and is careful to ensure that Waters emerges with intellectual, emotional and moral credit; but Price's viewpoint, appearing as it does at the play's climax, is inevitably the most emphatic and arresting.

It emerges rather the more strongly from Act III, too. This is a winding-up of both plot and argument, dramatically far less exciting than the scene preceding it, but absolutely necessary. First, Challenor offers his adjudication, and brushes briefly with Waters, who disagrees profoundly with his conclusions but knows it is no use complaining to headquarters. As a strong union man, he has always been unpopular with Challenor's Comedy Artists and Managers' Federation, a syndicate with monopolist ambitions. Then, there is a prolonged discussion between Waters and Price, in which the former accuses the latter's act of 'drowning in hate', and the latter accuses the former of having lost touch with his roots as both man and comedian – 'Hunger, diphtheria, filth, unemployment, means tests, bedbugs, head-lice'. And he adds: 'We're still caged, exploited, prodded and pulled at, milked, fattened, cut up, fed out. We still don't belong to ourselves. Nothing's changed. You've just forgotten, that's all.'

Up to this point the argument has been lucid enough, but now it begins to get slippery and confusing. Waters recalls visiting a death-camp while on a post-war tour of Germany. He felt it was 'the logic of our world, extended' and that 'there was no jokes left'. He was horrified, yet also, to his shame, sexually aroused: 'Something in me loved it, too.' His conclusion was that 'we gotta get deeper than hate, hate's no good'; and hence his view of comedy as medicine for the hurt, fearful or oppressed. But Price is not persuaded. He still thinks Waters has gone soft in a world which only hardness will change. Unlike the Jews at the gas chambers, he will 'stand in no line'. He will 'refuse my consent', both to the Challenors and to the Waters's. Instead, he will carry on in his dead-end job and 'wait for it to happen'. By 'it' he presumably means revolution.

His exit isn't quite the end of the play. On comes the bewildered Pakistani who earlier intèrrupted proceedings and, at the time, seemed little more than a device for getting Waters offstage. Now he rouses the glum teacher's spirits with a joke about a starving Hindu who pretends that a cow is a horse in order to be able to eat it. It is, in fact, the kind of crack that fits in with his comic philosophy, and he promptly offers the Pakistani a place in his next class. Perhaps, as Griffiths himself tentatively suggests, it shows the liberal moving into a new area of endeavour, and thereby preventing blacks from achieving their own revolution; or perhaps it simply demonstrates the resilience of Water's brand of humanism. Whatever the truth, it brings to an intriguing and provocative close a play that simultaneously offers fun and uses it to mount a moral and political debate of remarkable sweep.

Select Bibliography

The Plays

Barrie: *The Admirable Crichton*, Pilot Books, Hodder and
    Stoughton (1967).

Shaw: *Man and Superman*, in *The Bodley Head Bernard Shaw,*
    Collected Plays with their prefaces, vol. 2 (also includes *The Devil's*
    Disciple, Caesar and Cleopatra, Captain Brassbound's Conversion,
    and *John Bull's Other Island*), Max Reinhardt (1971); also
    Penguin (1971).
—— *Major Barbara*, in *The Bodley Head Bernard Shaw*, vol. 3 (also
    includes *The Doctor's Dilemma, Getting Married* and short plays),
    Max Reinhardt (1971); also Penguin (1969).
—— *Pygmalion*, in *The Bodley Head Bernard Shaw*, vol. 4 (also
    includes *Misalliance, Fanny's First Play, Androcles and the Lion,*
    and short plays), Max Reinhardt (1972); also Penguin (1969).
—— *Heartbreak House*, in *The Bodley Head Bernard Shaw*, vol. 5
    (also includes *Back to Methuselah* and short plays), Max
    Reinhardt (1972); also Penguin (1970).
—— *Saint Joan*, in *The Bodley Head Bernard Shaw*, vol. 6 (also
    includes *The Apple Cart, Too True to be Good, On the Rocks,*
    The Millionairess and short plays), Max Reinhardt (1973);
    also Penguin (1969); and Longmans (1964).

Granville-Barker: *The Voysey Inheritance*, Hereford Plays,
    Heinemann Educational (1967).

Synge: *The Playboy of the Western World*, in *Complete Plays*, Eyre
    Methuen (1963); Everyman (1969); and Oxford (1969); with
    Riders to the Sea, Hereford Plays, Heinemann Educational

(1961); and Unwin (1979); alone, New Mermaid Series, Benn (1975); and Eyre Methuen (1975).

Galsworthy: *Strife*, Duckworth (1977); also in *Galsworthy's Ten Best Plays* (with *The Silver Box, Justice, The Skin Game, Loyalties, Joy, Windows, Old English, Escape* and *The Roof*), Duckworth (1976).

Houghton: *Hindle Wakes*, in *Late Victorian Plays 1890–1914* (also includes Pinero's *The Second Mrs Tanqueray*, Jones's *The Liars*, Davies's *The Mollusc*, Hankin's *The Cassilis Engagement* and Galsworthy's *Justice*), Oxford University Press (1972).

Lawrence: *The Widowing of Mrs Holroyd*, with *The Daughter-in-Law*, Hereford Plays, Heinemann Educational (1968); with *The Daughter-in-Law* and *A Collier's Friday Night*, Penguin (1969).

Brighouse: *Hobson's Choice*, Hereford Plays, Heinemann Educational (1964).

Joyce: *Exiles*, Cape (1972); and Panther (1979).

Maugham: *The Circle*, in *Selected Plays* (also includes *The Constant Wife, Our Betters, The Sacred Flame* and *Sheppey*), Pan (1976).

O'Casey: *Juno and the Paycock*, with *The Shadow of a Gunman* and *The Plough and the Stars*, Macmillan (1965); and Pan (1980).
—— *The Silver Tassie*, with *Purple Dust* and *Red Roses for Me*, Macmillan (1965).

Coward: *Hay Fever*, in *Collected Plays*, vol. 1 (also includes *The Vortex, Fallen Angels* and *Easy Virtue*), Eyre Methuen (1979).
—— *Private Lives*, in *Collected Plays*, vol. 2 (also includes *Bitter-Sweet, The Marquise* and *Post-Mortem*), Eyre Methuen (1979).

Travers: *Rookery Nook*, W. H. Allen (1977); also in *Five Plays* (includes *A Cuckoo in the Nest, Thark, Plunder* and *The Bed before Yesterday*), Penguin (1979).

Sherriff: *Journey's End*, Hereford Plays, Heinemann Educational (1958).

Bridie: *Tobias and the Angel*, Constable (1976).

Eliot: *Murder in the Cathedral*, Faber (1938); pbk 1968.
—— *The Cocktail Party*, Faber (1974); pbk 1968.

Priestley: *An Inspector Calls*, in *Four Plays* (also includes *Time and*

the Conways, I Have Been Here Before and *The Linden Tree*),
Penguin (1969); alone, Hereford Plays, Heinemann
Educational (1965).

Fry: *The Lady's Not for Burning*, in *Three Plays* (also includes *Thor,
With Angels* and *A Phoenix Too Frequent*), Oxford University
Press (1969).

Whiting: *Saint's Day*, in *Collected Plays*, vol. 1 (also includes
Conditions of Agreement, A Penny for a Song and *Marching Song*),
Heinemann Educational (1969); alone, Hereford Plays,
Heinemann Educational (1963).

Rattigan: *The Deep Blue Sea*, in *Collected Plays*, vol. 2 (also
includes *The Browning Version, Harlequinade, Adventure Story* and
Who Is Sylvia?), Hamish Hamilton (1953).

Beckett: *Waiting for Godot*, Faber (1956); original version in
French, Harrap (1974).
—— *Endgame*, Faber (1964).
—— *Not I*, Faber (1973).

Behan: *The Quare Fellow*, in *Complete Plays*, Eyre Methuen
(1978); alone, Eyre Methuen (1956).

Osborne: *Look Back in Anger*, Evans Bros (1957); and Faber
(1960).
—— *Inadmissible Evidence*, Evans Bros (1966); Faber (1965);
pbk 1967.

Wesker: *Trilogy*, Cape (1960); and Penguin (1969).

Arden: *Sergeant Musgrave's Dance*, Eyre Methuen (1973); also in
John Arden's Plays, vol. 1 (includes *The Workhouse Donkey* and
Armstrong's Last Goodnight), Eyre Methuen (1977).

Pinter: *The Caretaker*, Eyre Methuen (1967); also in *Harold
Pinter's Plays*, vol. 2 (includes *Night School, The Dwarfs,
The Collection* and *The Lover*), Eyre Methuen (1977).
—— *The Homecoming*, Eyre Methuen (1966); also in *Harold
Pinter's Plays*, vol. 3 (includes *Tea Party, The Basement,
Landscape* and *Silence*), Eyre Methuen (1966).
—— *Old Times*, Eyre Methuen (1972).

Bolt: *A Man for All Seasons*, Hereford Plays, Heinemann
Educational (1967); and Drama Library, Heinemann

Educational (1980); also in *Three Plays* (with *Flowering Cherry* and *The Tiger and the Horse*), Heinemann Educational (1967).

Orton: *Loot*, Eyre Methuen (1973); also in *Complete Plays*, Eyre Methuen (1976).

Bond: *Saved*, Eyre Methuen (1969): also in *Bond's Plays*, vol. 1 (includes *Early Morning* and *The Pope's Wedding*), Eyre Methuen (1977).
—— *Lear*, Eyre Methuen (1972); also in *Bond's Plays*, vol. 2 (includes *The Sea* and *Narrow Road to the Deep North*), Eyre Methuen (1978).

Stoppard: *Rosencrantz and Guildenstern Are Dead*, Faber (1968).
—— *Jumpers*, Faber (1972).

Storey: *The Contractor*, with *In Celebration*, Penguin (1982).

Ayckbourn: *Absurd Person Singular*, in *Three Plays* (with *Absent Friends* and *Bedroom Farce*), Penguin (1979).

Brenton: *The Churchill Play*, Eyre Methuen (1974).

Griffiths: *Comedians*, Faber (1976); pbk 1979.

The following plays are also available in Samuel French's acting editions: *The Admirable Crichton; Hobson's Choice; The Circle; Juno and the Paycock; Hay Fever; Private Lives; Rookery Nook; Journey's End; An Inspector Calls; The Deep Blue Sea; The Caretaker; The Homecoming; A Man for All Seasons; Rosencrantz and Guildenstern Are Dead; Absurd Person Singular.*

Further Reading

BARRIE
Birkin, Andrew, *J. M. Barrie and the Lost Boys* (London, 1979); Dunbar, Janet, *J. M. Barrie: The Man Behind the Image* (London, 1970).

SHAW
Bentley, Eric, *Bernard Shaw* (New York, 1957, revised British ed. London, 1967); Berst, Charles A., *Bernard Shaw and the Art of Drama* (Urbana, Ill., 1973); Evans, T. F. (ed.), *Shaw, The Critical Heritage* (London 1976); Gibbs, A. M., *Shaw* (Edinburgh, 1969);

Henderson, Archibald, *G. B. Shaw: Man of the Century* (New York, 1956); Kronenberger, Louis (ed.), *Shaw: A Critical Survey* (New York, 1953); MacCarthy, Desmond, *Shaw: The Plays* (London, 1951); Meisel, Martin, *Shaw and the 19th-Century Theatre* (Princeton, N.J. 1963); Morgan, Margery M., *The Shavian Playground* (London, 1972); Pearson, Hesketh, *Bernard Shaw* (London, 1942); Shaw, Bernard, *The Prefaces* (London, 1934) (the prefaces and other relevant writings by Shaw are also available in the *Bodley Head Collected Plays*); Smith, J. Percy, *The Unrepentant Pilgrim* (Boston, 1965); Zimbardo, Rose (ed.), *Twentieth-Century Interpretations of Major Barbara* (Englewood Cliffs, N.J., 1970).

GRANVILLE-BARKER

Morgan, Margery M., *A Drama of Political Man: The Plays of Harley Granville-Barker* (London, 1961); Purdom, C. B., *Harley Granville-Barker: Man of the Theatre, Dramatist and Scholar* (1955).

SYNGE

Grene, Nicholas, *Synge: A Critical Study of the Plays* (Totowa, N.J., 1975, London, 1976); Kilroy, James, *The Playboy Riots* (Dublin, 1971); Mikhail, E. H. (ed.), *J. M. Synge: Interviews and Recollections* (London, 1977); Price, Alan, *Synge and Anglo-Irish Drama* (London, 1961); Saddlemyer, Ann, *J. M. Synge and Modern Comedy* (Dublin, 1968); Skelton, Robin, *The Writings of J. M. Synge* (London, 1971).

GALSWORTHY

Dupré, Catherine, *John Galsworthy* (London, 1976); Mottram, R. H., *John Galsworthy* (London, 1953).

LAWRENCE

Delavenay, Emile, *D. H. Lawrence: The Man and his Work* (London, 1972): Sagar, Keith, *The Art of D. H. Lawrence* (Cambridge, 1966); Sklar, Sylvia, *The Plays of D. H. Lawrence* (London, 1975); Spilka, Mark (ed.), *D. H. Lawrence: A Collection of Critical Essays* (Englewood Cliffs, N.J., 1963).

BRIGHOUSE

Brighouse, Harold, *What I Have Led: Chapters in Autobiography* (London, 1953).

JOYCE

Benstock, Bernard, *The Undiscovered Country* (Dublin, 1977); Deming, Robert, H., *James Joyce, The Critical Heritage*, vol. 1

(London, 1970); Ellmann, Richard, *James Joyce* (Cambridge, 1959); Hodgart, Matthew, *James Joyce, A Students' Guide* (London, 1978); Mason, Ellsworth, and Ellmann, Richard, *The Critical Writings of James Joyce* (London, 1959).

MAUGHAM
Barnes, Ronald E., *The Dramatic Comedy of William Somerset Maugham* (The Hague, 1968); Cordell, Richard, *Somerset Maugham: A Biographical and Critical Study* (London, 1961); Curtis, Anthony, *The Pattern of Maugham* (London, 1974).

O'CASEY
Armstrong, William A., *Sean O'Casey* (London, 1967); Ayling, Ronald (ed.), *Sean O'Casey: Modern Judgements* (London, 1969); Benstock, Bernard, *Paycocks and Others: Sean O'Casey's World* (New York, 1976); Cowasgee, Saros, *Sean O'Casey: The Man Behind the Plays* (Edinburgh, 1963) and *O'Casey* (Edinburgh, 1966); Krause, David (ed.), *The Letters of Sean O'Casey*, vol. 1 (New York and London, 1975), vol. 2 (New York and London, 1980) and *Sean O'Casey: The Man and his Work* (London, 1960); O'Casey, Sean, *Mirror in My House: Autobiographies* (New York, 1956).

COWARD
Morley, Sheridan, *A Talent to Amuse* (London, 1969).

TRAVERS
Travers, Ben, *Vale of Laughter, An Autobiography* (London, 1957) and *A-Sitting on a Gate, An Autobiography* (London, 1978).

SHERRIFF
Sherriff, R. C., *No Leading Lady, An Autobiography* (London, 1968).

BRIDIE
Bannister, Winifred, *James Bridie and his Theatre* (London, 1955); Luyben, Helen L., *James Bridie: Clown and Philosopher* (Philadelphia, 1965).

ELIOT
Bradbrook, M. C., *T. S. Eliot* (London, 1950); Browne, E. Martin, *The Making of T. S. Eliot's Plays* (Cambridge, 1969); Coghill, Nevill, commentary to *Cocktail Party* in Faber edition (London, 1974); Eliot, T. S. *The Sacred Wood* (1920), *Selected Essays* (1932) and *On Poetry and Poets* (1957); Frye, Northrop,

T. S. Eliot (Edinburgh, 1963); George, A. G., *T. S. Eliot: His Mind and Art* (London, 1962); Jones, David E., *The Plays of T. S. Eliot* (London, 1961); Smith, Carol H., *T. S. Eliot's Dramatic Theory and Practice* (Princeton, N.J., 1963); Smith, Grover, *T. S. Eliot's Poetry and Plays* (Chicago, 1956).

PRIESTLEY

Hughes, David, *J. B. Priestley: An Informal Study of his Work* (London, 1958); Lloyd Evans, Gareth, *J. B. Priestley the Dramatist* (London, 1964); Priestley, J. B., *The Art of the Dramatist* (London, 1957); Young, Kenneth, *J. B. Priestley* (London, 1977).

FRY

Stanford, D., *Christopher Fry, An Appreciation* (London, 1951).

WHITING

Hayman, Ronald, *John Whiting* (London, 1969); Salmon, Eric, *The Dark Journey: John Whiting as Dramatist* (London, 1979); Trussler, Simon, *The Plays of John Whiting* (London, 1966); Whiting, John, *The Art of the Dramatist* (London, 1970) and *John Whiting on Theatre* (London, 1966).

RATTIGAN

Darlow, Michael, and Hodson, Gillian, *Terence Rattigan: The Man and his Work* (London, 1979).

BECKETT

Alvarez, A., *Beckett* (London, 1974); Bair, Deirdre, *Samuel Beckett: A Biography* (London, 1978); Barnard, G. C., *Samuel Beckett: A New Approach* (London, 1970); Cohn, Ruby, *Back to Beckett* (Princeton, N.J., 1973) and *Samuel Beckett: The Comic Gamut* (New Brunswick, N.J., 1962); Doherty, Francis M. J., *Samuel Beckett* (London, 1971); Fletcher, Beryl, *et al*, *A Students' Guide to the Plays of Samuel Beckett* (London 1978); Fletcher, John, and Spurling, John, *Beckett: A Study of his Plays* (London, 1972); Graver, Lawrence and Federman, Raymond (eds.), *Samuel Beckett: The Critical Heritage* (London, 1979); Kenner, Hugh, *Samuel Beckett: A Critical Study* (London, 1962); Knowlson, James, and Pilling, John, *Frescoes of the Skull: The Late Prose and Drama of Samuel Beckett* (London, 1979); Mayoux, Jean-Jacques, *Samuel Beckett* (London, 1974); Pilling, John, *Samuel Beckett* (London, 1976).

BEHAN

Jeffs, Rae, *Brendan Behan: Man and Showman* (London, 1966); O'Connor, Ulrick, *Brendan Behan* (London, 1970); Porter, Raymond J., *Brendan Behan* (New York, 1973).

OSBORNE

Banham, Martin, *Osborne* (Edinburgh, 1969); Carter, Alan, *John Osborne* (Edinburgh, 1969); Hayman, Ronald, *John Osborne* (London, 1968); Trussler, Simon, *The Plays of John Osborne* (London, 1969).

WESKER

Hayman, Ronald, *Arnold Wesker* (London, 1970); Leeming, Glenda, and Trussler, Simon, *The Plays of Arnold Wesker: An Assessment* (London, 1971).

ARDEN

Arden, John, *To Present the Pretence: Essays on the Theatre* (London, 1977); Hunt, Albert, *Arden: A Study of his Plays* (London, 1974); Leeming, Glenda, *John Arden* (London, 1974); Trussler, Simon, *John Arden* (New York, 1973).

PINTER

Baker, William, and Tabachnik, Stephen Ely, *Harold Pinter* (Edinburgh, 1973); Esslin, Martin, *The Peopled Wound* (London, 1970); Ganz, Arthur (ed.), *Pinter: A Collection of Critical Essays* (Englewood Cliffs, N.J., 1972); Hayman, Ronald, *Harold Pinter* (London, 1968); Hinchliffe, Arnold, *Harold Pinter* (London, 1976); Lahr, John (ed.), *A Casebook on Harold Pinter's The Homecoming* (New York, 1971); Quigley, Austin E., *The Pinter Problem* (Princeton, N.J., 1975); Trussler, Simon, *The Plays of Harold Pinter* (London, 1973).

BOLT

Hayman, Ronald, *Robert Bolt* (London, 1969).

ORTON

Lahr, John, *Prick Up Your Ears* (London, 1978).

BOND

Coult, Tony, *The Plays of Edward Bond* (London, 1977); Hay, Malcolm, and Roberts, Philip, *Bond: A Study of his Plays* (London, 1980); Trussler, Simon: *Edward Bond* (London, 1976).

STOPPARD

Bigsby, C. W. E., *Tom Stoppard* (London, 1976); Dean, Joan Fitzpatrick, *Tom Stoppard: Comedy as a Moral Matrix* (Columbia, Mo., 1981); Hayman, Ronald, *Tom Stoppard* (London, 1977).

STOREY

John Russell Taylor, *David Storey* (London, 1964).

AYCKBOURN

Watson, Ian, *Conversations with Ayckbourn* (London, 1981).

General Books

Archer, William, *The Old Drama and the New* (London, 1923); Beerbohm, Max, *Around Theatres* (London, 1924), *More Theatres* (London, 1969) and *Late Theatres* (London, 1970); Brown, John Russell, *Theatre Language: A Study of Arden, Osborne, Pinter and Wesker* (London, 1972); Brustein, Robert, *Seasons of Discontent: Dramatic Opinions, 1959–65* (London, 1966), *The Theatre of Revolt* (Boston, 1964), and *The Third Theatre* (New York, 1969); Bryden, Ronald, *The Unfinished Hero* (London, 1969); Donoghue, Denis, *The Third Voice: Modern British and American Verse Drama* (Princeton, N.J., 1959); Ellis-Fermor, U., *The Irish Dramatic Movement* (London, 1939, revised 1954); Elsom, John, *Post-War British Theatre* (London, 1976); Esslin, Martin, *Brief Chronicles* (London, 1970) and *The Theatre of the Absurd* (London 1962, revised 1968); Goetsch, Paul, *English Dramatic Theories: 20th Century* (Tübingen, 1972); Hayman, Ronald, *British Theatre Since 1955* (Oxford, 1979), *Playback* (London, 1973) and *Playback 2* (London 1973); Hinchliffe, Arnold, *British Theatre 1950–70* (Oxford, 1974); Hunt, Hugh, *et al* (eds.), *The Revels History of Drama in English, vol 7: 1880 to the Present Day* (London, 1978); Itzin, Catherine, *Stages in the Revolution* (London, 1980); Kitchin, Laurence, *Drama in the Sixties* (London, 1966); Lloyd Evans, Gareth, *The Language of Modern Drama* (London, 1977); Lumley, Frederick; *New Trends in 20th-Century Drama* (London, 1967, revised 1972); Marowitz, Charles, *Confessions of a Counterfeit Critic* (London, 1973); Marowitz, Charles, *et al.* (eds.), *New Theatre Voices of the Fifties and Sixties* (London, 1981); Marowitz, Charles, and Trussler, Simon, (eds.), *Theatre at Work* (London, 1973); Montague, C. E., *Dramatic Values* (London, 1910, revised

1925); Morgan, Geoffrey, *Contemporary Theatre: A Selection of Reviews 1966–7* (London, 1968); Morley, Sheridan, *Review Copies: Plays and Players in London 1970–4* (London, 1974); Nicoll, Allardyce, *English Drama 1900–30* (Cambridge, 1973); Reynolds, Ernest, *Modern English Drama* (London, 1949); Roberts, Patrick, *The Psychology of Tragic Drama* (London, 1975); Taylor, John Russell, *Anger and After* (London, 1962, revised 1969), *The Rise and Fall of the Well-Made Play* (London, 1967) and *The Second Wave* (London, 1971); Trewin, J. C., *Dramatists of Today* (London, 1953) and *The Edwardian Theatre* (Oxford, 1976); Trussler, Simon (ed.), *New Theatre Voices of the Seventies* (London, 1981); Tynan, Kenneth, *Curtains* (London, 1961) and *Tynan Right and Left* (London, 1967); Wager, Walter (ed.), *The Playwrights Speak* (London, 1967); Weales, Gerald, *Religion in Modern English Drama* (Philadelphia, 1961); Williams, Raymond, *Drama from Ibsen to Brecht* (London, 1968); Williamson, Audrey, *Theatre of Two Decades* (London, 1951); Worth, Katherine, *Revolutions in Modern English Drama* (London, 1973).

Index